D0374822

NOV 2 0 2001

DISCARD

Modern Critical Views

Modern Critical Views

JOHN MILTON

Modern Critical Views

JOHN MILTON

Edited with an introduction by

Harold Bloom

Sterling Professor of the Humanities
Yale University

CHELSEA HOUSE PUBLISHERS
Philadelphia

THE COVER:
The opaque eyes, Satanic and sublime, center Gustave Doré's vision of Milton's fallen angels, the heroic but ruined host who followed their tragic leader into the Abyss.—H.B.

PROJECT EDITORS: Emily Bestler, James Uebbing
ASSOCIATE EDITOR: Maria Behan
EDITORIAL COORDINATOR: Karyn Gullen Browne
EDITORIAL STAFF: Laura Ludwig, Linda Grossman, Peter Childers
DESIGN: Susan Lusk

Cover by Susan Lusk

Copyright © 1986 by Chelsea House Publishers, a subsidiary of Haights Cross Communications.

Introduction copyright © 1986 by Harold Bloom

The Chelsea House World Wide Website address is
http://www.chelseahouse.com

All rights reserved. No part of this publication may be reproduced or transmitted, in any form or by any means, without the written permission of the publisher.

Printed and bound in the United States of America

10   9   8   7   6

Library of Congress Cataloging in Publication Data

John Milton.
 (Modern critical views)
 Bibliography: p.
 Includes index.
 1. Milton, John, 1608–1674—Criticism and interpretation—Addresses, essays, lectures.
I. Bloom, Harold.   II. Series.
PR3588.J64   1986   821'.4   85-7908
ISBN 0–87754–653–3

Contents

Editor's Note

This volume offers a representative selection of the best literary criticism devoted to the work of John Milton over the last thirty years. The editor's "Introduction," published in an earlier version in 1962, is an attempt to bring the Romantic reading of Milton up to that date. The chronological sequence begins with F. T. Prince's sensitive and formalist investigation of the Minor Poems (more "major" than almost any other poet's major efforts). Isabel G. MacCaffrey's mythic account of Satan as a voyager follows, an essay which can be regarded as one of the summits of the myth criticism of the fifties.

The late Sir William Empson's fierce and canny assault upon Milton's God begins the criticism of the sixties, and is followed here by Thomas Greene's very different and subtly learned delineation of the place of *Paradise Lost* in the epic sequence of angelic descents. Northrop Frye's majestic reading of the typology of *Paradise Regained* fitly ends the representation here of that increasingly troubled decade, in which criticism necessarily mirrored the cultural chaos that descended upon the academies.

With the seventies, Milton criticism entered into the wilderness of a more strictly intellectual dislocation, as new modes of description and analysis began to change both the context and the nature of what once was called the literary object. Geoffrey H. Hartman's exegesis of what he calls the Miltonic counterplot is already deeply informed by Continental models of critical discourse. With Angus Fletcher's Orphic allegorizings of *Comus*, and Stanley E. Fish's exposition of the reader's share in Milton's prose, further vistas of revisionist modes are clearly evident. These revisionist tendencies are amplified in Leslie Brisman's analysis of Edenic time in Milton's epic of temporal anxiety, and in the editor's own antithetical narrative of Milton's transumptions of his precursors. The highly dialectical reading of psychic division in *Samson Agonistes* by Mary Ann Radzinowicz brings the criticism of the seventies to a close.

I have tried to give a rather full coverage of current criticism by gathering together six instances of work done during the first half of the eighties. A lifetime of critical meditation upon the arts of poetic meditation culminates in Louis L. Martz's deeply informed reading of *Samson Agonistes*. John Hollander, certainly our most learned student of poetic allusion and echo, carries on the mode of Fletcher in his advanced treatment of the scheme of echo in *Paradise Lost*. A similarly advanced Freudian perspective, subtly tempered by imaginative priorities, is provided by William Kerrigan, the first critic to show some of the true uses of psychoanalytic concepts in the reading of Freud's favorite poet. Three younger critics end the volume with excellent versions of work-in-progress. In contrasting yet strangely supportive ways, they all analyze the conflict in Milton between a natural or personal monism and an inherited dualism. Sanford Budick's perspective is theological, Peter M. Sacks's reading is elegiac and Freudian, and William Flesch's analysis is romantic, yet chastened by deconstruction with its sense of the problematical in every literary representation. Together they give a sense of the ongoing challenge that our language's greatest poet of the Sublime mode will always present to every variety of criticism that can arise.

Introduction

By 1652, before his forty-fourth birthday and with his long-projected major poem unwritten, Milton was completely blind. In 1660, with arrangements for the Stuart Restoration well under way, the blind poet identified himself with the prophet Jeremiah, as if he would "tell the very soil itself what her perverse inhabitants are deaf to," vainly warning a divinely chosen people "now choosing them a captain back for Egypt, to bethink themselves a little, and consider whither they are rushing." These words are quoted from the second edition of *The Ready and Easy Way*, a work which marks the end of Milton's temporal prophecy and the beginning of his greater work, the impassioned meditations upon divine providence and human nature. In these [meditations] Milton abandons the field of his defeat, and leaves behind him also the songs of triumph he might have sung in praise of a reformed society and its imaginatively integrated citizens. He changes those notes to tragic, and praises, when he praises at all, what he calls the better fortitude of patience, the hitherto unsung theme of Heroic Martyrdom. Adam, Christ and Samson manifest an internal mode of heroism that Satan can neither understand nor overcome, a heroism that the blind Puritan prophet himself is called upon to exemplify in the England of the Restoration.

Milton had planned a major poem since he was a young man, and he had associated his composition of the poem with the hope that it would be a celebration of a Puritan reformation of all England. He had prophesied of the coming time that "amidst the hymns and hallelujahs of the saints some one may perhaps be heard offering at high strains in new and lofty measures to sing and celebrate thy divine mercies and marvellous judgements in the land throughout all ages." This vision clearly concerns a national epic, very probably on a British rather than a Biblical theme. That poem, had it been written, would have rivaled the great poem of Milton's master, Spenser, who in a profound sense was Milton's "Original," to cite Dryden's testimony. *Paradise Lost* is not the poem that Milton had prophesied in the exuberance of his youth, but we may guess it to be a greater work than the one we lost, for the unwritten poem would not have had the Satan who is at once the aesthetic glory and the moral puzzle of Milton's epic of loss and disillusion.

The form of *Paradise Lost* is based on Milton's modification of Vergil's attempt to rival Homer's *Iliad*, but the content of Milton's epic has a largely negative relation to the content of the *Iliad* or the *Aeneid*. Milton's "one greater Man," Christ, is a hero who necessarily surpasses all the sons of Adam, including Achilles and Aeneas, just as he surpasses Adam or archetypal Man himself. Milton delights to speak of himself as soaring above the sacred places of the classical muses and as seeking instead "thee *Sion* and the flow'ry brooks beneath," Siloam, by whose side the Hebrew prophets walked. For *Paradise Lost*, despite C. S. Lewis's persuasive assertions to the contrary, is specifically a Protestant and Puritan poem, created by a man who finally became a Protestant church of one, a sect unto himself. The poem's true muse is "that eternal Spirit who can enrich with all utterance and knowledge, and sends out his seraphim, with the hallowed fire of his altar, to touch and purify the lips of whom he pleases." This Spirit is one that prefers for its shrine, in preference to all Temples of organized faith, the upright and pure heart of the isolated Protestant poet, who carries within himself the extreme Christian individualism of the Puritan Left Wing. Consequently, the poem's doctrine is not "the great central tradition" that Lewis finds it to be, but an imaginative variation on that tradition. Milton believed in the doctrines of the Fall, natural corruption, regeneration through grace, an aristocracy of the elect, and Christian Liberty, all of them fundamental to Calvinist belief, and yet Milton was no orthodox Calvinist, as Arthur Barker has demonstrated. The poet refused to make a sharp distinction between the natural and the spiritual in man, and broke from Calvin in his theory of regeneration. Milton's doctrine of predestination, as seen in *Paradise Lost*, is both general and conditional; the Spirit does not make particular and absolute choices. When regeneration comes, it heals not only man's spirit but his nature as well, for Milton could not abide in dualism. Barker makes the fine contrast between Milton and Calvin that in Calvin even good men are altogether dependent upon God's will, and not on their own restored faculties, but in Milton the will is made free again, and man is restored to his former liberty. The hope for man in *Paradise Lost* is that Adam's descendants will find their salvation in the fallen world, once they have accepted Christ's sacrifice and its human consequences, by taking a middle way between those who would deny the existence of sin altogether, in a wild freedom founded upon a misunderstanding of election, and those who would repress man's nature that spirit might be more free. The regenerated descendants of Adam are to evidence that God's grace need not provide for the abolition of the natural man.

To know and remember this as Milton's ideal is to be properly prepared to encounter the dangerous greatness of Satan in the early books of *Paradise Lost*. The poem is a theodicy, and like *Job* seeks to justify the ways of Jehovah to man, but unlike the poet of *Job* Milton insisted that reason could comprehend God's justice, for Milton's God is perfectly reasonable and the perfection of man in Christ would raise human reason to a power different only in degree from its fallen status. The poet of *Job* has an aesthetic advantage over Milton, for most readers rightly prefer a Voice out of a Whirlwind, fiercely asking rhetorical questions, to Milton's sophistical Schoolmaster of Souls in Book III of *Paradise Lost*. But Milton's God is out of balance because Satan is so magnificently flawed in presentation, and to account for the failure of God as a dramatic character the reader is compelled to enter upon the most famous and vexing of critical problems concerning *Paradise Lost*, the Satanic controversy itself. Is Satan in some sense heroic, or is he merely a fool?

The anti-Satanist school of critics has its great ancestor in Addison, who found Satan's sentiments to be "suitable to a created being of the most exalted and most depraved nature. . . . Amid those impieties which this enraged spirit utters . . . the author has taken care to introduce none that is not big with absurdity, and incapable of shocking a religious reader." Dr. Johnson followed Addison with more eloquence: "The malignity of Satan foams in haughtiness and obstinacy; but his expressions are commonly general, and no otherwise offensive than as they are wicked." The leading modern anti-Satanists are the late Charles Williams, and C. S. Lewis, for whom Milton's Satan is to some extent an absurd egoist, not altogether unlike Meredith's Sir Willoughby Patterne. So Lewis states "it is a mistake to demand that Satan, any more than Sir Willoughby, should be able to rant and posture through the whole universe without, sooner or later, awaking the comic spirit." Satan is thus an apostle of Nonsense, and his progressive degeneration in the poem is only the inevitable working-out of his truly absurd choice when he first denied his status as another of God's creatures.

The Satanist school of critics finds its romantic origins in two very great poets profoundly and complexly affected by Milton, Blake and Shelley. This tradition of romantic Satanism needs to be distinguished from the posturings of its Byronic-Napoleonic cousin, with which anti-Satanists have loved to confound it. The greatest of anti-Satanists (because the most attracted to Satan), Coleridge, was himself guilty of this confusion. But though he insisted upon reading into Milton's Satan the lineaments of Bonaparte, Coleridge's reading of the Satanic character has never been equaled by any modern anti-Satanist:

> But in its utmost abstraction and consequent state of reprobation, the will becomes Satanic pride and rebellious self-idolatry in the relations of the spirit to itself, and remorseless despotism relatively to others; the more hopeless as the more obdurate by its subjugation of sensual impulses, by its superiority to toil and pain and pleasure; in short, by the fearful resolve to find in itself alone the one absolute motive of action, under which all other motives from within and from without must be either subordinated or crushed.

Against this reading of the Satanic predicament we can set the dialectical ironies of Blake in *The Marriage of Heaven and Hell* and the imaginative passion of Shelley in his Preface to *Prometheus Unbound* and *A Defence of Poetry*. For Blake the Satan of Books I and II supremely embodies human desire, the energy that alone can create. But desire restrained becomes passive, until it is only a shadow of desire. God and Christ in *Paradise Lost* embody reason and restraint, and their restriction of Satan causes him to forget his own passionate desires, and to accept a categorical morality that he can only seek to invert. But a poet is by necessity of the party of energy and desire; reason and restraint cannot furnish the stuff of creativity. So Milton, as a true poet, wrote at liberty when he portrayed Devils and Hell, and in fetters when he described Angels and God. For Hell is the active life springing from energy, and Heaven only the passive existence that obeys reason.

Blake was too subtle to portray Satan as being even the unconscious hero of the poem. Rather, he implied that the poem can have no hero because it too strongly features Milton's self-abnegation in assigning human creative power to its diabolical side. Shelley went further, and claimed Satan as a semi-Promethean or flawed hero, whose character engenders in the reader's mind a pernicious casuistry of humanist argument against theological injustice. Shelley more directly fathered the Satanist school by his forceful statement of its aesthetic case: "Nothing can exceed the energy and magnificence of Satan as expressed in *Paradise Lost*." Whatever else, Shelley concluded, might be said for the Christian basis of the poem, it was clear that Milton's Satan as a moral being was far superior to Milton's God.

Each reader of *Paradise Lost* must find for himself the proper reading of Satan, whose appeal is clearly all but universal. Amid so much magnificence it is difficult to choose a single passage from *Paradise Lost* as surpassing all others, but I incline to the superlative speech of Satan on top of Mount Niphates (Book IV, ll.32–113), which is the text upon which the anti-Satanist, Satanist or some compromise attitude must finally rest. Here Satan makes his last choice, and ceases to be what he was in the early books of the poem. All that the anti-Satanists say about him is true *after* this point; all or almost all claimed for him by the Satanists is true *before* it. When this speech is concluded, Satan has become Blake's "shadow of desire," and he is on the downward path that will make him "as big with absurdity" as ever Addison and Lewis claimed him to be. Nothing that can be regenerated remains in Satan, and the rift between his self-ruined spirit and his radically corrupted nature widens until he is the hissing serpent of popular tradition, plucking greedily at the Dead Sea fruit of Hell in a fearful parody of Eve's Fall.

It is on Mount Niphates again that Satan, now a mere (but very subtle) tempter, stands when he shows Christ the kingdoms of this world in the brief epic, *Paradise Regained*. "Brief epic" is the traditional description of this poem (published in 1671, four years after *Paradise Lost*), but the description has been usefully challenged by several modern critics. E. M. W. Tillyard has warned against judging the poem by any kind of epic standard and has suggested instead that it ought to be read as a kind of Morality play, while Arnold Stein has termed it an internal drama, set in the Son of God's mind. Louis L. Martz has argued, following Tillyard, that the poem is an attempt to convert Vergil's *Georgics* into a mode for religious poetry, and ought therefore to be read as both a didactic work and a formal meditation on the Gospel. *Paradise Regained* is so subdued a poem when compared to *Paradise Lost* that we find real difficulty in reading it as epic. Yet it does resemble *Job*, which Milton gave as the possible model for a brief epic, for like *Job* it is essentially a structure of gathering self-awareness, of the protagonist and hero recognizing himself in his relation to God. Milton's Son of Man is obedient where Milton's Adam was disobedient; Job was not quite either until God spoke to him and demonstrated the radical incompatibility involved in any mortal's questionings of divine purpose. Job, until his poem's climax, is an epic hero because he has an unresolved conflict within himself, between his own conviction of righteousness and his moral outrage at the calamities that have come upon him despite his righteousness. Job needs to overcome the temptations afforded him by this conflict, including those offered by his comforters (to deny his own righteousness) and by his finely laconic wife (to curse God and die). The temptations of Milton's Son of God (the poet's fondness for this name of Christ is another testimony to his Hebraic preference for the Father over the Son) are not easy for us to sympathize with in any very dramatic way, unlike the temptations of Job who is a man like ourselves. But again Milton is repeating the life-long quest of his poetry; to see man as an integrated unity of distinct natures, body and soul harmonized. In Christ these natures are perfectly unified, and so the self-realization of Christ is an image of the possibility of human integration. Job learns not to tempt God's patience too far; Christ learns who he is, and in that moment of self-revelation Satan is smitten with amazement and falls as by the blow of a Hercules. Milton had seen himself in *Paradise Lost* as Abdiel, the faithful Angel who will not follow Satan in rebellion against God, defying thus the scorn of his fellows. Less consciously, something crucial in Milton had found its way into the Satan of the opening books, sounding a stoic defiance of adversity. In *Paradise Regained* Milton, with genuine humility, is exploring the Jobean problem within himself. Has he, as a Son of God also, tried God's patience too far, and can he at length overcome the internal temptations that beset a proud spirit reduced to being a voice in the wilderness? The poet's conquest over himself is figured in the greater Son of God's triumphant endurance, and in the quiet close of *Paradise Regained,* where the Savior returns to his mother's house to lead again, for a while, the private life of contemplation and patience while waiting upon God's will, not the public life forever closed to Milton.

Published with *Paradise Regained* in 1671, the dramatic poem *Samson Agonistes* is more admired today than the brief epic it accompanied. The poem's title, like the *Prometheus Bound* of Aeschylus, refers to the episode in the hero's life upon which the work is centered. The reference (from the Greek for athletic contestants in public games) is to Samson's ordeal before the Philistines at their Feast of Dagon, where he is summoned for their sport to demonstrate his blind strength, and where his faith gives him light enough to destroy them. *Samson* is Milton's Christian modification of Athenian drama, as *Paradise Lost* had been of classical epic. Yet Milton's drama is his most personal poem, in its experimental metric and in its self-reference alike. Modern editors cautiously warn against overstressing the extent to which Samson represents Milton, yet the representation seems undeniable, and justly so, to the common reader. Milton's hatred of his enemies does not seem particularly Christian to many of his modern critics, but its ferocious zeal fits both the Biblical story of Samson and the very bitter situation that the blind Puritan champion had to face in the first decade of the Restoration. The crucial text here is the great Chorus, ll.652–709, in which Milton confronts everything in the world of public events that had hurt him most. The theodicy of *Paradise Lost* seems abstract compared to the terrible emotion conveyed in this majestic hymn. The men solemnly elected by God for the great work of renovation that is at once God's glory and the people's safety are then evidently abandoned by God, and indeed thrown by Him lower than He previously exalted them on high. Milton had lived to see the bodies of his great leaders and associates, including Cromwell, dug up and hanged on the gallows to commemorate the twelfth anniversary of the execution of Charles I. Sir Henry Vane, for whom Milton had a warm and especial admiration, had been executed by order of "the unjust tribunals, under change of times, / And condemnation of the ingrateful multitude." *Samson Agonistes* give us not only the sense of having experienced a perfectly proportioned work of art, but also the memory of Milton's most moving prayer to God, which follows his account of the tribulations of his fellow Puritans:

> So deal not with this once thy glorious Champion,
> The Image of thy strength, and mighty minister.
> What do I beg? how hast thou dealt already?
> Behold him in this state calamitous, and turn
> His labours, for thou canst, to peaceful end.

F. T. PRINCE

Milton's Minor Poems

With the exception of the mature sonnets and some of the translations of the Psalms, Milton's minor poems belong to the first thirty years of his life and represent for the most part a sustained effort of self-education in writing English verse. It is not impossible, however, to distinguish between those which are predominantly deliberate exercises in poetry and those which have drawn also upon deeper sources of inspiration. Thus *L'Allegro* and *Il Penseroso* and *Comus*—to take examples from the finest poems of this sort—are clearly written in what Keats called 'an artful or rather artist's humour'; while the hymn *On the Morning of Christ's Nativity* and *Lycidas* seem to mark, not only stages in Milton's acquisition of technical skill, but also important advances in imaginative power.

It is natural that, in a process of self-improvement such as the minor poems represent, the poet should produce some work of a kind which he does not repeat, and that much should appear which does not appear in quite the same guise in his later verse. So, to examine the minor poems in order to trace the ways in which Milton assimilated the Italian poetry he admired, is to find that many of them more obviously illustrate other things. If one considers Milton's English verse as a whole up to 1638, it shows that his chief purpose was to assimilate as much of the English poetic heritage as he found worthy and capable of being turned to his own use. The poetry of this period attempts less to absorb Italian technique (except in a few important cases) than to plunder Shakespeare, Spenser, Fletcher, and Ben Jonson of treasures with which Milton could

From *The Italian Element in Milton's Verse*. Copyright © 1954 by Oxford University Press.

build a more lofty, polished, and condensed poetic style than had yet been achieved in English.

Spenser and Jonson are taken by Milton as his masters in the earliest English poems. The influence of Spenser prevails in the specifically religious pieces: *On the Death of a Fair Infant, On the Morning of Christ's Nativity*, and *The Passion*. Jonson's influence is stronger in the more secular or courtly: *At a Vacation Exercise, An Epitaph on the Marchioness of Winchester, On Shakespeare, On the University Carrier*. Milton's cultivation of English verse begins appropriately under the joint auspices of these two poets, for they alone among the great Elizabethans and Jacobeans held the lofty Renaissance ideal of a learned poetry; and they alone upheld and applied critical theories which Milton could respect.

Milton's direct recourse to Italian poetry for technical lessons is, however, apparent even among the first group of his youthful poems. It is possible to trail the workings of this idiosyncrasy and to distinguish the results from those of the more diffused Italian influence which comes through Spenser and his school. The hymn *On the Morning of Christ's Nativity* illustrates this reflection of Italian form in the Spenserian tradition; the lines *Upon the Circumcision* show that at the same time Milton was willing to go directly to Tuscan poetry; and the lines *On Time* and *At a Solemn Musick* show the interplay of the two influences: they could not have been written as they were without Italian exemplars, but they indicate that Milton will henceforth prefer to follow only those Italian lyric forms which he can modulate in his own way.

In all the early poems, except the early sonnets, the following of Italian verse affects the prosody rather than the diction. Indeed, Milton's adaptation of devices of Italian diction, which is all-important to the understanding of his mature verse, does not begin until *Lycidas*, the last poem of his youth.

II

A glance at the hymn *On the Morning of Christ's Nativity* will show that what Italianisms we find in these youthful poems may be ascribed almost wholly to Milton's following of Spenser. The Spenserian quality of the language and the rhythms of the hymn is a commonplace of criticism. It appears in nothing more clearly than in the management of adjectives; and such usages as 'dark foundations deep', 'flowre-inwov'n tresses torn', and 'Timbrel'd Anthems dark', which Spenser derived from the Italians, Milton accepts as proven elements in English poetic diction. The stanza itself reveals the same origins. The concluding alexandrine seals its Spenserian character, and both this and the preceding octosyllable would be impossible in any strict adherence to the methods of the Italian *canzone*. Yet the pattern and movement of the stanza, and the very notion of employing such a stanza for a solemn ode of this sort, could only derive from the tradition of the *canzone*. Spenser himself took similar liberties in the *Epithalamion* and the *Prothalamion*, which nevertheless remain his tribute to the power of the *canzone* form. Milton may well have considered that such variations as alexandrines and octosyllables, as well as occasional rhythms such as

> And then at last our bliss
> Full and perfect is,

were desirable in an English adaptation of Italian prosody. And perhaps he was right, and may have been confirmed in his instinct by mature experience; for there is reason to believe that the much greater licence of the choruses of *Samson* represents his later version of the rhythmic complexity of Italian verse.

The confidence of the hymn *On the Morning of Christ's Nativity* is often contrasted with the relative failure of two experiments which must have closely followed it: the lines *Upon the Circumcision* and *The Passion*. There can be little doubt that the young Milton, fired by the sense of self-discovery and of poetic power conferred by his celebration of the birth of Christ, set out to hail in the same way those feasts of the Church which recorded the chief events in the scheme of Redemption. The poet's acceptance of defeat in this plan came with his relinquishment of the poem on *The Passion*, which has nothing to tell us of his technical progress. But this unsuccessful experiment must have been preceded in the New Year by the lines *Upon the Circumcision*, which, within their narrow limits, provide interesting evidence of the poet's methods.

It has never yet been noticed that these two stanzas, each of fourteen lines, reproduce as closely as possible the stanza used by Petrarch in his *canzone* to the Blessed Virgin. The only modification Milton makes, and it is a modification only for the eye, is to make two lines out of the two sections into which Petrarch's last line falls. Petrarch's last line is linked to its predecessor by *rimalmezzo* (medial rhyme); Milton follows the rhyme-pattern, but changes the accepted Italian way of setting out the verse, no doubt because he decided that it would be unfamiliar and unpleasing to English readers. A comparison between the first stanzas of the two poems makes the relationship clear and brings out other points.

Petrarch writes:

Vergine bella, che di Sol vestita,	a
Coronata di stelle, al sommo Sole	b
Piacesti sì che'n te sua luce ascose;	c
Amor mi spinge a dir di te parole,	b
Ma non so 'ncominciar senza tu' aita	a
E di Colui ch'amando in te si pose.	c
Invoco lei che ben sempre rispose,	c
Chi la chiamò con fede.	d
Vergine, s'a mercede,	d
Miseria extrema de l'umane cose	c
Già mai ti volse, al mio prego t'inchina;	e
Soccorri a la mia guerra,	f
Bench'i' sia terra,—e tu del ciel regina.	(f)e

And Milton:

Ye flaming Powers, and winged Warriours bright,	a
That erst with musick, and triumphant song	b
First heard by happy watchful Shepherds ear,	c
So sweetly sung your Joy the clouds along	b
Through the soft silence of the list'ning night;	a
Now mourn, and if sad share with us to bear	c
Your fiery essence can distill no tear,	c
Burn in your signs, and borrow	d
Seas wept from our deep sorrow,	d
He who with all Heav'ns heraldry whileare	c
Enter'd the world, now bleeds to give us ease;	e
Alas, how soon our sin	f
Sore doth begin	f
His Infancy to sease!	e

The lines *Upon the Circumcision* have the distinction of being Milton's only attempt to follow an Italian model in exactly this manner: that is to say, copying a complex stanza which must be repeated throughout the poem. Petrarch's *canzone* is 137 lines long; the fact that Milton, taking a stanza designed for a poem of this length, repeats it only once, may be a mere accident. There is nothing to indicate that his poem was intended to be longer than it is. But the brevity of the poem, and its unique fidelity to such a stanza-form, may well suggest that Milton's talent did not function easily on such a basis. The only stanza-form he continued to use was that of the sonnet, and then only in a manner which very considerably modified its stanzaic character.

The comparison between Milton's and Petrarch's stanzas shows also that Milton's are not articulated in the traditional manner. In the first stanza he does not observe the pause at the end of the sixth line which in Petrarch marks the end of the *fronte* of the stanza and the beginning of the *sirima* or *coda*. Either Milton at this time had not appreciated the significance of these divisions (which had indeed been blurred in many *canzoni* of the sixteenth century), and when he came to do so, decided against the attempt to imitate such complexities in English; or he found the attempt in this poem uncongenial and unsuccessful, and forswore such metres for ever.

For the two other pieces of this period are indeed sufficiently Italianate, but they take as their basis an Italian form, the madrigal, which is less exacting than the *canzone*, and which Milton can develop with characteristic power. *On Time* and *At a Solemn Musick* have a sonority, a sustained emphasis of statement, and a rhythmic weight which give an assurance that Milton is again on the right track, finding means of expression which will bring out his full powers. *On Time*, which the Trinity manuscript tells us was conceived as an inscription for a clock-case, derives from a branch of Italian poetry much cultivated in the later sixteenth century by Tasso, Marino, and others: the madrigal, used to reproduce the Greek epigram. Like many of their originals, these madrigals drew their subjects from pictures or statues and preserved the link between epigram and inscription. Drummond of Hawthornden was the only poet writing in English who had closely imitated the madrigals and epigrams of Tasso and his followers; Milton was not likely to be impressed by his pedestrian versions of these witty trifles. Yet his own more ambitious use of the form follows its essential features. In both these poems he builds up a triumphant epigrammatic close, which is marked by an alexandrine; both have an element of 'wit-writing', though this is outweighed by a religious gravity and fervour.

The madrigal in its origin was as it were merely one stanza of a *canzone*—a stanza which was not repeated; and it shared with the *canzone* the metrical basis of hendecasyllables and heptasyllables which had proved useful in English verse. Milton preserves the general nature of the form, but modifies it significantly, not only in his concluding alexandrines, but in his handling of the shorter lines. The Italian heptasyllable had found its theoretic equivalent in English in a line of six syllables and three stresses. Milton experiments, not only with this accepted equivalent, but with lines of four stresses. These are slightly tentative in the lines *On Time*:

> With an individual kiss;

and

> Then all this Earthy grosnes quit,

but provide the first magnificent climax of the second poem:

> With those just Spirits that wear victorious Palms,
> Hymns devout and holy Psalms
> Singing everlastingly;
>
> (*At a Solemn Musick*, ll. 14–16.)

These modulations are indicative of a feeling on Milton's part that full sonority in these Italianate forms could not be attained by pedantic imitation, and that he for his part could achieve the effect he wanted rather by a certain disciplined improvisation. The significance of the two poems is increased when we notice how this disciplined improvisation has enabled Milton to develop the long and elaborate sentence which is to be a structural element in all his mature poetry. *At a Solemn Musick* in particular shows his resources:

> That we on Earth with undiscording voice
> May rightly answer that melodious noise;
> As once we did, till disproportion'd sin
> Jarr'd against natures chime, and with harsh din
> Broke the fair musick that all creatures made
> To their great Lord, whose love their motion sway'd
> In perfect Diapason, whilst they stood
> In first obedience, and their state of good.

The poet who can draw upon such a syntax and rhythm as this has little need of intricate rhyme or stanzaic form; at this point the poem slips into what we can scarcely call couplets, but what the Italians would call *rime baciate*, which are seldom used lavishly in Italian lyrics except as a sort of dizzy climax or conclusion (as in the *sonetto caudato*). The importance of *On Time* and *At a Solemn Musick* is that they point forward to *Lycidas* and the choruses of *Samson Agonistes*, and foreshadow Milton's exploitation of syntax as a structural element both in those later lyrics and in his blank verse.

In these youthful poems may be seen the deliberation with which Milton sets himself to learn what he needs from Italian verse. This deliberation is very marked also in his first sonnets, that is to say the Sonnet to the Nightingale, the sonnets in Italian, and the Sonnet on his twenty-third birthday. But these must be considered with the sonnets as a whole. Here it need only be remarked that after this first phase of serious imitation of Italian verse Milton turns to English poetry and drama, and makes a thorough investigation of what they have to offer him.

III

The poems we associate with Milton's period of study at Horton display the results of this deliberate saturation in Elizabethan and Jacobean verse. Shakespeare, Jonson, and Fletcher are Milton's chief literary inspiration in *L'Allegro* and *Il Penseroso*; the titles are there to remind us of his special leaning towards Italian, but the metre and diction of these poems owe little to Italian verse, except perhaps a certain solidity and resonance which might equally well be attributed to Milton's cultivation of Latin.

Jonson is the presiding influence in *Arcades*, and determines the fundamental structure even of *Comus*, though *Comus* draws impressively on so many other sources. In its plan and in the texture of its verse *Comus* is based firmly on English masques and dramas; its relation to Italian pastoral drama, to Tasso's *Aminta* and Guarini's *Il Pastor Fido*, is indirect and subordinate. That Milton knew *Aminta* and *Il Pastor Fido* goes without saying; but his own poem owes more to Fletcher's *Faithful Shepherdess*, to Ben Jonson's masques and Shakespeare's plays, and to Spenser's blend of chivalry, pastoral and Renaissance philosophy.

Comus is by virtue of its length and the variety of its verse one of the most important illustrations of Milton's art before his visit to Italy. In the blank verse dialogues there is much that remains apparent in his mature epic verse. But there is a distinction to be made between this blank verse and that of *Paradise Lost*, which may help to bring out the specifically Italian element in the latter. Dr. Johnson remarks in connexion with *Comus* that

> Milton appears to have formed very early that system of diction, and mode of verse, which his maturer judgement approved, and from which he never endeavoured nor desired to deviate.

But the diction and the versification of the blank verse of *Comus* are not in fact identical with those of the great epics. Milton's feeling for the English language, the peculiar weight of his verse, these are of course fully present. We find his skill in constructing elaborate and extended verse-paragraphs, and his delight in an overwhelming fullness of expression. Many passages convey a sense of discovery as well as achievement, a reaching out towards a new style:

> Within the navil of this hideous Wood,
> Immur'd in cypress shades a Sorcerer dwels
> Of *Bacchus* and of *Circe* born, great *Comus*,
> Deep skill'd in all his mothers witcheries,
> And here to every thirsty wanderer,

By sly enticement gives his banefull cup,
With many murmurs mixt, whose pleasing poison
The visage quite transforms of him that drinks,
And the inglorious likenes of a beast
Fixes instead, ummoulding reasons mintage
Character'd in the face; this have I learn't
Tending my flocks hard by i'th hilly crofts,
That brow this bottom glade, whence night by night
He and his monstrous rout are heard to howl
Like stabl'd wolves, or tigers at their prey,
Doing abhorred rites to *Hecate*
In their obscured haunts of inmost bowres.
(Comus, ll. 520–36.)

This has Shakespeare's plenitude and weight, invaluable in dramatic verse. But it has these qualities to excess, because Milton's prime purpose is not dramatic but literary, and he is working towards the creation of a style essentially unsuited to drama. 'It is a drama in the epick style, inelegantly splendid', says Dr. Johnson. Milton's special preoccupation here is clearly to extend the limits of the sentence, as he is to find means of doing, more appropriately, in his epic verse.

Yet it is worth observing that the wonderful elaboration of this blank verse style in *Comus* is achieved without making use of many of the devices of *Paradise Lost*. Astonishing periods are constructed almost entirely without the 'Miltonic inversions' to be derived later from Virgil and the Italian experiments in epic diction. Lines and sequences of lines may be found almost everywhere which could occur also in the later blank verse; there is no consistent difference in the prosodic basis, though certain 'liberties' appear, both here and in the dialogues of *Samson Agonistes*, which suggest that Milton distinguished between dramatic blank verse and blank verse in narrative poetry. It would be difficult to demonstrate that the blank verse of *Comus* is a different metre from that of the epics. But it is sung to a different tune, as it were; has a different movement and pitch; it has behind it a different pattern. *Paradise Lost* has the movement and tone of Virgil, and it has the pattern of Italian *versi sciolti* of the sixteenth century. *Comus* observes the tone and movement of Shakespeare's blank verse, adapting also inflexions from lesser dramatists.

The lyrics of *Comus*, like those of *Arcades*, are related primarily to Jonson and Fletcher; if any affinities could be traced with contemporary Italian lyrics, they would probably be found to be due to the common musical tradition.

The importance of *Comus* for our study of the development of Milton's verse is that it illustrates copiously his relation to the Elizabethans and Jacobeans. It shows him consciously assimilating what he could of these native beauties. He had no Italian models in mind on this occasion; if he had had any idea of reproducing in English the special qualities of the Italian pastoral dramas, the result would assuredly have been very different from what we have.

IV

Lycidas follows Comus and immediately precedes Milton's Italian journey; its formal significance is worthy of separate treatment. After its composition Milton abandons the study and assimilation of English poetry which he undertook, among many other labours, in the Horton period. Henceforth his poetry is to be planned entirely under the influence of the two classical literatures and of Italian, the authority of which he considers equal to theirs. This settled view of his is reflected in the tractate *Of Education*, which he first printed in 1644, and which was written after his return from the Continent.

In this plan of a complete intellectual equipment, Italian is the only modern language to be set beside Greek, Latin, and Hebrew ('whereto it would be no impossibility to add the *Chaldey*, and the *Syrian* Dialect'). Italian and classical poetry are to be studied in the light of sixteenth-century Italian criticism and its classical sources, Aristotle and Horace. Milton's imaginary pupils would thus learn 'what the laws are of a true *Epic* Poem, what of a *Dramatic*, what of a *Lyric*, what Decorum is, which is the grand masterpiece to observe'. And they would thus know what to think of their native literature: 'Thus would make them soon perceive what despicable creatures our common Rimers and Playwriters be, and shew them, what religious, what glorious and magnificent use might be made of Poetry both in divine and humane things.'

This is where Milton stands at the end of his long experience of education and self-education; and from this point of view he conceives and finally carries out his mature work.

ISABEL G. MACCAFFREY

Satan's Voyage

In Books II to IV of *Paradise Lost*, Milton has given his version of one of the basic mythological themes: the quest, second stage of the "celestial cycle" of loss, search, and return. "The perpetual stumble of conjecture and disturbance in this our dark voyage" was portrayed earlier in the woodland wanderings of *Comus*. But the theme did not find its most profound incarnation until Satan voyaged out of Hell to light. His is a journey conjectural and disturbed enough, the original instance and subsequent type of fallen man's endeavor. Satan is the archetypal exile; the theme is transferred to man at the end of the poem, as the dark voyage of the race of Adam is adumbrated in the great panorama of Old Testament wanderings in the final books, which illustrate in history "the exile of temporal life."

Satan is not, obviously, *the* hero of *Paradise Lost*. But the story of his voyage is told by Milton *as if* he were one of the questing heroes of legend, while at the same time we are reminded of his position in the moral scheme of the poem as a whole. The elements of his character that Milton borrowed from heroic legend and epic link his adventures with those of the archetypal hero-figure; the elements that belong to the Devil of Christianity help us to see the hero himself in proper perspective, as one who makes the best of a fallen and sin-bound condition; though, once more, the short-comings of Satan's methods show up sharply against the humility and resolve of fallen Adam at the end of the poem. Heroism and heroic energy are virtues only in a world where struggle, doubt, and danger are real; one would not call the heavenly host heroic, nor God

From *Paradise Lost as 'Myth.'* Copyright © 1959 by The President and Fellows of Harvard College. Harvard University Press.

energetic. But Milton's epic, in its broad outlines, was to be a *complete* rendering of the types of human experience, and to be complete it had to include an account of life "as the state of man now is," as well as a picture of the happy state as it once was and a forecast of happiness to come. The life of fallen man could not, however, be enacted by a human hero, unless the poem's temporal and structural unity were to be sacrificed; Paradise knew nothing of the dark voyage. To show the results of the Fall graphically in the human offspring of Adam and Eve would have trammelled the poem with an unwieldly time-scheme and an inartistic break in the action.

Milton's solution shows an inspired simplicity. The dark voyage is transplanted to the life of the first fallen being. Human pain, struggle, confusion, and (one must add) energy and courage, are brought together in a creature who, while not technically human, shares the relevant human condition: he is sinful and hedged about with limitations. Satan carries this theme, of faltering and seeking "natural man," until, after the Fall, Adam is ready to assume its burden. The hero of myth, it has been said,

> must be one who is sufficiently "human" to be imagined as representative of mankind in its strivings and failures. Such are Aeneas—Dante himself—Adam—Faust. It is perhaps the one inherent weakness of Milton's myth that Adam, in his perfect innocence and ignorance of evil before the Fall, is a figure so remote from all our experience that it is well-nigh impossible to invest him with real interest.

This complaint is frequently lodged against Adam as hero. But Milton, we may think, anticipated Adam's remoteness, and so made Satan joint-hero of the poem, precisely because he was "sufficiently human" to be recognized as an exemplar of our predicament. After the middle of Book X Satan disappears, his part ended, leaving Adam to suffer and contend as the true wayfaring hero.

The continuous parallel between the fall of the angels and the fall of man is, of course, one of the major structural and moral principles of the poem; the imaginative linking of Satan's "wandering quest" with our own fate as voyagers through the unknown is, therefore, not difficult. Milton prepares us for this equation at the beginning of *Paradise Lost*, through a gradual change in the tone of his descriptions of Hell. Although, in the first part of Book I, the tone is one of remoteness and terror, by the time the first book ends we are feeling much more at home, among pilasters, Doric pillars, and bossy sculptures; Pandemonium is all too like the brassy and barren splendors of our own public occasions. This modulation from the remote to the familiar has been criticized as one of Milton's famous inconsistencies, but in fact the angels must be brought closer to our own level if we are to accept a quasi-identification between Satan and ourselves. In Book I, the progression is deliberate and artful; its hinge is the long account of the pagan gods, which brings the fallen angels literally into the context of the known world. When Pandemonium is likened to Babel, Babylon, and Cairo, the transition is almost complete, but it is advanced still further as Book II moves on. The soil of Hell in Book I has a nightmare ambiguity—neither land, liquid, nor fire; but in Book II the landscape takes on more familiar contours with the help of classical and Biblical reminiscences: it becomes "a frozen Continent" with "four infernal rivers." Inconsistent it may be; but, like the time-table in *Othello*, faithful to the psychological necessities of the poem.

The pastimes of Hell's inmates, once they have risen from the burning lake, are clearly human. The games, included principally to match the funeral games of ancient epic, and to point up the fruitless, frivolous nature of activity in Hell, also help to establish a parallel with the human or semi-divine heroes of myth. Two passages are especially pertinent. One is the section on the "vain wisdom" of the angels' philo sophical discussions, which "found no end, in wandering mazes lost."

> Of good and evil much they argu'd then,
> Of happiness and final misery,
> Passion and Apathie, and glory and shame,
> Vain wisdom all, and false Philosophie.
> (ii.562–65)

Of these scenes in Hell, G. Wilson Knight remarks, "It is, indeed, our own fallen world that Milton depicts," and adds: "The Satanic party are mankind in its fruitless struggles." It is always necessary, in reading *Paradise Lost*, to remember that Milton maintains almost constantly a dual point of view; he sees the world simultaneously from a vantage-point outside time, and from the dusty arena where the struggle is real, neces- sary, and an inevitable recourse of resilient if short-sighted human nature. Philosophy may be false, but humanity will go on philosophizing; struggle may be fruitless (though it is not always), but it will be engaged in as long as men exist. The angels' philosophy is, of course, especially vain because they are irredeemable, cut off hopelessly from good. But chiefly, in these lines, Milton is describing *human* preoccupations, including his own: good and evil, happiness and misery, glory and shame—they are the universal themes of legend and myth, of *Paradise Lost* itself. These mixed, opposing concepts are inevitably objects of speculation in a world where value and disvalue "grow up almost inseparably"; Hell is the first where such duplicity is known, but not the last. Two notes are struck in this passage: in the first three lines, a familiar one that brings us closer to a scene in which we (as Satan) are shortly to participate; and in the fourth line, the deeper tone of the timeless setting, where the vanity of these puny philosophers reverberates hollowly within the grand structure of universal truth. The double point of view is characteristic of irony, and the first three books of *Paradise Lost* together form one of the most sustained ironic passages in our literature. Irony is fundamentally tragic; it calls out simultaneously our sympathetic emotions and our critical intellects. Above all, the ironic vision of life refuses to permit a simple attitude. Hence, all arguments as to where our sympathies lie in the early books of Milton's epic are vain; they lie *both* with the follies of the fallen, and with the rigors of reason and discipline that are necessary for our salvation as reasonable beings.

The fallen angels, like fallen men, are wanderers in a maze, searching in vain for an end. From being wanderers in thought, they soon become wanderers in action:

> Thus roving on
> In confus'd march forlorn, th' adventrous Bands
> With shuddring horror pale, and eyes agast
> View'd first thir lamentable lot, and found
> No rest: through many a dark and drearie Vaile
> They pass'd, and many a Region dolorous,
> O're many a Frozen, many a Fierie Alpe,
> Rocks, Caves, Lakes, Fens, Bogs, Dens, and shades of death.
>   (ii.614–21)

The geography has become even more recognizable, the entire picture miserably familiar. Mankind in the wilderness of the world views his lamentable lot with the same shuddering horror, passes through a "drearie Vaile" of tears; the dolorous regions form part of the scenery of Malory's melancholy magic world, of *Sir Gawain, The Faerie Queene, Pilgrim's Progress.* Everyman, like Hell's angels, traverses the valley of the shadow, though unlike them he may attain the Heavenly City. God's mercy and man's repentance add a new dimension to the fate of these angels, but they do not change the initial stages of the journey; the Slough of Despond has still to be crossed and the sickness unto death undergone. Milton's passage reproduces in small compass the wider voyage of Satan, where the true prototype of the dark journey will be enacted; it brings us to the very brink of the abyss where that voyage is to take place.

In both of the passages examined above, the fallen angels are seekers; in the first, for an "end"—both literally and teleologically—in the second, for rest. *Seek, find, discover, search:* these recur persistently in Milton's epic vocabulary. They point to the same goals nearly always: rest, peace, ease. The activities of Hell are a vain attempt to achieve quietness, each angel seeking "where he may likeliest find Truce to his restless thoughts" (ii.525–26). Behind *truce* are images of warfare and division that sprang to life when Heaven and Hell were sundered. With Satan's followers began the eternal restlessness that is the result of imperfection striving to regain, or attain, perfection. The association between lack of rest and loss of virtue can be found in *Comus,* where Milton says of evil,

> It shall be in eternal restless change
> Self-fed and self-consum'd.
> (596–97)

Change enters a changeless universe only with sin, i.e., imperfection in action. The lost, homeless state of man came to seem his peculiar curse, and Milton's lines on the wandering angels are confirmed in "The Pulley" and "Man" by his contemporaries George Herbert and Henry Vaughan.

At two places in Book I the total meaning of *rest* for Milton's design emerges clearly. There is the melancholy, sighing rhythm of a few lines when we first see Hell:

> Regions of sorrow, doleful shades, where peace
> And rest can never dwell, hope never comes
> That comes to all.
> (i.65–67)

The poignancy is in the repeated *never,* for this negative of the happy eternity of Heaven was unknown until this moment. The elliptical phrase, "that comes to all," is there to remind us of the essential *difference* between ourselves and the fallen angels, which is brought out more strongly at the end of the poem; our struggles do have an end in rest, while theirs last eternally. The angel Abdiel, in his exchange with Satan, predicts a dateless future:

> Apostat, still thou errst, nor end wilt find
> Of erring, from the path of truth remote.
> (vi.172–73)

The *likeness* between the sin of men and of angels, on the other hand, is emphasized in another appearance of *never,* with a still more threatening undertone, just before Eve meets the serpent; again, the idea of rest accompanies it.

> Thou never from that houre in Paradise
> Foundst either sweet repast, or sound repose.
>
> (ix.406–07)

Rest makes its second important appearance in Book I in a parenthetical remark of Satan as he urges his followers toward the "dreary Plain":

> Thither let us tend
> From off the tossing of these fiery waves,
> There rest, if any rest can harbour there.
>
> (i.183–85)

Milton's verb, harbour, strengthens the suggestion of the quest for security and calm by making the angels mariners seeking a haven from a stormy ocean. Later, the idea of "no rest" for the weary is allegorized in the incessantly barking offspring of Sin, who complains, "Rest or intermission none I find" (ii.802). The antithesis of the harassments in Hell is found in Eden as Adam leads Eve to the bower:

> Fair Consort, th' hour
> Of night, and all things now retir'd to rest
> Mind us of the like repose, since God hath set
> Labour and rest, as day and night to men
> Successive.
>
> (iv.610–14)

The idea is several times repeated in Milton's account of Paradise; and at the Creation itself, a kind of cosmic rest emerges from restless Chaos. Raphael begins his account with a picture of the achieved, "poised" stillness of the quiet earth itself:

> As yet this world was not, and Chaos wilde
> Reignd where these Heav'ns now rowl, where Earth now rests
> Upon her Center pois'd.
>
> (v.577–79)

The tremor of restlessness re-enters, however, with Satan, who is warned by Michael, "think not here To trouble Holy Rest" (vi.271–72). Satan's intention is exactly that, nevertheless; he has first "disturb'd Heav'ns blessed peace" (vi.266–67), and now turns to trouble the rest of the Garden. The unquiet of evil is manifest in its disregard for the orderly cycles of rest and waking that are the basis of health in living things; hostile to life, it seeks to destroy the processes by which life maintains itself. An earlier example of this intent, not quite so explicit, is found in Comus, who appears at sunset to ask, "What hath night to do with sleep?"

(122). Satan's temptation in Eve's dream follows the same line—"Why sleepst thou Eve?" Night, moon, and stars prevail,

> in vain,
> If none regard; Heav'n wakes with all his eyes,
> Whom to behold but thee, Natures desire . . .
> (v.43–45)

The angels who come to foil his designs observe that he is "imploi'd it seems to violate sleep" (iv.883)—the very original of Comus.

After the first day's battle in Heaven, the rebels withdraw, already fatally afflicted.

> *Satan* with his rebellious disappeerd,
> Far in the dark dislodg'd, and void of rest.
> (vi.414–15)

So, after the Fall, we find Adam and Eve:

> thir shame in part
> Coverd, but not at rest or ease of Mind,
> They sate them down to weep.
> (ix.1119–20)

The end sought in vain by the fallen angels is given to man, however, and with it his place of rest. We suffer,

> till we end
> In dust, our final rest and native home.
> (x.1084–85)

The last variation on this theme comes in a passage from the final book. In it, Milton ties up neatly several threads of diction and imagery; it illustrates the nature of the journey and its goal. Jesus will quell

> The adversarie Serpent, and bring back
> Through the worlds wilderness long wanderd man
> Safe to eternal Paradise of rest.
> (xii.312–14)

Every word is significantly connected with the mythological themes of the poem. "Bring back" suggests the circular journey; *wilderness*, with its reminiscence of the forest and the maze, along with *safe*, indicate its danger. *Long* brings in the temporal dimension necessary to this part of the myth. And in the last phrase, the time-ridden win eternity, the outcasts Eden, the tired wanderers rest.

The word *wander* has almost always a pejorative, or melancholy, connotation in *Paradise Lost*. It is a key word, summarizing the theme of the erring, bewildered human pilgrimage, and its extension into the prelapsarian world with the fallen angels. As pagan gods, they are seen "wandring ore the Earth" (i.365); in Hell after Satan's departure, they "disband, and wandring, each his several way Pursues" (ii.523–24), or becomes lost in philosophic mazes. The theme here meshes with a closely allied though minor image, a persistent favorite with Milton, the laby-rinth. It stands for the difficulties of the dark voyage, the stage where the monster is encountered and the deceitful sorcerer appears with "baits and seeming pleasures." In *Comus*, the "Sunclad power of Chastity" shines forth even from the labyrinthine "huge Forrests, and unharbour'd Heaths";

> Yea there, where very desolation dwels
> By grots, and caverns shag'd with horrid shades,
> She may pass on with unblench't majesty.
> (428–30)

Almost all the images of danger that surround the journey of life are here: forest, desert, hills, caves. Later, Milton used the image in prose, empha-sizing the difference between the straightness of heaven and the dangerous crookedness of earth: "the ways of the Lord straight and faithful as they are, not full of cranks and contradictions, and pitfalling dispenses." But the most dangerous labyrinth is in the human soul, "the wily subtleties and refluxes of man's thoughts." Mazes, crooked ways, labyrinths, and "refluxes," are all to be found on a larger scale in *Paradise Lost*; they indicate the wayward and misleading powers of error, of which the serpent himself is the physical embodiment.

> Lead then, said *Eve*. Hee leading swiftly rowld
> In tangles, and made intricate seem straight,
> To mischief swift. Hope elevates, and joy
> Bright'ns his Crest, as when a wandring Fire
> Compact of unctuous vapor, which the Night
> Condenses, and the cold invirons round,
> Which oft, they say, some evil Spirit attends,
> Hovering and blazing with delusive Light,
> Misleads th' amaz'd Night-wanderer from his way.
> (ix.631–40)

The intrusion of cold and night into a pastoral scene of "blowing Myrrh and Balme" casts a sudden chill over Eden, and the intricate tangles of the serpent, the wandering course, hark back to the "brazen foulds" of the gate in Pandemonium (i.724) and the "scaly fould" of Sin (ii.651); the passage also looks ahead to Adam's perplexity after the Fall.

> All my evasions vain
> And reasonings, though through Mazes, lead me still
> But to my own conviction.
>
> (x.829–31)

Not only moral values, but the intellectual values on which they depend, can be objectified in Milton's topography, by the identification of physical and spiritual "wandering." Error is the linking word. The Paradise of Fools, "o're the backside of the World," includes follies that are defined as errors in the physical sense—wanderings off course, mistaking one place for another.

> Here Pilgrims roam, that stray'd so farr to seek
> In Golgotha him dead, who lives in Heav'n.
>
> (iii.476–77)

There is, too, the errant Satan, "from the path of truth remote," and his complement, Abdiel, who refuses to "swerve from truth" (v.902). Adam foresees an endless happiness, remote from "all anxious care" and confusion,

> unless we our selves
> Seek them with wandring thoughts, and notions vaine.
> But apte the Mind or Fancie is to roave
> Uncheckt, and of her roaving is no end.
>
> (viii.186–89)

In the end, despite his momentary wisdom, he is the victim of "wandring vanitie" (x.875). Milton carries the same images and diction into Samson Agonistes to indicate the doubt and perplexity from which Samson's ancestor, Adam, had prayed to be delivered, and to which his contemporaries had fallen prey, who

> give the rains to wandring thought,
> Regardless of his glories diminution;
> Till by thir own perplexities involv'd
> They ravel more, still less resolv'd,
> But never find self-satisfying solution.
>
> (300–09)

These wanderers are the lineal descendants of the angels in Hell who found themselves lost in wandering mazes.

The most memorable instance of Milton's use of wander is the phrase "wandring steps and slow" at the close of Paradise Lost; almost equally suggestive is Eve's speech as the recognition of her loss becomes part of her consciousness.

> From thee
> How shall I part, and whither wander down
> Into a lower World, to this obscure
> And wilde, how shall we breath in other Aire
> Less pure, accustomed to immortal Fruits?
> (xi.281–85)

Milton's adjectives call on the archetypes already established in the major action, to characterize the new, strange world: *obscure*, because farther removed from the fountain of light, and because the planets that illuminate it have been turned oblique; *wilde*, because nature is now hostile; its air *less pure* than the clear brilliance of Paradise.

The lesser perplexities and wanderings of *Paradise Lost* are anticipations or echoes of Satan's flight to earth; in Francis Fergusson's phrase, they are "analogous actions," with Satan the ultimate analogue. His voyage, in turn, reinforces the parallel between the two falls. In the nature of Satan's journey we can find, perhaps, one of the sources of our sympathy, or empathy, with him—a sympathy that has been excused, applauded, justified, and denied, but will never be explained to everyone's satisfaction. Some of Milton's most intimate feelings were certainly involved in his portrait of Satan, but the nature of those feelings may have been more universal than his rebellious Puritan independence. Satan's pilgrimage through the dark toward Paradise re-traces the necessity that life imposes on us all. His cry, "Long is the way and hard, that out of Hell leads up to light," speaks to an emotion almost universal, the same that answers Dante's verses—

> salimmo suso, ei primo ed io secondo,
> tanto ch' io vidi delle cose belle
> che porta il ciel, per un pertugio tondo;
>
> e quindi uscimmo a riverder le stelle.

> We mounted up, he first and I second, so far that I distinguished through a round opening the beauteous things which Heaven bears; and thence we issued out, again to see the Stars.
> (*Inferno*, xxiv.136–139. Translated by John Aitken Carlyle.
> The Temple Classics [London, 1941], pp. 390–91)

The urge to regain "the Archetype of the Vanishing Garden" "draws sustenance from the unplumbed depths of our individual and collective unconscious." Satan, exiled from Heaven, seeks compensation in man's Garden for his lost glory, tracing in the process the first of many quests.

The idea of Satan as outcast and wanderer was, of course, traditional, and evidently appealed to Milton from the beginning. In his youthful poem, *In quintum Novembris*, the Devil is described as "aethero vagus exul Olympo." We can see a faint shadow of a more distant voyage in his circling of the globe, and in his journey to Rome the ghost of his primordial quest.

> Hactenus; & piceis liquido natat aere pennis;
> Qua volat, adversi praecursant agmine venti,
> Densantur nubes, & crebra tonitrua fulgent.
>   Iamque pruinosas velox superaverat alpes,
> Et tenet Ausoniae fines.

This and no more; then with his pitch-black wings he swims in the liquid air. Wherever he flies, warring winds in battalions race before him, the clouds thicken, and the thunder and lightning are incessant.

And now he had swiftly passed over the ice-mantled Alps and was within the borders of Ausonia.

(ll.45–59. Translated by N. G. McCrea)

Milton's lines call to mind another seeker of the Ausonian land, in whose story was embedded the mythological theme of a journey toward a promised land.

> Vivite felices, quibus est fortuna peracta
> iam sua; nos alia ex aliis in fata vocamur.
> Vobis parta quies; nullum maris aequor arandum
> arva neque Ausoniae semper cedentia retro
> quaerenda.

Fare ye well, ye whose own destiny is already achieved; we are still summoned from fate to fate. Your rest is won. No ocean plains need ye plough, no ever-retreating Ausonian fields need ye seek.

(*Aeneid* ii.493–97. Translated by H. Rushton Fairclough.
Virgil, I, 380–81)

Whether it is the vanishing garden or the ever-vanishing Ausonian shore, the object of the quest is really the same: a home, a haven, safety, rest; or, if one likes, "the womb's security."

The voyage of Books II and III is Milton's greatest "original" creation. There was precedent for the journey motif in epic tradition, but no real parallel to a voyage by Satan in the Christian literature on which Milton drew. The germ of the theme may have been suggested by Grotius' *Adamus Exul*, which opens with "Sathan" proclaiming his intensions in soliloquy.

> Hac spe, per omnes Orbis ibo terminos,
> Hac spe citatus, clausa littoribus vagis

Transibo maria, saevus ut rictu Leo
Patulo timendus per locorum devia
Quaerit quod avido dente dilaniet pecus.

In this hope, I shall go through all the Globe's wide bounds;
Spurr'd by this hope I'll cross the seas, hemm'd in
By wandering shores; just as a cruel lion seeks
Through wandering ways, with formidable open jaws,
Some hapless flock that he may rend with greedy fangs.
(Translated by Watson Kirkonnell. *The Celestial Cycle*
[Toronto, 1952], pp. 98–99)

There were, too, contemporary "influences" at work on Milton, as Marjorie Nicolson has reminded us. "Satan's voyage through Chaos is one of the great 'cosmic voyages' of a period that sent imaginary mariners to the moon and planets in search of other worlds and other men." Milton's conception of Satan's journey remains unique, however, and more powerfully suggestive than any comparable treatment.

Complexity and suggestiveness enter at the start when we consider Chaos, the primordial ocean. Satan's traverse of it is an attempt to heal his impaired perfection, whether that be interpreted psychologically as a defeat by "the archiac forces of the unconscious," or morally as a fall into the disorder of sin which, Milton once wrote, is "as boundless as that vacuity beyond the world." Satan is, of course, going about the repair in the wrong way; he supposes that the achievement of Paradise or "some milde Zone" will divest him of gloom and anguish, not realizing that with his loss of Heaven he has also lost the sympathy with outward things that will allow them to touch and influence him. The nature of his quest and its failure are both indicated in an observation by Milton as Satan, entering the Garden, perches on the Tree of Life, "like a Cormorant."

Yet not true Life
Thereby regaind, but sat devising Death
To them who liv'd; nor on the vertue thought
Of that life-giving Plant, but only us'd
For prospect, what well us'd had bin the pledge
Of immortalitie.
(iv. 196–201)

Satan has been seeking a return to the immortal life he lost; and Milton includes in these lines a hint to more fortunate pilgrims that God's gifts, "well us'd," *can* lead to Paradise regained. Unregenerate, Satan brings his Hell with him.

His mission is, nevertheless, the traditional one of the hero, who seeks to renew or restore the kingdom for his people by winning some "treasure hard to attain." The images accord, therefore, with traditional accounts of the quest; the two basic ones, sea (Chaos) and pilgrimage, are really inseparable. Satan's role as pilgrim requires the dolorous regions through which he will pass. In accordance with epic precedent, the journey is expressed quite consistently in the imagery of a voyage, though the desert and wooded wilderness, also suitable quest-scenes, are never far away. Satan's first proposal of the search for Paradise, in the council of Hell, is like the previews in fairy tales, legend, and romance, of the perilous quest to be undertaken by the knight.

> What strength, what art can then
> Suffice, or what evasion bear him safe
> Through the strict Senteries and Stations thick
> Of Angels watching round?
>
> (ii.410–13)

A similar prospect confronts the Red Cross Knight setting out through the Wood of Error for the redemption of a symbolic city hedged about with perils, though his chief peril is not an angel, but a reincarnation of the old Serpent himself, who has changed his role to that of challenger. Another analogue is the hero of the *Romance of the Rose* attempting to enter a garden defended by allegorical sentries. The path to be followed by them all is "the Road of Trials," "a dream landscape of curiously fluid, ambiguous forms"; it is the "dim domain that has been for milleniums the holy goal of all the great questing heroes, from Gilgamesh to Faust."

As the final quotation suggests, the later heroes of myth usually reversed Satan's path, their first "holy goal" being the realm of death, from whose perils they returned to gain their reward in the shape of regained Paradise. Satan has ventured down, too, but his descent was involuntary. And his reascending quest is motivated by destructive rather than constructive impulses; though he starts out to seek a place where he can heal the scars of Hell, or reintegrate his personality, he ends by wanting merely to destroy the place, and his final fall is a further ignominious disintegration. Satan fails, as he must always fail; but his inverted image, with a successful end, is the pilgrim of *The Divine Comedy*. Our hopes and fears may not extend as high as Dante's or as low as Satan's, but we are bound on the same route. For man, the object of God's mercy as well as his wrath, trial may be "that which purifies us." But it is still a trial: "the way seems difficult and steep to scale" (ii.71).

Satan anticipates the trials awaiting him, in his speech accepting "alone the dreadful voyage." There is the void of Night, in which he will be threatened with "utter loss of being"—the descent into a pre-personal world where selfhood is swallowed up in the "abortive gulf" of unconscious and racial memory. There follows the journey through the unknown land.

> If thence he scape into what ever world,
> Or unknown Region, what remains him less
> Then unknown dangers and as hard escape.
> (ii.442–44)

After all, Satan's voyage is very like traditional "descents," even though he starts from deep Hell and not, like earthly heroes, from the light of day. In his speech to his angels, he makes Hell seem almost a haven, compared to the dangers awaiting him outside, and his entry into Chaos is as devastating as a true descent to the underworld. The grim guardians of Hell Gate are the first of his obstacles, and in his encounter with them we can see clearly for the first time Milton's design for his voyage. Once Satan has been allowed by God to escape from Hell, there is really no reason why he should not be immediately transferred to Paradise, where the main action of the Fall will begin. No reason, that is, except Milton's intention of including the great archetype of the journey in his poem. To be faithful to it, he had to include the trials of traditional quest-literature, and so Sin, Death, and the kingdom of Chaos are stationed in Satan's path. Like other heroes, he finds monsters in the Deep. Sin, with her scaly folds, is a combination of the old serpent of the ocean and another dream-figure, the siren or lamia, "who infatuates the lonely wanderer"; Milton's description of her accords with old illustrations of lamias, as well as with verbal accounts. Northrop Frye has said that the "darkness, winter and dissolution phase" of the universal myth contains as two of its standard subordinate characters "the ogre and the witch"; they, too, probably find ancestors in Milton's Sin and Death.

It is interesting, too, that allegorical beings, whose introduction into *Paradise Lost* has distracted so many critics, should inhabit the section of the poem that contains the favorite theme of allegory. Satan, a fallen creature, is already beginning to live in a world of allegorical symbols instead of myth. There is a family resemblance between Milton's Sin and Death and the traditional personages of allegory to whom they stand as grandparents, and the similarity has tended to obscure their place in *Paradise Lost.* Johnson, who considered "this unskilful allegory . . . one of the greatest faults of the poem," recognized, though he did not applaud, the untraditional character of Milton's figures.

> To exalt causes into agents, to invest abstract ideas with form, and animate them with activity has always been the right of poetry. But such

airy beings are for the most part suffered only to do their natural office, and retire; Thus Fame tells a tale and Victory hovers over a general or perches on a standard; but Fame and Victory can do no more. To give them any real employment or ascribe to them any material agency is to make them allegorical no longer, but to shock the mind by ascribing effects to nonentity.

Johnson's idea of allegory was, indeed, more circumscribed than it should have been; but more liberal standards cannot quite accommodate Milton's Sin under the conventional label of allegory, either. She is larger and more solid even than most of Bunyan's characters, the very incarnation of whatever is horrible and fascinating in evil. In the total context of *Paradise Lost*, she and Death are, as Johnson said, "allegorical no longer," but it is because Milton's "abstractions" are always substances, not because they are nonentities. When we first encounter them, with Satan, they call up so many echoes of others of their species that we seem to be already in a familiar world of disembodied abstractions. Later, however, when they enter the fallen world, we can see that they represent the last stage of Milton's *mythical* presentation. He had promised to tell how the Fall "brought Death into the World" and, since the story in its main outlines was mythical, the invasion of earth's frail shell by a literal, concrete Death was necessary, as had been the literal birth of Sin from Satan described in Book II. Once the Fall has taken place, the myth recedes into memory, to be replaced by new modes of experience, and it is at the point where it begins to recede that Sin and Death build their bridge. These two creatures live on the borderline between myth and allegory, between a world where physical and spiritual forces are identical, and a world where spiritual force is merely indicated by physical. They are neither wholly mythic nor completely allegorical. Sin can already separate her body from her power, because the quality embodied in her has been shattered by man's sin and distributed through the many bodies of the mortally stricken universe.

> Mean while in Paradise the hellish pair
> Too soon arriv'd, *Sin* there in power before,
> Once actual, now in body, and to dwell
> Habitual habitant.
>
> (x.585–88)

With Eve's sin (that is, when, with a sinful act, Sin became "actual"), a part of the archetype is separated from itself, and the fragment lodged in the human soul. Henceforth, because sin will be so widespread, no single representation of her can be complete; Milton's is the last full-length portrait before the destruction of archetypes.

The whole of Book X, indeed, hovers on the threshold between literal and figurative, and it is impossible to accept the bridge from Hell quite as unreservedly as "real," as the cosmography of Book III. This change seems to be reflected even in the style; the description of the bridge-building has struck many readers as odd, and is in fact much more particular and specialized than Milton's ordinary mythical language. Mr. Empson objects to the passage about "Gorgonian rigor" on the ground that it "shows the process of finding concrete for abstract caught half-way"; this is an exact account of what is really happening at that moment in the world of the poem, and Milton's style can be justified by saying that he was reproducing in it the half-real, half-imaginary quality of his subject.

Though their ontological status is ambiguous, Sin and Death, by their presence in Book II, help us to translate Satan's voyage into the terms of more familiar earthly pilgrimages. The process is assisted by Milton's allusions; a collection of famous voyagers make the voyaging Satan recognizable. Sin becomes an Homeric monster:

> Far less abhorrd then these
> Vex'd *Scylla* bathing in the Sea that parts
> *Calabria* from the hoarce *Trinacrian* shore.
> (ii.659–61)

Far into Chaos, Satan is beset by warring elements; he is, once more, Odysseus, and also Jason:

> Harder beset
> And more endanger'd, then when *Argo* pass'd
> Through *Bosporus* betwixt the justling Rocks:
> Or when *Ulysses* on the Larbord shunnd
> *Charybdis*, and by th' other whirlpool steard.
> (ii.1016–20)

He has already likened earth to "the happy Ile" (ii.410); the association is made again as he approaches Eden.

> Or other Worlds they seemd, or happy Iles,
> Like those *Hesperian* Gardens fam'd of old.
> (iii.567–68)

Earth is one Paradise among the starry Islands of the Blest that were the objects of nostalgia for the classical world. Their number and beauty gives a sense of almost dizzying opulence, as though Satan were swimming in the very atmosphere of a dream-paradise. As islands, the stars reinforce the image of the voyage; as Paradise, they support its spiritual intention.

Sometimes the inspiration for the imagery of these books comes not from other myths, but from the excitement of an opening world that had pricked the imaginations of poets for a century or more. Milton's geographical interests find ample scope in Satan's voyage along the unknown "coasts of dark destruction." The flagship for which Satan's spear in Book I provided a mast taller than the tallest Norwegian pine, becomes a whole fleet as he launches into Chaos, in the simile of the merchants on the "Trading Flood" (ii.636 ff.). By the time he comes in sight of the new world, he is weather-beaten, "glad that now his Sea should find a shore" (ii.1011), however brief his sojourn there.

> *Satan* with less toil, and now with ease
> Wafts on the calmer wave by dubious light
> And like a weather-beaten Vessel holds
> Gladly the Port, though Shrouds and Tackle torn.
> (ii.1041–44)

In the last lines of Book II, the voice of Milton speaks through the imagery to characterize this vessel; it is "full fraught with mischievous revenge" (ii.1054). Finally, as he is about to enter the Garden, Satan is a wolf and a thief, but he is also the mariner off the Cape of Good Hope, cheered by the grateful smell of Araby the Blest (iv.159 ff.).

Just as significant mythologically are the passages in which Satan's voyage is transported to land, and the theme is carried by images of the quest in the desert.

> Wandring this darksome Desart, as my way
> Lies through your spacious Empire up to light,
> Alone, and without guide, half lost, I seek
> What readiest path . . .
> (ii.973–76)

The major image of Book III is of Satan as a wilderness wanderer.

> As when a Scout
> Through dark and desert wayes with peril gone
> All night; at last by break of chearful dawne
> Obtains the brow of some high-climbing Hill . . .
> (iii.543–46)

After Book IV, the quest images cease, to resume after the Fall when man, too, has become a wanderer. There is a last allusion to Satan as a "great adventurer" awaited by his host (x.440); and Milton did not finally abandon the image until he had used it of the Satan of *Paradise Regained*. The Devil is still fruitlessly wandering the earth, finding no end; the "eternal restless change" of evil is incarnate in him, forcing from him a final despairing cry:

> I would be at my worst; worst is my Port,
> My harbour and my ultimate repose,
> The end I would attain, my final good.
>   (iii.209–11)

Paradise Regained is an "answer" to *Paradise Lost* in several ways; the answer is stated mythically in the "wilderness" imagery that makes Christ an instance of the hero beset by dangers. It is clear that Milton intended his Christ, wandering a "pathless Desert, dusk with horrid shades" (*P.R.*, i.296), to be the counterweight to Satan in *Paradise Lost*, also a pilgrim, but an erring one. Together they enact man's fate. An appropriate, if tempo-- rary, close is achieved in the last line of *Paradise Regained*, where Jesus is brought "home to his Mothers house"; the house is an ancient and natural enough emblem for the goal, resting-place, or harbor sought by the traveler. The most profound parallel between Satan and Christ, Milton did not choose to depict in his poetry; but the descent of the Savior to the lower regions is alluded to in traditional mythological terms in the *Christian Doctrine*.

> Hence it appears that baptism was intended to represent figuratively the painful life of Christ, his death and burial, in which he was immersed, as it were, for a season.

The waters of death received Christ, as the "waters" of Chaos had received Satan.

Into the adventures and exploits of Satan in the first four books of *Paradise Lost*, Milton incorporated not only explicit images of voyaging and pilgrimage, but also a number of motifs familiar to us in the literature of our own perplexed lives. Satan encounters and experiences, in anticipation or simile, the sinful world he is to create; indeed, we see him creating it as he goes along. After the colloquy with Sin and Death, with its forecast of "Pestilence and Warr" (ii.711), he comes upon the Anarch, Chaos, and "Sable-vested Night, eldest of things," whose arrival on earth will make the good things of day begin to droop and drowse and force a prayer from the benighted traveler; witness the Elder Brother of *Comus*, invoking moon and stars:

> Stoop thy pale visage through an amber cloud,
> And disinherit *Chaos*, that raigns here
> In double night of darkness and of shades.
>   (733–35)

The episode of the Paradise of Fools and its procession of future human trumpery is similarly prophetic. Satan also wears many of the guises he is to put on in the world's legends; he is, almost from the start of the voyage, the "specious object" against whom Eve is warned (ix.361). In his meeting with Uriel, he is the transformed wizard, ancestor of Archimago and Duessa—"the first That practisd falshood under saintly shew" (iv.121–22). Here he is a cherub; elsewhere a "Vultur on *Imaus* bred . . . to gorge the flesh of Lambs" (iii.431–34); shapeshifted again, a toad; and once more, "a Lion now he stalkes with fierie glare, Then as a Tyger," anticipating the hostile environment where beasts will threaten "gentle Fawnes at play" (iv.402–4). The mount of Paradise, assaulted by this "prowling Wolfe," suggests all the other enclosed treasures destined to fall prey to Satan's descendants. The accumulation of references to our familiar delusions and perils—the will-o'-the-wisp and Leviathan are others, placed elsewhere in the poem—shows once more the usefulness to Milton's scheme of the Satan sub-plot, in drawing into the mythical "present" of the poem the "future" of legend and history.

In the middle books of *Paradise Lost*, Milton is occupied with the still, changeless image of Paradise, and with the War, first on the soil of Heaven, then in the soul of man. Books IV through VIII are a still center of his turning world; Satan's quest leads up to them, and man's quest—both for the Paradise within, and for the lost Garden itself—leads away, down into the lower world of Biblical history. Dryden was perhaps the first to notice the modulation at the close of *Paradise Lost* into the symbolism of *The Faerie Queene* and its peers. He would have ranked Milton higher, he said, "if the giant had not foiled the knight, and driven him out of his stronghold, to wander through the world with his lady errant." This was a fanciful way of stating his objection to the "unhappy" ending of *Paradise Lost*; but the observation itself is accurate, and we may see a special virtue in the integration of the great Christian myth with the most universal of mythological themes. Dryden's statement indicates the ease with which the *dénouement* of *Paradise Lost* can be translated into the familiar terms of courtly romance, and thence into the allegory of Everyman. Tillyard has developed the idea in his remark that, at the end of the poem, Milton "in the manner of Spenser" presents Adam and Eve as "Everyman and Everywoman . . . setting out on their earthly quest for a mental paradise."

Milton dovetails his two journeys—the proto-human and the human—in a pointed line as Satan achieves, for the moment, his goal: "His journies end and our beginning woe" (iii.633). Time, in the consciousness of the first fallen creature, has led up to this moment, and time and struggle, the keynotes of fallen human consciousness, will follow. The transference of the quest theme from Satan to man is made plain later in the poem's action, but it is epitomized in this line. The nature of the "beginning woe," the life journey, is shown in the prophecy of Book III, where the shift of the pilgrim's progress to man's soul is described by God:

> And I will place within them as a guide
> My Umpire *Conscience*, whom if they will hear,
> Light after light well us'd they shall attain,
> And to the end persisting, safe arrive.
>
> (iii. 194–97)

This reads almost like a summary of Christian's safe arrival at the Heavenly City; it is echoed in the final book—

> Through the worlds wilderness long wanderd man
> Safe to eternal Paradise of rest.
>
> (xii. 313–14)

The quests of the Old Testament have, by this time, provided concrete examples of mankind's characteristic fate; the last books are full of journeys. Adam's phrase for Noah suggests again "the worlds wilderness": the patriarch is seen "wandring that watrie Desert" (xi. 779), the prototype of later travelers for whom Milton had once invoked the aid of Lycidas—"all that wander in that perilous flood." The endless Biblical pilgrimages related by Michael include Moses leading the Israelites, and Abraham,

> Not wandring poor, but trusting all his wealth
> With God, who call'd him, in a land unknown.
>
> (xii. 133–34)

All these, taken together, telescope the theme of the life journey, which is to be continued through the generations until "long wanderd man" is brought safely home.

The two most striking "interludes" in the main structure of *Paradise Lost* are both essential to the success of Milton's epic as a mythological poem. The introduction, at the beginning, of Satan's voyage, and at the end, of history seen in panorama, spatially rather than temporally, allow him to include the second major area of the Christian myth in his "architectural" plan. They give us a vision of human history in a form that is non-historical. The life of man is encompassed within the very walls of the City of God, on which Milton founded his changeless, eternal structure.

WILLIAM EMPSON

Heaven

We are often told nowadays that Milton's attitude to Satan must have been perfectly simple, but it is clear that when writing *Paradise Lost* he had plenty more evidence for God's connivance with Satan which he chose not to use. The reason why this game can be played, of course, is that the Old Testament is a rag-bag of material from very different stages of development; one would think Milton after his thorough study must have understood that, but his main allies were committed to relying on the text, to oppose the traditions of Rome. The furthest he went in writing was to conjecture that God allowed the text of his Word to become corrupt so as to force upon our attention the prior importance of our own consciences (*De Doctrina*, Chapter XXX).

No scholastic philosopher, said Sir Walter Raleigh, "could have walked into a metaphysical bramble-bush with the blind recklessness that Milton displays"; he seems to have been the first to make this very central point. But I do not think anyone who has read the *De Doctrina* will regard Milton's treatment as due to ignorance or stupidity. The effect is that of a powerful mind thrashing about in exasperation. Perhaps I should have recognized earlier a scholastic position which he would consider elementary; we are not to think that God forces the will of individuals merely because he foreknows what they will do. God's foreknowledge was universally admitted, even by believers in free will, such as Milton had become when he wrote the epic. The idea in itself is not remote from common experience; many a mother has felt with horror that she can 'see' her son is going to take to bad courses. We find a greater difficulty in the case of a Creator, as was said in lapidary form by Aquinas:

From *Milton's God*. Copyright © 1961 by William Empson. New Directions Books.

> Knowledge, as knowledge, does not imply, indeed, causality; but, in so far as it is a knowledge belonging to the artist who forms, it stands in the relation of causality to that which is produced by his art.

This too is not beyond our experience, especially if we firmly regard the Creator as a Father; who will often fear, without even blaming Mother, a recurrence of his own bad tendencies or perhaps those of the wicked uncles. Besides, an ancient tradition allows us to say that an author may be too inspired quite to foresee what he is producing by his art. But a parent who 'foresaw' that the children would fall and then insisted upon exposing them to the temptation in view would be considered neurotic, if nothing worse; and this is what we must ascribe to Milton's God.

Waldock, I think, first remarked that he seems anxious to prove he does not cause the Fall; "indeed, never to the end of the poem does he succeed in living down this particular worry". I had perhaps better document this argument. God says in his first speech:

> So without least impulse or shadow of Fate,
> Or aught by me immutably foreseen,
> They trespass, Authors to themselves in all
> Both what they judge and what they choose; for so
> I formed them free, and free they must remain,
> Till they enthrall themselves.
>
> (III. 120)

All this upbraiding of them is done before they have fallen, and God again protests his innocence as soon as they have done it:

> no Decree of mine
> Concurring to necessitate his Fall,
> Or touch with lightest moment of impulse
> His free will, to her own inclining left
> In even scale.
>
> (X.45)

Can it be the uneasy conscience of God or of Milton which produces this unfortunate metaphor of the scales, actually reminding us of the incident when he forced his troops to expose mankind to the tempter? Before the Creation, he gives what is perhaps a slightly different account of his power:

> Boundless the Deep, because I am who fill
> Infinitude, nor vacuous the space.
> Though I uncircumscribed myself retire,
> And put not forth my goodness, which is free
> To act or not, Necessity and Chance
> Approach not mee, and what I will is Fate.
>
> (VII.170)

This is one of the main bits used by M. Saurat to show the profundity, or
the impersonality and pantheism, of Milton's God; and God's claims do
feel better if we identify him with Fate and the Absolute and the primeval
matter of Chaos. But surely the story we are reading inspires a simpler
reflection. Chaos is also a person, and though he acts out of resentment,
so that God would not need to tip him off about the situation, he does
exactly what God wants of him; he lets Satan pass for the corruption of
mankind. As for making Sin and Death the guardians of Hell Gate, Sir
Walter Raleigh remarked with casual elegance:

> No one has plausibly explained how they came by their office. It was
> intended to be a perfect sinecure; there was no one to be let in and no
> one to be let out. The single occasion that presented itself for a neglect
> of their duty was by them eagerly seized.

—though later he approves of the absurdity, because "they are the only
creations of English poetry which approach the Latin in grandeur." Surely
the explanation is very simple; God always intended them to let Satan
out. Critics somehow cannot bring themselves to recognize that Milton
does this steadily and consistently, after announcing that he will at the
start. As a believer in the providence of God, Milton could not possibly
have believed in the huge success-story of Satan fighting his way to
Paradise. The chains of Hell, Sin, Death, Chaos and an army of good
angels hold Satan back, but all this stage machinery is arranged by God to
collapse as soon as he advances upon it, just as the fire cannot harm
Siegfried when he has courage enough to walk through it to Brunhild.
Chaos indeed jeers at the heroic piece of space-travel when he directs
Satan to the newly created world:

> If that be your walk, you have not far.
>   (II. 1010)

(By the way, Yvor Winters could not have called this line 'meaningless
inflation'.) We have thus no reason to doubt that Milton also intended the
final paradox of the series, after Satan has reached Eden, when God
cheats his own troops to make certain that the Fall occurs. As to what
God means by saying that none of his busy activity affects their free will, I
suppose he means that he does not actually hypnotize them, as Svengali
did Trilby; though he lets Satan do to Eve as much as a hypnotist really
can do.

A particularly impressive example of this poetic technique is given
by a detail about the chains, which I think must have made Mr T. S.
Eliot decide that the treatment of the chains is not sufficiently imagist.

The first words of God in the poem insist that he cannot control Satan, and mention these chains as among the things that Satan has escaped from. We might indeed suppose that Milton has 'made a slip', forgotten his story and his theology, whether from lack of imaging or not. The reason why this will not do, I think, is that he is writing so frightfully well; his feelings are so deeply involved that the sound effects become wonderful. *Wide interrupt can hold* is like the cry of sea-mews upon rocks; it has what I think is meant by the term 'plangency'. We have to suppose it meant something important to him.

> Only begotten Son, seest thou what rage
> Transports our adversary, whom no bounds
> Prescrib'd, no bars of Hell, nor all the chains
> Heapt on him there, nor yet the main Abyss
> Wide interrupt can hold; so bent he seems
> On desperate revenge, that shall redound
> Upon his own rebellious head. And now
> Through all restraint broke loose he wings his way
> Nor far off Heav'n, in the Precincts of Light,
> Directly towards the new created World,
> And man there plac'd . . .
>
> (III. 80)

The only consistent view, after the firm statement at I. 210 for example, is that this is the first of God's grisly jokes. The passage, I think, is the strongest bit of evidence for the view of C. S. Lewis, that Milton intended Satan to be ridiculous; but even so it does not feel very like a joke. Milton might have some wish to confuse his simpler readers, and God to confuse the loyalist angels, who have been summoned to hear him; one might think God could not want to look weak, but he may be wanting to justify his revenge. Nobody says that it is a joke, as the Son does after God expresses fear of losing his throne; but there is no opportunity, because what God goes on to say is so lengthy and appalling. His settled plan for punishment comes steadily out, and the verse rhythm becomes totally unlike the thrilling energy of this first sentence. In his first reply to the Son, we find him talking in rocking-horse couplets, using the off-rhymes which were re-invented by Wilfred Owen to describe the First World War, with the same purpose of setting a reader's teeth on edge:

> This my long sufferance and my day of grace
> They who neglect and scorn, shall never taste;
> But hard be hardened, blind be blinded more,
> That they may stumble on, and deeper fall.
>
> (III. 200)

This is also where we get the stage-villain's hiss of "Die he or Justice must". God is much at his worst here, in his first appearance; but he needs to be, to make the offer of the Son produce a dramatic change. I do not know what to make of his expressing the Calvinist doctrine that the elect are chosen by his will alone, which Milton had appeared to reject; it has a peculiar impact here, when God has not yet even secured the Fall of Adam and Eve. One might argue that he was in no mood to make jokes; and besides, the effect here is not a sardonic mockery of Satan, which can be felt in the military joke readily enough, but a mysterious and deeply rooted sense of glory. A simple explanation may be put forward; Milton felt that this was such a tricky bit to put over his audience, because the inherent contradictions were coming so very near the surface, that he needed with a secret delight to call on the whole of his power. This is almost what Shelley took to be his frame of mind; and it is hard to accept, with the *De Doctrina* before us, without talking about Milton's Unconsciousness. But we may be sure that there is a mediating factor; if he had been challenged about the passage, he would have said that he was following the Old Testament scrupulously, and allowing God to mock his foes.

This has often been said about the jokes of Milton's God, or at least about the one which can't be ignored because it is explained as a joke (V. 720); and one can make a rough check from the Concordance at the end of a Bible. The only important case is from Psalm ii; here again we meet the ancient document in which the King of Zion is adopted as the son of God:

> Why do the heathen rage . . . ? The kings of the earth set themselves, and the rulers take counsel together, against the Lord, and against his anointed. . . . He that sitteth in the heavens shall laugh; the Lord shall have them in derision.

This is echoed in Psalms xxxvii. 13 and lix. 8, and perhaps in Proverbs i.26, where Wisdom and not God mocks the worldly rather than a powerful aggressor; but after trying to look under all the relevant words I do not find that the Concordance ever ascribes the sentiment to the Prophets. It was thus an ancient tradition but one treated with reserve, as Milton would understand. Naturally his intention in putting so much weight on it has been found especially hard to grasp.

The views of M. Morand about the divine characters have been neglected and seem to me illuminating. In the same year as *De Comus A Satan* he published a pamphlet in English, *The Effects of his Political Life on John Milton*, concerned to show that a certain worldly-mindedness entered

Milton's later poetry as a result of his rather sordid experience of government, politics, and propaganda. What chiefly stands out in this lively
work, I think, is an accusation that Milton himself had smuggled into a
later edition of *Eikon Basilike* the prayer, derived from Sidney's *Arcadia*, for
which he then so resoundingly denounced King Charles in *Eikonoclastes*;
we are given a shocking picture of an English expert getting the evidence
of a Dutch researcher ignored by gentlemanly bluff. Mr Robert Graves
used the main story in *Wife to Mr Milton*, but I had not realized that the
evidence for it was so strong; indeed, Mr Graves often seems too disgusted
by Milton to be convincing—disagreeable in many ways he may have been,
but surely not a physical coward. I don't feel that the action is too bad for
Milton; he would think the divine purpose behind the Civil War justified
propaganda tricks, and need not have thought this a particularly bad one.
The King was dead, and the purpose of the cheat was merely to prevent
the people from thinking him a martyr. He hadn't written any of the book
really, and Milton suspected that at the time, so it was only a matter of
answering one cheat with another. Milton must in any case have been
insincere in pretending to be shocked at the use of a prayer by Sidney,
given in the story as that of a pagan, but so Christian in feeling as to be
out of period (it assumes that God may be sending us evil as a test or tonic
for our characters, which even if to be found in Aeschylus or Marcus
Aurelius is not standard for Arcadia). Milton might comfort himself with
the reflection that he wasn't even damaging the man's character in the
eyes of fit judges, only making use of a popular superstition—as Shelley
expected on another occasion. However, M. Morand finds that this kind
of activity brought about a Fallen condition, as one might say, in the
mind of the poet, and such is what *De Comus A Satan* examines throughout the later poetry.

There is an assumption here that to do Government propaganda
can only have a bad effect upon a poet's mind, and I feel able to speak on
the point as I was employed at such work myself in the Second World War,
indeed once had the honour of being named in rebuttal by Fritzsche
himself and called a curly-headed Jew. I wasn't in on any of the splendid
tricks, such as Milton is accused of, but the cooked-up argufying I have
experienced. To work at it forces you to imagine all the time what the
enemy will reply; you are trying to get him into a corner. Such a training
cannot narrow a man's understanding of other people's opinions, though it
may well narrow his own opinions. I should say that Milton's experience
of propaganda is what makes his later poetry so very dramatic; that is,
though he is a furious partisan, he can always imagine with all its force
exactly what the reply of the opponent would be. As to his integrity, he

was such an inconvenient propagandist that the Government deserves credit for having the nerve to appoint and retain him. He had already published the Divorce Pamphlets before he got the job; well now, if you are setting out to be severe and revolutionary on the basis of literal acceptance of the Old Testament, the most embarrassing thing you can be confronted with is detailed evidence about the sexual habits of the patriarchs; it is the one point where the plain man feels he can laugh. Milton always remained liable to defend his side by an argument which would strike his employers as damaging; his style of attack is savagely whole-hearted, but his depth of historical knowledge and imaginative sympathy keep having unexpected effects. He was not at all likely to feel that he had forfeited his independence of mind by such work. M. Morand therefore strikes me as rather innocent in assuming that he was corrupted by it, but I warmly agree that it made his mind very political. Professor Wilson Knight has also remarked that Milton wrote a political allegory under the appearance of a religious poem, though he did not draw such drastic consequences from the epigram.

On the Morand view, God is simply a dynastic ruler like those Milton had had to deal with; Cromwell had wanted his son to inherit, no less than Charles. M. Morand does not seem to realize it, but the effect is to make Milton's God much better. His intrigues and lies to bolster his power are now comparatively unselfish, being only meant to transfer it unimpaired to his Son, and above all he feels no malignity towards his victims. His method of impressing the loyalist angels will doom almost all mankind to misery, but he takes no pleasure in that; it simply does not bother him. The hypocrisy which the jovial old ruffian feels to be required of him in public has not poisoned his own mind, as we realize when he permits himself his leering jokes. This does, I should say, correspond to the impression usually made by the poem on a person not brought up as a Christian, such as my Chinese and Japanese students. The next step is to regard the debate in Heaven, where the Son, but no angel, offers to die for man, as a political trick rigged up to impress the surviving angels; the Son is free to remark (III. 245) that he knows the Father won't let him stay dead, so that the incantatory repetition of the word *death* comes to seem blatantly artificial. (We find in the *De Doctrina* Chapter XII that Milton includes "under the head of death, in Scripture, all evils whatsoever . . ."). Nobody is surprised at the absence of volunteers among the good angels, whereas Satan, during the parallel scene in Hell (II. 470), has to close the debate hurriedly for fear a less competent rebel put himself forward. Otherwise the two scenes are deliberately made alike, and the reason is simply that both are political:

Ce qui frappe, c'est le parallelisme des moyens employées, conseils, discours. Même souci de garder pour soi tout gloire.

On reaching *Paradise Regained*, M. Morand is interested to learn how the Son grew up. In *Paradise Lost* he often seems half ashamed of the auto- cratic behaviour of his Father, because his role is to induce the subject angels to endure it; but when he is alone on the earth-visit which has been arranged for him we find he has merely the cold calculating pride which we would expect from his training. However, we already find this trait, decides M. Morand, at the early public moment when he offers his Sacrifice; he is unable to avoid presenting himself as solely interested in his own career. As the Creation for which he was the instrument has already happened, he might at least speak as if he could tell a man apart from a cow, but he says that his Father's grace visits "all his creatures" (III. 230). Satan, on the parallel occasion, was at least genuinely con- cerned to get the job done, whoever did it; and M. Morand decides that the ringing repetition of ME in the speech of sacrifice of the Son is a little too grotesque, however perfectly in character. Milton

> n'eût pas pensé à ce que peut contenir de ridicule ce martellement du moi.
>> De personnages extra-terrestres, le moins éloigné de la modestie est encore Satan.

This is at least a splendid reply to the argument that pride is the basic fault of all the characters who fall.

The Morand line of argument can be taken an extra step, to argue that the Son too is being cheated by the Father; and this excites a suspicion that there is something inadequate about it. He says nothing of the means of his death, and speaks as if he is going to remain on earth till the Last Day:

> Behold mee then, mee for him, life for life
> I offer, on mee let thine anger fall;
> Account mee man; I for his sake will leave
> Thy bosom, and this glory next to thee
> Freely put off, and for him lastly die
> Well pleas'd, on me let Death wreck all his rage;
> Under his gloomy power I shall not long
> Lie vanquisht; thou hast giv'n me to possess
> Life in my self for ever, by thee I live,
> Though now to Death I yield, and am his due
> All of me that can die, yet that debt paid,
> Thou wilt not leave me in the loathsome grave
> His prey, nor suffer my unspotted Soul

For ever with corruption there to dwell;
But I shall rise Victorious, and subdue
My Vanquisher, spoild of his vaunted spoil;
Death his death's wound shall then receive, and stoop
Inglorious, of his mortal sting disarm'd.
I through the ample Air in Triumph high
Shall lead Hell Captive maugre Hell, and show
The Powers of darkness bound. Thou at the sight
Pleas'd, out of Heaven shalt look down and smile,
While by thee rais'd I ruin all my Foes,
Death last, and with his Carcass glut the Grave:
Then with the multitude of my redeemd
Shall enter Heaven long absent, and return,
Father, to see thy face, wherein no cloud
Of anger shall remain, but peace assur'd,
And reconcilement; wrath shall be no more
Thenceforth, but in thy presence Joy entire.

(III. 240)

Our chief impression here, surely, is not that he is too little interested in mankind but that he does not know what is going to happen, except for a triumph at which he can rejoice. If the Jews had not chosen to kill him, he would presumably have remained on earth till the Last Day, making history less bad than the poem describes it as being; and what they will choose can be foreknown by the Father only. The Son expects to find no frown upon the face of God on Judgement Day, the *Dies Irae* itself, so we can hardly doubt that he expects things to turn out better than they do. His prophecy appears to be continuous narrative: "not long lie . . . rise victorious . . . then . . . then", as if he will lead the blessed to Heaven very soon after the Resurrection. Among human speakers 'lastly die' is a natural way to express pathos, though a tautology; but a meaning which would make it a correct description of the career of the Son is hard to invent. It may be possible to interpret the whole speech as a true forecast, and Milton may have planned to leave his alternative open; but it is a more natural reading to suppose the Son ignorant, and Milton denies him foreknowledge in *De Doctrina* Chap. V.

We must compare the speech to what Michael tells Adam at XII.410, not long after hearing it. The angel has now been told of the Crucifixion, and explains that soon after it, while ascending to Heaven, Christ will surprise Satan in the air and drag him in chains, then resume his seat at God's right hand till the Second Coming. This clears up part of the Son's narrative; and if he is to remain on earth after the Second Coming for the Millennium, finally returning with his Saints, that explains 'long absent'. Milton seems rather doubtful about this doctrine, as Michael says that Christ will receive the faithful into bliss 'whether in Heaven or Earth'. *De Doctrina* Chapter XXXIII says that the glorious reign of Christ on earth will begin at the start of the Last Judgement and 'extend a little beyond its conclusion'; then the chapter goes on to name the thousand years, then it gives a still grander interpretation. Only the blessed will be revived for the Millennium (Revelation xx. 5), which might explain why the Son expects no frown when he leads them to Heaven after a thousand years. At any rate, if he expects to labour so long for mankind, we can hardly agree with M. Morand that he betrays lack of interest in them.

It often happens with a formative piece of criticism that one needs to consider why it seemed so true, after apparently refuting it. The mere repetition of *me* when offering oneself for sacrifice cannot be enough to prove self-centredness, even in the style of Milton, because Eve does it in a speech of splendid generosity. Surely the reason why Milton's treatment here seems cold, compared to a Good Friday service which is the natural comparison, is that no one throughout the long 'scene in Heaven' ever mentions that the Son is to die by torture. Even Michael does not describe the Cross to Adam as painful, only as 'shameful and accurst'. Death for a day and a half any of us might proffer, but we would find slow torture worth mentioning even given a doctor in attendance who guaranteed recovery after unconsciousness had finally supervened. I do not know whether there is a standard explanation for this lack in the poem, and do not remember to have seen it noticed. The reason for it, surely, is that Milton would not dirty his fingers with the bodily horror so prominent in the religion. We need not be surprised, because all his heroes fiercely refuse to let the prospect of pain so much as enter their minds while deciding what they ought to do; his devils are so superior to pain that we actually cannot remember they are all the time in bodily agony. This steady blaze of moral splendour must I am afraid be called unreal but at least makes the religion feel a good deal cleaner. The Son regularly talks like a young medieval aristocrat eager to win his spurs, and like him is not expected to mention pain. No doubt the singing angels (III. 375) would mention the Crucifixion if they had been told of it, but it could mean little to them as they have never experienced pain; God has only just invented it, and only applied it to rebels. Clearly God has given at least Michael further information before he speaks to Adam. But there is no dignified enough procedure by which God could tell the angels that he has made a huge increase in his demand upon the Son after accepting the Son's offer. To cheat his own Son into death by torture would be too bad even for the God of M. Morand; it would be bad propaganda. Thus I think we should apply here too the principle of Mr Rajan, that the correct interpretation is always the multimost one; Milton considered death by torture such a trivial sacrifice that he thought the Son must have offered a longer mission than the Father decided to require of him. Even if the Son does not know about the Crucifixion, he knows a good deal about the consequences of his offer; if we suppose the Father to have told him this beforehand we must still picture them, as M. Morand does, hammering out in private the scene of propaganda dialogue which they will present to the assembled angels. But their background is impossible for us to envisage, and the Father may simply put into the mind of the Son as much foreknowledge as he chooses on the instant, so that the Son acts, as we would call it, spontaneously. The process might let the Son presume the happier alternative for mankind, out of a bold confidence in his power to convert them; but, even so, he must be above feeling wronged when he finds that the Crucifixion has been incurred. We need not after that join M. Morand in blaming him for hoping to deserve praise. Milton if he intended this high detail would have to regard it as visible only to very fit readers, such as could cross-question his text like M. Morand; the broad literary effect is rather one of tactfulness in keeping the Crucifixion out of sight. The motive of the Father in crucifying the Son is of course left in even deeper obscurity.

Milton did however I think mean to adumbrate a kind of motive by his picture of the Last Things. Professor C. S. Lewis once kindly came to a lecture I was giving on the half-finished material of this book; and at question time, after a sentence of charitable compunction, recognizing that the speaker wasn't responsible for this bit, he said "Does Phelps Morand think God is going to abdicate, then?" I tried to explain that M. Morand regarded this as the way Milton's dramatic imagination worked, after it had been corrupted by his patriotic labours, not as part of his theological system. The answer felt weak, and soon afterwards another difficulty drove me back to the book of M. Saurat, which I had probably not read since I was an undergraduate; I thus suddenly realized, what M. Saurat was not intending to prove, that Milton did expect God to abdicate. At least, that is the most direct way to express the idea; you may also say that he is an emergent or evolutionary deity, as has been believed at times by many other thinkers, for example Aeschylus and H. G. Wells.

There has been such a campaign to prove that only the coarsely worldly Victorians would even want the world to get better that I had better digress about that, or I may be thought to be jeering at Milton. We are often told that In Memoriam is bad because Tennyson tries to palm off progress in this world as a substitute for Heaven. But he says in the poem that he would stop being good, or would kill himself, if he stopped believing he would go to Heaven; it is wilful to argue that he treats the progress of the human race as an adequate alternative. Indeed, he seems rather too petulant about his demand for Heaven, considering that *Tithonus*, written about the same time (according to Stopford Brooke) though kept from publication till later, appreciates so nobly the hunger of mankind for the peace of oblivion. But the underlying logic of *In Memoriam* is firm. The signs that God is working out a vast plan of evolution are treated as evidence that he is good, and therefore that he will provide Heaven for Tennyson. To believe that God's Providence can be seen at work in the world, and that this is evidence for his existence and goodness, is what is called Natural Theology; it is very traditional, and the inability of neo-Christians to understand it casts an odd light on their pretensions. Tennyson has also been accused of insincerity about progress because in another poem he expressed alarm at the prospect of war in the air; but he realized the time-scale very clearly; while maintaining that the process of the suns will eventually reach a good end, it is only sensible to warn mankind that we are likely to go through some very bad periods beforehand. Now, when mankind seems almost certain to destroy itself quite soon, we cannot help wincing at a belief that progress is inevitable; but this qualification seems all that is needed. I think that reverence *ought* to be aroused by the thought that so long and large a process has recently produced ourselves who can describe it, and other-worldly persons who boast of not feeling that seem to me merely to have cauterized themselves against genuine religious feeling. The seventeenth century too would have thought that so much contempt for Providence verged upon the Manichean. Milton claimed to get his conception of progress from the Bible; but he would have found corroboration, one would think, in the *Prometheus*, which was well known. There is only one reference to the myth in the epic, and it is twisted into a complaint against women (IV. 720); but Mr R. J. Z. Werblowsky, in his broad and philosophical *Lucifer and Prometheus* (1952), may well be right to think that Milton tried to avoid direct comparison between Prometheus and his Satan.

At the point which seemed to me illuminating, M. Saurat was calling Milton 'the old incorrigible dreamer' (p. 165, 1944 edition), apparently just for believing in the Millennium on earth, though that only requires literal acceptance of Revelation xx; but he was quoting part of Milton's commentary in Chapter XXXIII of the *De Doctrina*, "Of Perfect Glorification", and no doubt recognized that Milton was somehow going rather further. Milton says:

It may be asked, if Christ is to deliver up the kingdom to God and the Father, what becomes of the declarations [quotations from Heb. i. 8, Dan, vii 14, and Luke i. 33] "of his kingdom there shall be no end". I reply, there shall be no end of his kingdom . . . till time itself shall be no longer, Rev. x. 6, until everything which his kingdom was intended to effect shall be accomplished . . . it will not be destroyed, nor will its period be a period of dissolution, but rather of perfection and consummation, like the end of the law, Matt. v. 18.

The last clause seems to recall the precedent of an earlier evolutionary step, whereby the New Dispensation of Jesus made the Mosaic Law unnecessary; it is clear that the final one, which makes even the Millennium unnecessary, must be of an extremely radical character. The Father, I submit, has to turn into the God of the Cambridge Platonists and suchlike mystical characters; at present he is still the very disagreeable God of the Old Testament, but eventually he will dissolve into the landscape and become immanent only. The difficulty of fitting in this extremely grand climax was perhaps what made Milton uncertain about the controverted time-scheme of the Millennium. The doctrine of the end of time, if one takes it seriously, is already enough to make anything but Total Union (or else Total Separateness from God) hard to conceive.

The question which Milton answers here is at least one which he makes extremely prominent in the speech of rejoicing by the Father after the speech of sacrifice by the Son (III. 320). The Father first says he *will* give the Son all power, then in the present tense "I give thee"; yet he had given it already, or at least enough to cause Satan and his followers to revolt. Without so much as a full stop, the Father next says that the time when he will give it is the Day of Judgement, and the climax of the whole speech is to say that immediately after that "God shall be All in All". The eternal gift of the Father is thus to be received only on the Last Day, and handed back the day after. This has not been found disturbing, because the paradox is so clear that we assume it to be deliberate; nor are interpretations of it hard to come by. But Milton would see it in the light of the passage in the *De Doctrina*; there "God shall be All in All" ends the Biblical quotation which comes just before Milton's mystical "reply":

> Then cometh the end . . . but when he saith, all things are put under him, it is manifest that he is excepted which did put all things under him; and when all things are subdued unto him, then shall the Son himself also be subject unto him that put all things under him, that God may be all in all. (I Corinthians xv. 24–28)

St. Paul is grappling with earlier texts here in much the same scholarly way that Milton did, which would give Milton a certain confidence about re-interpreting his results even though they were inspired because Biblical. After hearing so much from M. Morand about the political corruption of Milton's mind, one is pleased to find it less corrupt than St Paul's; Milton decided that God was telling the truth, and that he would keep his promise literally. At the end of the speech of the Father, Milton turns into poetry the decision he had reached in prose:

> The World shall burn, and from her ashes spring
> New Heav'n and Earth, wherein the just shall dwell . . .
> Then thou thy regal Sceptre shalt lay by,
> For regal Sceptre then no more shall need,
> God shall be All in All. But all ye Gods
> Adore him, who to compass all this dies,
> Adore the Son, and honour him as me.
>
> (III. 340)

I grant that the language is obscure, as is fitting because it is oracular; and, besides, Milton wanted the poem to be universal, so did not want to thrust a special doctrine upon the reader. But the doctrine is implied decisively if the language is examined with care. St Paul presumably had in mind a literal autocracy, but Milton contrives to make the text imply pantheism. The O.E.D. records that the intransitive use of the verb *need* had become slightly archaic except for a few set phrases; the general intransitive use needed here belongs to the previous century—e.g. "stopping of heads with lead shall not need now" 1545. But a reader who noticed the change of grammar from *shalt* to *shall* could only impute the old construction: "Authority will then no longer be needed"—not, therefore, from the Father, any more than from the Son. There is much more point in the last two lines quoted if the Father has just proposed, though in an even more remote sense than the Son, that he too shall die. *All* is rather a pet word in Milton's poetry but I think he never gives it a capital letter anywhere else, and one would expect that by writing "All in All" he meant to imply a special doctrine, as we do by writing "the Absolute". Then again, this is the only time God calls the angels Gods, with or without a capital letter. He does it here meaning that they will in effect become so after he has abdicated. The reference has justly been used as a partial defence of Satan for calling his rebels Gods, but we are meant to understand that his claim for them is a subtle misuse of the deeper truth adumbrated here. Taking all the details together, I think it is clear that Milton wanted to suggest a high mystery at this culminating point.

There was a more urgent and practical angle to the question; it was not only one of the status of the Son, but of mankind. You cannot think it merely whimsical of M. Morand to call God dynastic if you look up the words *heir* and *inherit* in the concordance usually given at the end of a Bible. Milton was of course merely quoting the text when he made the Father call the Son his heir (as in VI. 705); but the blessed among mankind are also regularly called 'heirs of God's kingdom' and suchlike. The word *heir* specifically means one who will inherit; it would be comical to talk as if M. Morand was the first to wonder what the Bible might mean by it. The blessed among mankind are heirs of God through their union with Christ; Milton's Chapter XXIV is 'Of Union and Fellowship with Christ and the Saints, wherein is considered the Mystical or Invisible Church', and he says it is 'not confined to place or time, inasmuch as it is composed of individuals of widely separated countries, and of all ages from the foundation of the world'. He would regard this as a blow at all priesthoods, but also regard the invisible union as a prefiguring of the far distant real one. We can now see that it is already offered in the otherwise harsh words by which the Father appointed the Son:

> Under his great Vice-regent reign abide
> United as one individual Soul
> For ever happy
>
> (V. 610)

As a means of achieving such unity the speech is a remarkable failure; but God already knew that men would be needed as well as angels before the alchemy could be done. When the unity is complete, neither the loyal angels nor the blessed among mankind will require even the vice-regency of the Son, still less the rule of the Father; and only so can they become 'heirs and inheritors of God's Kingdom'.

The texts prove, I submit, that Milton envisaged the idea, as indeed so informed a man could hardly help doing; but the poetry must decide whether it meant a great deal to him, and the bits so far quoted are not very good. Milton however also ascribes it to God in the one really splendid passage allotted to him. This is merely an earlier part of the same speech, but the sequence III. 80–345 is full of startling changes of tone. The end of the speech happens to let us see Milton's mind at work, because we can relate it to the *De Doctrina*, but the main feeling there is just immense pride; Milton could never let the Father appear soft, and his deepest yielding must be almost hidden by a blaze of glory. Just before advancing upon thirty lines of glory, he has rejoiced that his Son:

> though thron'd in highest bliss,
> Equal to God, and equally enjoying
> God-like fruition, quitted all to save
> A world from utter loss, and hast been found

> By Merit more than Birthright Son of God,
> Found worthiest to be so by being Good,
> Far more than Great or High; because in thee
> Love hath abounded more than Glory abounds,
> Therefore thy Humiliation shall exalt
> With thee thy Manhood also to this Throne;
> Here shalt thou sit incarnate, here shalt Reign
> Both God and Man, Son both of God and Man,
> Anointed universal King; all Power
> I give thee, reign for ever, and assume
> Thy Merits; under thee as Head Supreme
> Thrones, Princedoms, Powers, Dominions I reduce
> (III. 305)

It is a tremendous moral cleansing for Milton's God, after the greed for power which can be felt in him everywhere else, to say that he will give his throne to Incarnate Man, and the rhythm around the word *humiliation* is like taking off in an aeroplane. I had long felt that this is much the best moment of God in the poem, morally as well as poetically, without having any idea why it came there. It comes there because he is envisaging his abdication, and the democratic appeal of the prophecy of God is what makes the whole picture of him just tolerable.

I may be told that I am simply misreading; the Father is not giving Man his own throne, but the Son's, and Milton has made this clear just previously by recalling that the Son too is throned; indeed I think this is the only place in the poem where he is said to be 'throned' at the right hand of God. (When the Father tells the Son to rise and drive out the rebels, Milton mysteriously says that he addresses 'The Assessor of his Throne' VI. 680; but I can deduce nothing from that.) But the grandeur of the position of the Son needed emphasizing here in any case, and Milton is inclined to 'plant' a word in this way soon before it is used especially sublimely. The effect of repeating the word *throne* is not so obtrusive as to exclude the more tremendous meaning. Besides, the Father could not say that the Son will be exalted as a reward to the throne which the Son already occupies; and the sequence is "this throne . . . here . . . here . . . Head Supreme", very empty rhetoric if it does not refer to the supreme throne. I grant that the meaning is not obvious unless one realizes how much support it is given later in the speech.

Wondering where to stop my quotation, I was struck by how immediately the passage turns from generosity to pride of power. The distinction is perhaps an unreal one; all the lines are *about* pride. God is generous to give his throne, but Milton exults in the dignity given to Man. The last line of my quotation, except that it omits the Virtues for convenience, gives the same roll-call of the titles of the angels as Satan does in his rabble-rousing speech, no doubt this was the standard form in Heaven, but the effect is to make the reader compare the two offers. One must agree with M. Morand that it is all weirdly political; temporary acceptance of lower-class status is what the Son is being praised for, a severe thing in his mind, just as it is beneath Satan's class to become incarnate as a snake. As to torture, that might come your way in any class, and would only be a minor thing to boast about afterwards. But one dare not call this mode of thought contemptible, if it elevates, or makes proud enough to act well, all classes of the society in which it operates.

I can claim that this account gives the thought of the epic a much needed consistency. Thus it may be objected that Milton's own temperament, because of the pride so evident in his style, would be quite unattracted by an ideal of total union. But certainly; he presents it as very unattractive even to the good angels. Abdiel can only translate it into terms exasperating for Satan; and the blushing of Raphael now acquires considerable point, which after all one would expect so bizarre a detail to have. Though capable of re-uniting themselves with God the angels do not want to, especially because this capacity lets them enjoy occasional acts of love among themselves. It is fundamental to Milton's system that angels, like all the rest of the universe, are parts of God from which God willingly removed his will; these highest forms of life, he finds it natural to suppose, have an approximation to the divine power among themselves, so that they can love by total interpenetration. Presumably God can gobble them up as soon as look at them, which would make him an alarming employer, and perhaps they are relieved that he never expresses any affection for them—though even interpenetration with God would not actually mean death; the Son, like Satan, doubts whether any life can be totally destroyed, III. 165; so does Milton, De Doctrina Chapter VII. Thus they put up a timidly evasive but none the less stubborn resistance to dissolving themselves into God, like a peasantry under Communism trying to delay collectivization; and here too the state has the high claim that it has promised eventually to wither away. God must abdicate, in the sense of becoming totally immanent or invisible, before the plan of Total Union can seem tolerable to them; and it is bitter for them that this transcendence cannot be achieved without stirring into the brew the blessed among mankind. Exactly why the angels are so inadequate that God's programme is necessary remains obscure; Milton quotes in De Doctrina Chapter VII from Job iv. 18 "he put no trust in his servants, and his angels he charged with folly", which perhaps he felt to give authority to his picture. But it is intelligible that a stern period of training may be required before transcendence, and at any rate the story is a great boast for ourselves; we are not inclined to blame God for deciding that he needed us before he could abdicate conscientiously.

Thus, by combining the views of M. Saurat and M. Morand, the one attributing to Milton thoughts beyond the reaches of our souls and the other a harsh worldliness, we can I think partly solve the central problem about the poem, which is how Milton can have thought it to justify God. I think the 'internal' evidence of Milton's own writing enough to decide that he meant what I have tried to describe, because it makes our impression of the poem and indeed of the author much more satisfactory; but, even so, external evidence is needed to answer the objection that Milton could not have meant that, or could not have thought of it. I had best begin by saying what I learned from M. Saurat and where I thought his view inadequate. His main interest, as I understand, was to show that the European Renaissance could not have occurred without an underground influence from Jewish mystics beginning two or three centuries before Milton; the main reason for supposing that Milton had read the Zohar, even after textual evidence had been found, was that he was a man who habitually went to the sources of the ideas which he had already found floating about. The doctrine that matter was not created from nothing but was part of God M. Saurat considered fundamental to the Renaissance, because it allowed enough trust in the flesh, the sciences, the arts, the future before man in this world. Milton undoubtedly does express this doctrine, but it does not strike me as prominent in other poets of the time, except for the paradoxes of Donne's love-poetry. However, I want to answer a rebuttal of the Saurat position which I happened to come across in an informative and strictly philological work by G. N. Conklin, *Biblical Criticism and Heresy in Milton*, 1949. He says that Milton could not have been influenced by the *Zohar*, or by the mystics around him in the Commonwealth such as Fludd either, because he was "a Puritan, a logician, and, whatever else, assuredly no theosophist", and furthermore that it is mere justice to admit that Milton extracted his beliefs from the ancient texts of Holy Writ by scientific philological techniques, as he steadily claimed to do. Thus his crucial decision that matter was not created from nothing turned simply on an analysis of the Biblical words for *create*, chiefly but not only in Hebrew. Admittedly, this is what Milton claims in Chapter VII of *De Doctrina*, but he was accustomed to defend a position rhetorically, to convince other people, after arriving at it himself by a more conscientious assessment of the evidence. The philological argument here is only, and could only be, that previous uses of the word had not meant this unique concept before the attempt at expressing it was allegedly made; thus the word in the Bible does not have to mean what theologians say, and is never redefined by the Bible in a phrase or sentence as meaning that. Milton goes on to give other reasons for his conclusion that 'create' in the Bible does not mean 'from nothing', and by doing so he has in effect enough sense to admit that his negative argument does not make a positive one. These problems about sources are often very subtle, because a powerful mind grabs at a hint of what it needs; admittedly, the *Zohar* was not the only possible source of these large mystical ideas; and one could explain the verbal correspondences found by M. Saurat by supposing that Milton got some other learned man to answer his questions about the *Zohar*, and read some crucial bits out to him, after he had become blind.

All the same, such ideas undoubtedly were floating about. The trouble with M. Saurat's position, I think, is that he welcomes the liquefaction of God the Father, making him wholly immanent in his creation, and argues that Milton intended that in his epic, without realizing that Milton and his learned contemporaries would think the liquefaction of all the rest of us a prior condition. The idea of the re-absorption of the soul into the Absolute does get hinted at a good deal in the literature, if only in the form of complete self-abandonment to God; whereas the idea that God himself is wholly immanent in his creation belonged mainly to the high specialized output of the Cambridge Platonists. Marlowe's Faustus, in his final speech, desires to return his soul like a rain-drop to the sea rather than remain eternally as an individual in Hell, and this is a crucial image for grasping the Far-Eastern position; the same idea is quite noisy in the supposedly orthodox peroration of *Urn-Burial*: "if any have been so happy as truly to understand Christian annihilation . . . liquefaction . . . ingression into the divine shadow". When Lovewit at the end of *The Alchemist* rebuffs a superstitious fool by saying "Away, you Harry Nicholas" (the founder of the mystical Family of Love which maintained that any man can become Christ), the now remote figure is presumed to be familiar to a popular audience. The ideas which Milton hinted at in the bits of his epic which I have picked out were therefore not nearly so learned and unusual as they seem now; indeed, he probably treated them with caution because they might suggest a more levelling, more economic-revolutionary, political stand than he in fact took. But the Cambridge Platonists were not dangerous for property-owners in this way; they were a strand of recent advanced thought which deserved recognition in his epic; also they allowed of a welcome contrast to the picture of God which the Bible forced him to present, and gave a bit more body to the mysterious climax of the Fortunate Fall. The abdication of the Father was thus quite an important part of his delicately balanced structure, and not at all a secret heresy; and of course not 'unconscious' if it needed tact. At bottom, indeed, a quaintly political mind is what we find engaged on the enormous synthesis. Milton knows by experience that God is at present the grindingly harsh figure described in the Old Testament; after all, Milton had long been printing the conviction that his political side had been proved right because God had made it win, so its eventual defeat was a difficult thing to justify God for. But it was essential to retain the faith that God has a good eventual plan; well then, the Cambridge Platonists can be allowed to be right about God, but only as he will become in the remote future. It seems to me one of the likeable sides of Milton that he would regard this as a practical and statesmanlike proposal.

M. Saurat, on the other hand, wanted Milton to use the *Zohar* to drive the last remnants of Manichaeism out of Christianity, and therefore argued that God in the epic is already an ineffable Absolute or World-Soul dissolved into the formative matter of the universe. After a timid peep into one volume of a translation of the *Zohar*, I am sure that Milton would not find it as opposite from the Gnostics as black from white, which is what the eloquence and selection of M. Saurat lead us to suppose. Milton would regard it as further evidence that the Fathers had slandered the Gnostics, as he had been sure when he was young, just as Rome had behaved very wickedly to the Cathars; all these heretics probably had something to be said for them, though of course one must expect most of their stuff to be dead wood. And the Gnostics are reported as believing, no less than the Cabbalists of the *Zohar*, in an eventual reunion of the many with the One. The Saurat interpretation of the epic makes nonsense of most of its narrative, but that is better than giving it an evil sense; the point where one ought to revolt comes when the interpretation drives poor M. Saurat into uneasy brief expressions of bad feeling. He praises God's jokes (p. 192, 1944 edition) because the only relation of the Absolute to its creation which a poet can present is 'irony', and here the protean word has to mean mean-minded jeering. M. Saurat deserves to be released from this position; the idea of God as the Absolute is genuinely present in the poem, but only when God is adumbrating the Last Things.

The well-argued view of M. Morand, that the purblind Milton described God from his experience of Cromwell, also allows of an unexpectedly sublime conclusion. Milton's own political record, as I understand, cannot be found contemptible; he backed Cromwell and his Independents in the army against the Presbyterians in Parliament because he wanted religious freedom, but always remained capable of saying where

he thought Cromwell had gone wrong; for example, in refusing to dises-
tablish the Church. However, on one point Cromwell was impeccable,
and appears to be unique among dictators; his admitted and genuine
bother, for a number of years, was to find some way of establishing a
Parliament under which he could feel himself justified in stopping being
dictator. When Milton made God the Father plan for his eventual abdication, he ascribed to him in the high tradition of Plutarch the noblest
sentiment that could be found in an absolute ruler; and could reflect with
pride that he had himself seen it in operation, though with a tragic end.
Milton's God is thus to be regarded as like King Lear and Prospero,
turbulent and masterful characters who are struggling to become able to
renounce their power and enter peace; the story makes him behave much
worse than they do, but the author allows him the same purifying aspiration. Even the lie of God "Die he or Justice must", we may now charitably
reflect, is partly covered when Milton says that Satan

> with necessity
> The Tyrant's plea, excused his devilish deeds.
> (IV. 395)

It must be added at once that we cannot find enough necessity; the
poem, to be completely four-square, ought to explain why God had to
procure all these falls for his eventual high purpose. Such is the basic
question as it stood long before Milton handled it; but he puts the mystery
in a place evidently beyond human knowledge, and he makes tolerably
decent, though salty and rough, what is within our reach.

This I think answers the fundamental objection of Yvor Winters, . . .
Milton's poetical formula for God is not simply to copy Zeus in Homer
but, much more dramatically, to cut out everything between the two
ends of the large body of Western thought about God, and stick to
Moses except at the high points which anticipate Spinoza. The procedure
is bound to make God interesting; take the case of his announcing to the
loyal angels that he will create mankind to spite the devil. God must be
supposed to intend his words to suggest to the angels what they do to us,
but any angel instructed in theology must realize that God has intended
throughout all eternity to spite Satan, so that when he presents this plan
as new he is telling a lie, which he has also intended to tell throughout all
eternity. No wonder it will be 'far happier days' after he has abdicated
(XII. 465). Milton was well able to understand these contradictions, and
naturally he would want to leave room for an eventual solution of them.

Perhaps I find him like Kafka merely because both seem to have
had a kind of foreknowledge of the Totalitarian State, whether or not this

was what C. S. Lewis praised as his beautiful sense of the idea of social order. The picture of God in the poem, including perhaps even the high moments when he speaks of the end, is astonishingly like Uncle Joe Stalin; the same patience under an appearance of roughness, the same flashes of joviality, the same thorough unscrupulousness, the same real bad temper. It seems little use to puzzle ourselves whether Milton realizes he was producing this effect, because it would follow in any case from what he had set himself to do.

THOMAS GREENE

The Descent from Heaven

Most of the important epic poetry of the sixteenth century was written by Humanist authors working at a court or, like Spenser, under the long shadow of a court. Boiardo, Ariosto, and Tasso wrote for the dukes of Ferrara as Pulci had written for Lorenzo de' Medici. Ronsard, the very model of a court poet, received not only the encouragement of Charles IX and the benefice to afford him leisure, but found himself obliged to follow the royal preference for a decasyllabic line. D'Aubigné spent several years at the court of Henri III and remained the confidant of Henri IV until the latter's conversion. Even Sannazaro and Vida wrote with the patronage of the papal court. Camoens, to be sure, wrote much of Os Lusíadas in the Orient, but part of his youth was spent at court, and he received a small royal pension after his epic was published. In all these sixteenth century courts, with the possible exception of the papal, a balance of sorts was maintained between soldiering and learning, the camp and the library, a balance which naturally led the Humanist poet to subjects involving warfare. The ancient duality of *sapientia* and *fortitudo* was perpetuated, as Curtius has shown, by the Renaissance coupling of "arms and studies." The courtly interest in epic action was thus not simply antiquarian. The immediate audience of the epic pursued an equilibrium of valor and refinement not utterly unlike the equilibrium reflected in the *Odyssey*. The finest Christian epics of the sixteenth century—those of Tasso, Spenser, and d'Aubigné— mostly eschewed Biblical subjects in preference for those of interest to an educated professional soldier.

From *The Descent from Heaven: A Study in Epic Continuity.* Copyright © 1963 by Yale University Press.

In seventeenth century France the military caste tended to detach itself from the court, although the separation never became complete. As early a poem as Marino's *Adone*, written at the court of Louis XIII, signaled the taste for subjects which had nothing to do with violence. But Marino's mythographical eroticism was not influential. Epic poetry in the succeeding decades was divided, as we have seen, between tired perpetuations of the quasi-military epic (Scudéry's *Alaric*, Desmarets de Saint-Sorlin's *Clovis*, etc.)—poems which really betray the growing gap between courtier-poet and soldier—and on the other hand, bourgeois Biblical epics in the tradition of Sannazaro, Vida, and Du Bartas. The Pléiade had experimented with Biblical poetry—as in Du Bellay's *Monomachie de David et de Goliath*, but had only shown spasmodic interest in it. Now, with the growth of a middle class reading public, a bastard form of Biblical epic enjoyed a wide popularity.

The socio-literary development of England was very different. There a Humanist literary movement comparable to the continental explosion gathered force only after the court ceased to be a literary center. This fact is of great importance. The first thorough-going neoclassical epic in England—Cowley's *Davideis*—was not published before 1656, although it was probably written a decade or more earlier. In 1656, continental epic poetry was expiring, and there existed in England no audience devoted to "arms and letters," no audience as variously accomplished as the court for which Spenser wrote. This meant that the nature of heroism represented in the English epic was obliged to change, to idealize the efforts of will comprehensible to a devout bourgeois public. In 1656, moreover, the wind of prosaic rationalism was beginning to blow strong, that wind which was soon to wither epic poetry. Gusts of it flutter the pages of Crowley's poem, and its steady draft altogether blights the decorous quatrains of Davenant's *Gondibert*. Given this milieu, great epic poetry in seventeenth century England was an historical anomaly. *Paradise Lost* is only less anomalous than the Arthurian epic Milton planned to write. That poem would have had no *raison d'être*, no fit audience at all. *Paradise Lost* still had the dwindling core of an audience, but only the massive, proud, and isolated independence of a Milton could have brought even this poem into being.

In sixteenth century England a movement had arisen which opposed the imitation of classical modes in all genres, and which substituted in each case sacred subjects and modes. Rather than attempt the *mélange coupable* of classical and Christian, this program enforced a strict segregation which, in epic poetry, broke down completely only with Cowley and Milton. It is not remarkable that the pious and pedestrian Quarles betrays so little classical influence in his Biblical narratives (*Job Militant, The Historie of Samson*), but it is perhaps a little odd that a poet like Drayton (in his *Moses, David and Golia, Noah's Flood*) should not betray a great deal more. Giles Fletcher's underestimated *Christ's Victorie and Triumph* (1610), a poem somewhat more allegorical than Biblical, contains a celestial descent of sorts, in the passage of Mercie into Christ's breast (*Christ's Victorie on Earth*, 1–16), but for an extended conventional descent to represent the English epic before Cowley one would have to search out a forgotten poem by Thomas Robinson, *The Life and Death of Mary Magdalene* (1569). In any case, the important landmark, historically if not artistically, is Cowley's *Davideis*.

The angelic descent in that poem is memorable chiefly because of the criticism by which Dr. Johnson singled it out. It appears oddly at the very end of a book—the second of the twelve Cowley planned and of the four he completed. David, while still a young man and before taking the throne, has been vouchsafed a prophetic dream by heaven, a dream which summarizes Jewish history from his own lifetime to the advent of Christ. The account of this dream, which occupies over three hundred lines, is tedious. But if the reader concludes it with pleasure, David awakes with doubt about its import, and Gabriel must descend to explain and reassure:

> When Gabriel (no blest Spirit more kind or fair)
> Bodies and cloathes himself with thickned ayr.
> All like a comely Youth in lifes fresh bloom;
> Rare workmanship, and wrought by heavenly loom!
> He took for skin a cloud most soft and bright,
> That e're the midday Sun pierc'ed through with light:
> Upon his cheeks a lively blush he spred;
> Washt from the morning beauties deepest red.
> An harmless flaming Meteor shone for haire,
> And fell adown his shoulders with loose care.
> He cuts out a silk Mantle from the skies,
> Where the most sprightly Azure pleas'd the eyes.
> This he with starry vapours spangles all,
> Took in their prime e're they grow ripe and fall.
> Of a new Rainbow e're it fret or fade,
> The choicest piece took out, a Scarf is made.
> Small streaming clouds he does for wings display,
> Not Vertuous Lovers sighes more soft then They.
> These he gilds o're with the Suns richest rays,
> Caught gliding o're pure streams on which he plays.
>   Thus drest the joyful Gabriel posts away,
> And carries with him his own glorious day
> Through the thick woods; the gloomy shades a while

Put on fresh looks, and wonder why they smile.
The trembling Serpents close and silent ly,
The birds obscene far from his passage fly.
A sudden Spring waits on him as he goes,
Sudden as that by which Creation rose.
Thus he appears to David, at first sight
All earth-bred fears and sorrows take their flight.
In rushes joy divine, and hope, and rest;
A Sacred calm shines through his peaceful brest.
Hail, Man belov'ed! from highest heav'en (said he)
My mighty Master sends thee health by me.
The things thou saw'est are full of truth and light,
Shap'd in the glass of the divine Foresight.
Ev'n now old Time is harnessing the years
To go in order thus; hence empty fears;
Thy Fate's all white; from thy blest seed shall spring
The promis'd Shilo, the great Mystick King.
Round the whole earth his dreaded name shall sound,
And reach to Worlds, that must not yet be found.
The Southern Clime him her sole Lord shall stile,
Him all the North, ev'en Albions stubborn Isle.
My Fellow-Servant, credit what I tell.
   Straight into shapeless air unseen he fell.
                                    (792–837)

   I fear that nothing can be said for the flatness of Cowley's unheroic couplets; his use of them is reminiscent of the uninspired Joshua Sylvester, from whom he may well have taken his lead. One must equally regret the bland coyness of his manner:

   Of a new Rainbow e're it fret or fade.

the pleasantness substituted for energy:

   Where the most sprightly Azure pleas'd the eyes . . .

the empty neoclassical generality of the vocabulary:

   All like a comely Youth in lifes fresh bloom . . .
              the gloomy shades a while
   Put on fresh looks . . .

when, as in the use of *obscene* (817) to mean ill-omened, his vocabulary is not pendantically mannered. But it is graceless to belabor a dead author for the immature failures of his youth, and I shall not dwell long upon those of Cowley's shortcomings which were peculiar to himself alone. Dr. Johnson's strictures on lines 796–807 can scarcely be improved upon:

This is a just specimen of Cowley's imagery; what might, in general expressions, be great and forcible, he weakens and makes ridiculous by branching it into small parts. That Gabriel was invested with the softest or brightest colours of the sky, we might have been told, and been dismissed to improve the idea in our different proportions of conception; but Cowley could not let us go, till he had related where Gabriel got first his skin, and then his mantle, then his lace, and then his scarf, and related it in the terms of the mercer and tailor.

Cowley could not remember that epic poetry requires the subordination of part to whole; he constantly diverts the reader from his poem's main business by ornaments (like the fading rainbow or the lovers' sighs) for which, were they more truly witty, a lyric might find organic place, but which only clog heroic action.

This shortcoming is related to Cowley's lack of structural intelligence. For it is difficult finally to ascertain the "main business" of the poem at all, so divided is it into unlike episodes. In its unfinished form the plot has no shape or outline, and one wonders whether the completed poem would have acquired them. The poet explains in his preface that he intended to write the life of David only up to his elegy upon Saul and Jonathan, but it is evident from the text that he wanted to incorporate into his account most of Old Testament history. In this disastrous intent he was probably misled not so much by the older English history poems—Daniel's *Civil Wars* and Drayton's *Barons' Wars*—as by Vida and above all by Du Bartas' *Judit*, a poem of undistinguished literary merit but great historical influence. Cowley's vast design was further weakened by his lack of dramatic sense, a shortcoming which led him to introduce this anticlimactic and superfluous descent of Gabriel with extended description. The account of the angel's preparations and the miraculous "sudden Spring" which attends him (inspired perhaps by Sylvester's Fracostoro) would have befitted an event of high moment, but the effect of this descent is dissipated in its pointlessness.

Apart from Cowley's personal failings, the *Davideis* betrays other shortcomings—or as it seems to me, confusions—which are almost endemic to the Christian epic and with which Milton would also have to come to terms. The first of these involves the question of truthfulness. In the preface to his *Poems* (which included the epic), Cowley dwelt enthusiastically upon the Scriptures' unminded riches for poetry, and indignantly upon mythology's meretricious falsity:

When I consider this, and how many other bright and magnificent subjects of the like nature, the Holy Scripture affords and proffers, as it were, to Poesie, in the wise managing and illustrating whereof, the Glory of God Almighty might be joyned with the singular utility and noblest delight of Mankind; It is not without grief and indignation that I behold that Divine Science employing all her inexhaustible riches of Wit and Eloquence, either in the wicked and beggerly Flattery of great persons, or the unmanly Idolizing of Foolish Women . . . or at best on the confused antiquated Dreams of senseless Fables and Metamorphoses.

There is not so great a Lye to be found in any Poet, as the vulgar conceit of men, that Lying is Essential to good Poetry.

In the invocation to the *Davideis* he underscores his poem's veracity as its highest originality:

> But Thou, Eternal Word, hast call'd forth Me
> Th'Apostle, to convert that World to Thee;
> T'unbind the charms that in slight Fables lie,
> And teach that Truth is truest Poesie.
> (I.39–42)

But in practice Cowley departs from the truth, or from his own beliefs regarding the truth, and records the departures in his exhaustive notes. Thus he follows a debate on the location of the Queen of Sheba's realm with the tell-tale confession: "In fine, whatever the truth be, this opinion makes a better Sound in Poetry." And on the question of the harmony of the spheres he writes:

> In this, and some like places, I would not have the Reader judge of my opinion by what I say; no more than before in diverse expressions about Hell, the Devil, and Envy. It is enough that the Doctrine of the Orbs, and the Musick made by their motion had been received very anciently.

The issue of epic truthfulness which troubled Cowley can be related to issues which had been subject to international critical controversy for decades when he penned these various opinions. Critics were not agreed as to whether the heroic action should be based on actual history, or how closely it should follow history, or with how much of the marvelous it might be colored. Despite continuing debate, the cause of historical fidelity was markedly gaining ground on the continent by the mid-seventeenth century, at the expense of the imagination. During Cowley's years in France with the exiled Royalist party there appeared Scudéry's *Alaric* (1654) with its influential preface advocating a non-Biblical subject drawn from true Christian history. Four years earlier, the exchange between Davenant and Hobbes prefacing *Gondibert* laid stress on realism at the expense of machinery, fables, and fantasy. The greater zeal for truth in Cowley's preface, as compared with his poem and notes (probably composed earlier), may reflect his tendency to change with his age. In the poem itself he is far from proscribing "machinery," but his treatment of it is so cool, so detached, so manifestly lacking in awe, that it already represents a step toward realism.

There are ulterior difficulties. The preface patronizes the poems of Quarles and Heywood as misguided efforts to write sacred poetry, but the imputed reasons for their failures are not altogether clear. Cowley has been speaking of the books of the Bible:

> Yet, though they be in themselves so proper to be made use of for this purpose; None but a good Artist will know how to do it: neither must we think to cut and polish Diamonds with so little pains and skill as we do Marble. For if any man design to compose a Sacred Poem, by only turning a story of the Scripture, like Mr. Quarles's, or some other godly matter, like Mr. Heywood of Angels, into Rhyme; He is so far from elevating of Poesie, that he only abases Divinity. In brief, he who can write a prophane Poem well, may write a Divine one better; but he who can do that but ill, will do this much worse.

Quarles is guilty of having turned Scriptural stories into rhyme with too bald a simplicity. What should he have done? Evidently he should have mastered first the skills of his *métier*, the skills one can learn from profane poetry. Among other things, presumably Quarles should have imitated the classics. Cowley himself imitated them on every page and employed all the epic conventions; his notes are stuffed with allusions to Virgil and other antique poets, allusions intended to justify his own poetic procedures. But in the same preface he refers to "those mad Stories of the Gods and Heroes" which "seem in themselves so ridiculous," and numbers himself as one of those "who deride their Folly, and are weary'd with their Impertinences." Thus Cowley's whole relation to antique poetry constitutes a second crucial and symptomatic confusion. He refers in his poem to a revolt of giants against Baal and is obliged to annotate this mysterious mythology by appeal to comparative mythology:

> For Baal is no other than Jupiter. *Baalsemen Jupiter Olympius.* But I like not in an Hebrew Story to use the European Names of Gods.

Elsewhere the poem alludes to Fates and the note must turn about in the contrary direction:

> The Fates; that is, according to the Christian Poetical manner of speaking, the Angels, to whom the Government of this world is committed.

If the notes to Gabriel's descent contain a reference to Revelation and to Aquinas, they contain as well three references to Virgil, two to Homer, others to Ovid, Servius, Pliny, Strabo, to "the Rabbies," and to certain unnamed "magical Books." To the Christian poem which may well have contributed to the descent (Sylvester's Fracastoro), there is no reference at all. How Christian should a Christian epic be? Quarles must have seemed an amateur indeed.

The third of Cowley's confusions we have already encountered . . . perhaps it can be found less strikingly in Tasso as well. This is the confusion exemplified by these lines of Gabriel:

> The things thou saw'est are full of truth and light . . .
> Ev'n now old Time is harnessing the years
> To go in order thus; hence empty fears . . .

The problem lies in the dream of which Gabriel is speaking; truthful it may have been, but scarcely orderly and scarcely filled with light, scarcely calculated to banish all fears. However the poet lays emphasis on the virtuous successors of David, however he rejoices in conclusion at Mary's conception of Jesus, he cannot conceal the patternless violence and suffering of the history he chooses to retail. He wanted to assert a pattern, and assert light and victory and joy, because he thought they were demanded by the genre and exemplified by the *Aeneid*. But he failed to make comprehensible poetically the "Sacred Calm" he meant to inspire. I fear that he inspires rather secular indifference. Perhaps we may thank the *Davideis* most cordially for having fulfilled its author's valedictory hope:

> Sure I am, that there is nothing yet in our Language (nor perhaps in any) that is in any degree answerable to the Idea that I conceive of it. And I shall be ambitious of no other fruit from this weak and imperfect attempt of mine, but the opening of a way to the courage and industry of some other persons, who may be better able to perform it thoroughly and successfully.

The report has survived that Cowley, with Shakespeare and Spenser, were Milton's favorites among the English poets.

II

The convention of the celestial messenger is here concluded with the majestic descent of Raphael to Adam in Book Five of *Paradise Lost*. There is a propriety in this, since Milton concludes so very much more; the clangor of his high style sounds the closing of an immense door within the temple of history. His poem is the more moving because it seems almost to glimpse at instants its own momentous finality.

Milton's earlier poems contain fragmentary rehearsals of Raphael's descent: in the Attendant Spirit's soliloquy that opens Comus:—

> Swift as the Sparkle of a glancing Star,
> I shoot from Heav'n to give him safe convoy . . .
>
> (80 81)

in the flight of Fama concluding the Quintum Novembris, and in the charming stanza of the Nativity Ode which pictures Peace descending to comfort Nature:

> But he her fears to cease,
> Sent down the meek eyd Peace,
>   She crown'd with Olive green, came softly sliding
> Down through the turning sphear
> His ready Harbinger,
>   With Turtle wing the amorous clouds dividing,
> And waving wide her mirtle wand,
> She strikes a universall Peace through Sea and Land.
>
> (45–52)

The outlines for projected tragedies in the Cambridge manuscript also contain at least two scenes involving the descent of an angel, reflecting perhaps the influence of the Italian sacre rappresentazioni which commonly contained angelic epiphanies. Milton alludes to the descent convention moreover in Book Three of Paradise Lost; when Satan feigns therein an appearance to deceive Uriel, he makes himself up to resemble the messenger we have encountered so frequently:

> And now a stripling Cherube he appeers,
> Not of the prime, yet such as in his face
> Youth smil'd Celestial, and to every Limb
> Sutable grace diffus'd, so well he feignd;
> Under a Coronet his flowing haire
> In curles on either cheek plaid, wings he wore
> Of many a colour'd plume sprinkl'd with Gold,
> His habit fit for speed succinct, and held
> Before his decent steps a Silver wand.
>
> (III.636–44)

Milton's own messenger is to be less carefully described, but will possess a maturity and presence beyond the reach of the conventional, Tasso-esque "stripling." Is there a faint touch of scornful pride in the bedecking of Satan in these worn lineaments of literary tradition?

Satan's pretty disguise misleads Uriel only for an hour; he is driven from paradise, and on the morrow Eve is quickly restored from the painful dream he has authored. Adam and Eve proceed to pray and to work, and so engaged attract the eye of God:

> Them thus imploid beheld
> With pittie Heav'ns high King, and to him calld
> *Raphael*, the sociable Spirit, that deignd
> To travel with *Tobias*, and secur'd
> His marriage with the seav'ntimes-wedded Maid.
>   *Raphael*, said hee, thou hear'st what stirr on Earth
> *Satan* from Hell scap't through the darksom Gulf
> Hath raisd in Paradise, and how disturbd
> This night the human pair, how he designes
> In them at once to ruin all mankind.
> Go therefore, half this day as friend with friend
> Converse with *Adam*, in what Bowre or shade
> Thou find'st him from the heat of Noon retir'd,
> To respit his day-labour with repast,
> Or with repose; and such discourse bring on,
> As may advise him of his happie state,
> Happiness in his power left free to will,
> Left to his own free Will, his Will though free,
> Yet mutable; whence warne him to beware
> He swerve not too secure: tell him withall
> His danger, and from whom, what enemie
> Late fall'n himself from Heav'n is plotting now
> The fall of others from like state of bliss;
> By violence, no, for that shall be withstood,
> But by deceit and lies; this let him know,
> Least wilfully transgressing he pretend
> Surprisal, unadmonisht, unforewarnd.
>   So spake th'Eternal Father, and fulfilld
> All Justice: nor delaid the winged Saint
> After his charge receivd; but from among
> Thousand Celestial Ardors, where he stood
> Vaild with his gorgeous wings, up springing light
> Flew through the midst of Heav'n; th' angelic Quires
> On each hand parting, to his speed gave way
> Through all th'Empyreal road; till at the Gate
> Of Heav'n arriv'd, the gate self-op'nd wide
> On gold'n Hinges turning, as by work
> Divine the sovran Architect had fram'd.
> From hence, no cloud, or, to obstruct his sight,
> Starr interpos'd, however small he sees,
> Not unconform to other shining Globes,
> Earth and the Gard'n of God, with Cedars crownd
> Above all Hills. As when by night the Glass

Of *Galileo*, less assur'd, observes
Imagind Lands and Regions in the Moon.
Or Pilot from amidst the *Cyclades*
Delos or *Samos* first appeering kenns
A cloudy spot. Down thither prone in flight
He speeds, and through the vast Ethereal Skie
Sailes between worlds and worlds, with steddie wing
Now on the polar windes, then with quick Fann
Winnows the buxom Air; till within soare
Of Towring Eagles, to all the Fowles he seems
A *Phoenix*, gaz'd by all, as that sole Bird
When to enshrine his reliques in the Suns
Bright Temple, to *Aegyptian Theb's* he flies.
At once on th' Eastern cliff of Paradise
He lights, and to his proper shape returns
A Seraph wingd; six wings he wore, to shade
His lineaments Divine; the pair that clad
Each shoulder broad, came mantling ore his brest
With regal Ornament; the middle pair
Girt like a Starrie Zone his waste, and round
Skirted his loines and thighes with downie Gold
And colours dipt in Heav'n; the third his feet
Shaddowd from either heele with featherd maile
Skie-tinctur'd grain. Like *Maia's* son he stood,
And shook his Plumes, that Heav'nly fragrance filld
The circuit wide. Strait knew him all the Bands
Of Angels under watch; and to his state,
And to his message high in honour rise;
For on som message high they guessd him bound.
Thir glittering Tents he passd, and now is come
Into the blissful field, through Groves of Myrrhe,
And flouring Odours, Cassia, Nard, and Balme;
A Wilderness of sweets; for Nature here
Wantond as in her prime, and paid at will
Her Virgin Fancies, pouring forth more sweet,
Wilde above Rule or Art; enormous bliss.
Him through the spicie Forrest onward com
Adam discernd, as in the dore he sat
Of his coole Bowre . . .

(219–300)

The verse of *Paradise Lost,* and pre-eminently such a passage as this, manifests as spacious and grandiose an imagination as we are privileged to know. If, as I have suggested, a perpetual expansiveness is the habit of the epic sensibility, then Milton was supremely endowed for epic. His most typical arrangements of space do not contain the crowded complexity typical of Virgil—are not, as it were, so busy, but they compose an immensity which shrinks the cosmos of Virgil by comparison. This immensity is effected here partly by the play of perspective and the stress on seeing, by the inconspicuous tininess of earth to Raphael's sight, and his loftiness from the vantage of towering eagles. The immensity is also effected by a certain careless disposal of the astral spheres, here not arranged according to the Ptolemaic system, nor catalogued in order as they are by Dante or Tasso. The earth is

> Not unconform to other shining Globes . . .

The randomness of Milton's heaven, the lack of tidy symmetry, somehow extends further its limits. We know as readers that his heaven *is* orderly in the fundamental respects, but when he writes

> Down thither prone in flight
> He speeds, and through the vast Ethereal Skie
> Sailes between worlds and worlds . . .

or when he writes earlier of Satan's descent

> Down right into the Worlds first Region throws
> His flight precipitant, and windes with ease
> Through the pure marble Air his oblique way
> Amongst innumerable Starrs . . .
>
> (III.562–65)

Milton's cosmos expands to a greater, more intractable vastness, wild like paradise "above Rule or Art."

The immensity of the poem moreover is not simply physical; that vastness is complemented by the learning which has wearied some readers and to others has wrongly seemed matter in itself for praise. No praise is due to pedantry, and pedantry there is occasionally in *Paradise Lost*. But on the whole it is confined to a few *loci molesti*; the wonder is that so much breadth of knowledge is saved from pedantry, so much history introduced with the natural ease of genius, so many allusions brought together without any yoking by violence. The grim, categorical, and narrow version of human history in Books Eleven and Twelve is supplemented by scattered allusions in the rest of the poem to a fuller, more various history—like the allusions above to Galileo and the pilot of the Cyclades.

If we consider only the Judaic-Christian elements in these eighty lines, their range is impressive: the original myth from Genesis; Isaiah's vision of the six-winged seraphim; the homely and charming story of Tobit; echoes of the pseudo-Dionysius' angelology; the late Latin poem *De*

Ave Phoenice ascribed to Lactantius; the theology of Augustine, among others, the Christian epic of the Renaissance, and particularly Tasso. All of these elements appear without strain in this episode of classical derivation, because they seem to have co-existed harmoniously in Milton's sensibility with the fruit of his classical education. Lesser poets avoided the comparison with Mercury at all costs because they were too self-conscious and uncertain of their Christian Humanism. But Milton's sensibility was at peace with itself, and the uncomfortable divisions of his predecessors did not touch him. "Like Maia's son he stood," he writes of Raphael, just as he puts the Graces in Eden, and we read on untroubled. If the superb description of the angel's wings (277–85) imitates Isaiah (with a glance at Ezekiel 1, in the treatment of the second pair), the eccentricity and Asiatic remoteness of the Old Testament have been suppressed. The uppermost wings do not, as in Isaiah, cover Raphael's face, but come "mantling ore his brest with regal Ornament." In describing the angel's wings, Milton describes more than wings; he endows his creature with a grace and energy and poise and beauty beyond the concern of the prophet—qualities reminiscent rather of antique and high Renaissance sculpture. His speculative intellect may not have remained as serene, but his *intuitions* of antiquity and of Hebraic culture were so spontaneously fine that he achieved for once that miraculous fusion denied to the culture of England or of Europe as a whole.

The style of *Paradise Lost* is a product of analogous fusion. Intervolved, hypotactic, and compressed as it generally is, the style is still more flexible than it looks at first acquaintance, and while one critic may praise its classical simplicity, another speaks of its "verbal cleverness, grotesqueness and obscurity," its "primitive . . . zest." Both kinds of style, as well as others, can be found in the poem. Their diversity springs not only from Milton's acute sense of decorum but from the several conceptions of language which had once lain in incipient conflict within his mind.

The first of these was the rhetorical conception Milton learned as a boy at Saint Paul's and from his tutor Thomas Young. The training in classics given at a Renaissance school was based upon the idea, descended from Isocrates and Cicero, that the perspicuous and accomplished use of language fosters the dignity, wisdom, and even the moral elevation of men. If . . . the use of language always involves an implicit confrontation with the magical or demonic powers in words, then Humanist rhetoric took a middle position toward them. By stressing clarity and precision, and by systematically cataloguing tropes, rhetoric tethered the demonic elements with firm bonds while still not altogether paralyzing them.

Language, according to this position, is a creature of the human mind which remains its docile but immensely productive servant. The rhetoricians lived by the faith that language employed with discipline and study was an instrument for attaining truth, and the younger Milton bears witness in a score of passages to his participation in that faith.

But he was also influenced by divergent conceptions of language less compatible with that faith than he realized. On the one hand, certain passages of his prose reflect sympathy with that current of Puritanism which distrusted all rhetoric or ornamentation, a current which professed to find Scripture bare of tropes and which sought to quell the demonic elements with a strait jacket of stylistic "purity." Thus Milton in an early pamphlet refers to the "sober, plain, and unaffected stile of the Scriptures," and ridicules the prelates who seek refuge in church tradition from Scripture's accusing clarity:

> They feare the plain field of the Scriptures . . . they seek the dark, the bushie, the tangled Forrest, they would imbosk . . .

As he was forced to penetrate the tangled forest of controversy, forced to recognize the abuses of language by which his opponents (to his thinking) muddied truth, he became increasingly aware of the insidious deceptiveness of language, and lost a little of his rhetorical faith. In passage after passage of his prose, and even of his sonnets, he thunders against those perverse and barbarous manipulators of words who prostitute language for unworthy ends. The preface to his *Art of Logic* warns with disillusion that art may blunt as well as sharpen nature "when it is employed too anxiously and too subtly, and especially where it is unnecessary."

This conservative conception was at variance with still a third, which Milton entertained in his hopes of becoming a Christian poet-priest. This conception led him to a truer understanding of Old Testament language, with its dense orchestration of imagery, its poetic abandon, its visionary fire, not more restrained, as some Puritans thought, but less restrained than classical poetry. The implicit theory of Hebrew prophecy was inspirationalist; it denied study and rational control; it regarded the poet as a man possessed or driven by God to speak things his rational will resisted; it released the demonic powers within the word and made of it a searing, blazing, uncontrollable thing, an antisocial explosive. Milton played with that conception when in *The Reason of Church Government* he spoke of his intention to write a great sacred poem; he quoted Jeremiah:

> His word was in my heart as a burning fire shut up in my bones.

and he alluded to the calling of Isaiah when he prayed to

that Eternal Spirit who can enrich with all utterance and knowledge, and sends out his seraphim with the hallowed fire of his altar, to touch and purify the lips of whom he pleases . . .

He was moved by the same ideal when he pictured the sacred poet "soaring in the high region of his fancies with his garland and singing robes about him." Other passages in the same tract make clear that he was far from rejecting many of his Humanist-rhetorical beliefs, but the phrases I have quoted show him radically modifying or extending them.

All of these conceptions—the rhetorical, the Puritan, the inspirational—contributed to the style of *Paradise Lost* and were there harmonized. Of these the first is the most commonly recognized. The debt of Milton's style to classical Latin has become a truism, but the truism is meaningless if it fails to distinguish the effect of *Latin* poetry from the effect of *latinate* poetry in English. Milton enriched many English words by restoring to them their Latin meanings (like his use of *enormous*, in line 297 of Raphael's descent, to mean "exceeding the rule"), but in thus roughening his language he did not imitate Virgil. Virgil allowed his language a certain shadowiness when he chose, but never so much as to dim its continuous clarity. Virgil's language is seldom so *thick* as Milton's. Moreover the deliberate rearranging of normal English word order may *remind* you of Latin, but it creates an effect quite unlike Latin. English does not commonly permit the rearrangement Milton attempted, so that he arrived at something very unlike the Virgilian style. By adopting Tasso's theory of *asprezza* or "roughness" as a means to stylistic "magnificence," Milton moved away from the correctness which a later generation would associate with Virgil. His liberties with language in *Paradise Lost* are actually far greater than those authorized by antique precedent or by his education. He did not surrender rational control to inspirational abandon, but he allowed the demons in his language at least as much room as he allowed to those in his *dramatis personae*.

He had not, for all this, lost his conservative distrust of language, which had rather been deepening with the years. It affects both that style Milton accommodated to heaven and the other he accommodated to hell. In heaven it is reflected in the abstract and colorless speeches of God and the decorous choral hymns of the angels which aim at stark simplicity. Milton's own style in describing heaven (but not Raphael's style in describing the war) virtually eschews similes and his language, if elevated, is markedly less dense than elsewhere. Comparison is out of place in heaven, and even when poetry is descriptive, as in lines 247–56 of Raphael's descent, the visual brilliance is simply reported without ambiguity or metaphor or ulterior significance. We see few physical things in heaven, but those we see—such as the gate which opens to Raphael, or the angelic crowns strewn on the sea of jasper before God's throne (III.349 ff)—are shining and pure-colored and incapable of similitude to earthly copies. The style Milton used to describe heaven might well have pleased John Calvin.

In hell the distrust of rhetoric is reflected in just the opposite way. For the speeches of Satan and the other devils are brilliant textbook models of illogic, demagoguery, wrenched syllogisms, false conclusions, sleight-of-phrase, malicious abuse of words. The impressive description of Beelzebub at the Great Consult:

> . . . with grave
> Aspect he rose, and in his rising seemd
> A Pillar of State; deep on his Front engraven
> Deliberation sat and publick care;
> And Princely counsel in his face yet shone . . .
> (II.300–04)

is a misleading portrait of the ideal Ciceronian orator-statesman which anticipates the pose of Satan at the climax of his temptation of Eve, like "som Orator renound in Athens or free Rome" (IX.670–71). Both deceptive poses are successful.

If the style which describes heaven is "pure," that which describes hell is murkily accommodated to the darkness visible. We make out the dim, grey, physical forms through a fog of jagged syntax, deceptive similes, confusions of physical and abstract, straight-faced but withering irony. In heaven Milton would have us see face to face the truth that makes us free, but in hell darkly the confusion which enslaves us. This is why the syntax of Satan's opening speech resists parsing, and the first statement about Death (II.666–70) is no statement at all but a noun followed by conditional clauses trailing off to leave the sentence incomplete. This is why Satan and Belial begin to pun during the war, "scoffing in ambiguous words." It is this style which leads Prince to speak of "cleverness, grotesqueness, and obscurity" in *Paradise Lost*.

Milton's third style, that which is accommodated to earth, represents something of a mean between his celestial and infernal manners. Terrestrial vision after the fall is obscured by the:

> sideral blast,
> Vapour, and Mist, and Exhalation hot,
> Corrupt and Pestilent . . .
> (X.693–95)

and a pall of infernal confusion hovers correspondingly about the worried syntax of Adam's solliloquy:

> O miserable of happie! is this the end
> Of this new glorious World, and mee so late
> The Glory of that Glory, who now becom
> Accurst of blessed, hide me from the face
> Of God, whom to behold was then my highth
> Of happiness: yet well, if here would end
> The miserie, I deserv'd it . . .
>
> (X.720–26)

All of Adam's posterity will be pursued by that "Ev'ning Mist," curling up in the poem's closing lines, which

> Ris'n from a River ore the marish glides,
> And gathers ground fast at the Labourers heel
> Homeward returning.
>
> (XII.630–32)

Human vision after the fall is dimmed; the mist will darken "the glass of Galileo" when it,

> less assur'd, observes
> *Imagind* Lands and Regions in the Moon . . .

and so the pilot's sight is blurred when he

> from amidst the Cyclades
> Delos or Samos first appeering kenns
> A cloudy spot.

The pilot's uncertainty is imitated by the uncertain grammar, which leaves the reader peering to make out the construction. *Spot* might be considered as an appositive after *Delos* and *Samos*, taken as objects of *kenns*, but one could also consider *spot* the object, and "Delos or Samos first appeering" a parenthetical absolute phrase.

Such clouded vision is the effect of the fall. But even before it, the appearances of this world are capable of misleading, and the style is a little less transparent than in heaven. Raphael's own vision, to be sure, is faultless:

> From hence, no cloud, or, to obstruct his sight,
> Starr interpos'd, however small he sees,
> Not unconform to other shining Globes,
> Earth and the Gard'n of God, with Cedars crownd
> Above all Hills.

The detail of the cedars convinces us that he really does see the garden. But the syntax puts a strain on the act of vision, as soon as Raphael passes the gate of heaven, by confusing us momentarily with the absolute construction, "no cloud or . . . starr interpos'd," and by separating the adjective *small* so far from the nouns it modifies, *Earth* and *Gard'n*. But this strain is slight in comparison to the logical ambiguity surrounding the phoenix. Does Raphael literally take the form of this bird?

> till within soare
> Of Towring Eagles, to all the Fowles he seems
> A Phoenix, gaz'd by all, as that sole Bird
> When to enshrine his reliques in the Suns
> Bright Temple, to Aegyptian Theb's he flies.

If one stopped reading here, there would be no difficulty: Raphael is not flying to Thebes; he is carrying no relics; one could only read this passage as a simile in which the angel is tenor and the bird vehicle. But Milton continues:

> At once on th'Eastern cliff of Paradise
> He lights, and to his proper shape returns
> A Seraph wingd . . .

If Raphael returns to his proper shape then he *has* assumed literally the form of a phoenix, however lacking its burden and destination. Or has his flight simply deceived the "Fowles" who take him mistakenly for a superior bird? The text seems rather to support the former reading, and it appears that we must accustom ourselves to a phoenix both within and without the simile. Milton in any case has been less than ingenuous with his readers, and the more one reads him, the more disingenuous he appears. Why introduce a phoenix here at all, figurative or real? That too is unclear, but we remember at least the purpose of the angel's descent:

> By violence, no, for that shall be withstood,
> But by deceit and lies; this let him know . . .

This world is vulnerable to deceit, and Milton subtly underscores the passage from heaven to earth by heightening the demonic insidiousness of his language. The fallen reader's imperfect reason must strain to make out relations as the pilot strains with his physical eyes, as Galileo strains with his telescope, as the fowls gaze with mistaken recognition on the angel, as Adam and Eve will fail to strain and so blur all our vision.

Thus if Milton enriched the classical style with unorthodox and audacious liberties, he also passed judgment in a sense upon those liberties, and in his most "exalted" scenes attempted to dispense with them.

This latter procedure he carried even further in *Paradise Regained*, where the poetic treatment of Christ is comparably bare, and only the temptations make lovely but intermittent demands upon the senses.

III

Paradise Lost is the only epic to incorporate the celestial descent into a larger, and indeed a comprehensive pattern of imagery, a pattern which includes the poem's two major events—the falls of Satan and of Adam. Milton interweaves those events into a fabric of multitudinous references to height and depth, rising and falling, which appear on virtually every page and bind every incident of the narrative into a closer unity. Sometimes witty, sometimes ironic, sometimes simple and transparent, appearing now in an epithet, a phrase, a simile as well as in the sweeping lines of the action, the subtle workings of this pattern turn incessantly a moral or metaphysical mirror upon objective events, and conversely translate moral events into spatial terms.

Milton seems to have regarded this pattern—it might be called vertical imagery—as one of two patterns basic to his poem. The other is the ubiquitous imagery of light and dark. He couples them—and thereby associates his own creative act with the dramatic action—at the close of his first invocation:

> What in mee is dark
> Illumin, what is low raise and support . . .
> (I.22–23)

He couples them again in describing Satan during the temptation of Eve:

> Hope elevates, and joy
> Bright'ns his Crest . . .
> (IX.633–34)

And he seems to balance them in constructing Books Two and Three. Book Three is saturated with light imagery as Book Two is with vertical imagery. The hymn to light which opens Book Three is balanced by the opening of Book Two:

> High on a Throne of Royal State . . .
> Satan exalted sat, by merit rais'd
> To that bad eminence; and from despair
> Thus high uplifted beyond hope, aspires
> Beyond thus high, insatiat to persue
> Vain Warr with Heav'n . . .
> (II.1, 5–9)

Book Two ends with the punning verb *hies* as Book Three ends with the punning *lights*. In the rest of the poem the two patterns are mingled indiscriminately as they are in the first book, but the vertical imagery is perhaps the denser throughout.

Underlying this imagery is a paradox which had become a Biblical commonplace. Its most familiar forms are the prophecies of the second Isaiah:

> Every valley shall be exalted, and every mountain and hill shall be made low.

and of Christ:

> Whosoever shall exalt himself shall be abased; and he that shall humble himself shall be exalted.

But it takes many other forms: in the command to Ezekiel:

> Exalt him that is low, and abase him that is high.

in Mary's hymn of gratitude to God:

> He hath put down the mighty from their seats, and exalted them of low degree.

in the admonition of Peter:

> Humble yourselves therefore under the mighty hand of God, that he may exalt you in due time.

and in many other passages. The paradox appears in the poetry of men as different as Vaughan ("O let me climbe when I lye down") and Du Bartas, and it recurs in the prose of the paradox-loving Donne. But it found its most sophisticated expression—and the most relevant to Milton—in Saint Augustine:

> There is, therefore, something in humility which, strangely enough, exalts the heart, and something in pride which debases it. This seems, indeed, to be contradictory, that loftiness should debase and lowliness exalt. But pious humility enables us to submit to what is above us; and nothing is more exalted above us than God; and therefore humility, by making us subject to God, exalts us. But pride, being a defect of nature, by the very act of refusing subjection and revolting from Him who is supreme, falls to a low condition; and then comes to pass what is written: "Thou castedst them down when they lifted up themselves." For he does not say "when they had been lifted up" as if first they were exalted, and then afterwards cast down; but "when they lifted up themselves" even then they were cast down—that is to say, the very lifting up was already

a fall. And therefore it is that humility is specially recommended to the
city of God as it sojourns in this world, and is specially exhibited in the
city of God, and in the person of Christ its King; while the contrary vice
of pride, according to the testimony of the sacred writings, specially rules
his adversary the devil.

Paradise Lost plays continually with the paradoxical duality of
lowness—the lowness of humility and of moral degradation or despair—
and with the duality of height—of spiritual eminence or exaltation and of
pride. It plays also with the paradoxes of rising and falling, the abasement
that exalts and the pride that abases. When Adam and Eve fall prostrate to
the ground, confessing their sin with tears in humiliation meek, their
prayers rise successfully to heaven. When the Son offers to descend to a
mortal body, he is correspondingly elevated:

> because in thee
> Love hath abounded more than Glory abounds,
> Therefore thy Humiliation shall exalt
> With thee thy Manhood also to this Throne . . .
> (III.311–14)

But when Satan's ambition leads him to rebel, he enters a state of
perpetual pride and thus continuous, progressive degradation. The bitterest
ironies in hell are reserved for the devils' attempts to deny their fall, to
build up their downcast pride and by so doing unwittingly to deepen their
abasement. Here they are cheering themselves up:

> hee his wonted pride
> Soon recollecting, with *high* words, that bore
> Semblance of worth not substance, gently *rais'd*
> Thir fainted courage, and dispelld thir fears.
> Then strait commands that at the warlike sound
> Of Trumpets loud and Clarions be *upreard*
> His mighty Standard; that proud honour claimd
> Azazel as his right, a Cherube *tall*:
> Who forthwith from the glittering Staff unfurld
> Th'Imperial Ensign, which full *high* advanc't
> Shon like a Meteor streaming to the Wind . . .
> At which the universal Host *upsent*
> A shout that tore Hells Concave . . .
> All in a moment through the gloom were seen
> Ten thousand Banners *rise* into the Air
> With Orient Colours waving: with them *rose*
> A forrest huge of Spears . . .
>   Anon they move
> In perfet Phalanx to the Dorian mood

> Of Flutes and soft Recorders; such as *rais'd*
> To *highth* of noblest temper Hero's old
> Arming to Battel . . .
>
> (I.527–53)

When earlier Satan cries:

> . . . in this abject posture have ye sworn
> To adore the Conqueror? . . .
> Awake, arise, or be for ever fall'n.
>
> (I.322–23, 330)

his irony is swallowed in a greater irony. Each of the speakers at the Great Consult is really concerned with regaining his former height by various means: Moloch by armed invasions; Belial, whose "thoughts were low," by appeasement; Mammon, by attempting to "raise Magnificence;—and what can Heav'n shew more?"; Beelzebub, by corrupting man that the devils may "Joy upraise" in God's disturbance. This venture, says Beelzebub, "from the lowest deep will once more lift us up" (II.392–93). And Satan as he volunteers is one whom

> now transcendent glory rais'd
> Above his fellows, with Monarchal pride
> Conscious of highest worth . . .
>
> (II.427–29)

The consult disbands with its leaders "rais'd by false presumptuous hope," some of them to celebrate past deeds in song but others to retire to a hill, "in thoughts more elevate," there to reason high of fate and freedom. The symbolic answer to all this is the metamorphosis in Book Ten:

> They felt themselves now changing; down thir arms,
> Down fell both Spear and Shield, down they as fast,
> And the dire hiss renewd, and the dire form
> Catchd by Contagion, like in punishment,
> As in thir crime.
>
> (X.541–45)

The descent of Raphael typifies that celestial condescension which is opposed to demonic aspiration. It is a minor instance of the solicitous compassion for man whose major instance is Christ's sacrificial redemption. The episode's opening words:

> Them thus imploid beheld
> With pittie Heav'ns high King . . .

implicitly express the paradox of divine generosity. The epithet *high* is not perfunctory; it makes the necessary quiet contrast with *pittie*, God's affective descent to earth which precedes the angel's literal descent. Raphael is chosen in turn for that gracious mansuetude toward men which he will display again toward Tobias. That he deigns now to descend to extended conversation with Adam implies as well the height of man upon the scale of creation. When after the fall Michael descends to Paradise, Adam immediately remarks the severer aspect of his mien:

> yet not terrible,
> That I should fear, nor sociably mild,
> As Raphael, that I should much confide,
> But solemn and sublime . . .
>   (XI.223 36)

The fallen Adam will not be worthy then to receive the angel in "his shape Celestial" but "as Man clad to meet Man." Raphael's prelapsarian sociable mildness betokens both heavenly charity and human dignity.

That this height of dignity is threatened we are reminded by God's references to

> what enemie
> Late fall'n himself from Heav'n is plotting now
> The fall of others from like state of bliss . . .

But for the moment the threat is muted; man remains the felicitous enjoyer of God's garden, "with Cedars crownd above all hills," for whose welfare celestial emissaries post with zealous speed.

> Down thither prone in flight
> He speeds . . .

The adverb is stressed by its position. Raphael's magnanimity is further underscored by the revelation of his eminence in the angelic hierarchy. He is one to whom the lesser angels pay homage warranted both by his rank and his errand:

> Strait knew him all the Bands
> Of Angels under watch; and to his state,
> And to his message high in honour rise;
> For on som message high they guessed him bound.

Adam too will pay homage, although not such as to compromise his own rank:

> Mean while our Primitive great Sire, to meet
> His god-like Guest, walks forth, without more train
> Accompanied then with his own compleat
> Perfections; in himself was all his state . . .

> Neerer his presence Adam though not awd,
> Yet with submiss approach and reverence meek,
> As to a superior Nature, bowing low,
> Thus said . . .
>
>   (V.350–53, 358–61)

Both the rising of the angels and the bowing of Adam demonstrate the true and cheerful humility which, for Milton, remained consonant with self-respect and freedom.

The height of Adam's dignity before the fall is balanced by his abasement afterwards: first after Eve's sin when he "the Garland wreath'd for Eve down dropd" (X.892–93); then in the false humiliation of pride-concealing despair, when

> On the ground
> Outstretcht he lay, on the cold ground, and oft
> Curs'd his Creation . . .
>
>   (X.850–52)

and later in the true humiliation of repentance, when husband and wife

> Repairing where he judg'd them prostrate fell
> Before him reverent . . .
>
>   (X.1099–100)

Despite the mercy earned by that act, they must leave Paradise, and the closing lines show them led "down the Cliff . . . to the subjected Plaine" of suffering and death. This to be sure is not the ultimate conclusion; that will come only when

> New Heav'n and Earth shall to the Ages rise,
> Or down from Heav'n descend.
>
>   (X.647–48)

That is the conclusion the poem glimpses hopefully, but it remains in the distance. The true curve of the poem's major action follows the fallen couple down into the valley of humiliation.

In thus ending with a downward movement, *Paradise Lost* reverses the visionary ascent with which Milton almost habitually concluded his earlier poems. The youthful optimism of his Christian Humanism is reflected in the soaring visions of redemption which conclude *On Time*, *At a Solemn Musick*, *Epitaph on the Marchioness of Winchester*, *On the Death of the Bishop of Winchester*, *Manso*, *Damon's Epitaph*, *Lycidas*, and *Comus*. The same optimism informs the visionary conclusion of his first published prose work, *Of Reformation in England*. We can contrast that period of hope with the pessimism of twenty years later by noticing the downward movement with which *The Ready and Easy Way* concludes. The final words of that tract warn against the "precipice of destruction" to which the "deluge" of Royalist "epidemic madness would hurry us, through the general defection of a misguided and abused multitude." At the time these words were written, *Paradise Lost* was already well begun. The descent with which the epic concludes has none of the tract's desperate alarm, but their common movement downward is significant. In both works the poet struggles—as indeed he does in all the later works—to reconcile the high potentialities of man with his fallen perversity. The vertical imagery in *Paradise Lost* registers the progress of that noble and fearful struggle within a great man's moral imagination.

IV

The richness of Milton's similes is unique in epic poetry. The finest of them are marvels of compression, and their relationship to their respective tenors seems almost inexhaustible. They form thus a sharp contrast with the similes of the *Iliad* which, as we have seen, tend to provide relief from the narrative rather than commentary upon it. Virgil's similes do comment, in broad and generally moral terms, but they do not imitate the tenor in specific point after point; no ingenuity or wit has gone into their making. Milton's similes are immensely ingenious; they are little Chinese boxes of meaning. His conception of the simile may have been influenced less by the classical epics than by the theory and practice of George Chapman's translations. Chapman believed in the detailed correspondence between Homer's similes and their tenors, and tried to demonstrate his belief with desperate ingenuity in his translation as well as his notes.

Certain of Milton's literary and historical allusions are in themselves incipient similes, like the Tobias allusion which precedes Raphael's descent:

> Them thus imploid beheld
> With pittie Heav'ns high King, and to him calld
> Raphael, the sociable Spirit, that deignd
> To travel with Tobias, and secur'd
> His marriage with the seav'ntimes-wedded Maid.

Milton is implicitly comparing the two descents. The ostensible point of comparison is the sociability of Raphael discussed above, that quality by which he deigns "half this day as friend to friend" to converse with Adam just as he will deign to travel with Tobias. This is the ostensible point in common, but here as in most Miltonic similes, the ostensible point is not the most important. The purpose of Raphael's visit is to warn Adam against Satan, and we remember that in the Tobias story Raphael succeeds in bilking Satan. If we had forgotten it, an earlier allusion would have reminded us:

> So entertaind those odorous sweets the Fiend
> Who came thir bane, though with them better pleas'd
> Then Asmodeus with the fishie fume,
> That drove him though enamourd, from the Spouse
> Of Tobits Son, and with a vengeance sent
> From Media post to Aegypt, there fast bound.
>   (IV.166–71)

Asmodeus or Satan has sexual designs upon Sara, the spouse of Tobias, just as Satan designs to seduce Eve. Raphael appears in Tobit as the protector of a marriage ("secur'd his marriage with the seav'ntimes-wedded Maid."), the role which he is about to play here. When God considers Adam and Eve "thus imploid . . . with pittie," they stand as patterns of a perfect marriage. They have first manifested their conjugal harmony in the morning hymn, and now their cooperative labor involves a second kind of wedding:

> they led the Vine
> To wed her Elm; she spous'd about him twines
> Her mariageable arms, and with her brings
> Her dowr th'adopted Clusters, to adorn
> His barren leaves. Them thus imploid . . .
>   (V.215–19)

They deserve pity because they exemplify marriage threatened by the devil. Raphael's solicitude in *Tobit* for the uniquely human institution also graces the domestic scenes in Adam's bower. But this spouse he cannot protect.

The phoenix simile—since it *is* at least partly a simile—remains more difficult to elucidate because the history of the phoenix legend is immensely complex, and because Milton helps less to focus his meaning by qualifying particulars. The meaning of such an image really has an open end, and no one can know precisely at what point to delimit it; we cannot even be absolutely sure how much comparative mythology Milton knew. The texts most obviously in the background of the simile are Tasso's description of Armida (*Ger. Lib.*, 18.35), his beautiful *canzone, La Fenice*, and the simile from Vondel's descent [noted elsewhere]. All of these passages use the bird as an image of brilliance and beauty and éclat, qualities which Milton is at pains to confer upon his angel and which may in themselves have led him to the image. From the *Odyssey* and *Aeneid* downward, the descent convention involved a bird simile, and what more natural than to choose for *Paradise Lost* the most fabulous of birds, the unique, indeed the legendary king of birds?

Behind the Renaissance allusions lie the manifold descriptions in antique prose and verse. Among the fullest of these are the poems on the phoenix by Claudian and Lactantius, if the attribution to the latter is correct. In both of these poems much is made of the excitement engendered by the bird's arrival in Egypt, so precious and sacred was it considered to be. Not only is it greeted joyfully by men, but the very birds acclaim and escort it. Claudian's poem specifically names the eagle as a member of this escort, and the same poet returns to the image elsewhere in a passage strikingly close to Milton's:

> So when by that birth in death the Phoenix renews its youth and gathers its father's ashes and carries them lovingly in its talons, winging its way, sole of its kind, from the extreme east to Nile's coasts, the eagles gather together and all the fowls from every quarter to marvel at the bird of the sun; afar its living plumage shines, itself redolent of its father's fragrant pyre.

A reader familiar with such a passage as this would recognize in Milton's allusion the note of religious and joyful momentousness.

Neither the poets of antiquity—Ovid, Claudian, Lactantius—nor the prose authors—Herodotus, Pliny, Tacitus, etc.—who speak of the phoenix describe it as a celestial messenger, but this role was anciently assigned to it, or a bird like it, in the Orient and Egypt. An English scholar writes as follows of Egyptian beliefs regarding birds:

> The bird, of whatever kind, is the obvious choice for a messenger since it is essential to the whole idea of the reservoir of power that it should be unattainable by mere mortals. The traffic is both ways, the bird is the messenger from men to gods or, more exactly, the soul of the departed who traverses the boundary between the two worlds and the angel of the gods who comes from the divine numinous regions of power. In the latter case the message from the gods is the announcement of ineluctable fate, the re-appearance of some temporarily absent physical phenomenon—a star, a season, an inundation of the Nile, or it can be the declaration of a new age or phase of good or evil luck.

One bird singled out particularly for the role of messenger was the *Bn.w* bird, which seems to have been a mythographic ancestor of the phoenix.

> On the whole the *Bn.w* bird is an angel, announcing stellar events or dates and, by an extension, the fate of mankind.

Milton could not have known this belief in anything like its original form, but some derived version of it may conceivably have reached him. In any case the phoenix became an obvious symbol for a new age and for collective or individual renewal. Just as Vida had applied it to the resurrected Christ, so Milton would use it as a great climactic symbol of Samson's regeneration. It is suggestive that in his other verse reference to the phoenix, in the *Epitaphium Damonis*, he represents it watching the dawn arise. And when in *Paradise Lost* God predicts the end of the fallen world, he uses language which recalls the phoenix legend:

> The World shall burn, and from her ashes spring
> New Heav'n and Earth . . .
>
> (III.334–35)

Raphael's discourse to Adam will record the end of that earlier age which was closed by the angels' revolt, as well as the beginning of the new in the majestic *allegresse* of creation. His descent is vitalized by the sense of fresh and hopeful life springing from a great cosmic renewal. Perhaps it does not strain excessively the subtlety of Milton's imagery to associate the phoenix' "reliques" with the history Raphael is charged to communicate.

The reference to these relics introduces another curious element of the legend. Most antique writers repeat that version by which the bird dies not in fire but in a ball of spices. This ball it is which the offspring bears to the temple of the sun in Heliopolis (or as Milton has it, Thebes). The offspring's plumage is itself fragrant with spices; this detail appears both in the above quotation from Claudian and with more emphasis in his poem on the phoenix. It can be no coincidence that Raphael's wings also effuse fragrance:

> Like Maia's son he stood,
> And shook his Plumes, that Heav'nly fragrance filld
> The circuit wide.

What are more curious are the subsequent references to spices in Paradise, references which Professor Bush also associates with the phoenix material:

> Thir glittering Tents he passd, and now is come
> Into the blissful field, through Groves of Myrrhe,
> And flouring Odours, Cassia, Nard, and Balme;
> A Wilderness of sweets . . .

All four of the plants named here appear in Lactantius' *De Ave Phoenice*, and three of the four in Ovid. The resemblance is the more interesting when it is remembered that Lactantius and Claudian situated the birth and death of the phoenix in an oriental paradise protected from all evil.

In this paradise Lactantius places the spices which also flourish in Milton's
Eden. A favorite site for this other paradise was Arabia Felix, whose spicy
fragrance has been compared to the odors of Eden in an earlier simile:

> now gentle gales
> Fanning thir odoriferous wings dispense
> Native perfumes, and whisper whence they stole
> Those balmie spoiles. As when to them who saile
> Beyond the Cape of Hope, and now are past
> Mozambic, off at Sea North-East windes blow
> Sabean Odours from the spicie shoare
> Of Arabie the blest . . .
>
> (IV.156-63)

I am far from sure that these tantalizing parallels can be fitted into
a single coherent interpretation. It is possible that we have left interpretation behind and blundered into the psychology of poetic creation. But one
unpretentious conclusion is surely justified. To the instructed reader, the
phoenix simile intensifies the imagery of storied remoteness and oriental
lushness with which Milton saturates his Paradise. If his story is the true,
original, archetypal story which later history and myth fragment and
distort, the poet must nonetheless employ those distorted fragments to
reconstruct for us a living experience of the true. Milton would have
regarded the phoenix' paradise as such a distortion of the true, and he
edges as much of it into his poem as he needs to enrich the great
arch-image of the garden.

The spices contribute, quite apart from any legend, to a certain
lulling heaviness in the atmosphere of Paradise, a Keatsian excess of
pleasure which the ensuing lines intensify:

> A Wilderness of sweets; for Nature here
> Wantond as in her prime, and plaid at will
> Her Virgin Fancies, pouring forth more sweet,
> Wilde above Rule or Art; enormous bliss.

The scented air and tangled flowers are not calculated to permit hard work
much relevance. Thus the "Sabean Odours" of the Arabia Felix simile
invite the sailors to interrupt their work:

> with such delay
> Well pleas'd they slack thir course . . .
> (IV.163-64)

In Paradise as well the fragrance seems an invitation to indolence. It even
suggests an incipient sexuality. Adam's account of his first sexual union
with Eve will mention the same fragrance:

> fresh Gales and gentle Aires
> Whisperd it to the Woods, and from thir wings
> Flung Rose, flung Odours from the spicie Shrub,
> Disporting . . .
>
> (VIII.515–18)

and as early a poem as the *Elegia Quinta* associates odorous breezes with seductiveness. Indeed that poem's great central image—of Earth inviting and yearning for the embraces of Apollo—looks forward to Nature wantoning in Paradise.

But the nature of Paradise, redolent with a slightly drowsy sexuality, is not quite the nature of the rest of Milton's earth. From its first description, Paradise is a little enervating:

> Another side, umbrageous Grots and Caves
> Of coole recess, ore which the mantling Vine
> Layes forth her purple Grape, and gently creeps
> Luxuriant; mean while murmuring waters fall
> Down the slope hills, disperst, or in a Lake,
> That to the fringed Bank with Myrtle crownd,
> Her crystal mirror holds, unite thir streams.
> The Birds thir quire apply; aires, vernal aires,
> Breathing the smell of field and grove, attune
> The trembling leaves . . .
>
> (IV.257–66)

The waters murmur; the leaves tremble; the mantling vine creeps *gently*. One understands the artistic logic of this drowsiness. The loveliest paradise of our deepest fancy is of its essence dreamy. But Milton's nature as a whole, the nature without the garden, is *not* dreamy, before the fall or after it. The nature is vital, energetic. robust, dynamic, possessed of a Baroque joy in living movement. Such is the nature of the world whose creation is described in Book Seven. The creation is the setting in movement of a dance, the dance of jocund universal praise, wherein nothing is inert or heavy and nothing seems to rest. Its poetry is a poetry of verbs. The same vital dance is evoked—with what consistency is uncertain—by Adam and Eve in their great morning hymn:

> Moon, that now meetst the orient Sun, now fli'st
> With the fixt Starrs, fixt in thir Orb that flies,
> And yee five other wandring Fires that move
> In mystic Dance not without Song, resound
> His praise, who out of Darkness calld up Light.
> Aire, and ye Elements the eldest birth
> Of Natures Womb, that in quaternion run

Perpetual Circle, multiform, and mix
And nourish all things, let your ceasless change
Varie to our great Maker still new praise . . .
(V.175–84)

Milton's language is a magnificent reservoir of heroic energy which, when
he chooses, charges the world with the grandeur of God.

But Adam and Eve and the garden about them are not so charged.
To man is given the life of reason and love gratified by a wilderness of
sweets, but not the life of robust energy dancing in praise. Milton was
concerned, perhaps too concerned, with dramatizing the *loss* of Eden; he
wanted to overwhelm us with all that we might have had. And so he
conceived his great arch-image to resemble the gardens of Alcinous in the
Odyssey, the court of Alcina in Ariosto, the island of Cupid in Camoens,
Armida's garden in Tasso, Spenser's Bower of Bliss. But in these other
poems the garden is represented as a place where heroic activity is
interrupted or forgotten. None of those poets would have considered it
dignified to remain forever there where Nature wantoned so wildly. But
Milton represents it as dignified.

Raphael as he alights is brimming with divine vitality; it flows from
Messiah as he wages heavenly war; Satan too retains it before it gradually
drains from him in the later books. But to Adam, by art or accident,
Milton denies this more potent glory. Adam's life is circumscribed by the
walls of his garden, and his strength is not of that mobile or questing
temper which would lead him beyond.

This limitation remains with him and his posterity after his fall.
The heroism required of fallen man involves less active energy than the
passive strength of fortitude and patience. The heroes in Michael's foreview
of history—Abel, Enoch, Noah, Christ—are men whose wills govern
nothing beyond themselves. The heroic will is no longer ambitious to
extend its control. Milton's sarcastic dismissal of those heroic poems
which dissect "with long and tedious havoc fabl'd Knights in Battels
feignd" (IX.30–31) finds reinforcement in Michael's explanation of the
Israelite itinerary after leaving Egypt:

> the Race elect
> Safe towards Canaan from the shoar advance
> Through the wilde Desert, not the readiest way,
> Least entring on the Canaanite allarmd
> Warr terrifie them inexpert, and feare
> Return them back to Egypt, choosing rather
> Inglorious life with servitude; for life
> To noble and ignoble is more sweet
> Untraind in Armes, where rashness leads not on.
> (XII.214–22)

Milton betrays something like contempt for human military prowess, although he admires angelic prowess. Perhaps it is also significant that the vigor of his language flags, for whatever reason, in just these two concluding books where human history is related and heroism exemplified. In the poignant last lines of the poem, exceptionally tender for Milton, the courage of Adam and Eve is qualified by an almost childlike hesitancy which the faltering verse rhythms underscore. The quietness and pathos of the close make a pointed, self-conscious contrast with the traditional epic.

This separation of energy and human heroism seems to me one of the most distinctive qualities of *Paradise Lost*. In part it has led to the Satanist misunderstanding. Satan is unquestionably more vital than Adam, but in the end it is clear that he is less heroic—as the poem defines *heroic*. The only real question is whether such a definition, excluding the expansive, questing impulse of the ego, suppressing vital zest in favor of dogged, self-contained integrity—whether that definition is consonant with one's idea of epic heroism or even of moral elevation. The great paradox of *Paradise Lost* lies in Milton's withholding from his human characters that spacious power which ennobled his own imagination.

V

There is no need today to stress the heterodoxy of Milton's belief in the goodness of matter, the belief which led him to the mortalist heresy and the denial of creation *ex nihilo*. It is more useful to examine the tensions which that belief heightened within his own mind. For he attempted to straddle, both theologically and artistically, two forms of religious experience which generally tend to oppose each other. The two forms have been described thus:

> [Puritanism] was a return to the Augustinian tradition in which the relation between the individual soul and God is all that matters. This relationship has too often been taken as a purely intelligible affair to the exclusion of the senses. In this regard, Puritanism was what we might call a religion of the "ear," i.e., the *hearing* and *understanding* of the Word and of doctrine—hence the profusion of great Puritan preachers—and not a religion of the "eye," i.e., the seeing of the sensuous aspect of the world and the physical passion of Christ.
> (John E. Smith, "Poetry, Religion, and Philosophy," *Review of Metaphysics*, 9 [1955], 260)

Milton was typically Puritan in his neglect of the "physical passion," but he was un-Puritan when he evoked "the sensuous aspect of the world."

His religion of the eye, however, did not really diminish the great importance he laid upon the inner ear. This latter emphasis becomes immediately apparent if we think of the real purpose of Raphael's descent: to expound the truth. In this respect Milton's celestial messenger represents a unique departure from the convention. For he is dispatched neither to prod nor to encourage nor to punish but to explain, almost indeed to lecture. The success or failure of his mission will lead to visible, objective consequences, but these are actually secondary; they serve only to manifest the crucial consequences which are interior. Milton welcomed the triviality in the act of eating an apple because that triviality demonstrates the primacy of interior action. For that action all the visible imagery serves mainly as metaphorical equivalent. We have already seen how easily the transference is made by such devices as the vertical imagery.

Milton's artistic withdrawal from the visible world is implicit in Michael's scorn for physical heroism (a scorn which several passages confirm), as perhaps it is implicit in God's phrase to Raphael:

By violence, no, for that shall be withstood,
But by deceit and lies . . .

But the withdrawal is carried further than this. The poet's prayer must be taken seriously when he invokes the Celestial Light to shine inward

that I may see and tell
Of things invisible to mortal sight.
(III.54–55)

The blind consciousness is drawn nostalgically to the beautiful sensuous world denied it, but driven back thence to the world of things invisible. Adam will allude uncategorically to the inferiority of outward things:

For well I understand in the prime end
Of Nature her th'inferiour, in the mind
And inward Faculties, which most excell . . .
(VIII.540–42)

and Raphael later assures him that Eve, rightly governed, will "to realities yield all her shows" (VIII.575). More telling than these is the impatient remark of Michael which betrays Milton's imaginative weariness:

Much thou hast yet to see, but I perceave
Thy mortal sight to faile; objects divine
Must needs impaire and wearie human sense:
Henceforth what is to com I will relate . . .
(XII.8–11)

Henceforth almost to the very end the eye is neglected for the ear. Michael's discourse moves, the whole poem moves, as Barker tells us all of Milton's thought moves, toward the "Paradise within thee happier far," the paradise one cannot see.

If all epics are concerned with cosmic politics, *Paradise Lost* is pre-eminently concerned with them, but like other lesser poems of its century, it alters the traditional form of political struggle. God is impervious to violence, but to disobedience he is not so obviously impervious; his victory has to come in the long run. The struggle works itself out in those terms which have meaning for a devout, sedentary, urban public. In thus fulfilling the seventeenth-century tendency to shift the political medium from violence to morality, Milton implicitly rejected, it seems to me, part of the basis of epic itself—the balance of objective and subjective action, the balance of executive and deliberative. In the closing books of *Paradise Lost*, the books which define human heroism, the executive episodes almost disappear. This rejection need not in itself involve grounds for criticism. But it is important to see how the last of the great poems in conventional epic dress contained within itself, not accidentally but essentially, the seeds of the genre's destruction. One of these seeds was the internalization of action, the preference for things invisible. A second was the questioning of the hero's independence; a third was the detaching of heroism from the community, the City of man in this world. Both of these latter procedures need more comment.

Heroic independence in *Paradise Lost* is weakened by Milton's juggling with the theological categories of grace and merit. If we were to grant "the better fortitude of Patience and Heroic Martyrdom" as a proper notion of epic heroism, we should still want to feel that fortitude to be the painful achievement of the hero. But Milton in more than one passage suggests that this fortitude is the gift of God. It is a little anticlimactic for the reader, after following tremulously the fallen couple's gropings toward redemption in Book Ten, to hear from the Father's lips that he has decreed it—that all of this tenderly human scene, this triumph of conjugal affection and tentative moral searching, occurred only by divine fiat. One might have been tempted to alter his ideas of heroism to include Adam's contrition, did he not encounter God's own curt dismissal of it:

> He sorrows now, repents, and prayes contrite,
> My motions in him: longer then they move,
> His heart I know, how variable and vain
> Self-left.
>
> (XI.90–93)

And so the later exemplary figures in Michael's discourse lose most of their prestige from his prefatory warning·

> good with bad
> Expect to hear, supernal Grace contending
> With sinfulness of Men . . .
>
> (XI. 358–60)

It is true that we need not regard Adam and the Hebrew patriarchs as necessarily elect above the rest, recipients of that "peculiar grace" which ensures salvation, although Milton very likely did so regard most of them. Even if we choose to ignore that doctrine, the remaining ambiguity of grace and merit to which Milton's language leads effectually destroys the dramatic clarity and force which epic heroism requires. The interplay at the heart of the epic between individual excellence and limitation falters because so little ground is left for excellence. The announced intent, to turn the note to tragic, risks failure because tragedy implies a standard of human greatness surviving in spite of misfortune and even corruption. Milton maintains that standard only shakily and intermittently after the disaster of the fall. And he makes clear that man can do nothing to achieve the one thing worth achieving—nothing at least beyond the act of faith:

> his [Christ's] obedience
> Imputed becomes theirs by Faith, his merits
> To save them, not thir own, though legal works.
> (XII. 408–10)

This weakening of heroic prestige is abetted by the severing of the traditional bond between hero and community. It is true that the Son considered as hero is a benefactor of the widest possible community, and even Abdiel speaks in a sense for all the loyal angelic community in his defiance of Satan. But if we agree to limit heroic awe to the human sphere, then we must speak only of individual heroes, lonely men who mount the current of common perversity. Their goodness, as Milton describes them, stands over against the universal evil; no, more than this, it outweighs the evil. Adam's comment on the deluge is offensive and immoral but Milton did not so regard it:

> Farr less I now lament for one whole World
> Of wicked Sons destroyd, then I rejoyce
> For one Man found so perfet and so just,
> That God voutsafes to raise another World
> From him, and all his anger to forget.
> (XI. 874–78)

By the standards of Milton's arrogant moral aristocracy, the damnation of the community matters less than the salvation of the few.

Although the anatomy of evil in the poem is so brilliant as to be unsurpassed in its kind, the dramatization of goodness fails. When Michael, anticipating Saint Paul, refers to charity as "the soul of all the rest" of the virtues, we can only protest that we have seen little of it in the poem. We miss it chiefly in those places where Milton asserts it to exist. When it is scrutinized, God's generosity in dispatching Raphael turns out to be not at all a true magnanimity but a petty legalistic self-righteousness. Adam must not be allowed to "pretend surprisal, unadmonisht, unforewarnd." The majesty of Raphael's descent can only be appreciated if the awkwardness of its motive remains half-forgotten.

The aristocratic doctrine which prefers the few to the many leads directly to Adam's *felix culpa* speech and God's imputed victory over Satan. The meaning of that victory is contained in Satan's lines at the outset:

> If then his Providence
> Out of our evil seek to bring forth good,
> Our labour must be to pervert that end,
> And out of good still to find means of evil . . .
> (I.162–65)

Satan has perverted the good of the angelic creation by revolt; out of that evil comes the good of the human creation. Satan will pervert that too, but he still loses the poem, Milton tells us, through the good accruing from the Incarnation and Atonement. It matters not, from this viewpoint, if the great mass of souls are damned, since for the saints

> the Earth
> Shall all be Paradise, farr happier place
> Then this of Eden.
> (XII.463–65)

It is possible doubtless to share Adam's joy at this outcome, but one's participation is increased if he can personally look forward to that felicity. In this respect, I fear, by the poet's own doctrine, his audience is few indeed. For the rest of us, Michael's depressing recital of our forebears' tribulations mars the perfection of God's victory. At this point *Paradise Lost*, like so many other Christian epics, falls into that ambivalence of joy and pain which plagued the genre, as it now seems, almost inevitably. Theologically its conclusion asks us to applaud, but dramatically it brings us to tears.

This conflict finds a local solution in the concluding expulsion which I have already had occasion to praise. Here for once Milton's compassion is unmixed, and all the constituent feelings—nostalgia, resolution, remorse, bewilderment, timidity, and hope—these make a peace which owes its harmony to the poet's wise pity. These last twenty-five lines go far toward saving the great uneasy poem they conclude. But the mending is the work of image, rhythm, tone, and mood, instruments of local efficacity; as soon as we free ourselves of their atmosphere to reflect on those more abstract planes which the poem also embraces, we rediscover its profound and destructive divisions.

Perhaps however in the last analysis it is pedantic to dwell too long upon those divisions. Even if one chooses, with Sir Walter Raleigh, to regard *Paradise Lost* as a monument to dead ideas, or contradictory or even offensive ideas, one need not return to it out of wonder alone for its magisterial and insidious art. Milton's enlightened reverence for the Bible permitted him to entertain the possibility that his story was something like a myth. If we too consider it as that, in the fullest sense, if we read it with the detachment we bring to the myth of the *Iliad*, then we need not follow unmoved and unedified Milton's search for a measure and definition of human existence. The work in its plenary wholeness makes a richer definition than any one of its dogmatic parts. And just as Swift betrayed his concern for mankind by railing at it, Milton persuades us of his humanity even in his moments of passionate severity.

NORTHROP FRYE

Revolt in the
Desert

Among the least fully realized parts
of *Paradise Lost* is what seems a hurried and perfunctory summary of the
Bible in the latter part of Michael's revelation. The reason is that such
events as the Incarnation and the Last Judgment cannot be given their full
poetic resonance at that point in the *Paradise Lost* scheme, otherwise the
conclusion would become top-heavy. They must either be dramatized
separately or assumed to have their importance already understood by the
reader. *Paradise Regained* dramatizes the third of four epiphanies in which
Christ confronts Satan: it refers back to the original war in heaven as
recounted in *Paradise Lost*, and forward to the final binding of Satan
prophesied in the Book of Revelation. The defeat of Satan as tempter
fulfils the prophecy in Genesis that the seed of Adam shall "bruise the
serpent's head," which Satan refers to so light-heartedly in *Paradise Lost*.

This imagery suggests the romantic theme of a knight-errant killing
a dragon, and is one of several such images in the Bible. Besides the
serpent in Eden, the Old Testament speaks of a dragon or sea monster,
called "leviathan," or "Rahab," who was defeated once at the creation
and is to be destroyed, or, in the metaphor of the sea serpent, hooked and
landed, on the day of judgment. A comparison of Satan to the leviathan
appears early in *Paradise Lost*. Isaiah refers both to the previous and to the
future victories over this leviathan, and Ezekiel and Isaiah appear to
identify him with Egypt as the symbolic land of bondage. In the Book of
Revelation this figure becomes a dragon with seven heads and ten
horns, whose tail draws a third of the stars from heaven, the basis of

From *The Return of Eden*. Copyright © 1965 by University of Toronto Press.

Milton's account of Satan's fall. The connection of this dragon with Egypt in Milton is indicated in Michael's references to the Nile's seven mouths and to the plagues of Egypt as the ten wounds of the river dragon. In the symbolism of Revelation, again, the Satan of Job and the gospels, the serpent of the Eden story, and the leviathan of the prophecies, are all explicitly identified.

From this is derived the conventional symbol of Christ as a dragon-killer, such as we have in medieval sculptures portraying him with a dragon or basilisk under his feet. In the first book of *The Faerie Queene*, the story of St. George and the dragon is used as an allegory of the imitation of Christ by the church. St. George's dragon in Spenser is identified with the Satan-serpent-leviathan complex in the Bible, and as a result of St. George's victory the parents of his lady Una, who are Adam and Eve, are restored to their inheritance, the Garden of Eden, which is also the unfallen world. In *The Reason of Church Government* Milton refers to the allegory of St. George and "the king's daughter, the Church." Michael explains to Adam, however, that the contest of Christ and Satan will be not a physical but a spiritual and intellectual fight, the cutting weapons used being those of dialectic, and the true dragon being a spiritual enemy.

I mentioned [elsewhere] the passage in *The Reason of Church Government* in which Milton speaks of the literary genre of the "brief epic." As *Paradise Regained* is clearly Milton's essay in the brief epic, and as the model for that genre is stated by Milton to be the Book of Job, we should expect *Paradise Regained* to have a particularly close relation to that drama. In Job the contest of God and Satan takes the form of a wager on Job's virtue, and the scheme of *Paradise Regained* is not greatly different, with Christ occupying the place of Job. Satan, we notice, soon disappears from the action of Job, and when Job's mind is finally enlightened by God, God's speech consists very largely of discourses on two monsters, behemoth and leviathan, the latter of whom, the more important, is finally said to be "king over all the children of pride." These monsters seem to represent an order of nature over which Satan is permitted some control, but, in a larger perspective, they are seen to be creatures of God. By pointing these beasts out to Job, God has, so to speak, put them under Job's feet, and taken Job into his own protection. Thus the victory of Job is, in terms of this symbolism, a dialectical victory over both Satan and leviathan, Satan and leviathan being much the same thing from different points of view.

In more traditional views of the Incarnation the central point of the contest of Christ and Satan is located between Christ's death on the cross and his resurrection. It is then that he descends to hell, harrows hell, and achieves his final victory over hell and death. In medieval paintings of the harrowing of hell, hell is usually represented as leviathan, a huge open-mouthed monster into which, or whom, Christ descends, like the Jonah whom Christ accepted as a prototype of his own Passion. For Milton, however, the scriptural evidence for the descent into hell was weak, and besides, Milton believed that the whole of Christ's human nature died on the cross, with no soul or spirit able to survive and visit hell. In the synoptic gospels, the temptation immediately follows the baptism. Milton's view of baptism is an exception to his generally anti-sacramental attitude to biblical symbolism: he is willing to see in it a symbol of the three-day crisis of Christian redemption, death, burial and resurrection. So the temptation is what becomes for Milton the scripturally authorized version of the descent into hell, the passing into the domain of Satan, and the reconquest of everything in it that is redeemable. Certain features, such as the bewilderment of the forsaken disciples and the elegiac complaint of the Virgin Mary at the beginning of the second book, might seem more natural if Milton had followed medieval tradition in making *Paradise Regained* the harrowing of hell. In any case Christ's withdrawal from the world at this point is the opposite of a "fugitive and cloistered virtue," as he is being led directly into the jaws of hell itself, and not yet as a conqueror.

The Bible gives us two parallel versions of the fall and redemption of man. The first is the *Paradise Lost* version. Adam falls from the garden into a wilderness, losing the tree of life and the water of life. Christ, the second Adam, wins back the garden ("Eden raised in the waste wilderness") and restores to man the tree and river of life. This version is elaborated by Spenser as well as Milton, for in Spenser the fight between St. George and the dragon takes place at the boundary of Eden, and St. George is refreshed by the paradisal well of life and tree of life, which continue in the church as the sacraments of baptism and communion. As the natural home of Christ on earth is a fertile garden, the Eden in which he walked in the cool of the day, so the natural home of devils is the wilderness, "A pathless desert dusk with horrid shades," a blasted land like the country traversed in the *City of Dreadful Night* or by Browning's Childe Roland, the sort of scene one instinctively calls "God-forsaken," where the panic inspired by hunger, lost direction and loneliness would have unsettled the reason of most people in much less than forty days.

Inside the story of Adam comes the second version, the story of Israel, who falls from the Promised Land into the bondage of Egypt and Babylon. Besides being a second Adam, Christ is a second Israel, who wins back, in a spiritual form, the Promised Land and its capital city of Jerusalem. In this capacity the story of the Exodus, or deliverance of Israel from Egypt, prefigures his life in the Gospels. Israel is led to Egypt through a Joseph; Christ is taken to Egypt by a Joseph. Christ is saved from a wicked king who orders a massacre of infants; Israel is saved from the slaughter of Egyptian first-born. Moses organizes Israel into twelve tribes and separates it from Egypt at the crossing of the Red Sea; Christ gathers twelve followers and is marked out as the Redeemer at his baptism in the Jordan, which the Israelites also later cross. Israel wanders forty years in the wilderness; Christ forty days. The Israelites receive the law from Mount Sinai; the gospel is preached in the Sermon on the Mount, which in its structure is largely a commentary on the Decalogue. The Israelites are plagued by serpents and are redeemed by placing a brazen serpent on a pole. This, like the story of Jonah, is also accepted as a prototype of the Crucifixion by Christ himself. The Israelites conquer the Promised Land under Joshua, who has the same name as Jesus, corresponding to Christ's victory over death and hell, as, in the church's calendar, Easter immediately follows the commemorating of the temptation in Lent. Thus when the Angel Gabriel tells the Virgin Mary to call her child's name Jesus, or Joshua, the meaning is that the reign of the law is now over and the assault on the Promised Land has begun.

The death of Moses just outside the Promised Land represents the inability of the law alone to redeem mankind, as Milton emphasizes both in *Paradise Lost* and in *The Christian Doctrine*. The difficulty of the temptation for Christ, as *Paradise Regained* presents it, is complicated by the fact that Christ is still, at this stage of his career, within the law. His temptation is part of a much subtler process of separating, in his own mind, the law which is to be annihilated from the law which is to be fulfilled and internalized. Milton explicitly says that Christ in the wilderness "into himself descended," and employed his time in clarifying his own mind about the nature of his Messianic mission. We see little of what is actually passing in Christ's mind, but as his refusal of one after another of Satan's temptations drives Satan on to display his resources in a steadily rising scale of comprehensiveness and intensity, the poetic effect is that of negatively clarifying Christ's own thoughts. The climax of the temptation corresponds to the death of Moses: it is the point at which Jesus passes from obedience to the law to works of faith, from the last Hebrew prophet to the founder of Christianity.

The typical Old Testament figures who represent the law and the prophets, respectively, are Moses and Elijah, who accompany Jesus in the Transfiguration and are the two "witnesses" to his teaching in the Book of

Revelation. Both of them prefigured the forty-day retirement and fast of Jesus in their own lives. The Old Testament says that Elijah will come again before the Messiah, a prophecy fulfilled by John the Baptist, but in a sense Moses has to be reborn too, as the law is fulfilled in the gospel. The Bible suggests the possibility that Moses did not die but was, like Elijah, transported directly to Paradise. An early version of *Paradise Lost* was to have begun with some speculations on this point.

Christ has fasted for forty days, and, as Luke remarks with some restraint, "he afterward hungered." He has a Freudian wish-fulfilment dream, like Eve in *Paradise Lost*, in which memories of Old Testament stories of prophets are mingled with food. Still, he is not hungry until after the first temptation to turn stones to bread, which consequently has nothing to do with hunger but is superficially an appeal to his charity, corresponding to the miraculous provision of manna in the Exodus. Jesus' answer that man shall not live by bread alone is a quotation from a passage in Deuteronomy that refers to the giving of manna. A contrast is involved between the material bread of the law and the bread of life in the gospel. This contrast distinguishes the gospel from what, for Milton, was the sacramental fallacy, the tendency to translate the Jewish ceremonial code into Christian terms, the fallacy that produced the doctrine of transubstantiation, which Milton characterizes as a banquet of cannibals. Milton's interest in this first temptation, however, is less in the temptation as such than in the tactical manoeuvre which Satan makes after his disguise is penetrated.

Milton's most obvious source for *Paradise Regained*, apart from the Bible itself, was Giles Fletcher's poem *Christ's Victory and Triumph*, of which the temptation forms an episode. In Fletcher, the first temptation is primarily a temptation of despair, and hence closely follows the episode of Despair in the first book of *The Faerie Queene*. Milton's Christ uses only the term "distrust," but still Milton is here the poetic grandson of Spenser. Despair's argument in Spenser is based on the logic of law without gospel, i.e., sin is inevitable, and the longer one lives the more one sins. The emotional overtones are those of the indolence and passivity which is at the heart of all passion, and some of them are echoed in the argument of Comus to the Lady:

> Refreshment after toil, ease after pain.

Satan's argument in *Paradise Regained* is a refinement of Despair's. Good and evil are inseparable in the fallen world, and, in a world where all instruments are corrupted, one must either use corrupt instruments or not act at all. The use of evil or Satanic means being inevitable, Satan himself must be a reluctant agent of the will of God, as long as we can preserve a belief in the will of God. In terms of the law alone, which can discover but not remove sin, this argument is more difficult to refute than it looks—in fact it could be a clever parody of the central argument of *Areopagitica*. Christ's answer, leading up as it does to a prophecy of the cessation of oracles and the coming of the Word of God to the human heart, is based on the gospel or spiritual view of scripture. Satan has never met this view before, and is sufficiently baffled to retire and consult with his colleagues before going further.

The conflict in *Paradise Regained* is ultimately a spiritual one, but the basis of the human spirit is the physical body, and the body is the battlefield of the spirit. Milton is clear that the soul is the form of the body, and that there are not two essences in man. Another allegorical poem between *The Faerie Queene* and *Paradise Regained, The Purple Island,* by Giles Fletcher's brother Phineas, begins with a detailed allegory of the physical body and then expands into a psychomachia, in which the principals are Christ and the Dragon. This allegory is based on the defence of the House of Alma in the second book of *The Faerie Queene*, which presents the quest of Guyon, the knight of temperance or continence, the physical integrity which is not so much virtue as the prerequisite of virtue. The crucial ordeals of Guyon are the temptation of money in the cave of Mammon, mentioned by Milton in a famous passage in *Areopagitica*, and the Bower of Bliss, where the tempting agent is female and the temptation itself primarily erotic. In Giles Fletcher's version of the temptation of Christ the final temptation is modelled on the Bower of Bliss. Satan's rejection of Belial's proposal to tempt Christ with women indicates Milton's deliberate departure from Fletcher's precedent. Milton had already dealt with such themes in *Comus. Comus,* which leads up to Sabrina's deliverance of the Lady by sprinkling her with water, an act with some analogies to baptism, presents, so to speak, the temptation of innocence, where the assault on sexual continence is naturally central. *Paradise Regained* follows baptism, and presents the temptation of experience.

The sequence of temptations, which now proceeds unbroken to the end of the poem, begins, then, with an attack on the physical basis of Jesus' humanity. There are two of these temptations—a banquet and an offer of money; neither is in the gospels, and it is clear that the temptations of "Beauty and money" in the second book of *The Faerie Queene* are mainly responsible for them. They take place in a pleasant grove, and one line is a vestigial survival of the Bower of Bliss, with its triumph of artifice over nature:

> Nature's own work it seemed (Nature taught Art).

Attacks on temperance could be resisted by any genuine prophet or saint, or even by a virtuous heathen. Satan is an imaginative Oriental bargainer, and one has the feeling that although of course he would like to gain Christ as cheaply as possible, he is reconciled to seeing these temptations fail. His strategy, as we shall see, is cumulative, and individual temptations are expendable. The temptations of food and money continue the argument of the first temptation, in that they urge the necessary use of doubtful means for good ends. Their rejection establishes the principle, which is also in Spenser, that the moral status of the instrument depends on the mental attitude toward it. If the initial attitude is one of passive dependence, the instrument will become an illusory end in itself. It is not immediately apparent, however, why Satan has so much higher an opinion of food than of women as a temptation, even granting that there is really only one temptation of food.

We should be careful not to take anything in Satan's reply to Belial, such as his remark that beauty stands "In the admiration only of weak minds," at its face value. Nothing that Satan says in the poem is as trustworthy as that. He is, of course, right in thinking that Christ cannot be tempted to sins which are foreign to his nature; he can be tempted only to be some form of Antichrist, some physical or material counterpart of himself. But he is right for the wrong reasons.

. . . The initial attacks on Jesus are based on greed, and lust, in its primitive sexual form, is what is sacrificed in Satan's gambit. The reason is that Satan assumes Christ to be a hero of some kind, in view of what was said of him at the baptism. If he is designed to redeem Adam, he must be strong at Adam's weak point of susceptibility to "female charm." For Satan, heroic action means his own type of aggressive and destructive parody-heroism, which is a form of lust. His assumption that the Messiah's heroism will be in some way of this type, or can be easily diverted to it, is genuine, and he is consequently willing to give Jesus credit for a heroic contempt of "effeminate slackness," besides being unwilling to put him prematurely on his guard by presenting him with a relatively crude form of lust. Satan's own contempt for the kind of heroism that Christ seems to prefer is also genuine, and for anyone else this would be itself a major temptation, a form of shame. Faithful in Bunyan, for example, remarks that shame, in the sense of worldly contempt, was his worst enemy. Satan, the accuser of Israel, is what, since Milton's day, we have learned to call a Philistine. Both Satan and Christ divide the world into the material and the spiritual, but for Satan the material is real and the spiritual is imaginary, or, as he says, "allegoric." It is only from Christ's point of view that he is an Archimago or master of illusion: from ours he is consistently a realist.

Hence, just as Comus puns on the word "nature," so all the elements of the dialectical conflict are attached to a material context by Satan and to a spiritual one by Christ. By rejecting everything that Satan offers in Satan's sense, Christ gets it again in its true or spiritual form, just as Adam, if he had successfully resisted his temptation, would still have become as the gods (i.e., the true gods or angels), knowing good, and evil as the possible negation of good. In *The Christian Doctrine* Milton speaks of the virtue of urbanity and its opposing vice of obscenity, which, he says, consists of taking words in a double sense. In this context he means what we mean by the *double entendre*: still, Christ is the source of urbanity and Satan of obscenity, and something of the *double entendre*, the great words "the kingdom, the power and the glory" profaned to their worldly opposites, runs all through Satan's speeches. As in the previous conflict, Satan is "scoffing in ambiguous words."

The opening colloquy between Satan and Christ in the first book is already a clash of oracular powers. Satan's dialectical instrument is the evasive or quibbling oracle, which cheats its hearer, as it did Macbeth, by double meanings that would be bad jokes if their serious consequences did not make them obscene. Christ speaks throughout with the simplicity and plainness that, as we saw, Milton emphasizes so much in the gospels. The climax of *Paradise Regained*, when Satan falls from the pinnacle and Christ stands on it, is marked by two very carefully placed Classical allusions, almost the only mythological ones in the poem. One is to Hercules and Antaeus, of which more later; the other is to Oedipus and the Sphinx. Christ has not only overcome temptation, but, as the Word of God, he has solved the verbal riddle of human life, putting all the words which are properly attributes of God into their rightful context.

The temptations which follow are temptations to false heroic action, and fall into three parts: the temptation of Parthia, or false power; the temptation of Rome, or false justice; and the temptation of Athens, or false wisdom. One problem of interpretation is raised by Milton's curious proportioning of emphasis. The temptation of Parthia seems much the crudest of the three: it is not easy to think of Jesus as some kind of Genghis Khan. Yet it takes up the entire third book, while the other two are huddled with the third temptation into the fourth.

In Jesus' day, with the memory of the Maccabees still vivid, the question of armed rebellion against Roman power was very insistent; it was the course that most Jews expected the Messiah to take, and had already been in the mind of the youthful Christ:

> victorious deeds
> Flamed in my heart, heroic acts, one while
> To rescue Israel from the Roman yoke.

And, though even then Christ thought of putting down violence rather than of using violence, still Satan's arguments on this point are unanswerable: to defeat Roman power by arms requires princely virtues, and princely virtues, as Machiavelli demonstrated, are not moral virtues, far less spiritual ones; they are martial courage and cunning, both demonic gifts. What Satan unwittingly does for Christ in the temptations of Parthia and Rome is to dramatize the nature of that aspect of law that is to be annihilated by the gospel—law as a compelling external force in which spiritual authority is subject to and administered by temporal authority.

Satan is shrewd enough to throw in the suggestion that, by gaining the power of Parthia, Christ will be able to realize the patriotic dream of reuniting the lost ten tribes with the Jewish remnant. In rejecting this, Christ rejects also the legal conception of Israel as a chosen people and is ready to usher in the new Christian conception of Israel as the body of believers. But there seems also to be some personal reference, however indirect, to the great blighted hope of Milton's political life.

The final binding of Satan, the last phase of the total cycle, is prophesied in the Book of Revelation, where, in the twelfth chapter, we have again a wilderness, a symbolic female figure representing the church, and a threatening dragon beaten off by Michael, the angelic champion of Israel, in a repetition of the first encounter. Milton, like everyone else, took the Book of Revelation to be in part a prophecy of the troubles the church was to suffer after the apostolic period. In *The Reason of Church Government* he attacks the supporters of tradition because they do not understand that the Book of Revelation foretells an apostasy of the church and "the Church's flight into the wilderness." Several times in the prose pamphlets Milton refers to the rebellion against Charles I in terms of the Exodus from Egypt, and expresses a hope that England will be a new chosen people, chosen this time for the gospel instead of the law, the rescued apocalyptic church coming out of the wilderness with Michael into a new Promised Land. In this role the English nation would represent the returning lost tribes, a new Israel taking up the cross that the Jews had rejected. By the time he wrote *Paradise Regained*, the English had chosen, in the terrible phrase of *The Ready and Easy Way*, "a captain back for Egypt." Yet even Milton cannot allow Christ to dismiss the unfaithful tribes, who have lost their birthright rather than their home, without adding a few wistful cadences in another key, too gentle in tone to be a direct reply to Satan, and at most only overheard by him:

Yet he at length, time to himself best known,
Rememb'ring Abraham, by some wondrous call
May bring them back, repentant and sincere,
And at their passing cleave the Assyrian flood,
As the Red Sea and Jordan once he cleft,
When to the Promised Land their fathers passed;
To his due time and providence I leave them.

The temptation of Parthia, to ally the Messiah with an anti-Roman power in order to overthrow Rome, had thus been a temptation of Milton's as well as of Milton's Christ. . . . If Milton had written an epic around the time he wrote *The Reason of Church Government*, it would have been more closely affiliated to the epic-romance convention established by Boiardo, Ariosto, and Spenser, in which Arthur would have represented a crusader or Christian warrior and some heroine an aspect of "the king's daughter, the Church," like Spenser's Una. But the female figure over whom physical wars are fought is likely to be closer to the erotic conventions "inductive mainly to the sin of Eve," to courtly love, uxoriousness and lust. The rejected romance tradition appears in Milton's reference to "The fairest of her sex, Angelica," where we might expect the more familiar Helen of Troy or Guinevere. The shadowy and insubstantial landscape of Boiardo may be Milton's reason for choosing it rather than a more concretely historical theme.

In *Paradise Regained* Satan displays all his kingdom: consequently Christ must refuse all of it, including much that in other contexts he might handle fearlessly. Later in his career he shows no hesitation in providing miraculous food, sitting at table with sinners, or accepting money and other gifts. But he has not yet entered on his ministry: the teaching and healing Christ that we know, with his compassion and courtesy, his love of children, and his sense of humour, has no place in Satan's kingdom. The haughtiness and aloofness of Christ mean that, before Christ can work in the world, he must recognize and repudiate all worldliness. In *Paradise Regained* Christ is looking at the world as it is under the wrath, as the domain of Satan. Wrath is the reaction of goodness contemplating badness; it is disinterested and impersonal, and is the opposite of anger or irritation. If God is capable of wrath, he must be incapable of irritation. This is the real reason for the difficulty we stumbled over [elsewhere], the Father's being such a monster of indifference to his creation in *Paradise Lost* that he merely smiles when he observes that a third of his angels have revolted. The word "unmoved," so often applied to Christ in *Paradise Regained*, refers to his emotions as well as his intellect: Satan is condemned but not railed at. Christ cannot exercise mercy until he has separated it from sentimentality, and his comments on the misery of man under wrath are part of this separation. This means that once more we are faced with a contrast between the dramatic and the conceptual aspects of the situation. Dramatically, Christ becomes an increasingly unsympathetic figure, a pusillanimous quietist in the temptation of Parthia, an inhuman snob in the temptation of Rome, a peevish obscurantist in the temptation of Athens.

We said that when Adam decides to die with Eve rather than live without her, we are expected to feel some sympathy for Adam, to the point at least of feeling that we might well have done the same thing in his place, as, of course, we would. Conversely, one may almost say that the point at which the reader loses sympathy with Jesus in *Paradise Regained* is the point at which he himself would have collapsed under the temptation. All of us are, like Christ, in the world, and, unlike him, partly of it. Whatever in us is of the world is bound to condemn Christ's rejection of the world at some point or other. This aspect of the temptation story is the theme of the other great literary treatment of it, the Grand Inquisitor episode of *The Brothers Karamazov*, but it is present in Milton too.

Paradise Regained thus illustrates to the full the contrast between the dramatic and conceptual aspects of a situation that we have seen to be characteristic of Milton's temptation scenes. One might think that Milton had selected the temptation of Christ because it is, with the possible exception of the agony in the garden (on which Milton also meditated a "Christus patiens"), the only episode in which suspense and the feeling of the possible awful consequences of failure are consistently present. Christ's immediate discerning of Satan under his initial disguise, and his ability to reply "Why are *thou* solicitous?" to every temptation, destroy all opportunity for narrative suspense. Of course Christ, like Adam, must be "sufficient to have stood, though free to fall," and he can hardly be sufficient to have stood if, like Eve, he can be deceived by a disguise, or if, like Uriel, he is too simple to understand hypocrisy. In any case dramatic propriety is on the side of clear vision: the more objective one is, the more easily one may see the subjective motivations in others, and anyone with Christ's purity of motivation would know the thoughts of others, as in the gospels he is said to do. Narrative suspense and dramatic sympathy go together: we can have them in *Samson Agonistes*, but they must be renounced here.

The reader may feel that the effect is to make both Christ and Satan seem bored with their roles, and that such boredom is infectious. Of course in long poems there are two areas of criticism, the structure or

design and the poetic realization of details, and value-judgments established in one area are not transferable to the other. It is quite possible for
a poem to be, as *Paradise Regained* may be, a magnificent success in its
structure and yet often tired and perfunctory in its execution. In structure,
however, *Paradise Regained* is not only a success but a technical experiment that is practically *sui generis*. None of the ordinary literary categories
apply to it; its poetic predecessors are nothing like it and it has left no
descendants. If it is a "brief epic," it has little resemblance to the epyllion;
its closest affinities are with the debate and with the dialectical colloquy
of Plato and Boethius, to which most of the Book of Job also belongs. But
these forms usually either incorporate one argument into another dialecti-
cally or build up two different cases rhetorically; Milton's feat of constructing a double argument on the same words, each highly plausible and yet as
different as light from darkness, is, so far as I know, unique in English
literature. It is the supreme poetic statement of the dialectician in Milton,
the poet who defended the freedom of the press on the ground that "this
permission of free writing, were there no good else in it . . . is such an
unripping, such an anatomy of the shyest and tenderest particular truths,
as makes not only the whole nation in many points the wiser, but also
presents and carries home to princes, and men most remote from vulgar
concourse, such a full insight of every lurking evil."

The rejecting of the temptation of Rome forces Satan to relinquish
one of his trump cards, which is the appeal to opportunity, the panic
inspired by the ticking clock. The aspect of temptation which suggests the
temporal also has a connection with Milton's own life and the collision of
impulses to complete and postpone his masterpiece already referred to.
This problem, in itself peculiar to Milton as a poet, was for him also a
special case of the general principle that the Christian must learn to will
to relax the will, to perform real acts in God's time and not pseudo-acts in
his own. In the temptations of Adam and Samson the same theme recurs
of an action not so much wrong in itself as wrong at that time, a hasty
snatching of a chance before the real time has fulfilled itself. Christ is
older than Milton was at twenty-three when he wrote his famous sonnet,
and Satan is constantly urging him, from the first temptation on, to be his
own providence, to release some of his own latent energies. The discipline
of waiting is not only more difficult and inglorious, but constantly subject
to the danger of passing insensibly into procrastination.

The subtlest thing that Satan says in the poem is his remark that

> each act is rightliest done,
> Not when it must, but when it may be best.

The demonic hero judges the present by an intuitive sense of the immedi-ate future. He is distinguished from other men by his capacity to take thought for the morrow, to be in short a diviner. Thus Satan is a spokesman for that dark and forbidden future knowledge which we have spoken of as in the Classical epics gained from the gods below and not the gods above. We are not surprised to find that Satan's oracular powers in *Paradise Regained* include a knowledge of Christ's future "fate" gained by astrology. Christ's main scriptural ally in rejecting this temptation is Ecclesiastes, with its doctrine that there is a time for all things, but the sense of strain in waiting for God's time comes out in several places in the poem, from the reference to the lost tribes, already quoted, to the strain of the forty days' fast itself.

The temptation of Athens has, as its Antichrist core, the Stoic ideal, the "apathy" of the invulnerable individual who feels that the wise man in a bad world can only do the best he can for himself. This is the simple giving up of social action for individual improvement, which, as we saw [elsewhere], was not the real meaning of the impact of the Restoration on Milton. In rejecting this temptation, Christ also rejects the contemplative life as an end: Christ's aim is to redeem the world, not to live a morally sinless life, which he might conceivably have done as a philosopher. In the temptation of Athens the clash of the two oracular traditions, the prophetic and the demonic, reaches its climax. Here again it is Greek philosophy in its context as part of Satan's kingdom that is being rejected. A Christian working outward from his faith might find the study of Plato and Aristotle profitable enough; but if he were to *exchange* the direct tradition of revelation for their doctrines, which is what Christ is being tempted to do, he would find in them only the fine flower of a great speculative tree, with its roots in the demonic metaphysics and theology described in the second book of *Paradise Lost*.

The third temptation begins with a night of storm, not in itself a temptation but an indispensable preliminary to one. Its object is to impress Christ with Satan's power as prince of an indifferent and mindless order of nature, to suggest that his Father has either forsaken him or is unable to reach him in a fallen world. It is, in short, another suggestion of despair or distrust, but with the specific aim of making Christ feel lonely and deserted, hence isolated, hence the self-contained ego which is the form of pride. It demonstrates the fact that in a world of death and mutability the light of nature is surrounded by the darkness of nature; but as Christ has already rejected all arguments based on the analogy of natural and revealed wisdom, this fact comes as no great surprise. The placing of Christ on the pinnacle of the temple follows and is, as Satan makes clear, a temptation of Jesus purely in his capacity as Son of God, an ordeal that no simple human nature would be able to survive. Here, for once, we can cautiously accept what Satan says, although of course his motive in saying it is to drop a suggestion of arrogance into Christ's mind.

The temptation of the pinnacle is equally a bodily and a mental assault. Christ has been weakened by forty days of fasting and by the night of storm. We saw that Satan won over Eve by instilling thoughts into her mind while her consciousness was preoccupied with the wonder of a talking snake, so that Eve, when she came to search her own mind, found Satan's thoughts there and took them for her own. Christ is far more astute, but still the sequence of blinding visions of earthly glory may have left in his mind some faint trace of attachment, some unconscious sense of exaltation. If so, he will feel dizzy on the pinnacle. Mentally, then, Christ is being tested for *hybris*, or pride of mind. He is in the position of a tragic hero, on top of the wheel of fortune, subject to the fatal instant of distraction that will bring him down.

Physically, Christ is being tested for exhaustion, for a slight yielding to pressure that will make him stagger out of sheer weariness. Satan quotes the Psalms to show that the Messiah could fall, trusting in the support of angels; but Christ, though led by the Spirit into the wilderness, is not being led by the Spirit to fall off the pinnacle. That would be his own act, and the Antichrist core of it would be a trust not in angels but in his own fortune, or luck, and trusting to luck is the same thing as trusting Satan. It would perhaps be a reasonable definition of cowardice to say that a coward is a man whose instinct it is, in a crisis, to do what his enemy wants him to do. Christ's ordeal is one of fortitude as well as wisdom, and he has proved himself no coward; but even brave men have had traitors lurking within them, something that co-operated with an outward attack. If there is the smallest trace either of pride in Christ's mind or what we should now call the death-impulse in his body—the impulse that would make any other man accept the vinegar sponge on the cross—this final test will reveal it. If not, Christ is ready to be God's sacrificial victim, a martyr who, so far from being, like many martyrs, half in love with easeful death, dies as the implacable enemy of death.

Christ has thus far been tempted *quasi homo*, purely as man. For Milton, Christ, having resisted the whole of Satan's world, has done what man can do: he has come to the end of the negative and iconoclastic effort which is all that man as such can accomplish in aid of his own salvation. The only possible next step is for God to indicate acceptance of what has been done. Thus the fact that Christ successfully stands on the pinnacle is miraculous, but not a miracle drawn from his own divine nature, not an ace hidden up his sleeve, which is what Satan is looking for. It means that his human will has been taken over by the omnipotent divine will at the necessary point, and prefigures the commending of his spirit to the Father at the instant of his death on the cross.

Christ's answer, "Tempt not the Lord thy God," is the only remark Christ makes in the poem which employs ambiguity. Primarily, it means "Do not put the Father to unnecessary tests," the meaning of the passage in Deuteronomy which Jesus is quoting. But here the Son carries the name and nature of the Father, and the statement bears the secondary meaning "Do not continue the temptation of the Son of God." At this point, perhaps, Satan for the first time recognizes in Jesus his old antago-nist of the war in heaven. Earlier in the poem he had spoken of Christ as an opaque cloud which might be a cooling or shading screen between himself and the wrath of the Father. This is, not surprisingly, the direct opposite of Christ's true nature

> In whose conspicuous countenance, without cloud,
> Made visible, the Almighty Father shines.

So far from screening the fire of the Father, the Son is focusing it like a burning glass, the two natures of the Godhead united as closely as Milton's Christology will permit. And just as this last temptation was of Christ in his specific role as Son of God, so with his victory Satan is defeated in his own headquarters, the lower heaven or element of air which is the spatial limit of his conquest at the fall. That is why Christ's victory is immediately followed by a reference to the struggle of Hercules and Antaeus, in which Hercules (a prototype of Christ also in the Nativity Ode and elsewhere) overcame the monstrous son of earth in the air.

There is a hidden irony in Satan's quotation from the ninety-first Psalm. He quotes the eleventh and twelfth verses; the thirteenth reads: "Thou shalt tread upon the lion and adder; the young lion and the dragon shalt thou trample under feet." In his fall Satan assumes the position of the dragon under Christ's feet, the only place for him after his failure to gain entrance to Christ's body or mind. At this point a new centre of gravity is established in the world, as the gospel is finally separated from the law. Judaism joins Classical wisdom as part of the demonic illusion, as the centre of religion passes from the temple Christ is standing on into the Christian temple, the body of Christ above it. The destruction of the Garden of Eden at the flood showed that God "attributes to place no sanctity," and the later destruction of the temple, prefigured at this point, illustrates the same principle. Christ's casting the devils out of heaven prefigured the cleansing of the temple, with which, according to John, his

ministry began. Here, with the end of the temptation, Christ has chased
the devils out of the temple of his own body and mind and is ready to
repeat the process for each human soul.

The temptation of the pinnacle corresponds to the point in *Samson
Agonistes* at which Samson, after beating off Manoah, Delilah, and Harapha,
refuses to go to the Philistine festival. He is right in refusing, but he has
come to the end of his own will. At that point he appears to change his
mind, but what has happened is that God has accepted his efforts and
taken over his will. In *Samson Agonistes*, which is a tragedy, this point is
the "peripety": Samson is now certain to die, though also certain of
redemption. Jesus has also made it possible for himself to avoid death, as
his prototypes Elijah and perhaps Moses did; but *Paradise Regained* is not a
tragedy, but an episode in the divine comedy, and we need another term
for the crucial point of the action.

We have already met Milton's distinction between the literal and
what he calls the metaphorical generation of the Son by the Father. The
latter, we said, was epiphany, the manifesting of Christ in his divine
capacity to others, and it is this epiphany and not literal generation that is
taking place in the first chronological event of *Paradise Lost*. The same
distinction recurs in the Incarnation. Two of the Gospels, Matthew and
Luke, the two which give us the account of the temptation, are nativity
Gospels: they begin with Christ's infancy or physical generation in the
world. The other two, Mark and John, are epiphanic Gospels, and begin
with the baptism, where Jesus is pointed out to man as the Son of God.
(In the Western churches epiphany means particularly the showing of the
infant Christ to the Magi, but in the Eastern churches it means particularly the baptism.) Epiphany is the theological equivalent of what in
literature is called "anagnorisis" or "recognition." The Father recognizes
Jesus as the Son at the baptism: Satan recognizes him on the pinnacle in a
different, yet closely related, sense. The action of *Paradise Regained* begins
with the baptism, an epiphany which Satan sees but does not understand,
and ends with an epiphany to Satan alone, the nature of which he can
hardly fail to understand.

With the end of the temptation, Christ's work is essentially accomplished. The Passion itself, and more particularly the crucifixion, is also
epiphanic, an exhibition to mankind of what Christ is and what he has
done. The two poles of Christ's career on earth are the baptism and the
crucifixion, both public events. And just as the crucifixion was followed
by the resurrection, which was esoteric, shown only to Christ's followers,
so the baptism is followed by a hidden event in which Christ disappears
from the sight of mankind and then "Home to his mother's house private

returned," the fate of the world having been changed in the meantime. *Paradise Regained* is the definitive statement in Milton of the dialectical separation of heaven from hell that reason based on revelation makes, and the individual nature of every act of freedom. To use terms which are not Milton's but express something of his attitude, the central myth of mankind is the myth of lost identity: the goal of all reason, courage and vision is the regaining of identity. The recovery of identity is not the feeling that I am myself and not another, but the realization that there is only one man, one mind, and one world, and that all walls of partition have been broken down forever.

GEOFFREY H. HARTMAN

Milton's Counterplot

Milton's description of the building of Pandemonium ends with a reference to the architect, Mammon, also known to the ancient world as Mulciber:

> and how he fell
> From Heav'n, they fabl'd, thrown by angry *Jove*
> Sheer o'er the Crystal Battlements: from Morn
> To Noon he fell, from Noon to dewy Eve,
> A Summer's day; and with the setting Sun
> Dropt from the Zenith like a falling Star,
> On *Lemnos* th'Ægæan Isle.
> *(Paradise Lost* 1.740–46)

These verses stand out from a brilliant text as still more brilliant or emerge from this text, which repeats on several levels the theme of quick or erring or mock activity, marked by a strange mood of calm, as if the narrative's burning wheel had suddenly disclosed a jeweled bearing. Their subject is a fall, and it has been suggested that Milton's imagination was caught by the anticipation in the Mulciber story of a myth which stands at the center of his epic. Why the "caught" imagination should respond with a pastoral image, evoking a fall gradual and cool like the dying of a summer's day and the sudden, no less aesthetically distant, dropping down of the star, is not explained. One recalls, without difficulty, similar moments of relief or distancing, especially in the cosmic fret of the first books: the comparison of angel forms lying entranced on the inflamed sea with autumnal leaves on Vallombrosa's shady brooks; or the simile of springtime bees and of the dreaming peasant at the end of Book 1; or the

From *English Literary History* (1958). Copyright © 1958 by Johns Hopkins University Press.

applause following Mammon's speech in Book 2, likened to lulling if hoarse cadence of winds after a storm; or even the appearance to Satan of the world, when he has crossed Chaos and arrives with torn tackle in full view of this golden-chained star of smallest magnitude.

The evident purpose of the Mulciber story is to help prick inflated Pandemonium and, together with the lines that follow, to emphasize that Mammon's building is as shaky as its architect. This fits in well with the plot of the first two books, a description of the satanic host's effort to build on hell. But the verses on Mulciber also disclose, through their almost decorative character, a second plot, simultaneously expressed with the first, which may be called the counterplot. Its hidden presence is responsible for the contrapuntal effects of the inserted fable.

The reader will not fail to recognize in Milton's account of the progress of Mulciber's fall the parody of a biblical rhythm: "And the evening and the morning were the (first) day." The thought of creation is present to Milton, somehow associated with this fall. Moreover, the picture of angry Jove blends with and gives way to that of *crystal* battlements and the imperturbability of the summer's day through which the angel drops:

> from Morn
> To Noon he fell, from Noon to dewy Eve,
> A Summer's day:

while in the last part of his descent an image of splendor and effortlessness outshines that of anger or ignominy:

> and with the setting Sun
> Dropt from the Zenith like a falling Star.

In context, of course, this depiction is condemned as mere fabling, and there is nothing splendid or aloof in the way Milton retells the story:

> thus they relate,
> Erring; for he with his rebellious rout
> Fell long before; nor aught avail'd him now
> To have built in Heav'n high Tow'rs; nor did he scape
> By all his Engines, but was headlong sent
> With his industrious crew to build in hell.
>
> (1.746–51)

Yet for a moment, while moving in the charmed land of pagan fable, away from the more literal truth in which he seeks supremacy over all fable, Milton reveals the overwhelming if not autonomous drive of his imagination. Mulciber draws to himself a rhythm reminiscent of the

account of the world's creation, and his story suggests both God and the
creation undisturbed (Crystal Battlements . . . dewy Eve) by a fall which
is said to occur later than the creation yet actually preceded it. Here,
surely, is a primary instance of Milton's automatically involving the idea
of creation with that of the Fall. But further, and more fundamental, is
the feeling of the text that God's anger is not anger at all but calm
prescience, which sees that no fall will ultimately disturb the creation,
whether Mulciber's fabled or Satan's real or Adam's universal fall.

Milton's feeling for this divine imperturbability, for God's omnipotent knowledge that the creation will outlive death and sin, when expressed in such an indirect manner, may be characterized as the counterplot.
For it does not often work on the reader as an independent theme or
subplot but lodges in the vital parts of the overt action, emerging from it
like good from evil. The root feeling (if *feeling* is the proper word) for
imperturbable providence radiates from many levels of the text. It has
been given numerous interpretations in the history of criticism, the best
perhaps, though impressionistic, by Coleridge: "Milton is the deity of
prescience: he stands *ab extra* and drives a fiery chariot and four, making
the horses feel the iron curb which holds them in." Satan's fixed mind
and high disdain are perverted reflectors of this same cold passion, but
doomed to perish in the restlessness of hell and its compulsive gospel of
the community of damnation. So deep-working is this spirit of the "glassy,
cool, translucent wave," already invoked in *Comus*, that other poets find
it hard to resist it and, like Wordsworth, seek to attain similar virtuosity in
expressing "central peace, subsisting at the heart/Of endless agitation."
Milton's control is such that, even in the first dramatic account of Satan's
expulsion, he makes the steady flame of God's act predominate over the
theme of effort, anger, and vengefulness: in the following verses "Ethereal
Sky" corresponds to the "Crystal Battlements" of Mulciber's fall, and the
image of a projectile powerfully but steadily thrust forth (evoked in part by
the immediate duplication of stress, letter and rhythmic patterns) recreates the imperturbability of that other, summer space:

> Him the Almighty Power
> Hurl'd headlong flaming from th'Ethereal Sky
> With hideous ruin and combustion down
> To bottomless perdition, there to dwell
> In Adamantine Chains and penal Fire . . .
> (1.44–48)

One of the major means of realizing the counterplot is the simile.
Throughout *Paradise Lost*, and eminently in the first two books, Milton

has to bring the terrible sublime home to the reader's imagination. It would appear that he can only do this by analogy. Yet Milton rarely uses straight analogy, in which the observer and observed remain, relative to each other, on the same plane. Indeed, his finest effects employ magnifying and diminishing similes. Satan's shield, for example, is described as hanging on his shoulder like the moon, viewed through Galileo's telescope from Fiesole or in Valdarno (1.284–91). The rich, elaborate pattern of such similes has often been noted and variously explained. Certain details, however, may be reconsidered.

The similes, first of all, not only magnify or diminish the doings in hell but invariably put them at a distance. Just as the Tuscan artist sees the moon through his telescope, so the artist of *Paradise Lost* shows hell at considerable remove, through a medium which, while it clarifies, also intervenes between reader and object. Milton varies points of view, shifting in space and time so skillfully that our sense of the reality of hell, of its power vis-à-vis man or God, never remains secure. Spirits, we know, can assume any shape they please; and Milton, like Spenser, uses this imaginative axiom to destroy the idea of the simple location of good and evil in the spiritual combat. But despite the insecurity, the abyss momentarily glimpsed under simple events, Milton's main effort in the first books is to make us believe in Satan as a real and terrible agent, yet never as an irresistible power. No doubt at all of Satan's influence: his success is writ large in religious history, which may also be one reason for the epic enumeration of demonic names and place names in Book 1. Nevertheless, even as we are closest to Satan, presented with the hottest view of hell's present and future appeal, all suggestion of irresistible influence must be expunged if Milton's two means of divine justification—man's free will and God's foreknowledge of the creation's triumph—are to win consent.

These two dominant concepts, expressed through the counterplot, shed a calm and often cold radiance over all of *Paradise Lost*, issuing equally from the heart of faith and the center of self-determination. The similes must persuade us that man was and is "sufficient to have stood, though free to fall" (3.99): that his reason and will, however fiercely tempted and besieged, stand on a pinnacle as firm and precarious as that on which the Christ of *Paradise Regained* (4.541 ff) suffers his last, greatest, archetypal temptation. They must show the persistence, in the depth of danger, passion, or evil, of imperturbable reason, of a power working ab extra.

This the similes accomplish in several ways. They are, for example, marked by an emphasis on place names. It is the *Tuscan* artist who views the moon (Satan's shield) from the top of *Fiesole* or in *Valdarno* through his optic glass, while he searches for new Lands, Rivers, Mountains on the spotty globe. Do not the place names serve to anchor this observer and set him off from the vastness and vagueness of hell, its unnamed and restless geography, as well as from his attempt to leave the earth and rise by science above the lunar world? A recital of names is, of course, not reassuring of itself: no comfort accrues in hearing Moloch associated with *Rabba*, *Argob*, *Basan*, *Arnon*, or sinful Solomon with *Hinnom*, *Tophet*, *Gehenna* (1.397–405). The point is that these places were once neutral, innocent of bloody or holy associations; it is man who has made them what they are, made the proper name a fearful or a hopeful sign (cf. 11.836–39). Will *Valdarno* and *Fiesole* become such bywords as *Tophet* and *Gehenna*? At the moment they are still hieroglyphs, words whose ultimate meaning is in the balance. They suggest the inviolate shelter of the created world rather than the incursions of a demonic world. Yet we sense that, if Galileo uses the shelter and Ark of this world to dream of other worlds, paying optical rites to the moon, Fiesole, Valdarno, even Vallombrosa may yield to the tug of a demonic interpretation and soon become a part of hell's unprotected marl.

Though the figure of the observer *ab extra* is striking in Milton's evocation of Galileo, it becomes more subtly patent in a simile a few lines further on which tells how the angel forms lay entranced on hell's inflamed sea

> Thick as Autumnal Leaves that strow the Brooks
> In *Vallombrosa*, where th'Etrurian shades
> High overarch't imbow'r; or scatter'd sedge
> Afloat, when with fierce winds *Orion* arm'd
> Hath vext the Red-Sea Coast, whose waves o'erthrew
> *Busiris* and his *Memphian* Chivalry,
> While with perfidious hatred they pursu'd
> The sojourners of *Goshen*, who beheld
> From the safe shore thir floating Carcasses
> And broken Chariot Wheels . . .
>
> (1.302–11)

A finer modulation of aesthetic distance can hardly be found: we start at the point of maximum contrast, with the angels prostrate on the lake, in a region "vaulted with fire" (298), viewed as leaves fallen seasonally on a sheltered brook vaulted by shade; go next to the image of seaweed scattered by storm; and finally, without break of focus, see the Israelites watching "from the safe shore" the floating bodies and parts of their pursuers. And, as in music, where one theme fades, another emerges to its place; while the image of calm and natural death changes to that of violent and supernatural destruction, the figure of the observer *ab extra* becomes explicit, substituting for the original glimpse of inviolable peace.

Could the counterplot be clearer? A simile intended to sharpen our view of the innumerable stunned host of hell, just before it is roused by Satan, at the same time sharpens our sense of the imperturbable order of the creation, of the coming storm, and of the survival of man through providence and his safe-shored will. Satan, standing clear of the rout, prepares to vex his legions to new evil:

> on the Beach
> Of that inflamed Sea, he stood and call'd
> His Legions, Angel Forms, who lay intrans't
> Thick as Autumnal Leaves . . .

but the scenes the poet himself calls up mimic hell's defeat before Satan's voice is fully heard, and whatever sought to destroy the calm of autumnal leaves lies lifeless as scattered sedge. The continuity of the similes hinges on the middle image of Orion, which sketches both Satan's power to rouse the fallen host and God's power to scatter and destroy it. In this plot/counterplot the hand of Satan is not ultimately distinguishable from the will of God.

A further instance, more complex still, is found at the end of Book 1. Milton compares the host gathered in the gates of Pandemonium to bees at springtime (1.768 ff). The wonder of this incongruity has been preserved by many explanations. It is clearly a simile which, like others we have adduced, diminishes hell while it magnifies creation. The bees are fruitful, and their existence in the teeth of Satan drowns out the sonorous hiss of hell. Their "straw-built Citadel" will survive "bossy" Pandemonium. As Dr. Johnson kicking the stone kicks all excessive idealism, so Milton's bees rub their balm against all excessive demonism. But the irony may not end there. Are the devils not those bees who bring food out of the eater, sweetness out of the strong (Judg. 14:5–14)?

It may also be more than a coincidence that the most famous in this genre of similes describes the bustle of the Carthaginians as seen by storm-exiled Aeneas (*Aeneid*, 1.430–40). Enveloped in a cloud by his divine mother, Aeneas looks down from the top of a hill onto a people busily building their city like a swarm of bees at summer's return and is forced to cry: "O fortunati, quorum iam moenia surgunt [Oh fortunate people, whose walls are already rising]!" Then Virgil, as if to dispel any impression of despair, adds: "mirabile dictu [a wonder]!" Aeneas walks among the Carthaginians made invisible by divine gift.

Here the counterplot thickens, and we behold one of Milton's amazing transpositions of classical texts. Aeneas strives to found Rome, which will outlast Carthage. The bees building in Virgil's text intimate a spirit of creativity seasonally renewed and independent of the particular civilization; the bees in Milton's text represent the same privilege and promise. Aeneas wrapped in the cloud is the observer ab extra, the person on the shore, and his impatient cry is of one who desires to build a civilization beyond decay, perhaps even beyond the wrath of the gods. An emergent, as yet invisible figure in Milton's text shares the hero's cry: he has seen Mammon and his troop build Pandemonium, Satan's band swarm triumphant about their citadel. Despite this, can the walls of creation outlive Satan as Rome the ancient world?

All this would be putative or extrinsic if based solely on the simile of the bees. For this simile, like the middle image of Orion vexing the Red Sea, is indeterminate in its implications, a kind of visual pivot in a series of images which act in sequence and once more reveal the counterplot. Its indeterminacy is comparable to Milton's previously mentioned use of proper nouns and his overall stylistic use of the pivot, by means of which images and words are made to refer both backward and forward, giving the verse period unusual balance and flexibility. The series in question begins with the trooping to Pandemonium, and we now give the entire modulation which moves through several similes:

> all access was throng'd, the Gates
> And Porches wide, but chief the spacious Hall
> (Though like a cover'd field, where Champions bold
> Wont ride in arm'd, and at the Soldan's chair
> Defi'd the best of *Paynim* chivalry
> To mortal combat or career with Lance)
> Thick swarm'd, both on the ground and in the air,
> Brusht with the hiss of rustling wings. As Bees
> In spring time, when the Sun with *Taurus* rides,
> Pour forth thir populous youth about the Hive
> In clusters; they among fresh dews and flowers
> Fly to and fro, or on the smoothed Plank,
> The suburb of thir Straw-built Citadel,
> New rubb'd with Balm, expatiate and confer
> Thir State affairs. So thick the aery crowd
> Swarm'd and were strait'n'd; till the Signal giv'n,
> Behold a wonder! they but now who seem'd
> In bigness to surpass Earth's Giant Sons
> Now less than smallest Dwarfs, in narrow room
> Throng numberless, like that Pigmean Race
> Beyond the *Indian* Mount, or Faery Elves,
> Whose midnight Revels, by a Forest side

Or Fountain some belated Peasant sees,
Or dreams he sees, while over-head the Moon
Sits Arbitress, and nearer to the Earth
Wheels her pale course, they on thir mirth and dance
Intent, with jocund Music charm his ear;
At once with joy and fear his heart rebounds.
(1.761–88)

The very images which marshall the legions of hell to our view reveal simultaneously that the issue of Satan's triumph or defeat, his real or mock power, is in the hand of a secret arbiter, whether God and divine prescience or man and free will. In the first simile the observer ab extra is the Soldan who, as a type of Satan, overshadows the outcome of the combat between pagan and Christian warriors in the "cover'd field." The second simile is indeterminate in tenor, except that it diminishes the satanic thousands, blending them and their warlike intents with a picture of natural, peaceful creativity, Sun and Taurus presiding in place of the Soldan. "Behold a wonder!" echoes the *mirabile dictu* of Virgil's story and prepares the coming of a divine observer. The mighty host is seen to shrink to the size of Pigmies (the third simile), and we know that these—the "small infantry," as Milton had called them with a pun reflecting the double perspective of the first books—can be overshadowed by Cranes (1.575–76). The verse period then carries us still further from the main action as the diminished devils are also compared to Faery Elves glimpsed at their midnight revels by some belated Peasant. From the presence and pomp of hell we have slowly slipped into a pastoral.

Yet does not this static moment hide an inner combat more real than that for which hell is preparing? It is midnight, the pivot between day and day, and in the Peasant's mind a similar point of balance seems to obtain. He is not fully certain of the significance or even reality of the Fairy ring. Like Aeneas in Hades, who glimpses the shade of Dido (*Aeneid*, 6.450–55), he "sees, Or dreams he sees" something barely distinguishable from the pallid dark, obscure as the new moon through clouds. What an intensity of calm is here, reflecting a mind balanced on the critical pivot, as a point of stillness is reached at greatest remove from the threats and reverberations of hell! But even as the man stands uncertain, the image of the moon overhead becomes intense: it has sat there all the time as arbiter, now wheels closer to the earth, and the Peasant's heart rebounds with a secret intuition bringing at once joy and fear.

The moon, clearly, is a last transformation of the image of the observer ab extra—Soldan, Sun and Taurus, Peasant. What was a type of Satan overshadowing the outcome of the real or spiritual combat is converted into a presentment of the individual's naïve and autonomous power of discrimination, his free reason, secretly linked with a superior influence, as the moon overhead. The figure of the firmly placed observer culminates in that of the secret arbiter. Yet this moon is not an unambiguous symbol of the secret arbiter. A feeling of the moon's uncertain, changeable nature—incorruptible yet spotty, waxing and waning (1.284–91; 2.659–66; see also "mooned horns," 4.978, quoted below)—is subtly present. It reflects this series of images in which the poet constantly suggests, destroys and recreates the idea of an imperturbably transcendent discrimination. The moon that "Sits Arbitress" seems to complete the counterplot, but is only the imperfect sign of a figure not revealed till Book 4. Thus the whole cycle of to and fro, big and small, Pigmies or Elves, seeing or dreaming, far and near, joy and fear—this uneasy flux of couplets, alternatives, and reversals—is continued when we learn, in the final lines of Book 1, that far within Pandemonium, perhaps as far from consciousness as hell is from the thoughts of the Peasant or demonic power from the jocund if intent music of the fairy revelers, Satan and the greatest of his Lords sit in their own, unreduced dimensions.

We meet the Peasant once more in *Paradise Lost*, in a simile which seems to want to outdo the apparent incongruity of all others. At the end of Book 4, Gabriel and his files confront Satan apprehended squatting in Paradise, a toad at the ear of Eve. A heroically contemptuous exchange follows, and Satan's taunts finally so incense the Angel Squadron that they

> Turn'd fiery red, sharp'ning in mooned horns
> Thir Phalanx, and began to hem him round
> With ported Spears, as thick as when a field
> Of *Ceres* ripe for harvest waving bends
> Her bearded Grove of ears, which way the wind
> Sways them; the careful Plowman doubting stands
> Lest on the threshing floor his hopeful sheaves
> Prove chaff. On th'other side *Satan* alarm'd
> Collecting all his might dilated stood,
> Like *Teneriff* or *Atlas* unremov'd:
> His stature reacht the Sky, and on his Crest
> Sat horror Plum'd; nor wanted in his grasp
> What seem'd both Spear and Shield: now dreadful deeds
> Might have ensu'd, nor only Paradise
> In this commotion, but the Starry Cope
> Of Heav'n perhaps, or all the Elements
> At least had gone to rack, disturb'd and torn
> With violence of this conflict, had not soon

Th'Eternal to prevent such horrid fray
Hung forth in Heav'n his golden Scales, yet seen
Betwixt *Astrea* and the *Scorpion* sign,
Wherein all things created first he weigh'd,
The pendulous round Earth with balanc'd Air
In counterpoise, now ponders all events,
Battles and Realms . . .

(4.978–1002)

The question of Satan's power does not appear to be academic, at least not at first. The simile which, on previous occasions, pretended to illustrate hell's greatness but actually diminished hell and magnified the creation, is used here just as effectively against heaven. Milton, by dilating Satan, and distancing the spears of the angel phalanx as ears ready for reaping, creates the impression of a balance of power between heaven and hell. Yet the image which remains in control is neither of Satan nor of the Angels but of the wheatfield, first as its bearded ears bend with the wind, then as contemplated by the Plowman. Here the counterplot achieves its most consummate form. *Paradise Lost* was written not for the sake of heaven or hell but for the sake of the creation. What is all the fuss about if not to preserve the "self-balanc't" earth? The center around which and to which all actions turn is whether man can stand though free to fall, whether man and the world can survive their autonomy. The issue may not therefore be determined on the supernatural level by the direct clash of heaven and hell but only by these two arbiters: man's free will and God's foreknowledge. The ripe grain sways in the wind; so does the mind which has tended it. Between ripeness and ripeness gathered falls the wind, the threshing floor, the labor of ancient *ears*, the question of the relation of God's will to man's will. The ears appear to be at the mercy of the wind; what about the thoughts, the "hopeful sheaves" of the Plowman? The fate of the world lies between Gabriel and Satan, but also between the wind and the ripe ears and between man and his thoughts. Finally God, supreme arbiter, overbalances the balance with the same pair of golden scales (suspended yet between Virgin and Scorpion) in which the balanced earth weighed at its first creation.

ANGUS FLETCHER

The Transcendental Masque

That *Comus* is no ordinary masque has
long been felt. In dedicating the published work to John, Lord Viscount
Brackley, Lawes said that although *Comus* was "not openly acknowledged
by the author, yet it is a legitimate offspring, so lovely, and so much
desired, that the often copying of it hath tired my pen to give my several
friends satisfaction, and brought me to a necessity of producing it to the
public view." These friends found an excellence posterity has confirmed.
Yet beyond the eloquence of the "series of lines," to use Johnson's phrase,
Comus has presented a problematic aspect in both theme and form.

The extraordinary bulk of critical commentary on the Miltonic
treatment of chastity, a critique as subtle as it is learned—much if not all
of it leading into the mysteries of Christian or Neoplatonic theology—will
bear witness to the ambiguity of themes in *Comus*. We may perhaps be
impatient with the questions, proofs, and counterproofs of thematic criticism. But we cannot dismiss the crisis implied in this lore. No simple way
out of tangled Miltonic image and theme will be forthcoming, and if a
formal approach to *Comus* is proposed, it should be constantly attuned to
the complications of theme which have made the work so tantalizing to its
readers. What needs to be done, following Robert M. Adams' lead, is to
explain the doubts of critics about *Comus*, yet without explaining them
away. Generations of critics are never, taken as a whole, wrong. They are
responding to something, and the historical critic in his turn should
respond to this continuity of critical awareness. In dealing with *Comus*
there is no need to deny its dramatic force. *Comus*, naïvely viewed, is a

From *The Transcendental Masque: An Essay on Milton's Cosmos*. Copyright © 1971 by
Cornell University Press.

markedly dramatic piece. But how so? Perhaps it would be useful to take Dr. Johnson seriously and ask if, as he called it, *Comus* is not "a drama in the epic style."

Woodhouse wisely referred criticism of *Comus* to the remarkable passage of *An Apology for Smectymnuus* where Milton recounts the progress of his almost obsessive concern with idea of chastity. Among several striking personal reminiscences there runs a key motif: Milton set the problem of chastity in the context of a largely literary experience. He began his education in purity in the poetic world of "the two famous renowners of Beatrice and Laura," and proceeded in due time ("whither my younger feet had wandered") to "those lofty fables and romances which recount in solemn cantos the deeds of knighthood founded by our victorious kings," and thence "from the laureate fraternity of poets, riper years and the ceaseless round of study and reading led me to the shady spaces of philosophy, but chiefly to the divine volumes of Plato and his equal, Xenophon." Throughout the account we sense not only the pursuit of the "abstracted sublimities" of knowledge and virtue, but in the course of this pursuit, the sublimation of thought into character, so that we can well believe the poet when he announces his early won creed: "that he who would not be frustrate of his hope to write well hereafter in laudable things, ought himself to be a true poem, that is, a composition and pattern of the best and honorablest things; not presuming to sing high praises of heroic men or famous cities unless he have in himself the experience and practice of all that which is praiseworthy." This is not hermetic pretension, though there is a smell of the magus about the poet as sublime poem; Milton here betrays that characteristically total involvement of his whole self with his thought, an involvement mediated by his poetic vocation. For through the poetic second voice, he would discover the self defined by all the prior patterns and compositions of the best and most honorable things.

The Johnsonian epithet comes into focus. A drama written in epic style would first of all flow like a narrative poem, and secondly it would be a drama raised above the requirements of realistic decorum to a level of inspired, prophetic, or epic voice, that is, raised to the vehement level of style described in Longinus' famed treatise. Johnson did not clarify the distinction between the usual dramatic genres and the epic drama, but Thomas Warton did, when in his edition of Milton (1791) he said that "*Comus* is a suite of Speeches, not interesting by discrimination of character; not conveying a variety of incidents; not gradually exciting curiosity; but perpetually attracting attention by sublime sentiment, by fanciful imagery of the richest vein, by an exuberance of picturesque description, poetical allusion, and ornamental expression." The prime mover of the drama in epic style would seem to be the "sublime sentiment," with its usual picturesque accompaniments.

In *Comus*, therefore, Milton is "unfolding those chaste and high mysteries" which, in conjunction with the Holy Scriptures, veil and reveal the secrets of divine wisdom. In the terms of Pico della Mirandola the poet is at once both magus and *interpres*. Chastity must be envisioned in the most sacred languages, and, by conversion, the language of the poet, arising in the devotion to the ideal of the chaste, must achieve sublimity if it is to equal the transcendental challenge. Milton writes about chastity continuously, in tracts on marriage, love, and divorce—even on freedom of speech and thought—and in his major poems, all of which deal with virtue as an effluence of chastity. The *Apology* suggests something even more radical about the Miltonic career: that it was the literary enactment of one vast, many-sided *personal* struggle for the comprehension of the idea of the chaste mystery, and therefore that as a career the life of Milton indeed has the prime requisite of a poem: namely, it has a hero. Milton becomes a poet-poem in this heroic manner. The idea of chastity is for him a burning, luminous, radiant core of energy, and the recurrent theme of temptation, on which Frye has commented so eloquently, is but the dramatic trial of the chaste vision. For chastity, like grace (if that is in any ordinary sense a "virtue"), metaphorically permits only perfect motion: that is, motion which redeems the wandering, mazy, labyrinthine error of ordinary life. Chastity finds its model of movement in the circular form of the Ptolemaic universe; it is perfect, like a sphere, with no beginning and no end. How then express its forms and implications? This is the mystery that Milton wished to suggest, and went so far as to describe, in the *Apology*.

Milton imagines himself living and acting on heroic lines. Frye has pointed out the difference between his "radical, revolutionary temperament" and the conservative temperament of Spenser.

> The radical or revolutionary artist impresses us, first of all, as a tremendous personal force, a great man who happened to be an artist in one particular field but who would still have been a remarkable man whatever he had gone into. His art has in consequence a kind of oratorical relation to him: his creative *persona* reveals his personality instead of concealing it. He does not enter into the forms of his art like an indwelling spirit, but approaches them analytically and externally, tearing them to pieces and putting them together again in a way which expresses his genius and not theirs. In listening to the Kyrie of the Bach B Minor Mass we feel what amazing things the fugue can do; in listening to the finale of Beethoven's Opus 106, we feel what amazing things can

be done with the fugue. This latter is the feeling we have about *Comus* as a masque, when we come to it from Jonson or Campion. Because the art of the revolutionary artist follows a rhythm of personal development external to itself, it goes through a series of metamorphoses: the revolutionary artist plunges into one "period" after another, marking his career off into separate divisions.

The continuous revelation of a giant personality behind the mask is crucial to the work of an artist like Milton. But in assessing the work itself, we need a notion like "the transcendental." The formal peculiarity of this style of work is again finely suggested in Frye's distinction between the conservative and revolutionary aspects of poetry.

> The revolutionary aspect of Milton also comes out in that curious mania for doing everything himself which led him to produce his own treatise on theology, his own national history, his own dictionary and grammar, his own art of logic. . . . Both kinds of genius may seek for an art that transcends art, a poetry or music that goes beyond poetry or music. But the conservative artist finds—if this metaphor conveys anything intelligible to the reader—his greatest profundities at the centre of his art; the radical artist finds them on the frontier. . . . Milton, like Beethoven, is continually exploring the boundaries of his art, getting more experimental and radical as he goes on.

Comus fits into this radical experimentation; it transcends by formal pressures on the normal boundaries of the masque. It "transcends art" in this sense precisely, and I would hold that the other transcendence, of which Frye rightly speaks, is only the fulfillment of the more limited possibilities of classical selectivity and repose. There is, perhaps, a further distinction to be made, though it does not really contradict Frye's notion, between the transcendence of the radical style and the perfectionism of the conservative style. The former issues, as Frye suggests, in a revolutionary attitude toward tradition, the latter in a neoclassic piety toward rules—at least if the energy of creation is not coequal with the energies of self-expression.

Comus, should it fit this broad view of Miltonic creativity, can be only partially illuminated by historical "sources" which are supposed to explain its power and its complexity. To argue that Milton had various models is to repeat the obvious, unless one further asks, What was his experimental attitude toward those models? For the transcendental recreation of an inherited form is always so new and revolutionary in feeling and form that it will yield none of its secrets to the critic who is, at bottom, unconcerned with the radical mentality bringing such a work into being. In the case of *Comus*, as we shall see, the obvious use of a whole range of magic devices, persons, and scenes provides the setting for the radical encounter with masque as genre. Milton picks exactly the theme and variations which will permit him to exercise a virtuoso control over his masque. . . .

THYRSIS: THE ORPHIC PERSONA

Orpheus had been a central character in Campion's The Lords Maske (1613) where he served a purpose rather similar to the Daemon's purpose in Comus. Both figures command the powers of song and can summon the agents of perfect incantation. But while the singing magician is the happier version of Orpheus, he has another, less happy side, in line with other myths of the culture bringer. Besides "building the lofty rime" he can suffer the Orphic death, and Adonis-like, become the sacrificial victim whose highest parallel is Christ—a similitude Milton draws upon for Lycidas, which he significantly designates a monody. The Orphic persona thus has a double valence, which complicates and deepens his use for the utterance of the poet's "second voice." In commenting on the importance of the Orphic legend for Virgilian creativity, Berger has stressed the phrase from the Aeneid, Book IV, describing the loss of Euridice: Orpheus respexit ("Orpheus looked back"). "Here respicere means to look back unguardedly, in longing, toward the object of love. The poet must learn to look back at the beloved past without destroying its life, or his own happiness and control. Respicere can also mean to look back, in the sense of reflecting on, or, to look again, in the sense of re-vising." In Comus we find a parallel situation: here the "looking back" is conveyed, as we shall see, in sonorous form, in the resonating mirror of the echo song. In both cases we are dealing with a deep irony in the culture bringer's passion. What he values is never to be directly his, since to possess the loved object would be to destroy it; it can only be his if it is reflected, recreated, resonated. The Orphic design is, in this light, a myth of resonance. Fulfillment is an echo.

The mystery of repetition is the secret of the Virgilian respicere. Kierkegaard asked, Is repetition possible? The myth of Orpheus embodies one set of answers to that question. It is thus significant that Orpheus was the hero of heroes for early opera, that most expressive art form. John Arthos has recently argued for an affinity between Monteverdi's operatic work and Samson Agonistes. Gretchen Finney has shown operatic analogies between Comus and the Catena d'Adone. These parallels are haunting chiefly because in the Orphic aspect of Thyrsis, Milton seems to be projecting a mythic meaning that was strongly projected by the first operas. Kerman has described their mythic basis:

> The myth of Orpheus, furthermore, deals with man specifically as artist, and one is drawn inevitably to see in it, mirrored with a kind of proleptic vision, the peculiar problems of the opera composer. Initially Orpheus is the supreme lyric artist. In the classic view he is the ideal of the prize-winning *kitharista*—or, in Christian allegory, the evangelical psalmist who charmed the melancholy Saul. To the fourteenth century, he is the minstrel who exacts his boon from the Fairy King; to the sixteenth, perhaps, the madrigalist; to the nineteenth, proud Walther who persuades the German pedants. The eighteenth century painted him, tremulously, as the amiable singer of Metastasio's faint verses who entranced the King of Spain. But for Orpheus the lyric singer, the crisis of life becomes the crisis of his lyric art: art must now move into action, on to the tragic stage of life. It is a sublime attempt. Can its symbolic boldness have escaped the musicians of 1600, seeking new power in the stronger forms of drama? Orpheus' new triumph is to fashion the lament that harrows hell out of his own great sorrowing emotion—this too they must have specially marked, wrestling as they were with new emotional means, harrowing, dangerous to manage. But the fundamental conflict of the myth transcends that time and this medium, and extends to every artist. It is the problem of emotion and its control, the summoning of feeling to an intensity and communicability and form which the action of life heeds and death provisionally respects. All this Orpheus as artist achieves. But as man he cannot shape his emotions to Pluto's shrewd decree; face to face with the situation, he looks back, and fails. Life and art are not necessarily one.

Kerman goes on to show that the mythic failure of Orpheus is by no means clear or self-evident in its significance. Yet the failure is a great operatic crux. "To be sure, this 'problem of control' is an abstraction; few artists, and certainly not Monteverdi or Gluck, have drawn so clean and scientific an issue. Nor did Orpheus, in the simple, unelaborated myth. It is the dramatist's task to clarify the issue for Orpheus." And we can say, with Milton in mind, it is the masque maker's task to clarify the Orphic failure by treating the masque as "defense and resource."

Barber has said that if *Comus* fails, "it fails by a failure of rhythm . . . mere vehemence, mere assertion . . . and where our imagination is allowed to rest on the merely literal or merely intellectual contest, the defense of chastity lacks the final cogency of pleasure." Barber finds this vehemence in Comus himself—perhaps according to Milton's design. Barber would seem to support the view of song as liberating spell: "It is notable that the images which suggest a benign sexual release refer to song." Milton has accorded success to his benign magician, the Attendant

Spirit. But evidence of the Attendant Spirit's power is not apparent in a mere reading of his imagery. We have to w all his rhythms, and besides, we have to make use of our surviving musical manuscripts of Comus in order to discover the metrical style Milton and Lawes together created. For here will be the antidote to all false vehemence and spurious assertiveness. To restate Barber's question, the masque has to achieve the natural grace of its own chosen *metron*. Compared with the use of verse and music, the use of dance is minimal, even negligible.

It may even be misleading to suggest that Comus has much in common with the earlier dance-drama of the typical court masques. Unlike them, Comus could be presented without dances—a loss which would obliterate many earlier masques—although the spectacle and the meaning do in fact profit, in due measure, from the two dances that Milton did allow. Whereas the earlier models, Jonsonian especially, carried a weight of meaning in their dances and spectacle, Milton's work has displaced this burden and given it to the imagery of the speeches and the recitative music of their declamation.

Seeking the source of this "musical" style in the mythography of the work, we would associate expressivity with the Orphic voice. Orpheus sings in suffering. The music he makes is not instrumental: in *Ad Patrem*, Milton praises to his father the true Orphic bard (the *vates*), who sang at ancient festal occasions. He asks: "In brief, of what use is the idle modulation of the voice if it lacks words and sense and rhythmical speech? That kind of music suits woodland singers, not Orpheus, who by his song, not his lyre, held back rivers, gave ears to the oak trees, and by his singing drew tears from the shades of the dead. Such fame he owes to song" (ll. 50–55). This distinction Ficino had made.

> In his treatise on divine madness, he states that the human soul acquires through the ears a memory of that divine music which is found first in the eternal mind of God, and second, in the order and movements of the heavens. There is also a twofold imitation of that divine music among men, a lower one through voices and instruments, and a higher one through verse and metre. The former kind is called vulgar music, whereas the latter is called by Plato serious music and poetry.

Milton was to espouse the higher music in his own works, where he forged "willing chains and sweet captivity." *At a Vacation Exercise* makes perfectly clear the equation in Milton's mind between music and the verse of his native language, which remains independent of any strictly musical accompaniment. Even when he praises the singing of Leonora Baroni, the great Roman singer, he does so in terms that place the standard of beauty in a celestial frame. God or the Holy Ghost, he tells her, "moves with secret power in your throat—moves with power, and graciously teaches mortal hearts how they can insensibly become accustomed to immortal sounds. But, if God is all things and interpenetrates all, in you alone he speaks, and in silence holds all else" (ll. 5–10). The second epigram to Baroni confers on her the power of reanimating the dead Pentheus, the archetypal victim of maenadic bacchic rage. To give Pentheus life is to make harmony the means of salvation. Milton imagines this sublime sacrificial act in ambivalent terms, for it was Orpheus whom the maenads tore to pieces.

Perhaps only in *Samson Agonistes* and its choral inventions did Milton control the full flood of this ambivalence. There the Orphic voice is committed equally to salvation and self-destruction. An unwitting yet half-chosen suicide rewards the singer who descends into the underworld. It is not clear how much of a sense of this descent is left in *Samson Agonistes*; this is a skewed myth, but Samson's doom elicits pure outcries. Samson is the ultimate Orphic hero; his blindness drives him into a totally auditory world of hearing and speaking. As for persona, it is not unwarranted to question the parallels between the hero and his poet. The choice of Samson as tragic voice, for all its risk of dramatizing the stasis of tragic energy rather than its motions, is still the most daring of Milton's choices. Now he can fully utter the drama of an entangled self-consciousness; now it is proper for the hero to be in part the poet himself, and equally proper for the poet to voice his absolute command of the poetic medium. The final twist in this triumph of a rational self-awareness (and its mystery) is the invention of the Chorus, for this Chorus is planned on the principle of echo, to give resonance—to provide a resonating surface and mirror—to the second voice of the poet.

The particulars of every Miltonic work differ, but common to them all is a penchant for enclosed vastness. That the poet understood his own will to encompass may be seen throughout his writings, since he is generally so conscious of what, as a writer, he is attempting. No better example could be given than the encomium upon Cromwell in *The Second Defence of the People of England*, where, expanding on a traditional rhetorical topic, Milton uses the terminology of enclosure and expansion:

> It is not possible for me in the narrow limits in which I circumscribe myself on this occasion, to enumerate the many towns which he has taken, the many battles which he has won. The whole surface of the British empire has been the scene of his exploits, and the theatre of his

triumphs; which alone would furnish ample materials for a history, and want a copiousness of narration not inferior to the magnitude and diversity of the transactions.

Later, observing that "the title of king was unworthy the transcendent majesty of your character," Milton defines the problem of naming the surpassing glory: "Actions such as yours surpass, not only the bounds of our admiration, but our titles; and, like the points of the pyramids, which are lost in the clouds, they soar above the possibilities of titular commendation." Cromwell had to let himself be called Lord Protector because it was "expedient, that the highest pitch of virtue should be circumscribed within the bounds of some human appellation." In *Tetrachordon*, Milton describes the practical problem of "the abundance of argument that presses to bee utter'd, and the suspense of judgement what to choose, and how in the multitude of reason, to be not tedious." It is the trial of superabundance, of genius conscious that it generates.

Johnson was right. It was in Milton's character always to choose subjects "on which too much could not be said, on which he might tire his fancy without censure of extravagance." Inheriting a large literary capital, Milton put this imagistic wealth to work. The capitalistic analogy is hardly a metaphor here. Milton treats literary tradition like an entrepreneur, investing one work in another, continuously making "mergers." This parodistic takeover particularly colors the Ovidian elements of *Comus*, which show that myth is a currency convertible from one generation to another. Comus the seducer replays Leander's sermons of love to Hero. Suddenly, the poem of *Hero and Leander* rises like an apparition, staring Comus in the face. We shall need to speculate further on this mirroring.

Then, too, Milton has the power of extreme concentration. He holds a whole tradition of exegesis suspended in the little speech on haemony, where Thyrsis knowingly refers to "that Moly / Which Hermes once to wise Ulysses gave." It was to this moly that the Stoic philosopher Cleanthes applied an early allegorical gloss, perhaps about 200 B.C. (and in transcribing Cleanthes' view, Apollonius the Sophist made what may be the earliest use of the term *allegoria*): "Cleanthes the philosopher says that Reason is indicated allegorically, by which the impulses and passions are mollified." Haemony is more than moly, as scholars have labored to show. It acts magically in the framework of a dramatic action. But it has the effect of a *logical* power as well. It is entangled in a kind of witchcraft, the verbal spell, for as Milton would know from the *Remedia Amoris*, Ovid had said: "If anyone thinks that the beneficial herbs of Haemonia and the arts of magic can avail, let him take his own risk. That is the old way of witchcraft; my patron Apollo gives harmless aid in sacred songs." One can no longer tell if haemony is a drug or a word. *Comus* is full of such terms. Extravaganza without extravagance results. The richness of commentary on the *Maske* itself suggests that wealth is one aim of transcendental form.

STANLEY E. FISH

Reason in "The Reason of Church Government"

My description of *The Reason of Church Government* is a curious one by any of the standards we usually apply to controversial prose—sentences without verbs, conclusions before arguments, points made by declining to make them—but in the context of the tradition we have been following [here], it falls perfectly into place as a work that undermines its own pretensions and repeatedly calls attention to what it is *not* doing. It does not express truth, or contain it, or process it. Indeed, its elaborate rational machinery operates only to emphasize how independent truth is of the validation that reason and rational structures can confer. At best, it turns the mind of the reader (and then only of the reader who is predisposed) in the direction of truth.

In a curious way, then, I agree with Hamilton when he implies that *The Reason of Church Government* doesn't say anything at all ("a lack of real intellectual content"), but this is not the same thing as concluding that it doesn't mean anything at all. It is simply that the locus of meaning is not the printed page, where literally nothing is happening, but the mind of the reader, where everything is happening. I make it a point to ask my students what they remember of their previous night's reading of *The Reason of Church Government*; and invariably they answer not with propositions or chains of inferences, but with words, and groups of words, that come tumbling out haphazardly, and yet arranged somehow in the patterns of relationship we have observed [elsewhere]. I cannot recreate their response in all its associative spontaneity, but an equivalent effect is

From *Self-Consuming Artifacts*. Copyright © 1972 by The Regents of the University of California. University of California Press.

produced simply by rehearsing, in the order of their appearance, two lists
of opposing phrases and images:

> gross, patched, varnished, embellishings, veil, sumptuous, tradition, show,
> visibility, polluted, idolatrous, Gentilish rites, cermonies, feather, brav-
> ery, hide, deformed, plumes, pomp, flesh, outward, ceremonial law,
> delusions, particolored, mimic, custom, specious, sophistical, names,
> fallacy, mask, dividing, schismatical, forked, disfigurement, Egyptian,
> overcloud, scales, false, glitter, beads, art, sweet, dim, reflection, fleshly
> wisdom, garb, defaced, overcasting, copes, vestures, gold robes, sur-
> plices, adorn, corporeal resemblances, clothing, maskers, gaudy glister-
> ings, delude, carnal, high, sensual, fermentations, worldly, external,
> flourishes, counterfeit, crafty, artificial, appearance, outward man, skin,
> defile, ignorance, pride, temples, carpets, tablecloth, slimy, confections,
> profane, faulty, false-whited, gilded, vanities, dross, scum, luggage, in-
> fection, formal outside, greasy, brazen, temporal, oil over, besmear,
> corrupt, shadow, darkened, obscured.

And on the other side:

> plainly, clearness, eternal, invariable, inspired, open, spiritual eye, in-
> ward, plain, clear, evident, pure, spiritual, simple, lowly, internal, faith,
> homogeneous, even, firm, unite, truth, steadfastness, perfection, unity,
> seamless, unchangeable, constancy, light, sacred, illumination, luster,
> inspiration, revelation, eye-brightening, inward prompting, divine, bright,
> belief, common sense, simplicity, clear evidence, naked, inward holi-
> ness, inward beauty, bareness, lowliness, purity of Doctrine, wisdom of
> God, glory, enlightened, true knowledge, holy, cleansed, health, purge,
> God's word.

What will strike the reader of these two lists at once, I think, is the
presence of an argument, even in the absence of a discursive syntax.
Statements of relationships form themselves unbidden simply because the
words and phrases so obviously belong together; and this continues to be
true even when they *are* implicated in a syntactical structure: "however in
show and *visibility* it may seeme a part of his Church, yet in as much as it
lyes thus unmeasur'd he leaves it to be trampl'd by the Gentiles, that is to
be *polluted* with *idolatrous* and *Gentilish rites* and *ceremonies* (761, emphasis
mine)." The order of the [italicized] words is the order of their (consecu-
tive) appearance in the list; and the impression they make in the two
contexts is remarkably similar. In one, the mere fact of their contiguity
suffices to generate connections; and in the other, the connections sup-
plied by the syntax are overwhelmed by the connections they themselves
generate. Were one asked to form a sentence of these words, the result
would no doubt be something like this: "The show and visibility of

Gentilish rites and ceremonies are evidence of the pollution of idolatry "
And this is exactly the import of the sentence in which they do, in fact,
appear. The organizing pressure of the "however . . . yet" construction
makes little difference, for the construction is finally not the agency of
relationship. Its only effect is to focus our attention on the indeterminate
"it," a neutral counter which draws to itself the multiple and complementary associations of the surrounding words. They *are* the sentence at the
same time that their interrelationships are independent of its structure.
The source of the fellowship they so obviously (self-evidently) share is to
be found outside the framework that happens, for the moment, to contain
them. And what is true of these words and a single sentence is true of the
full list and the entire tract.

In fact one can rewrite the entire tract by rearranging the two lists
into a table of natural contraries:

carnal	spiritual
false	true
sight	faith
varnished	plain
outer	inner
darkness	light
polluted	pure
idolatrous	holy
hid	open
covered	naked
earthly	divine
veil	clear
schism	unity
sophistical	simple
pride	lowliness
clothing	bareness
profane	sacred
slimy	clean

This is by no means complete, and even if there were space enough to
continue indefinitely, the result would still be a distortion; for not only
does each term interact with its opposing fellow, it is also, by virtue of the
vertical equivalences (carnal=false=polluted) implicated in all the order
single oppositions. Obviously the entire complex of interrelationships
could not be represented on the printed page (mine or Milton's), for it is
not linear. Its true medium, because it is the only medium flexible enough
to hold in solution all of the shifting patterns, is the reader's conscious-

ness. I return, by a kind of back door, to the idea of a progress in *The Reason of Church Government*; not, of course, to the "ratiocinative progress" whose absence Hamilton deplores, but to a progressive enlargement of the understanding. Hamilton and I agree, in our different ways, that the reader who negotiates these sixty or so pages is not following an argument. And yet he must be doing something, and what he is doing, with varying degrees of self-consciousness, is accumulating and cross-referencing pairs of coordinate words and images on either side of a great divide; and as these pairs succeed one another, not on the page but in the mind, they lose their discreteness and become, in the process of (reading) time, interchangeable. That is to say, at some point (and I will not specify it), one reads "Prelacy" in (not into) the word "profane," and "profane" in the word "Prelacy," and both in the phrase "fair outsides"; and conversely "Presbyter" in the word "pure," and "pure" in the word "Presbyter," and both in "inward." The reader proceeds in space and time and from point to point, but always to find the same unchanging essences shining through their local manifestations.

Again, this is possible only because the ligatures of logical thought are binding rather than directing; they help the flow of the prose along, but they do not structure it. For another example, one longer than a single sentence, consider the opening of the second chapter of the second book:

> That which next declares the heavenly power, and reveales the deep mistery of the Gospel, is the pure simplicity of doctrine, accounted the foolishnes of this world, yet crossing and counfounding the pride and wisdom of the flesh.
>
> (826)

Typically, the main verb and the construction it supports make little claim on the reader's attention. The real work of the sentence is done by the sequence of phrases—"heavenly power," "deep mistery of the Gospel," "pure simplicity of doctrine," "foolishnes of this world," "crossing and counfounding," "pride and wisdom of the flesh"—and by the several patterns of relationship in which they become implicated. The first pattern forms when the conjunction "and" joins not only the verbs "declares" and "reveales" (near synonyms in Milton's lexicon), but also "heavenly power" and "deep mistery." For a moment, "pure simplicity of doctrine" makes a third in this series, before it combines with "foolishnes of this world" into a new pattern, a pattern of opposition. But almost immediately "foolishnes of this world" separates itself to enter into a fellowship with "pride and wisdom of the flesh," and this pair then stands in obvious contrast to "heavenly power," "deep mistery of the Gospel," and "pure simplicity of the time" (that pattern is now reestablished).

All of these patterns can operate more or less simultaneously because the pressure of the syntax is so minimal that nothing in the sentence is confined to one place or to one relationship; and the possibility of the whole dividing too neatly into halves is forestalled by "crossing and counfounding," a strongly rhythmic phrase that is not a part of the shifting configurations of contraries and correspondences "Crossing and counfounding," however, establishes a pattern of its own, a pattern of doublets and alliteration that soon dominates the chapter. "Pride and wisdom" (made one by the "and") are drawn into it immediately to be joined in succeeding sentences by "worship and service," "presumption of ordering," "traditions and ceremonies," "defeated and counfounded," "proudest and wisest," "bulwark and stronghold":

> And wherein consists this fleshly wisdom and pride? in being altogether ignorant of God and his worship? No surely, for men are naturally asham'd of that. Where then? it consists in a bold presumption of ordering the worship and service of God after mans own will in traditions and ceremonies. Now if the pride and wisdom of the flesh were to be defeated and confounded, no doubt, but in that very point wherin it was proudest and thought it self wisest, that so the victory of the Gospel might be the more illustrious. But our Prelats instead of expressing the spirituall power of their ministery by warring against this chief bulwark and strong hold of the flesh, have enter'd into fast league with the principall enemy against whom they were sent, and turn'd the strength of fleshly pride and wisdom against the pure simplicity of saving truth.
>
> (826–827)

The ruling doublet remains "pride and wisdom." In the company of "flesh" (and derivative forms) it weaves a way in between the others, undergoing a series of permutations, from "pride of wisdom of the flesh" to "fleshy wisdom and pride" back to "pride and wisdom of the flesh," made adjectival (and superlative) in "proudest and wisest" (flesh has for a moment attached itself to "bulwark and stronghold") until finally it ends the sequence as "fleshly pride and wisdom," opposed, not surprisingly, to the "pure simplicity of saving truth."

This is also the opposition of the chapter's concluding sentence:

> Thus we see again how Prelaty sayling in opposition to the main end and power of the gospel doth not joyn in that mysterious work of Christ, by lowliness to confound height, by simplicity of doctrin the wisdom of the world, but contrariwise hath made it self high in the world and the flesh to vanquish things by the world accounted low, and made itself wise

in tradition and fleshly ceremony to confound the purity of doctrin which
is the wisdom of God.

(829–830)

Here the word "opposition" itself controls the first of two polarizing
motions, aligning "Prelaty" against "gospel" and "work of Christ," "lowli-
ness" against "height," and "simplicity" against worldly wisdom. At this
point the second polarizing motion is introduced by "contrari*wise*" (a pun
anticipates the transformation of worldly wisdom) and the sentence winds
its way through the smaller contraries of "high" and "low," "fleshly" and
"purity," "ceremony" and "doctrin," before coming to rest on the ca-
denced rhythm of "wisdom of God." ("Wisdom" has, in the course of the
chapter, been redefined and baptized.)

The first words of this sentence—"thus we see"—contain something I have spoken of before, the suggestion of a challenge to the reader
who *doesn't* see. To be sure, the pressure on the reader is slight, but it is
enough to place him in the action, as it were, poised somewhat uneasily
between the contending parties, their modes of apprehension, and their
indigenous patterns of imagery. This is a position he occupies literally in
the concluding sentences of the third chapter of the first book, which are,
incidentally, nearly indistinguishable from the passage we have just analyzed:

> If the religion be *pure, spirituall, simple,* and *lowly,* as the Gospel most
> truly is, such must the face of the ministery be. And in like manner if
> the forme of the Ministery be *grounded* in the *worldly* degrees of autority,
> honour, *temporall* jurisdiction, we see it with our eyes it will turne the
> *inward* power and *purity* of the Gospel into the *outward carnality* of the
> *law;* evaporating and exhaling the *internall* worship into empty conformi-
> ties, and *gay shewes.*
>
> (766, emphasis mine)

Here the syntax does not even pretend to do anything more than hold in
place the words I have italicized; *they* carry the argument, moving in a
kind of dance from one pattern of relationships to another; first ranging
themselves formally in lines of battle, "pure," "spirituall," "simple," "lowly"
against "grounded" (the metaphor becomes literal in the company of its
fellows), "worldly," "temporall," and then separating into opposing pairs
which engage each other in hand-to-hand combat: inward vs. outward,
purity vs. carnality, internall vs. gay shewes. These smaller oppositions
operate to flesh out the more abstract opposition of the Gospel to the law
which, in turn, feeds into the ever-present opposition of Prelaty to
Presbyterianism. And exactly in the middle of the sentence, and therefore
in the middle of the smaller and larger coordinates, stands the reader or,

more properly, his eyes which are declared responsible ("we see it with our eyes") for judging between the "faces" of the two ministries. The responsibility, however, is limited, since the judgment is already imbedded in the imagery and the reader can only approve it or become its object. The sentence pressures us to choose between alternatives that are implicitly self-revelatory. Are your eyes "pure," "spirituall," "inward," or are they "carnal," "worldly," and "outward"? Are they answerable to that which "most truly is" or to "gay shewes"? And, of course, the reader's response (he can hardly withhold it) not only places him in a hierarchy of vision, but commits him to a whole series of attendant positions: for the Presbyters and against Prelacy, for the inner light and against priestly ceremony, for the immediate validation of illumined eyes and against the worldly machinery of reasons formally set down.

Thomas Kranidas has observed that "a study of the prose of Milton becomes in large part a study of the way things are complexly unified or related." *The Reason of Church Government* not only provides support for this statement, but, as an object, itself exemplifies the principle of unity that is, as Kranidas points out, one of Milton's "obsessions." There is a perfect and sustained correspondence between the two structures of the tract (inner and outer), the two ecclesiastical structures that are its subject, the two ways of knowing (reason and illumination) that support those structures, and the two patterns of imagery that reflect their properties. The final (and activating) links in this chain of correspondences are, of course, the two sets of readers whose differing visions are reflected in and answerable to every one of these patterned oppositions. Thus the reader who inclines to the party of the Prelates will be the reader who attends carefully to the order of the numbered chapters and to the unfolding argument they presumably carry, while to the eye of the Presbyterian (or illumined) reader, these divisions will be less pressuring than the truths that imply themselves at every point. In a way, then, *The Reason of Church Government* is nothing more (or less) than an elaborate and continuing eye test. It validates not reasons, but visions, and it is always reaching conclusions not about systems of church government (a matter closed to disquisition), but about *you*.

Indeed, it would not be too much to say that you are finally the subject of the tract, since your discerning (or not discerning) is its only real issue, although it is not the issue of record until the concluding chapter of the second book: "*That Prelatical jurisdiction opposeth the reason and end of the Gospel and State.*" Prelatical jurisdiction, the jurisdiction of courts and judgments, would impose the outward censure of a worldly authority, and it is opposed (predictably) to the inner censure of a man's "own severe and modest eye upon himselfe" (842). This is merely an extension and reformulation of the familiar correspondences and oppositions. The outward and formal censure of Prelatical jurisdiction is, like the superstructure of reasons and proofs, superfluous to those whose court of jurisdiction sits within. It is to this court and to that "severe and modest eye" that the tract has been speaking all along, and the lengthy discussion here is merely a reconfirmation in more explicit terms of everything that has gone before. It is also an additional explanation (hardly required at this point) of the absence in the tract of a sustained and coercive argument: for if the judgment of the inner eye is sufficient and necessary, any judgment rendered or urged by a body of print will be either unnecessary, if the inner eye is indeed illumined and severely modest, or inefficacious, if it is not. *The Reason of Church Government* does not pretend to correct eyes—only the inner mechanism of "honourable shame" can do that—it merely tests eyes and issues interim reports on the visions of its two sets of readers.

It reports also on Milton's vision, for the question the prose is always asking—"you see don't you?"—contains an implied declaration, "*I do!*" Milton is continually affirming the illumination of his own eyesight, indirectly whenever his independence of reasons formally set down is implied, and directly in the famous autobiographical digression, which is really not a digression at all since its argument is no more (or less) than the argument of the preceding seven chapters—those who have eyes will see. Technically these pages constitute the author's "defense for writing," but it is the writing itself that is finally put on the defensive. Rather than proclaiming (and documenting) his fitness for the task at hand, Milton declares that the business at hand is beneath him, because it is beneath the capacities he has been given by God. It is a kind of arrogant humility, in which the emphasis is not on his powers but on their source in divine inspiration. The question for Milton is "how and in what manner he shall dispose and employ those summes of knowledge and illumination, which God hath sent him into this world to trade with" (801). Immediately, the burden of proof is shifted from Milton to any reader who would challenge his credentials, which are now revealed to have been issued by God. The identification of Presbyterianism with the revealed word is here extended to the poet, but with a more literal force. The Holy Spirit has, in effect, appropriated Milton and made of him an instrument of the divine will:

> For surely to every good and peaceable man it must in nature needs be a hatefull thing to be the displeaser, and molester of thousands; much better would it like him doubtless to be the messenger of gladnes and contentment, which is his chief intended busines, to all mankind, but

that they resist and oppose their own true happinesse. But when God commands to take the trumpet and blow a dolorous or a jarring blast, it lies not in mans will what he shall say, or what he shall conceal.

(803)

This is a conventional claim of the inspired (and reluctant) prophets to whom Milton refers and with whom he identifies himself, but it takes on added force when we recall that at crucial points in the body of the tract the sense of a personal voice recedes to be replaced by the voiceless proclaiming of a universal and self-validating truth. Of course the personal Milton is heard here, in this digression, but his tone is not exactly as commentators have described it. This is no program for a later career (although the accidents of literary history have made this misinterpretation inevitable), but a complaint, tempered by resignation, against the interruption of a career that may never be resumed. The emphasis is not on his hopes, but on their frustration. He is not concerned chiefly to tell us what he will do in the future, but what he is not doing now. He is not now writing something which "aftertimes" will not willingly let die (810); he is not now inbreeding and cherishing "in a great people the seeds of vertu" (816); he is not now "Teaching over the whole book of sanctity" (817) or making "the paths of honesty and good life . . . appeare . . . easy and pleasant" (818). And, above all, he is not now engaged in those higher pursuits whose reward is the "beholding the bright countenance of truth" (821).

Once again, the validation of eyesight has as its reverse consequence the invalidation of the tract. "Clubbing quotations" is not only distasteful, and far below his abilities, it is also useless and irrelevant:

I trust hereby to make it manifest with what small willingnesse I endure to interrupt the pursuit of no lesse hopes then these . . . to come into the dim reflexion of hollow antiquities sold by the seeming bulk, and there be fain to club quotations with men whose learning and belief lies in marginal stuffings, who when they have like good sumpters laid ye down their hors load of citations and fathers at your dore, with a rapsody of who and who were Bishops here or there, ye may take off their packsaddles, their days work is don, and episcopacy, as they think, stoutly vindicated.

(822)

With such men as these, one may wage a war of citations, and win, without effecting the chief end, the inculcation of belief. Those who believe that a system of church government can be vindicated by marginal stuffings (or formal reasons) may be forced to yield a point and still remain *inwardly* unpersuaded; and insofar as Milton enters this arena and parades this kind of learning, he commits himself to an impossible task.

Why, then, does he do it? The assumptions that dictate the strategy of *The Reason of Church Government* entail the futility of the entire enterprise. There are only two kinds of readers in Milton's audience, those for whom the reasons imply themselves, and those so unregenerate that no reason, of man or God, will convince them. When Milton asks "What need I conclude?" he might as well be asking "What need I write?" And the answer to that question is the answer to all the questions this tract raises and declines to prosecute: the first and greatest reason is because God hath so commanded, and "when God commands" (803), even though the service be inglorious and of doubtful issue, his servant obeys: "But were it the meanest under-service, if God by his Secretary conscience injoyn it, it were sad for me if I should draw back" (822). In *Paradise Lost*, the angels loyal to God evidence their faith by persevering in an action they know to be unnecessary in response to a command— drive out the rebel host—which they find themselves incapable of carrying out. That perseverance entitles them to the epithet "hero," and to the extent that his situation in *The Reason of Church Government* parallels theirs, it is Milton's epithet too, and presumably he will someday be the recipient of the praise God bestows on Abdiel:

> Servant of God, well done.
> (*P.L.*, VI, 29)

Meanwhile, however, Milton stands alone, or with those of his audience who, like him, are "eye-brightened" and the prose continues to pressure the reader to enroll himself in that number:

> And if ye think ye may with a pious presumption strive to goe beyond God in mercy, I shall not be one now that would dissuade ye. Though God for lesse then ten just persons would not spare *Sodom*, yet if you can finde after due search but only one good thing in prelaty either to religion, or civil goverment, to King or Parlament, to Prince or people, to law, liberty, wealth or learning, spare her, let her live, let her spread among ye, till with her shadow, all your dignities and honours, and all the glory of the land be darken'd and obscurd. But on the contrary if she be found to be malignant, hostile, destructive to all these, as nothing can be surer, then let your severe and impartial doom imitate the divine vengeance; rain down your punishing force upon this godlesse and oppressing government: and bring such a dead Sea of subversion upon her, that she may never in this Land rise more to afflict the holy reformed Church, and the elect people of God.
>
> (861)

In an important sense, *The Reason of Church Government* is a self-consuming artifact only in one direction: for while it does invalidate its own claims to process knowledge and illumination, it does not provoke the self of the reader to change, merely to acknowledge his position in the polarities it continually uncovers. The tract does not persuade or convert; rather it bullies, and in this final paragraph the basic pattern of the reader's experience is rehearsed for the last time. First he is asked to choose between two alternatives, as he was asked in the beginning to choose between two forms of church government, but no sooner is one of them proffered (and indeed urged) before its terrible consequences are visited: "with her shadow, all your dignities and honours, and all the glory of the land be darken'd and obscurd." The choice is, as it has been so many times before, no choice at all, and its rhetorical pretense is further subverted by the parenthetical "as nothing can be surer" which introduces the downward sweep of the concluding sentence. The form of that sentence is conditional ("If she be found to be malignant"), but because all the conditions have already been fulfilled, it becomes a command ("rain down your punishing force"), a command which has all the more impact because we have been implicitly included in the group in whose name it is issued, the elect people of God.

Inclusion is also the motion of Burton's prose in *The Anatomy of Melancholy*, but in his vision there are no elect, and God is prominent only by his absence.

LESLIE BRISMAN

Edenic Time

Ah! lost! lost! lost! for ever!
So Leutha spoke. But when she saw that Enitharmon had
Created a New Space to protect Satan from punishment;
She fled to Enitharmons Tent & hid herself. Loud raging
Thunder'd the Assembly dark & clouded, and they ratify'd
The kind decision of Enitharmon & gave a Time to the Space,
Even Six Thousand years; and sent Lucifer for its Guard.
But Lucifer refus'd to die & in pride he forsook his charge
And they elected Molech, and when Molech was impatient
The Divine hand found the Two Limits: first of
Opacity, then of Contraction
Opacity was named Satan, Contraction was named Adam.
— BLAKE, Milton

The depiction of stasis depends on the awareness of time. Moments of arrest are measured by some simultaneous ongoingness; turns take place along the distances of time lost; stasis in song is distinguished from the satanic attempt to carry it out of time into space; and the temptation to poetic arrest is woven into the continuity of verse or narrative. One could say simply that the fallen world is a world of temporality, in which presentness is apprehended only as it is passing away, in which choice is realized only as it passes into determinateness. But one would then have to identify Milton with Blake, finding Creation itself the Fall—a misreading a little more fallen than creative. We

From *Milton's Poetry of Choice and its Romantic Heros.* Copyright © 1973 by Cornell University. Cornell University Press.

need to turn from fictional arrest to historicity in Milton's poetics of choice.

Such a perspective is necessitated most plainly by the extent to which Milton makes time a part of paradise. Were presentness and choice in simple opposition to the awareness of time, perhaps one could turn to the descriptions of paradise before the Fall for a longer look at stasis; the moment could have "extension" without a sense of contradiction. Paradise, the eternal present, would know no time. But Milton deliberately makes Adam and Eve aware of time past, and it is an awareness intimately connected with the concept of choice.

EDENIC TIME

The account of the Fall does not restrict events to a single day, let alone the day of creation; the first parents have inhabited paradise for some time, long enough to see the rhythmic recurrence of days and nights as a measure of ongoingness. Eve, moderately absorbed in her own being and her own time, questions the reason for the stars shining while she and Adam are asleep, and is answered:

> Those have thir course to finish, round the Earth,
> By morrow Ev'ning, and from Land to Land
> In order, though to Nations yet unborn,
> Minist'ring light prepar'd, they set and rise;
> Lest total darkness should by Night regain
> Her old possession, and extinguish life.
>   (PL, IV.661–666)

The first four lines are rich with awareness of time future; the next two add—not really future possibility, though they are richer for that suggestion—awareness of time past. The exchange occurs after Eve's great lyric in which love becomes man's opportunity to share the divine perspective outside of time: "With thee conversing I forget all time, / All seasons and thir change, all please alike." One can only forget what was once known, and the knowledge of time passed is the basis of the love relationship. Adam and Eve have a little past in common, the awareness they share of days gone by that constitute the remembered, and therefore imaginative, reality that is the realm of love.

In the love lyric preceding Eve's question all nature is consummately praised as if joying in mere being, and then turned and made to be contingent on Adam. In a way the twenty lines form a passage of extended repetition, which, like those discussed [elsewhere], seems to arrest time, capturing the moment in the turn on "but": "Sweet is the breath of morn . . . pleasant the sun . . . But neither breath of morn . . . nor rising sun . . . without thee is sweet." The extended hold on all of nature is dependent on the pleasure she takes in Adam's company, as though all times, past and to come waited on his presence. The second "but" that introduces her question ("But wherefore all night long shine these?") returns contemplation to time. A remark of Kierkegaard's helps explain how Milton uses the question to emphasize the scene's underlying innocence: "When you begin to notice that a certain pleasure or experience is acquiring too strong a hold upon the mind, you stop a moment for the purpose of remembering."

Eve is not quite aware that her relationship to Adam or to anything in paradise could acquire "too strong a hold upon the mind." In itself the question about the stars seems rather to be the passage closest to expressing her self-absorption, her mistaking the conscious time she shares with Adam for all time. In this it is like the lines that introduce her song ("With thee conversing I forget all time"), slightly suspect because forgetting all time sounds like satanic arrest, the kind of stasis we have associated with Comus and passion. Such overtones remind the reader of the incipient Fall, and help to make the song paradisal. But Eve herself is free from such knowledge; "I forget all time" turns out to mean, in the next lines, that she forgets what specific time it is, not what existence in time has been, for she goes on to describe exquisitely the times of day. In unfallen speech, what is ignored is not past and future but the fleetingness of the present.

Against this temporal background Eve's question creeps in like a miniature of the moment of choice the serpent presents. The beauty of her exchange with Adam depends partly on our recognition that here are the same problems we face in the fallen world but delicately turned around. While the task of the "uncouth swain" of "Lycidas" is to redeem the sense of the pastness of the past, to make the past "present," Adam's task is to make the present past. It is, in the most humanistic way, an anticipation of the educative function of Raphael and Michael. Adam is talking about the stars shining now, and he explains the present by making it seem a part of Eve's past:

> Millions of spiritual Creatures walk the Earth
> Unseen, both when we wake, and when we sleep:
> All these with ceaseless praise his works behold
> Both day and night: how often from the steep
> Of echoing Hill or Thicket have we heard

> Celestial voices to the midnight air,
> Sole, or responsive each to other's note
> Singing thir great Creator.
> (*PL*, IV.677–684)

Adam reminds Eve of what they oft have heard, giving the new insight—ancestor of Socrates that he is—with the implication that she knew that already.

While Adam speaks to Eve, making the present seem part of their past, Milton makes that past seem present to us, and we read lines like "Millions of spiritual Creatures walk the Earth" forgetting all time between Eden and us till we are recalled by the authorial voice reminding us of the pastness of the past: "Thus talking hand in hand alone they pass'd / On to thir blissful Bower." We are tolled back to poetic time primarily by the reintroduction of the past, narrative tense—"they pass'd"—secondarily by the imagery of hands that must always be read forward and back in this poem ("her rash hand in evil hour"; "from her husband's hand her hand / Soft she withdrew"; "they hand in hand with wand'ring steps and slow"). Lastly, the comparative past is introduced to emphasize the choiceness of this moment: "it was a place [the poet, stepping away, speaks in narrative past] chosen [in some more distant past] by the sovran Planter, when he framed [when was that? further back? no, for Him there is no gap between good intentions and bad choices] all things to man's [we are with Adam here] delightful use."

Narrative attention to lengths of time preceding the temptation, far from diminishing the decisiveness of that moment, augments its significance. The choice of the fruit may be distinguished from the more immediate kind of option which does not gather all the past into it—what Kierkegaard calls "aesthetic choice": "The only absolute either/or is the choice between good and evil, but that is also ethical. The aesthetic choice is either entirely immediate, or it loses itself in the multifarious. . . . When one does not choose absolutely one chooses only for the moment, and therefore can choose something different the next moment." *Paradise Lost* must convince that the first ethical choice, the "absolute either/or," carries with it the psychological impossibility of choosing something different the next moment, and the epic therefore suggests a length of time for Eve's deliberation and a substantial gap between her first taste and Adam's fall. The description of what Adam does "the while" Eve "so long delay'd" extends that period and points to the new, fallen sense of duration in time as a bane. Suddenly the clock ticks too slowly; or, more accurately, suddenly there is an intrusion of measured time in which man is extended where before there was an easy commerce of old and new. Eve's first fallen words to Adam describe time with the new and indelible sense of loss:

> Hast thou not wonder'd, *Adam*, at my stay?
> Thee I have misst, and thought it long, depriv'd
> Thy presence, agony of love till now
> Not felt.
>
> (IX.856–859)

Where their past was previously present, where they were in each other's presence, there is now "the pain of absence," a dearly bought awareness like the "Knowledge of good bought dear by knowing ill" (IV.222). The absolute either/or puts an end to aesthetic or momentary choice and introduces the pain of irrevocability, the distance between present and past. An end to immediacy, the new temporality is prepared for by an awareness of the immediacy of the past in the form of memory. What Adam tells Eve, what Raphael tells them both, establishes the sense of time that is brought to the moment of the Fall, the sense of time that it will be the task of the last two books of the epic to re-establish.

Other references to past time in paradise shadow these educative encounters. After Adam answers Eve, the two pass to their bower, where

> in close recess
> With Flowers, Garlands, and sweet-smelling Herbs
> Espoused *Eve* deckt first her Nuptial Bed. . . .
>
> (IV.708–710)

Reading just so much, one might momentarily mistake this approach to the nuptial bed for the first. But the poet goes on:

> And heav'nly Choirs the Hymenaean sung,
> What day the genial Angel to our Sire
> Brought her in naked beauty more adorn'd,
> More lovely than *Pandora*.

The syntactical difficulty, the way the sentence restructures itself as it goes on, affects the way the reader shares the experience of time in paradise. It turns out (we already knew, but such passages can make it seem first awareness) that this is not the first day Adam led Eve, that the description is really in the past perfect, another reference to antecedent time. The choirs do not sing about the nuptial day, for "What day" is not the object of "sung" but a prepositional phrase, "on an earlier day, when . . ." Eve was not "more adorn'd" than she is now but "more adorn'd" than Pandora, so that remembered time melts into imaginative time in which Pandora and Eve are one. How does Eve compare with Pandora? or with

Delia, Juno, Helen, Pomona, Nausicaa, Proserpina? Associations are poised between the delightful and the damning, and the reader confronts choice in working backward to the associational typology, as well as forward to the moral resonances of a given poetic moment. Literary allusion is less a demystification of a moment's uniqueness than a slight mystification in which the determined strength of the past blurs into an "indefinite abstraction" of choice. Is Eve to be seen as more lovely or more hapless—perhaps more guilty—than Pandora? For the moment the openness of the choice is both ours and hers. In the above passage the real and the imagined coexist in the further abstraction between "What day" and this day, for Eve was presented to Adam by God, and invoking a presentation by a genial angel is an imaginative softening of a perhaps too real "Heavenly Maker" (VIII.485).

Later references to past experience in paradise are specifically about heavenly visitations and heighten the sense of what has passed by contrasting the visits. The Son greets Adam after the Fall:

> Where art thou Adam, wont with joy to meet
> My coming seen far off? I miss thee here,
> Not pleas'd, thus entertain'd with solitude,
> Where obvious duty erewhile appear'd unsought:
> Or come I less conspicuous, or what change
> Absents thee, or what chance detains?
>
> (X.103–108)

Ultimately, his mission is grace, and the Son begins by recalling what is gone, because psychologically, "memory plays the same supernatural role as Grace in Christian thought. It is this inexplicable phenomenon that comes to apply itself to a fallen nature, irremediably separated from its origins. . . . Remembrance is 'a succour from on high' which comes to the being in order 'to draw him from the nothingness out of which, by himself, he would not have been able to emerge.' " But if God and memory in the end work to draw man from nothingness, the immediate effect of recalling the past here is to confront its nothingness, to confront loss itself. The relationship of awareness of loss to redemption is reflected in the experience of the reader, for when the Son addresses Adam, the reader awakens with surprise to the realm of what is past, suddenly seeing that there was duration in paradise, time during which the Son visited habitually. The change that absents Adam opens up an imaginative realm precisely when it is seen to be presently closed.

The sense of loss imbues Eve's reference to past days after her Satan-inspired dream.

                                                    I this Night
Such night till this I never pass'd, have dream'd,
If dream'd, not as I oft am wont, of thee,
Work of day past, or morrow's next design,
But of offense and trouble, which my mind
Knew never till this irksome night.

                                                    (V.30–35)

Describing the effect of this night, Eve makes us aware that there have
been previous nights, and enough of them to have established in her mind
a pattern of what "I oft am wont." We are not really getting a new piece of
information, but as Eve says the words "Such night till this," we perceive
the heavy change in a way we did not "till this." The new awareness of
the difference, of what has changed, is like a dream of the difference that
will be actualized with the Fall. As the Fall turns untroubled experience
into a thing of the past, the dream anticipates the Fall by seeing untroubled
sleep as past. But more than a foreshadowing, a type of the association of
choice, fall, and a sense of the past, Eve's dream creates a past that can be
brought, in memory, to the moment of temptation. As such it gives, in
terms of "mimic fancy," a sense of things that have been, a sense of
history like that which Raphael's rational discourse more overtly presents.
Just as Raphael speaks to both parents, so the dream that is recounted by
Eve to Adam presents a sense of past to them both; but whereas the
angel's reason suits Adam more than Eve, the means of fancy are properly
Eve's own.

    Eve presents another premonition of the Fall that is associated
with an awareness of the past when she recounts to Adam her earliest
memory. In innocent outgoingness she is offering love—the attempt to
recapture and share one's past—as Adam later expresses his love to
Raphael by desiring to detain him with reminiscence. At the same time
Eve's memory also intimates the distance between the first parents which
later, in spatial and psychic terms, will bring about the Fall. "We all
cannot remember the same things. . . . Memory, which allows us by
analogy to understand one another, also keeps us apart." Eve begins in the
tone of one who has been peacefully living in paradise rather than that of
a newcomer there: "That day I oft remember, when from sleep / I first
awak't" (IV.449–450). The past gives a sense of continuity, of what is
habitual and oft remembered; "that day" implies an intervening period of
some time. The whole speech shows to what extent choice is dependent
upon an awareness of remembered days and a remembered other self. Eve
tells of her first moments when, seeing her image and starting back in
surprise and delight, she came close, not only to the self-destructiveness of

Narcissus, but to the destructiveness of Satan in love with sin as image of himself:

> but pleas'd I soon return'd,
> Pleas'd it return'd as soon with answering looks
> Of sympathy and love; there I had fixt
> Mine eyes till now, and pin'd with vain desire,
> Had not a voice thus warn'd me, What thou seest,
> What there thou seest fair Creature is thyself.
> (IV.463–468)

The repetition in the last two lines grammatically expresses the arrest that is passion. She is drawn out of self-love by a voice that introduces time when it introduces Adam—who is significantly at a spatial remove, just as he is temporally distanced by having been created earlier and by having superior knowledge of the intervening time.

When, after her fall, Eve refers to her new sense of the "pain of absence," what is new is the pain that accompanies absence rather than the feeling, which she already knew, that someone or some event is not physically or temporally present. Eve's account of her first awakening presents physical absence—her distance from the image in the water— and, in larger terms, her psychic distance from Adam as she first saw him. Telling her story is a recognition of temporal absence, of certain feelings and events as past. It measures her remove from that time in Wordsworthian fashion:

> so wide appears
> The vacancy between me and those days
> Which yet have such self-presence in my mind,
> That, musing on them, often do I seem
> Two consciousnesses, conscious of myself
> And of some other Being.
> (Prelude, II.28–33)

Eve's history serves in little the purpose of the large historical narrations, creating a sense of "self presence in my mind" as the ground of self-consciousness needed for choice. The conditions of freedom are established when the self sees itself and another, when two identities become simultaneously present rather than "determined" in chronological sequence. The context of the passage from The Prelude is particularly relevant to Eve. Wordsworth muses:

> Ah! is there one who ever has been young,
> Nor needs a warning voice to tame the pride
> Of intellect and virtue's self-esteem?

One is there, though the wisest and the best
Of all mankind, who covets not at times
Union that cannot be?

(II.19–24)

Eve originally coveted such union, and the memory of the whole lakeside episode takes the place of the youth she never had. Eve needs such a "warning voice," something Milton cries for, not right before the Fall in Book IX, but at the beginning of Book IV, before the warning which we can hear in Eve's narration.

Her first reaction to Adam is also her first experience of loss. Called away from the image of herself, she follows till she sees him,

fair indeed and tall,
Under a Platan, yet methought less fair,
Less winning soft, less amiably mild,
Than that smooth wat'ry image; back I turn'd,
Thou following.

(IV.477–481)

In terms of symbolic sexuality, it seems especially appropriate that Eve should be given this first recognition of loss; in Kierkegaard's categories, "woman explains finiteness, man is in chase of infinitude." Eve recaptures the sense of finitude when, describing Adam as he was then but addressing him now, she faces and turns from her past in recognition of what is present. The original experience of finitude was her impression that Adam was "less fair," for if following him is to represent the first choice, it must involve recognition of something renounced for something else. There is no choice if the rejected alternative does not have an appeal of its own, so the incident is Eve's first lesson that what is immediately more appealing is not necessarily best. Not that there was a real choice at that moment; but looking back, Eve can carry with her the association of alternative with renunciation. "Non-being always appears within the limits of a human expectation"; having seen herself first, and expected a form as fair, Eve is aware of the element of negation in turning to a man, "less fair." Many a reader of *Paradise Lost*, as well as Adam himself, has felt the attraction of the chivalric gesture of falling with Eve. Northrop Frye parallels Aeneas' meeting with Dido in hell, pointing to the generalization that a great author polarizes reality, not trivially, but in a way that implicates loss with determination. There is no choice where it is not necessary to say "no" to one alternative, so the first parents are prepared with an awareness of past or hypothetical experience, alternatives to which time has said "no."

Eve herself is not misled about how open her first choice was. She admits, "what could I do / But follow straight, invisibly thus led?" And she notes how Adam wisely gave her little time to make up her mind:

> with that thy gentle hand
> Seiz'd mind, I yielded, and from that time see
> How beauty is excell'd by manly grace.
> (IV.489–491)

If yielding does not look like the result of an open option, it does set the background for seeing choice as the alternative to determinacy. Recalling how she was guided then, we can see the difference, see that she herself must choose her fall. Satan, unlike Adam, does not seize but insinuates: "if thou accept / My conduct, I can bring thee thither soon" (IX.629–630). Eve chooses: "Lead then." Once that choice is made, once the Fall takes place, the openness of choice again seems lost. In contrast to her semireluctant yielding to Adam originally is the unself-conscious eagerness with which she responds after the Fall. Adam seizes her hand, and "to a shady bank . . . / He led her nothing loath" (IX.1037, 1039). Reservation is the mark of openness of possibility, of freedom; when feelings are unambiguous, choice seems dead.

In Book V, Raphael comes to create a sense of futurity and possibility, and to create a sense of past and the openness of choice. He provides the memory of the fall of the angels that allows the two alternatives "fall" and "no fall" to be simultaneously present to the choosing consciousness. Providing the material for memory itself acts, not to break continuity, but to establish it. Poulet says, "By remembering, man escapes the purely momentary; by remembering, he escapes the nothingness that lies in wait for him between moments of existence."

Everything about Raphael's visit is designed to make it a confrontation of experience in time rather than a break in continuity. The hour is specified as noon, while Eve "within, due at her hour prepar'd / For dinner" (V.303–304). Laurence Stapleton notes that "the particular indications of days and hours in all the scenes that take place in Paradise are indispensable in creating an effect of continuity"; the description of Eve at a housekeeping task adds to the sense of regularity and ongoingness. In a way time does have to be suspended to give a "picture" of history, and books V through VIII of the epic halt narrative time to make the past "present" to the reader as Raphael makes it present to Adam. Thus Adam sees the coming of the angel as a break in time, "another Morn / Ris'n on mid-noon (V.310–311), just as later he suggests that light "longer will delay to heare thee tell" (VII.101). Eve, on the other hand, is femininely at one with the rhythm of time and serves as the reminder that even heavenly revelation is something absorbed into human history rather than an interruption of it. She reminds Adam that there is little need for preparations or storage when provision is always present, at hand, in season.

In the scene that ensues, the choiceness of the present is related to the concept of choice through the awareness of the linear sequentiality of present moments. Eve is concerned

> What choice to choose for delicacy best,
> What order, so contriv'd as not to mix
> Tastes, not well join'd, inelegant, but bring
> Taste after taste upheld with kindliest change.
>   (V.333–336)

One may be surprised to learn that it is necessary to plan this vegetarian menu, but Eve's experience with fruit is preparation for the choice when one alternative will be the forbidden fruit and the unkindliest change it brings. "Taste after taste" is harmonious experience in time, and such change, "for delicacy best," like the cycle of days in heaven, "for change delectable, not need" (V.629), contrasts with the fallen world where the fullness of daily activity and housekeeping concerns may have to be renounced for the one thing that is needful. Kierkegaard explains, "There is only one situation in which either/or has absolute significance, namely when truth, righteousness, and holiness are lined up on one side, and lust and base propensities and obscene passions and perdition on the other; yet it is always important to choose rightly, even as between things one may innocently choose." Eve's housekeeping involves such little, aesthetic, innocent choices which prepare us, if not her, for the absolute either/or and weave intimations of it into daily experience. "How wide the gulf and unpassable," Blake says, "between simplicity and insipidity."

A familiar "simplicity" is the line "No fear lest Dinner cool" (V.396). There is no hurry and no worry over passing time in the unfallen world, in contrast to the way a line like "Home to his Mother's house private return'd" (PR, IV.639) makes the re-entry of daily time startling. More important, the intrusion of colloquial tone and concern is not felt as an intrusion into the purity of Eden and does not have to be renounced, the way lines which suggested any modulation in the tone of Comus were excised. The line does interject our time, poet's and reader's, into a description of paradise, but the poet's mediation turns pedestrian fact into the smallest sorrow more beautiful than beauty's self. Experiencing the occurrence of such a turn in the most homey of details, we share the richness of paradise. But more, when Milton stands between Eden and us, he establishes a continuity between his reaction and ours which replaces the discontinuity of paradise lost.

He mediates again in exclaiming over naked Eve ministering to Adam and Raphael:

> O innocence
> Deserving Paradise! if ever, then,
> Then had the Sons of God excuse to have been
> Enamour'd at that sight.
>
> (V.445–448)

Scholars have remarked that Milton enters the controversy over the meaning of Genesis 6 : 1–2. "And it came to pass, when men began to multiply on the face of the earth, and daughters were born unto them, That the sons of God saw the daughters of men that they were fair; and they took them wives of all which they chose." Why does Milton bring that up here? The intervention of the exegetical problem itself contrasts with the innocence of Raphael's intervention. An unusual turn has taken place in literature's customary position of being, at best, commentary on the Word, for at this point in *Paradise Lost* the problem raised by Genesis and its commentators seems to come from outside, seems to be in marginal relation to the text of the poem. Raphael is not to be tempted, but the poet captures the indeterminacy of poetry, its implication of moral choice, in opening the option of introducing commentary into the text. Milton may have known that each of the kabalistic *sephiroth*, or emanations of God, is associated with a body of angels as well as a specific archangel; for the eighth emanation, Splendor, the order of angels is the Sons of God, and the archangel is Raphael.

The point of such association, whether or not it can legitimately be included in the patristic debate over the Sons of God, is the renuncia-tion that must be made of its relevance. The poet's intervention seems to penetrate so much closer to the center of biblical truth than do the labyrinthine byways of hermeneutic conjecture. "If ever there were excuse for angels to be tempted by mortals" joins with "If ever there were reason to bring up the issue of temptation." The "if" is the conditional in which poet and reader share the indeterminacy of paradise. "Then" is a word introducing hypothetical consequence, but its repetition (more than a Latin trope) serves as temporal pointer: "then,/Then"—at that moment, not of fictional arrest, but of Edenic history. Milton's imagined scene has become the real truth to point to while we let fade the Sons of God and the fallen history they inaugurate. We regret realizing that Eve will be

more easily tempted by Satan than Raphael is by her. But sorrow at the loss
of innocence is transcended by the sublimity of the loss of intervening
time as we are rapt beyond logical and theological consequence into direct
perception of unfallen time.

Raphael's visit is one of many events that make historicity the
boon, not the bane, of unfallen man. Careful always to distinguish the
sense of time from the sense of loss, Milton makes a week elapse between
Raphael's visit and Satan's return. For Adam to have freedom of choice,
time must elapse between the guidance and the temptation, alternatives
be taken out of dictated sequentiality into the indeterminate order of
memory. It is as if the first parents were given a push and must go a way
before their motion can be called their own.

The lines that specify the time elapsed describe the voyage of
Satan—"The space of seven continu'd Nights he rode. . . . On th' eighth
return'd"—and picture his re-entry in terms designed to disentangle the
incipient loss from the effect of time:

> There was a place
> Now not, though Sin, not Time, first wrought the change,
> Where *Tigris* at the foot of Paradise
> Into a Gulf shot under ground, till part
> Rose up a Fountain by the Tree of Life.
>
> (IX.69–73)

The period of his wandering (represented in poetic time by the description
of place) is the time the first parents spend in uninterrupted presentness
before the crucial day. It is their opportunity to contemplate past and
future, to recall and rehearse what Raphael has told them. Memory
requires the sense of interim and the chance to forget; "forgetting is the
true expression for an ideal process of assimilation by which the experience is reduced to a sounding-board for the soul's own music." About
another writer for whom remembrance of things past was crucial, one
critic has said that he "wrote at length in order to create within the frame
of his novel an interval of *oubli*, the forgetting which would allow the
reader a true experience of remembering and recognizing."

HAROLD BLOOM

Milton and His Precursors

No poet compares to Milton in his intensity of self-consciousness as an artist and in his ability to overcome all negative consequences of such concern. Milton's highly deliberate and knowingly ambitious program necessarily involved him in direct competition with Homer, Virgil, Lucretius, Ovid, Dante and Tasso, among other major precursors. More anxiously, it brought him very close to Spenser, whose actual influence on *Paradise Lost* is deeper, subtler and more extensive than scholarship so far has recognized. Most anxiously, the ultimate ambitions of *Paradise Lost* gave Milton the problem of expanding Scripture without distorting the Word of God.

A reader, thinking of Milton's style, is very likely to recognize that style's most distinctive characteristic as being the density of its allusiveness. Perhaps only Gray compares to Milton in this regard, and Gray is only a footnote, though an important and valuable one, to the Miltonic splendor. Milton's allusiveness has a distinct design, which is to enhance both the quality and the extent of his inventiveness. His handling of allusion is his highly individual and original defense against poetic tradition, his revisionary stance in writing what is in effect a tertiary epic, following after Homer in primary epic and Virgil, Ovid, and Dante in secondary epic. Most vitally, Miltonic allusion is the crucial revisionary ratio by which *Paradise Lost* distances itself from its most dangerous precursor, *The Faerie Queene*, for Spenser had achieved a national romance, of epic greatness, in the vernacular, and in the service of moral and theological beliefs not far from Milton's own.

The map of misprision move[s] between the poles of *illusio—*

From *A Map of Misreading*. Copyright © 1975 by Oxford University Press.

irony as a figure of speech, or the reaction-formation I have termed
clinamen—and allusion, particularly as the scheme of transumption or
metaleptic reversal that I have named *apophrades* and analogized to the
defenses of introjection and projection. As the common root of their
names indicates, *illusio* and allusion are curiously related, both being
a kind of mockery, rather in the sense intended by the title of
Geoffrey Hill's poem on Campanella, that "Men are a mockery of Angels." The history of "allusion" as an English word goes from an initial
meaning of "illusion" on to an early Renaissance use as meaning a pun, or
word-play in general. But by the time of Bacon it meant any symbolic
likening, whether in allegory, parable or metaphor, as when in *The
Advancement of Learning* poetry is divided into "Narrative, representative,
and allusive." A fourth meaning, which is still the correct modern one,
follows rapidly by the very early seventeenth century, and involves any
implied, indirect or hidden reference. The fifth meaning, still incorrect
but bound to establish itself, now equates allusion with direct, overt
reference. Since the root meaning is "to play with, mock, jest at,"
allusion is uneasily allied to words like "ludicrous" and "elusion," as we
will remember later.

Thomas McFarland, formidably defending Coleridge against end-
lessly repetitive charges of plagiarism, has suggested that "plagiarism"
ought to be added as a seventh revisionary ratio. Allusion is a comprehensive enough ratio to contain "plagiarism" also under the heading of
apophrades, which the Lurianic Kabbalists called *gilgul*, as I explained
[previously]. Allusion as covert reference became in Milton's control the
most powerful and successful figuration that any strong poet has ever
employed against his strong precursors.

Milton, who would not sunder spirit from matter, would not let
himself be a receiver, object to a subject's influencings. His stance against
dualism and influence alike is related to his exaltation of unfallen *pleasure*,
his appeal not so much to his reader's senses as to his reader's yearning for
the expanded senses of Eden. Precisely here is the center of Milton's own
influence upon the Romantics, and here also is why he surpassed them in
greatness, since what he could do for himself was the cause of their
becoming unable to do the same for themselves. His achievement became
at once their starting point, their inspiration, yet also their goad, their
torment.

Yet he too had his starting point: Spenser. Spenser was "the
soothest shepherd that e'er piped on plains," "sage and serious." "Milton
has acknowledged to me, that Spenser was his original," Dryden testified,
but the paternity required no acknowledgment. A darker acknowledgment

can be read in Milton's astonishing mistake about Spenser in *Areopagitica*, written more than twenty years before *Paradise Lost* was completed:

> . . . It was from out the rind of one apple tasted, that the knowledge of good and evil, as two twins cleaving together, leaped forth into the world. And perhaps this is that doom which Adam fell into of knowing good and evil, that is to say of knowing good by evil. As therefore the state of man is, what wisdom can there be to choose, what continence to forbear, without the knowledge of evil? He that can apprehend and consider vice with all her baits and seeming pleasures, and yet abstain, and yet distinguish, and yet prefer that which is truly better, he is the true warfaring Christian. I cannot praise a fugitive and cloistered virtue, unexercised and unbreathed, that never sallies out and sees her adversary, but slinks out of the race, where that immortal garland is to be run for, not without dust and heat. Assuredly we bring not innocence into the world, we bring impurity much rather; that which purifies us is trial, and trial is by what is contrary. That virtue therefore which is but a youngling in the contemplation of evil, and knows not the utmost that vice promises to her followers, and rejects it, is but a blank virtue, not a pure; her whiteness is but an excremental whiteness; which was the reason why our sage and serious poet Spenser, whom I dare be known to think a better teacher than Scotus or Aquinas, describing true temperance under the person of Guyon, brings him in with his palmer through the cave of Mammon, and the bower of earthly bliss, that he might see and know, and yet abstain. . . .

Spenser's cave of Mammon is Milton's Hell; far more than the descents to the underworld of Homer and Virgil, more even than Dante's vision, the prefigurement of Books I and II of *Paradise Lost* reverberates in Book II of *The Faerie Queene*. Against Acrasia's bower, Guyon enjoys the moral guidance of his unfaltering Palmer, but necessarily in Mammon's cave Guyon has to be wholly on his own, even as Adam and Eve must withstand temptation in the absence of the affable Raphael. Guyon stands, though at some cost; Adam and Eve fall, but both the endurance and the failure are independent. Milton's is no ordinary error, no mere lapse in memory, but is itself a powerful misinterpretation of Spenser, and a strong defense against him. For Guyon is not so much Adam's precursor as he is Milton's own, the giant model imitated by the Abdiel of *Paradise Lost*. Milton re-writes Spenser so as to *increase the distance* between his poetic father and himself. St. Augustine identified memory with the father, and we may surmise that a lapse in a memory as preternatural as Milton's is a movement against the father.

Milton's full relation to Spenser is too complex and hidden for any rapid description or analysis to suffice, even for my limited purposes in this [essay]. Here I will venture that Milton's transumptive stance in regard to all his precursors, including Spenser, is founded on Spenser's resourceful and bewildering (even Joycean) way of subsuming his precursors, particularly Virgil, through his labyrinthine syncretism. Spenserian allusiveness has been described by Angus Fletcher as collage: "Collage is parody drawing attention to the *materials* of art and life." Fletcher follows Harry Berger's description of the technique of *conspicuous allusion* in Spenser: "the depiction of stock literary motifs, characters, and genres in a manner which emphasizes their conventionality, displaying at once their debt to and their existence in a conventional climate—Classical, medieval, romance, etc.—which is archaic when seen from Spenser's retrospective viewpoint." This allusive collage or conspicuousness is readily assimilated to Spenser's peculiarly metamorphic elegiacism, which becomes the particular legacy of Spenser to all his poetic descendants, from Drayton and Milton down to Yeats and Stevens. For Spenser began that internalization of quest-romance that is or became what we call Romanticism. It is the Colin Clout of Spenser's Book VI who is the father of Milton's *Il Penseroso*, and from Milton's visionary stem the later Spenserian transformations of Wordsworth's Solitary, and all of the Solitary's children in the wanderers of Keats, Shelley, Browning, Tennyson and Yeats until the parodistic climax in Stevens' comedian Crispin. Fletcher, in his study of Spenser, *The Prophetic Moment*, charts this genealogy of introspection, stressing the intervention of Shakespeare between Spenser and Milton, since from Shakespeare Milton learned to contain the Spenserian elegiacism or "prophetic strain" within what Fletcher calls "transcendental forms." In his study of *Comus* as such a form, *The Transcendental Masque*, Fletcher emphasizes the "enclosed vastness" in which Milton, like Shakespeare, allows reverberations of the Spenserian resonance, a poetic diction richly dependent on allusive echoings of precursors. *Comus* abounds in *apophrades*, the return of many poets dead and gone, with Spenser and Shakespeare especially prominent among them. Following Berger and Fletcher, I would call the allusiveness of *Comus* still "conspicuous" and so still Spenserian, still part of the principle of echo. But, with *Paradise Lost*, Miltonic allusion is transformed into a mode of transumption, and poetic tradition is radically altered in consequence.

Fletcher, the most daemonic and inventive of modern allegorists, is again the right guide into the mysteries of *transumptive allusion*, through one of the brilliant footnotes in his early book, *Allegory: The Theory of a Symbolic Mode* (p.241, n.33). Studying what he calls "difficult ornament" and the transition to modern allegory, Fletcher meditates on Johnson's ambivalence towards Milton's style. In his *Life of Milton*, Johnson observes that "the heat of Milton's mind might be said to sublimate his learning." Hazlitt, a less ambivalent admirer of Milton, asserted that Milton's learning had the effect of intuition. Johnson, though so much more grudging, actually renders the greater homage, for Johnson's own immense hunger of imagination was overmatched by Milton's, as he recognized:

> Whatever be his subject, he never fails to fill the imagination. But his images and descriptions of the scenes or operations of Nature do not seem to be always copied from original form, nor to have the freshness, raciness, and energy of immediate observation. He saw Nature, as Dryden expresses it, *through the spectacles of books*; and on most occasions calls learning to his assistance. . . .
> . . . But he does not confine himself within the limits of rigorous comparison: his great excellence is amplitude, and he expands the adventitious image beyond the dimensions which the occasion required. Thus, comparing the shield of Satan to the orb of the Moon, he crowds the imagination with the discovery of the telescope, and all the wonders which the telescope discovers.

This Johnsonian emphasis upon allusion in Milton inspires Fletcher to compare Miltonic allusion to the trope of transumption or metalepsis, Puttenham's "far-fetcher":

> Johnson stresses allusion in Milton: "the spectacles of books" are a means of sublimity, since at every point the reader is led from one scene to an allusive second scene, to a third, and so on. Johnson's Milton has, we might say, a "transumptive" style. . . .

Here is the passage that moved Johnson's observation, *Paradise Lost*, Book I, 283–313. Beelzebub has urged Satan to address his fallen legions, who still lie "astounded and amazed" on the lake of fire:

> He scarce had ceas't when the superior Fiend
> Was moving toward the shore; his ponderous shield
> Ethereal temper, massy, large and round,
> Behind him cast; the broad circumference
> Hung on his shoulders like the Moon, whose Orb
> Through Optic Glass the *Tuscan* Artist views
> At Ev'ning from the top of *Fesole*,
> Or in *Valdarno*, to descry new Lands,
> Rivers or Mountains in her spotty Globe.
> His Spear, to equal which the tallest Pine
> Hewn on *Norwegian* hills, to be the Mast
> Of some great Ammiral, were but a wand,
> He walkt with to support uneasy steps
> Over the burning Marl, not like those steps
> On Heaven's Azure, and the torrid Clime

Smote on him sore besides, vaulted with Fire;
Nathless he so endur'd, till on the Beach
Of that inflamed Sea, he stood and call'd
His Legions, Angel Forms, who lay intrans't
Thick as Autumnal Leaves that strow the Brooks
In *Vallembrosa*, where th' *Etrurian* shades
High overarch't imbow'r; or scatter'd sedge
Afloat, when with fierce Winds *Orion* arm'd
Hath vext the Red-Sea Coast, whose waves o'erthrew
Busiris and his *Memphian* Chivalry,
While with perfidious hatred they pursu'd
The Sojourners of *Goshen*, who beheld
From the safe shore thir floating Carcasses
And broken Chariot Wheels, so thick bestrown
Abject and lost lay these, covering the Flood,
Under amazement of thir hideous change.

The transumption of the precursors here is managed by the juxta-position between the far-fetching of Homer, Virgil, Ovid, Dante, Tasso, Spenser, the Bible and the single near-contemporary reference to Galileo, "the Tuscan artist," and his telescope. Milton's aim is to make his own belatedness into an earliness, and his tradition's priority over him into a lateness. The critical question to be asked of this passage is: why is Johnson's "adventitious image," Galileo and the telescope, present at all? Johnson, despite his judgment that the image is extrinsic, implies the right answer: because the expansion of this apparently extrinsic image crowds the reader's imagination, by giving Milton the true priority of *interpretation*, the powerful reading that insists upon its own uniqueness and its own accuracy. Troping upon his forerunners' tropes, Milton com-pels us to read as he reads, and to accept his stance and vision as our origin, his time as true time. His allusiveness introjects the past, and projects the future, but at the paradoxical cost of the present, which is not voided but is yielded up to an experiential darkness, as we will see, to a mingling of wonder (discovery) and woe (the fallen Church's imprison-ment of the discoverer). As Frank Kermode remarks, *Paradise Lost* is a wholly contemporary poem, yet surely its sense of the present is necessar-ily more of loss than of delight.

Milton's giant simile comparing Satan's shield to the moon alludes to the shield of Achilles in the *Iliad*, XIX, 373–80:

. . . and caught up the great shield, huge and heavy next, and from it
the light glimmered far, as from the moon.
And as when from across water a light shines to mariners from a blazing
fire, when the fire is burning high in the mountains in a desolate

standing, as the mariners are carried unwilling by storm winds over the
fish awarming sea, far away from their loved ones,
so the light from the fair elaborate shield of Achilleus shot into the high
air.

(Lattimore version)

Milton is glancing also at the shield of Radigund in *The Faerie
Queene*, V, v, 3:

> And on her shoulder hung her shield, bedeckt
> Upon the bosse with stones, that shined wide,
> As the faire Moone in her most full aspect,
> That to the Moone it mote be like in each respect.

Radigund, Princess of the Amazons, is dominated by pride and
anger, like Achilles. Satan, excelling both in his bad eminence, is seen
accurately through the optic glass of the British artist's transumptive
vision, even as Galileo sees what no one before him has seen on the
moon's surface. Galileo, when visited by Milton (as he tells us in
Areopagitica), was working while under house arrest by the Inquisition, a
condition not wholly unlike Milton's own in the early days of the Restoration. Homer and Spenser emphasize the moonlike brightness and shining
of the shields of Achilles and Radigund; Milton emphasizes size, shape,
weight as the common feature of Satan's shield and the moon, for
Milton's post-Galilean moon is more of a world and less of a light. Milton
and Galileo are *late*, yet they see more, and more significantly, than
Homer and Spenser, who were *early*. Milton gives his readers the light,
yet also the true dimensions and features of reality, even though Milton,
like the Tuscan artist, must work on while compassed around by experiential darkness, in a world of woe.

Milton will not stop with his true vision of Satan's shield, but
transumes his precursors also in regard to Satan's spear, and to the
fallen-leaves aspect of the Satanic host. Satan's spear evokes passages of
Homer, Virgil, Ovid, Tasso and Spenser, allusions transumed by the
contemporary reference to a flagship ("ammiral") with its mast made of
Norwegian fir. The central allusion is probably to Ovid's vision of the
Golden Age (Golding's version, I, 109–16):

> The loftie Pyntree was not hewen from mountaines where it stood,
> In seeking straunge and forren landes to rove upon the flood.
> Men knew none other countries yet, than where themselves did keepe:
> There was no towne enclosed yet, with walles and ditches deepe:
> No horne nor trumpet was in use, no sword nor helmet worne.
> The worlde was suche, that souldiers helpe might easily be forborne.

The fertile earth as yet was free, untoucht of spade or plough,
And yet it yeelded of it selfe of every things inough.

Ovid's emblem of the passage from Golden Age to Iron Age is reduced to "but a wand," for Satan will more truly cause the fall from Golden to Iron. As earlier Satan subsumed Achilles and Radigund, now he contains and metaleptically reverses the Polyphemus of Homer and of Virgil, the Tancredi and Argantes of Tasso, and the proud giant Orgoglio of Spenser:

> a club, or staff, lay there along the fold—
> an olive tree, felled green and left to season
> for Kyklops' hand. And it was like a mast
> a lugger of twenty oars, broad in the beam—
> a deep-sea-going craft—might carry:
> so long, so big around, it seemed.
> (Odyssey, IX, 322–27, Fitzgerald version)

> . . . we saw
> upon a peak the shepherd Polyphemus;
> he lugged his mammoth hulk among the flocks,
> searching along familiar shores—an awful
> misshapen monster, huge, his eyelight lost.
> His steps are steadied by the lopped-off pine
> he grips. . . .
> (Aeneid, III, 660–66; Mandelbaum version,
> 849–55)

These sons of Mavors bore, instead of spears,
    Two knotty masts, which none but they could lift;
Each foaming steed so fast his master bears,
    That never beast, bird, shaft, flew half so swift:
Such was their fury, as when Boreas tears
    The shatter'd crags from Taurus' northern clift:
Upon their helms their lances long they brake,
And up to heav'n flew splinters, sparks, and smoke.
    (Jerusalem Delivered, VI, 40, Fairfax version)

So growen great through arrogant delight
    Of th'high descent, whereof he was yborne,
    And through presumption of his matchlesse might,
    All other powres and knighthood he did scorne.
    Such now he marcheth to this man forlorne,
    And left to losse: his stalking steps are stayde
    Upon a snaggy Oke, which he had torne
    Out of his mothers bowelles, and it made
His mortall mace, wherewith his foemen he dismayde.
    (Faerie Queene, I, vii, x)

The Wild Men, Polyphemus the Cyclops and the crudely proud Orgoglio, as well as the Catholic and Circassian champions, Tancredi and Argantes, all become late and lesser versions of Milton's earlier and greater Satan. The tree and the mast become interchangeable with the club, and all three become emblematic of the brutality of Satan as the Antichrist, the fallen son of God who walks in the darkness of his vainglory and perverts nature to the ends of war-by-sea and war-by-land, Job's Leviathan and Behemoth. Milton's present age is again an experiential darkness—of naval warfare—but his backward glance to Satanic origins reveals the full truth of which Homer, Virgil, Tasso give only incomplete reflections. Whether the transumption truly overcomes Spenser's Orgoglio is more dubious, for he remains nearly as Satanic as Milton's Satan, except that Satan is more complex and poignant, being a son of heaven and not, like the gross Orgoglio, a child of earth.

The third transumption of the passage, the fiction of the leaves, is surely the subtlest, and the one most worthy of Milton's greatness. He tropes here on the tropes of Isaiah, Homer, Virgil and Dante, and with the Orion allusion on Job and Virgil. The series is capped by the references to Exodus and Ovid, with the equation of Busiris and Satan. This movement from fallen leaves to starry influence over storms to the overwhelming of a tyrannous host is itself a kind of transumption, as Milton moves from metonymy to metonymy before accomplishing a final reduction.

Satan's fallen hosts, poignantly still called "angel forms," most directly allude to a prophetic outcry of Isaiah 34:4:

> And all the host of heaven shall be dissolved, and the heavens shall be rolled together as a scroll; and all their host shall fall down, as the leaf falleth off from the vine, and as a falling fig from the fig tree.

Milton is too wary to mark this for transumption; his trope works upon a series of Homer, Virgil, Dante:

> . . . why ask of my generation?
> As is the generation of leaves, so is that of humanity.
> The wind scatters the leaves on the ground, but the fine timber
> burgeons with leaves again in the season of spring returning.
> So one generation of men will grow while another dies. . . .
> (*Iliad*, VI, 145–50, Lattimore version)

> thick as the leaves that with the early frost
> of autumn drop and fall within the forest,
> or as the birds that flock along the beaches,
> in flight from frenzied seas when the chill season
> drives them across the waves to lands of sun.

> They stand; each pleads to be the first to cross
> the stream; their hands reach out in longing for
> the farther shore. But Charon, sullen boatman,
> now takes these souls, now those; the rest he leaves;
> thrusting them back, he keeps them from the beach.
> (*Aeneid*, VI, 310–19; Mandelbaum version,
>   407–16)

. . . But those forlorn and naked souls changed color, their teeth chat-
tering, as soon as they heard the cruel words. They cursed God, their
parents, the human race, the place, the time, the seed of their begetting
and of their birth. Then, weeping loudly, all drew to the evil shore that
awaits every man who fears not God. The demon Charon, his eyes like
glowing coals, beckons to them and collects them all, beating with
his oar whoever lingers.

As the leaves fall away in autumn, one after another, till the
bough sees all its spoils upon the ground, so there the evil seed
of Adam: one by one they cast themselves from that shore at signals,
like a bird at its call. Thus they go over the dark water, and before
they have landed on the other shore, on this side a new throng
gathers.

> (*Inferno*, III, 100–120, Singleton version)

Homer accepts grim process; Virgil accepts yet plangently laments,
with his unforgettable vision of those who stretch forth their hands out of
love for the farther shore. Dante, lovingly close to Virgil, is more terrible,
since his leaves fall even as the evil seed of Adam falls. Milton remembers
standing, younger and then able to see, in the woods at Vallombrosa,
watching the autumn leaves strew the brooks. His characteristic metonymy of shades for woods allusively puns on Virgil's and Dante's images of
the shades gathering for Charon, and by a metalepsis carries across Dante
and Virgil to their tragic Homeric origin. Once again, the precursors are
projected into belatedness, as Milton introjects the prophetic source of
Isaiah. Leaves fall from trees, generations of men die, because once
one-third of the heavenly host came falling down. Milton's present time
again is experiential loss; he watches no more autumns, but the optic glass
of his art sees fully what his precursors saw only darkly, or in the vegetable
glass of nature.

By a transition to the "scattered sedge" of the Red Sea, Milton
calls up Virgil again, compounding two passages on Orion:

> Our prows were pointed there when suddenly,
> rising upon the surge, stormy Orion
> drove us against blind shoals. . . .
> (*Aeneid*, I, 534–36; Mandelbaum version,
>   753–55)

> . . . he marks Arcturus,
> the twin Bears and the rainy Hyades,
> Orion armed with gold; and seeing all
> together in the tranquil heavens, loudly
> he signals. . . .
> (*Aeneid*, III, 517–21; Mandelbaum
> version, 674–78)

Alastair Fowler notes the contrast to the parallel Biblical allusions:

> He is wise in heart, and mighty in strength: who hath hardened himself
> against him, and hath prospered?
> . . . Which alone spreadeth out the heavens, and treadeth upon the waves
> of the sea.
> Which maketh Arcturus, Orion, and Pleiades, and the chambers of
> the south.
> (Job 9:4, 8–9)

> Seek him that maketh the seven stars and Orion, and turneth the
> shadow of death into the morning, and maketh the day dark with night:
> that calleth for the waters of the sea, and poureth them out upon the
> face of the earth: The LORD is his name. . . .
> (Amos 5:8)

In Virgil, Orion rising marks the seasonal onset of storms. In the
Bible, Orion and all the stars are put into place as a mere sign-system,
demoted from their pagan status as powers. Milton says "hath vexed" to
indicate that the sign-system continues in his own day, but he says
"o'erthrew" to show that the Satanic stars and the hosts of Busiris the
Pharaoh fell once for all, Pharaoh being a type of Satan. Virgil, still
caught in a vision that held Orion as a potency, is himself again transumed
into a sign of error.

I have worked through this passage's allusions in some detail so as
to provide one full instance of a transumptive scheme in *Paradise Lost*.
Johnson's insight is validated, for the "adventitious image" of the optic
glass is shown to be not extrinsic at all, but rather to be the device that
"crowds the imagination," compressing or hastening much transumption
into a little space. By arranging his precursors in series, Milton figuratively
reverses his obligation to them, for his stationing crowds them between
the visionary truth of his poem (carefully aligned with Biblical truth) and
his darkened present (which he shares with Galileo). Transumption mur-
ders time, for by troping on a trope, you enforce a state of rhetoricity or
word-consciousness, and you negate fallen history. Milton does what
Bacon hoped to do; Milton and Galileo become ancients, and Homer,
Virgil, Ovid, Dante, Tasso, Spenser become belated moderns. The cost is
a loss in the immediacy of the living moment. Milton's meaning is

remarkably freed of the burden of anteriority, but only because Milton himself is already one with the future, which he introjects.

It would occupy too many pages to demonstrate another of Milton's transumptive schemes in its largest and therefore most powerful dimensions, but I will outline one, summarizing rather than quoting the text and citing rather than giving the allusions. My motive is not only to show that the "optic glass" passage is hardly unique in its arrangement, but to analyze more thoroughly Milton's self-awareness of both his war against influence and his use of rhetoricity as a defense. Of many possibilities, Book I, lines 670–798, seems to me the best, for this concluding movement of the epic's initial book has as its hidden subject both the anxiety of influence and an anxiety of morality about the secondariness of any poetic creation, even Milton's own. The passage describes the sudden building, out of the deep, of Pandaemonium, the palace of Satan, and ends with the infernal peers sitting there in council.

This sequence works to transume the crucial precursors again—Homer, Virgil, Ovid and Spenser—but there are triumphant allusions here to Lucretius and Shakespeare also (as Fowler notes). In some sense, the extraordinary and reverberating power of the Pandaemonium masque (as John Hollander terms it, likening it to transformation scenes in court masques) depends on its being a continuous and unified allusion to the very idea of poetic tradition, and to the moral problematic of that idea. Metalepsis or transumption can be described as an extended trope with a missing or weakened middle, and for Milton literary tradition is such a trope. The illusionistic sets and complex machinery of the masque transformation scene are emblematic, in the Pandaemonium sequence, of the self-deceptions and morally misleading machinery of epic and tragic convention.

Cunningly, Milton starts the sequence with a transumption to the fallen near-present, evoking the royal army in the Civil War as precise analogue to the Satanic army. Mammon leads on the advance party, in an opening allusion to Spenser's Cave of Mammon canto, since both Mammons direct gold-mining operations. With the next major allusion, to the same passage in Ovid's *Metamorphoses* I that was evoked in the Galileo sequence, Milton probes the morality of art:

> Let none admire
> That riches grow in Hell; that soil may best
> Deserve the precious bane. And here let those
> Who boast in mortal things, and wond'ring tell
> Of *Babel*, and the works of *Memphian* Kings,
> Learn how thir greatest Monuments of Fame,

> And Strength and Art are easily outdone
> By Spirits reprobate, and in an hour
> What in an age they with incessant toil
> And hands innumerable scarce perform.

Milton presumably would not have termed the *Iliad* or the *Aeneid* "precious bane," yet the force of his condemnation extends to them, and his anxiety necessarily touches his own poem as well. Pandaemonium rises in baroque splendor, with a backward allusion to Ovid's Palace of the Sun, also designed by Mulciber (*Metamorphoses* II, 1–4), and with a near-contemporary allusion to St. Peter's at Rome and, according to Fowler, to Bernini's colonnade in the piazza of St. Peter's. Mulciber, archetype not only of Bernini but more darkly of all artists, including epic poets, becomes the center of the sequence:

> Men call'd him *Mulciber*; and how he fell
> From Heav'n, they fabl'd, thrown by angry *Jove*
> Sheer o'er the Crystal Battlements: from Morn
> To Noon he fell, from Noon to dewy Eve,
> A Summer's day; and with the setting Sun
> Dropt from the Zenith like a falling Star,
> On *Lemnos* th' *Ægæan* Isle: thus they relate,
> Erring; for he with this rebellious rout
> Fell long before; nor aught avail'd him now
> To have built in Heav'n high Towrs; nor did he scape
> By all his Engines, but was headlong sent
> With is industrious crew to build in hell.

The devastating "Erring" of line 747 is a smack at Homer by way of the *errat* of Lucretius (*De rerum natura*, I, 393, as Fowler notes). The contrast with Homer's passage illuminates the transumptive function of Milton's allusiveness, for Homer's Hephaistos (whose Latin name was Vulcan or Mulciber) gently fables his own downfall:

> . . . It is too hard to fight against the Olympian.
> There was a time once before now I was minded to help you, and he caught
> me by the foot and threw me from the magic threshold,
> and all day long I dropped helpless, and about sunset
> I landed in Lemnos. . . .
>
> (*Iliad*, I, 589–93, Lattimore version)

Milton first mocks Homer by over-accentuating the idyllic nature of this fall, and then reverses Homer completely. In the dark present, Mulciber's work is still done when the bad eminence of baroque glory is turned to the purposes of a fallen Church. So, at line 756, Pandaemonium is called "the high capital" of Satan, alluding to two lines of Virgil

(*Aeneid*, VI, 836 and VIII, 348), but the allusion is qualified by the complex simile of the bees that continues throughout lines 768–75, and which relies on further allusions to *Iliad*, II, 87–90 and *Aeneid*, 430–36, where Achaian and Carthaginian heroes respectively are compared to bees. One of the most remarkable of Milton's transumptive returns to present time is then accomplished by an allusion to Shakespeare's *Midsummer Night's Dream*, II, i, 28ff. A "belated peasant" beholds the "Faery Elves" even as we, Milton's readers, see the giant demons shrink in size. Yet *our* belatedness is again redressed by metaleptic reversal, with an allusion to *Aeneid*, VI, 451–54, where Aeneas recognizes Dido's "dim shape among the shadows (just as one who either sees or thinks he sees . . . the moon rising)." So the belated peasant "sees, or dreams he sees" the elves, but like Milton we *know* we see the fallen angels metamorphosed from giants into pygmies. The Pandaemonium sequence ends with the great conclave of "a thousand demi-gods on golden seats," in clear parody of ecclesiastical assemblies re-convened after the Restoration. As with the opening reference to the advance-party of the royal army, the present is seen as fallen on evil days, but it provides vantage for Milton's enduring vision.

So prevalent throughout the poem is this scheme of allusion that any possibility of inadvertence can be ruled out. Milton's design is wholly definite, and its effect is to reverse literary tradition, at the expense of the presentness of the present. The precursors return in Milton, but only at his will, and they return to be corrected. Perhaps only Shakespeare can be judged Milton's rival in allusive triumph over tradition, yet Shakespeare had no Spenser to subsume, but only a Marlowe, and Shakespeare is less clearly in overt competition with Aeschylus, Sophocles, Euripides than Milton is with Homer, Virgil, Ovid, Dante, Tasso.

Hobbes, in his *Answer to Davenant's Preface* (1650), had subordinated wit to judgment, and so implied also that rhetoric was subordinate to dialectic:

> From knowing much, proceedeth the admirable variety and novelty of metaphors and similitudes, which are not possibly to be lighted on in the compass of a narrow knowledge. And the want whereof compelleth a writer to expressions that are either defaced by time or sullied with vulgar or long use. For the phrases of poesy, as the airs of music, with often hearing become insipid; the reader having no more sense of their force, than our flesh is sensible of the bones that sustain it. As the sense we have of bodies, consisteth in change and variety of impression, so also does the sense of language in the variety and changeable use of words. I mean not in the affectation of words newly brought home from travel,

but in new (and withal, significant) translation to our purposes, of those that be already received, and in far fetched (but withal, apt, instructive, and comely) similitudes. . . .

Had Milton deliberately accepted this as challenge, he could have done no more both to fulfill and to refute Hobbes than *Paradise Lost* already does. What Davenant and Cowley could not manage was a complete translation to their own purposes of received rhetoric; but Milton raised such translation to sublimity. In doing so, he also raised rhetoric over dialectic, *contra* Hobbes, for his farfetchedness (Puttenham's term for transumption) gave similitudes the status and function of complex arguments. Milton's wit, his control of rhetoric, was again the exercise of the mind through all her powers, and not a lower faculty subordinate to judgment. Had Hobbes written his *Answer* twenty years later, and after reading *Paradise Lost*, he might have been less confident of the authority of philosophy over poetry.

MARY ANN RADZINOWICZ

"Samson Agonistes": The Divided Mind

A strong emphasis upon outward stillness and inward movement is created by Milton's disposition of events. Blindness and fetters render Samson motionless once he has dismissed his silent guide, as immobile as Prometheus chained to the rock. He lies "with languish't head unprop't" (Act I); he leans "in low dejected state" (Act II); assailed by unseen visitors, he cannot move away and must ask the Chorus to prevent too close approach, "let [Dalila] not come near me" Act III); with his "heels . . . fetter'd" he is a fixed and stationary figure whose "manacles remark him, there he sits" (Act IV). Only at the climax, when he becomes aware of "rouzing motions," is Samson enabled to stand, to move, to act. Throughout the morning of the popular feast day which has been called so that Dagon may be magnified "as their God who hath deliver'd . . . Samson bound and blind into thir hands," the protagonist-agonist is absolutely still. His self-contempt finds expression precisely in this state: the vilest worm may creep, but he himself is still as a fool in the power of others. He cannot make even the simplest choice of moving or not moving. But while outwardly still, Samson is inwardly restless, assailed by a swarm of disturbing thoughts, thoughts his tormentors armed with deadly stings. His agony is internal but generates a great energy: within himself he struggles with weakness, despair, guilt, pride, self-hatred, and violence. So strong are these interior demons that Samson believes they are only to be buried when he is buried; forsaken by

From *Toward Samson Agonistes: The Growth of Milton's Mind.* Copyright © 1978 by Princeton University Press.

sleep, Samson sees his only cure in death's benumbing opium. He is locked in a self which both feels like a sepulcher and seethes with intellectual pain. His condition is that of hell: enchained, encased in sightless silence, confined to a single bank, enclosed in the dark dungeon of a body, assaulted by numberless inward griefs.

The action of *Samson Agonistes* is composed of encounters which, as debates, are metaphors or metonymies for serious inward change. The Chorus does not speak in interludes which divide sections of the action, it takes full part in the dialogue. The tragedy is stripped of spectacle. The only visual effect from movement available to the mind's eye lies in the approaches of the Chorus, their advance toward Samson and their accompaniment of the other limited number of characters a short distance away from him. They themselves describe the contrast between immobility and movement when they begin the fifth episode by saying:

> This Idols day hath bin to thee no day of rest,
>   Labouring thy mind
> More then the working day thy hands. . . .
>   (1297–99)

The impression which the overall disposition of the fable gives of having been devised to draw attention to an intellectual conflict within the mind of the protagonist, reflected outwardly in a series of disputations, is at once confirmed by the disposition within each of the smaller units of composition. The prologue simultaneously declares its difference from a hypothetical "average Greek tragedy" and its intentional classical form. Taken as a whole, the prologue is very long, constructed as a soliloquy, and spoken by the protagonist. Among the thirty-two extant Greek tragedies upon which Milton could model his prologue, the longest prologues appear in Euripides. Milton's is nearly double their average length. Nearly half begin with a soliloquy fulfilling an expository function, but such opening soliloquies are usually assigned to a neutral minor witnessing character. In no play of Aeschylus or Sophocles is the prologue spoken by the protagonist; in those plays of Euripides commencing with a soliloquy by the protagonist, the speech is a brief recital of antecedent events. Again, the protagonist opens a certain number of Greek tragedies—two Aeschylean, three Sophoclean, three Euripidean—but in these the practice is for the exposition to be communicated by dialogue. Milton's prologue therefore feels very Greek without being very Greek, conspicuously differing by its inwardness, intellectuality, and personal struggle. The prologue is immediately followed by a parode which is also contructed as a long soliloquy, balancing and echoing the material of the prologue.

Each assumes the internal form of debate; placed in juxtaposition, they play off their internal debates as an implicit dialogue which becomes explicit in the first episode.

All Milton's opening adaptations and variations are designed to achieve dialectic. It has often been remarked that *Samson Agonistes* is comparatively free of stichomythia, free not only in comparison with Greek practice but also in comparison with Milton's own practice in *Comus*. William Riley Parker conjectured that stichomythia is omitted because *Samson Agonistes* was not intended for the stage, "thrust and parry in bright monostich" being an obvious stage device. That may well be so, but it is also true that "thrust and parry" is an instrument of debate only between fixed and preestablished positions; it is not an instrument of intellectual discovery.

The internal structure of the prologue again confirms the suggestion of its overall design. The prologue is composed of well-articulated units functional to the exposition before the action commences, that is, functional in presenting the circumstances of time, place, occasion, state of mind, antecedent action, and the like. It is also intensely grieved and grieving: the amount of remorse it conveys and of intense sorrow binds the prologue so painfully into a unity that to separate it into its composite parts seems insensitive. But dissection is necessary in order to show the smaller structures through which Milton stimulates thought. At the center of the prologue is a strongly marked contrast between "Times past, what once I was, and what am now," introduced by two suspended sentences, each of eleven lines, the first hortatory and the second declarative. The opening sentence is addressed to the unnamed silent guiding hand which conducts Samson to the bank with choice of sun or shade before the prison, the quiet bank to which Samson withdraws from popular noise whenever he can. That apparently hortatory sentence nonetheless has the force of prayer. Behind its "lead me" and "leave me" echoes the prayer of the Psalmist: "Judge me, O God, and plead my cause against an ungodly nation; O deliver me from the deceitful and unjust man. / For thou art the God of my strength; why dost thou cast me off? Why go I mourning because of the oppression of the enemy? / O send out thy light and thy truth: let them lead me" (Psalm 43). Behind its "breath of Heav'n . . . with day-spring born" echoes the prophetic benediction of Zacharia: "the dayspring from on high has visited us, to give light to them that sit in darkness and in the shadow of death, to guide our feet into the way of peace." Samson's sense of how shamefully much he needs the help of a hand and how hopelessly far he must travel to emerge from darkness is conveyed, together with all the necessary circumambient conditions of the tragedy. The next, exactly symmetrical declarative sentence begins as though Samson had continued speaking to his outward guide, but in withdrawing from "the popular noise" to "this unfrequented place," the sentence modulates into solitude. It declares *I seek ease to the body and find none to the mind*, the reason being the ceaseless torture of contrasting "what once I was, and what am now."

The main body of the following soliloquy, spoken before Samson becomes aware of being no longer alone, is exactly divided into two sections of forty-three and a half lines each, the first looking back at the past, the second lamenting the present. Samson begins as if speaking to himself were a matter of one stable ego alone in self-communion expressed through simple monologue. But the sentence patterns through which the meditation on the past is rendered are not at all patterns with the force of *I tell myself what I know of myself as an integral person*. Two questions ("O wherefore was my birth . . . foretold" and "Why was my breeding order'd"), followed by an exclamation ("O glorious strength") and two imperatives ("Ask for this great Deliverer" and "Yet stay"), lead to a further question ("Whom have I to complain of"), an exclamation ("O impotence of mind"), a question and its answer ("But what is strength" and "God . . . hung it in my Hair"), followed by a final imperative ("But peace"). The last is a command so impossible to obey that in the middle of a line the imperative loses all force and drains into lament ("Would ask a life to wail"). These sentence patterns reveal a human being split within himself into several orders of being, a divided self, one aspect of whom proposes inflexible codes of behavior to the other. Both selves are present as subjects: "if I must die" are the words of a self-solicitous subject; "I must not quarrel" is the comment of a self-denying subject. But the tortured lament also carries a sense of self as object as well as subject:

> Promise was that *I*
> Should *Israel* from *Philistian* yoke deliver;
> Ask for *this* great Deliverer now, and find *him*
> Eyeless in *Gaza* at the Mill with slaves,
> *Himself* in bonds under *Philistian* yoke.
> (38–42; emphasis added)

Samson in conflict with himself experiences stress arising from external circumstances, stress from other persons' expectations and judgments impinging upon him, stress from the privately acknowledged contradictions in his own impulses toward duty and comfort. In experiencing the torments of his divided self, he tries to protect his vulnerable core by playing off his private self against a public self and by assuming an external role in public life, the role of laboring fallen hero. Heavy stress upon the contrasting *I* and *him* at the line ends gives the whole game away: Samson protects his innermost "I" by using it to condemn and even to taunt the failed Samson, "him." Within Samson is played an inner drama in which "I" mocks and disowns "him." Until he reintegrates the divisions in his own soul, Samson will be the objective, tormented fallen hero who reveals a split subjective self, half contemptuously rigorous and half remorsefully self-pitying, and he will be unable to act.

Samson's survey of his present griefs, contained in the next forty-three and a half lines, involves an integration resembling a total withdrawal, but that integration is one which must be put aside. It is subsumed formally under Samson's command to himself to be just to his God, who "Happ'ly had ends above my reach to know," but it swells into a terrible lyric of the grieved "I" expressing its full grief in a way which if it does not call the justice of God into doubt, certainly questions His mercy and goodness. Structured about five apostrophizing O's, it is powerfully reminiscent of Adam's nightlong struggle to justify God's treatment of him, in Book X of *Paradise Lost*. Samson's "O loss of sight," "O worse then chains," "O dark, dark, dark," "O first created Beam," "O yet more miserable" are like Adam's "O miserable of happie," "O voice once heard," "O fleeting joyes," "O welcom hour [of death]," "O thought horrid, if true"—but with the terrible addition that Samson's tolling strokes of despair in this long lamentation identify light and sight with life, and he is dark and blind with death. Yet once again, significantly breaking across the repeated exclamations, come two questions: "Why am I . . . bereav'd" of light and "Why was the sight to . . . th' eye confin'd." The questions are not *why did I* and *now how can I*, questions calling for self-analysis and resolution; they are questions of God's benevolence. They reverse the prayerful quality of the opening sentence of the soliloquy by standing on its head the moral lesson which the Church habitually drew from Samson's blindness. The order of readings for 13 April set as the first lesson the story of Samson from Judges and as the second lesson a passage from Luke which reads in part, "The light of the body is the eye: therefore when thine eye is single, thy whole body is also full of light; but when thine eye is evil, thy body also is full of darkness. Take heed therefore that the light that is in thee be not darkness." The physician Luke denied that sight is confined by God to the easily crushed eyeball, and he specifically affirmed that sight or the light of life *is* diffused in every part. To reverse Luke's assurance is to draw Samson's lament down to the lowest depths. Samson is dark with faithlessness; his loss of faith arises from his loss of sight, just as his loss of sight arose from his loss of faith. His lament is not only devoid of the sublimation Milton himself drew upon for courage in his own personal lyric lament at blindness, it contradicts it. Milton's description of his own case opens Book III of *Paradise Lost*:

> Thus with the Year
> Seasons return, but not to me returns
> Day, or the sweet approach of Ev'n or Morn,
> Or sight of vernal bloom, or Summers Rose,
> Or flocks, or herds, or human face divine;
> But cloud in stead, and ever-during dark
> Surrounds me, from the chearful waies of men
> Cut off, and for the Book of knowledg fair
> Presented with a Universal blanc
> Of Natures works to mee expung'd and ras'd,
> And wisdom at one entrance quite shut out.
> So much the rather thou Celestial light
> Shine inward, and the mind through all her powers
> Irradiate, there plant eyes, all mist from thence
> Purge and disperse, that I may see and tell
> Of things invisible to mortal sight.
>
> (III, 40–55)

Here Milton sublimates his loss of sight through the consideration that God may give to the blind a compensatory vision with the inner eye. Milton had been able, although imperfectly and perhaps intermittently, to free himself from an inherited system of harsh theology and could conceive of a relationship with God different from that of taskmaster-servant and nearer that of physician-patient, teacher-pupil, poet-audience. God had not blinded him as punishment, he himself had chosen blindness in fighting for the cause of liberty; God had not deserted him. The severest pain in Samson's lyric lament comes from his shocked and shocking conviction that God has "expos'd," "bereav'd," and "exil'd" him, has left him for dead: "My self, my Sepulcher, a moving Grave."

The last five lines of the prologue signal the speechless approach of the Chorus and underline the fearfulness with which the divided self must receive their advance upon his public personality. Samson's person will be insultingly stared at by enemies, while he remorsefully grieves at the death of his will and faith, tortured by the peremptory commands of the harsh authoritarian who shares his ego. Such an understanding of Samson's psychology is not something which a modern reader retrospectively reads into Milton's lines; it was present in scriptural models upon which Milton drew, present in the sense of loss and dread of the Psalmist— "why hast thou forsaken me. . . . But I am a worm, and no man; a

reproach of men, and despised of the people. All they that see me laugh
me to scorn. . . . They look and stare upon me" (Psalm 22)—and in the
sense of isolation, anxiety, and uneasiness of Job—"That which I am
afraid of cometh unto me. I am not at ease, neither am I quiet, neither
have I rest; but trouble cometh." The internal symmetries in the prologue
bring together such discordant forms of apprehension. Taken as a whole,
they achieve a portrait of a tragic hero who makes this kind of statement:
*I am alone. I am trying to understand how I came to the fallen state I occupy in
spite of all I was meant to be. But I cannot persist in these thoughts because my
grief is so great; it appears to me that I was meant to fail.* The structure
imitates a mind turning against itself and against God.

To focus, finally, on even smaller units of composition within the
parts of the prologue is to discover that Milton's style and his choice of
syntax, figures, and rhetorical devices also all tend to promote the impression of thought, internal intellectual struggle, and self-divided debate.
Milton has disposed line after line in such a way as to imitate active
thought. Apparently, only if Samson were actually to have said to himself
in soliloquy *in the first place, in the second place, on the other hand, ergo,
hence, therefore,* and *Q.E.D.*, could some readers consent to recognize his
intellectual activity. Milton, however, gave him in diction, construction,
and variety of ornamentation everything short of that. The diction of
Samson Agonistes marks the poem as dominantly plain in style. As in
Paradise Regained, Milton rejected "swelling Epithetes thick laid / As
varnish on a Harlots cheek." In the passage in *Of Education* recommend-
ing the study of poetics, Milton commends also the organic arts of logic
and rhetoric, of which rhetoric can "enable men to discourse and write
perspicuously, elegantly and according to the fittest style of lofty, mean,
or lowely." The distinction into three levels of style was a commonplace
of the period. According to Renaissance theorists, a poet would make his
choice of style according to a rigid application of the principles of decorum: tragedies *a priori* would demand the lofty style, for the speaker would
concern himself with "the noble gest and great fortunes of Princes and the
notable accidents of time. . . ." "All hymnes and histories and Tragedies
were written in the high stile," George Puttenham would write. Of course
there were some Renaissance theorists unwilling to tie themselves too
rigidly to divisions along these lines. Thus Roger Ascham stated, "The
trew difference of Authors is best knowne *per diuersa genera dicendi* that
euerie one used. And therefore here I will deuide *genus dicendi* not into
these three, *tenue, mediocre, et grande,* but as the matter of euri Author
requireth, as in *Genus: Poeticum, Historicum, Philosophicum, Oratorium.*"
Milton's rejection of the rigidity of earlier theories freed him to consider

the most appropriate style for tragedy to be that most imitative of discourse. In *Paradise Regained* Milton wrote of

> what lofty grave Tragoedians taught
> In *Chorus* or *Iambic*, teachers best
> Of moral prudence, with delight receiv'd
> In brief sententious precepts. . . .

The reference to "Iambic" suggests that Milton adopted Aristotle's view of tragedy as employing iambics, since they imitate conversation most aptly. Again, verisimilitude is the stylistic principle that takes precedence over decorum.

This is not to say that Milton's style does not conform to the recommendations of Aristotle, Horace, Tasso, and Castelvetro, for in the most general terms it does. But its dominant qualities arise not from careful reliance upon classical authorities—Parker could find few impressive verbal echoes in the play—but from experimental freedom. In general terms the style answers to Aristotle's recommendations. The diction is clear and not pedestrian; since it imitates speech, it uses those words most natural to conversation ("here I feel amends"; "here leave me to respire"; "I seek this unfrequented place to find some ease"; "why was my breeding order'd"; "if I must dye betray'd, captiv'd, and both my Eyes put out"), but it raises them above the pedestrian by the moderate use of metaphors ("dark steps"; "restless thoughts like a deadly swarm of Hornets"; "breath of Heav'n"; "day-spring"; "charioting his presence"; "myself . . . a moving Grave"), of unfamiliar words, that is, of words used in a sense unusual in English ("popular noise"; "delight annull'd"; "light extinct"; "vacant interlunar cave"; "eye so obvious"; "obnoxious to the miseries of life"), and of ornamental words ("air imprison'd also"; "blaze of noon"; "day-spring"; "Heav'n-gifted"). The drama's most boldly unadorned passages of sheerly conversational writing in plain style occur, as one would expect, when Samson's personal integration is most complete. He engages directly and confidently with an external adversary in poetry which approximates to the condition of prose while it retains a perfection of verse form. Samson achieves that integration in a passage culminating in the triumphant phrase "My self? my conscience and internal peace." That affirmation stands in conscious antithesis to the passage we have been examining, which ends with "My self, my Sepulcher, a moving Grave." But even in the divided and contorted expressions of the prologue, the conversational style is exceedingly plain, very sparingly ornamented.

There are, no doubt, a number of additional reasons for the concentration on plain style in *Samson Agonistes*, beside its suitability for thought, speech, and expression of passion, the authority of classical proscription, and the emerging new taste. One reason is that the play works closely from scriptural sources, and the plain style testifies to the strictly biblical quality of the fable. But beyond all these, the marked stylistic traits are adjustments of the poetry to the conveying of ethical truth through argument and to the characterizing of a speaker wrestling with intellectual problems at every stage in the play.

To begin at the level of words themselves, one notices that the meaning is carried by a series of abstract nouns ("*chance* relieves"; "*superstition* yields"; "*strength* put to the *labour*"; "call in doubt divine *Prediction*"; "*wisdom* bears command"; "*impotence* of mind"; "quarrel with the *will* of highest *dispensation*"), as though abstract nouns best display in themselves the vitality of conceptualizing or the energy of thought. Second, a number of single words are used by Samson in a literal sense but, because of the weight of biblical or liturgical significance they bear, are used by Milton in a metaphorical sense, words such as *guiding, hand, dark, blind, promise, sight, light, rest, bondage, ransom, deliver,* and *free.* The effect is not only to evoke a pervasive tragic irony as in place after place the reader catches the protagonist unconsciously predicting the final meaning of the play, but also to call forth an effort on the part of the reader to discover these differences and similarities and to interrelate them. In the *Art of Logic,* noting that "the metaphor is a similitude contracted to one word without signs," Milton showed himself sensible of the power of the single word to interrelate two concepts. *Samson Agonistes* is economically spare: one bare word may present conceptualizing or induce it.

But if the play is exceedingly austere in style, its austerity is variable among the characteristic three kinds of figures which contemporary readers would have considered appropriate for the tragedian to exploit, the kinds of figures which Puttenham, to take a convenient instance, called "auricular," "sensable," and "sententious" or "rhetorical." Auricular figures are perceived by the ear and not by the mind; they are among the most conspicuous and revolutionary devices Milton used, the highest signs of originality in the work and a source of delight to the reader. Sensable figures are perceived intellectually but are apprehended sensuously and include all *tropes* in contradistinction to *schemes.* It is in such figures that *Samson Agonistes* is most restrained, with the effect, of course, of throwing those images that are used into great prominence. Sententious figures are perceived by the ear and the intellect, and they are far and away the most numerous in the play. Individual words are arranged in the prologue as smaller structures within that substructure in a perpetual and arresting series of rhetorical patterns, all requiring that the reader hear and mark how ideas, conceits, and concepts interrelate.

The patterns of parallelism, repetition, antithesis, contradiction, disjunction, paradox, enumeration, continuation, and subordination can all be found within the first eighty lines. Structural patterns (such as: "a little onward . . . a little further on"; "I a prisoner chain'd . . . the air imprison'd also"; "ease to the body some, none to the mind"; "impotence of mind, in body strong"; "what once I was, and what am now"; "scarce half . . . to live, dead more then half"; "deliver . . . Deliverer"; "inferiour to the vilest . . . the vilest here excel"; "dark, dark, dark . . . irrecoverably dark") occur together with word echoes or contrasts across the lines (such as: "light . . . life . . . life . . . light"; "order'd and prescrib'd . . . design'd . . . Betray'd, Captiv'd . . . put out") or at the line ends ("with leave . . . I seek . . . some ease"). The names of the figures for all these relationships and for others were familiar to every contemporary student of the "organic arts" but have passed so out of usage that to revive them would be idle. My point is not simply that the prologue, like the entire drama, is artificial while seeming plain, although to be sure it is; nor that its artifice consists in a marked preference for rhythmical effects and rhetorical schemes over poetic tropes, although that too is the case. Rather, the density of artificial arrangements in logical patterns or schemes inevitably and intentionally prompts attention to mental operations. To notice that Samson's speech contains a perpetual and strenuous effort to arrange his thoughts in coherent patterns according to the principles of sententious expressiveness, *because his speech imitates the mind at work*, is to notice half of the force of the small structures in the prologue.

The other half of the prologue's force derives from the imitative syntax: the effort to order thought is expressed by a perpetual disturbance of normal word order. The disturbed syntax reflects intellectual difficulty and prompts intellectual effort. One instance may stand for many. Samson says

> Whom have I to complain of but my self?
> Who this high gift of strength committed to me,
> In what part lodg'd, how easily bereft me,
> Under the Seal of silence could not keep,
> But weakly to a woman must reveal it,
> O'recome with importunity and tears.
> (46–51)

The phrases and clauses, if divided, numbered, and rearranged in normal word order, make a pattern of desperate crisscrossing within Milton's poetic order. It is worthwhile taking up the general challenge made by Karl Shapiro, to parse at best this passage. The natural order rearranges Milton's phrases as:

> [I] who | could not keep | under the seal of silence | this high gift of strength | committed to me | [and] how easily bereft me | [and] in what part [it was] lodged | but | o'recome with importunity and tears | must reveal it | weakly | to a woman.

The sentence seems perhaps to substitute normal Latin word order for normal English word order, but even that, according to Milton's own *Accedence Commenct Grammar,* is hopelessly sprung in the middle. the initial copulative relative and the position of the verb are the only clearly Latin elements. The major complication lies in the specifications of what Samson could not keep secret; these have the force of internal exclamations, a lamenting exclamation—"how easily bereft me"—and a mournful exclamation—"in what part lodg'd." That complication indicates the functional purpose of the irregular syntax. Samson is indicting himself, but the indictment is painful and terrible, not easily spoken, but not to be eluded. He therefore protracts it and underlines it as he postpones it. He produces his self-indictment in thick gasps of two- and three-stress phrases and sweeps into the suspended sentence "who . . . could not keep" not only all the parts of the secret but all the sources of the pain within his total trouble of spirit: his strength was solemnly committed to him so that he knew his responsibility for it; it was strength which could only have been maintained by using his mind; such strength was a contingent high gift so that its efficacy was placed in his hair; he yielded the secret of his strength and of its location and of its contingency, not to a valiant or equal enemy under compulsion, but to a woman; he did so for no better reason than that he was overcome by the sentimental weapons of importunity and tears.

Milton did not interrupt normal word order merely for ornament and variety, as though he enjoyed the effect of backing through a sentence quite as much as going forward. He produced a knotted and contorted phrasing where each element of the thought could sting with its own hornet's attack, sometimes distorting syntax by beginning phrases, clauses, or sentences with adverbs of time ("this day"), place ("a little onward"), manner ("unwillingly this rest"), degree ("but O yet more miserable"), or frequency ("scarce half"; "daily"), as though to give preliminary warning of the quality of the relationship about to be predicated. At other times he distorts syntax by beginning with the object of predication ("whom have I to complain of") or even the verb itself ("suffices that") in order to direct attention and underline emphasis. The smallest units of composition in the prologue are so disposed as to confirm what the larger units suggest: Milton induces intense intellectual concentration by imitating knotty thought both rhetorically and syntactically.

The prologue ends with the blind Samson in a state of dread at the muffled approach of feet, his meditation on death disturbed by their sound. The feet do not march up but stand off; and the parode does not supply reassurance. The Chorus speaks in unison, not voice on voice, and its sixty-one lines function as a symmetrical parallel to the prologue, an objective commentary sometimes complementary and sometimes almost corrective. The prologue contains five logical units, the parode, three. The first of the three identifies Samson in eleven and a half lines ("This, this is he. . . . See how he lies. . . . Can this be hee?"); the second recalls his former greatness in twenty-five lines ("whom no strength . . . could withstand"); the third laments his present state in an equal number of lines ("Which shall I first bewail, thy Bondage or lost Sight"). The lines which identify Samson parallel the two opening parts of the prologue in which Samson described his coming to the unfrequented bank to seek ease to the body and find none to the mind. Like those lines, they are composed of exclamation ("O change"), imperatives ("let us not"; "see how he lies"), and questions ("do my eyes misrepresent"; "can this be hee"). The passage begins with careful self-imposed quiet in soft sibilants placed in a cadence in which caesural movement forms the primary rhythmical effect almost to the exclusion of stress. It begins with affirmation and ends with pretended doubt. The picture Samson gave of himself was of a man whose external sensations are limited to a change of air. The Chorus in complementary contrast looks at Samson from the outside to observe "how he lies at random, carelessly diffus'd, with languish't head unprop." To the image of Captive in Samson's speech is added the image of Sufferer. The phrase "with languish't head unprop" compels visualization and compels it in terms of latent contrast. Samson's posture is so expressive of despair as to constitute an icon of despair in contrast to an imagined posture with hypothetical "upright head propt," which would be an icon of positive thought. Michelangelo's tomb of Lorenzo de Medici comes irresistibly to mind, whether or not Milton visited it on either his first two-month stay in Florence or his second. Lorenzo is depicted as a thinker, upright, resting his well-held head lightly on his right hand; below him recline the two figures of Evening and Dawn. The description of Samson given by the Chorus is precisely that of Evening, leaning heavily slumped on his left elbow as he lies with his head turned down, unsupported, in vacant despair brooding "at random. . . . As one past hope, abandon'd, / And by himself given over." To the picture of the thoughttormented captive has been added its complement, the *brooding sufferer*, the man of melancholy.

The passage recalling Samson's former greatness likewise parallels Samson's own account of what he was, complementing Samson's emphasis on the prophecy of his birth and the appropriateness of his early breeding with the choral emphasis upon the deeds of his maturity. Together, the two speeches place all the antecedent action before the reader; where Samson spoke of himself as "design'd for great exploits," the Chorus describes his achievement of them. There is no suggestion in the parode that the Chorus is composed of men divided within themselves or among themselves; they think and speak in coherent accord. And yet Milton contrives to continue the sense of dialogue and debate by giving to the Chorus both affirmative and negative modes of description. They say that Samson's actions were positive and successful, unlike his enemies' negative actions. They communicate Samson's strength by perpetually contrasting it to other, baser uses of strength. Samson's ways as a warrior were unlike chivalric knightly conquests: he fought victoriously but "unarm'd . . . weaponless . . . in scorn of thir proud arms . . . with what trivial weapon came to hand." Moreover, by employing the same devices of syntactical dislocation and rhetorical patterning in both the prologue and parode, Milton protracts in the parode the themes of past strength and present loss introduced in the prologue in such a way as to imitate and recreate efforts of assessment and thought. A prominent instance of grammatical ambiguity prompting thought by imitation—not of the action described, but of the assessment of that action—is the passage

> But safest he who stood aloof,
> When insupportably his foot advanc't,
> In scorn of thir proud arms and warlike tools,
> Spurn'd them to death by Troops.
>
> (135–38)

Samson made a whole army foolish when he lifted up the support of one foot and insupportably (and punningly) kicked the enemy aside to their doom. In this passage the irresistible advancement of Samson's foot and his individual destruction of platoon by platoon is preceded by the hypothetical cautious withdrawal to safety of a general, "he," whom the Chorus has distinguished and whom the reader must distinguish from the specific Samson with "his foot." This is interlined by the adverbial phrase of manner, which delays the action to communicate its quality. The figurative austerity of Samson's own account of his past also prevails in the

Chorus's account. A Scripture-based comparison—"he rent [the lion] as he would have rent a Kid"—and a classical comparison of Samson carrying the gates of Gaza to Atlas—"like whom the Gentiles feign to bear up Heav'n"—are separated by nothing more than two metaphorical adjectives, Chalybean and Adamantean. But once again, schemes abound where tropes do not.

When the Chorus turns to the lamentation of Samson's present state, they again do so initially in the terms Samson himself used. But they *bewail* succinctly what Samson thought "would ask a life to wail," by coalescing and making concentric the two sources of his grief, "Prison within Prison." Although they speak of "inward light" only to dismiss it ("alas [it] Puts forth no visual beam"), they have at least mentioned the countertheme of compensatory illumination, the light of the mind. They conclude their lamentation with an interpretation of Samson's plight. This again is supplementary to the prologue. Samson could do no more than caution himself against attributing his fall to the will of God; the Chorus can describe it: "O mirror of our fickle state, . . . By how much from the top of wondrous glory, . . . To lowest pitch of abject fortune thou art fall'n." Their interpretation is close to Aristotle's definition of the tragic hero, and so Milton gives the Chorus an additional five final lines negatively explaining the nature of the true tragic hero. He is not the prince of noble line raised high by the wheel of fortune, but the Puritan aristocrat, the man with a talent, the elect given "strength, while vertue was her mate." With the Chorus's explanation of Samson's fall—that he fell to show how men regularly do fall—the thesis of Act I has been stated: there is a bleak and fatalistic meaning in the tragic fall of the great, and it moves those who observe it to pity. Samson speaks two lines of question, the Chorus moves closer to address him. Their identification of themselves and their errand answers the expression of fear with which Samson concluded his prologue, and it initiates the first episode, the dialogue of the first act, the Aristotelian beginning. They are friends, contemporaries, neighbors, and they have come to bring, if possible, "Counsel or Consolation" to Samson's troubled mind.

In the exchanges which follow, two important matters at issue are left latent, to be resolved in the course of the play. These are the cause of Samson's fall and the prospect of the remainder of his life. Alone, Samson dealt with the first to some effect ("O impotence of mind, in body strong"), but only to reenact it: mind is still powerless, for his thinking stings and makes no headway against suicidal despair. As for the second, since he is buried but not exempt thereby from torment and has desired the oblivion of death, he must be presumed to have made no progress at all. Alone, the Chorus had not touched on the cause of the fall but had begun with an estimate of Samson's prospects. He is to be an example of the irreparable, a mirror of man's fickle state; his future is fixed in failure. Now, together, they begin to juxtapose the cause of the fall and the prospect of the future.

Samson's first speech shows the alteration of mood which an objective but friendly audience necessarily brings. Samson enters into the physician-patient relationship which the Chorus offers. His physician is not wiser nor more experienced in his sort of complaint than he is, as will shortly be clear, but it can listen and reflect back to Samson what he can formulate. To formulate and to define is to begin to think purposefully. As Samson speaks, the divisions within himself are placed in a new context. He is encouraged to speak of them, and in expressing them, he can begin the process of readjusting and balancing them which will lead to their integration. He has said to himself that the most painful and wounding of his sufferings is his blindness, the symbol of his powerlessness; he now can say that his shame is an even greater torture, shame at recognizing himself and being seen by others as a fool. Stating the shame releases the power to compare his present crushed pride with its former flourishing, and he concludes:

> Immeasurable strength they might behold
> In me, of wisdom nothing more then mean;
> This with the other should, at least, have paird,
> These two proportiond ill drove me transverse.
>
> (206–9)

Milton's version of Samson's *hubris*—proudly exulting in the lesser faculty and taking no thought for the higher faculty—is exactly stated. But when Samson speaks of strength and wisdom as "proportiond ill," he appears to the Chorus to be shifting the responsibility away from himself and onto God, the ultimate disposer of such gifts. They quickly warn him, "tax not divine disposal," before offering him some quite common human comfort, the knowledge that "wisest Men have err'd, and by bad Women been deceiv'd." Ordinary human weakness does not warrant such powerful self-condemnation, their lines continue: "Deject not then so overmuch thy self." Their words carry the implication that since future heroism is impossible, it is better to be a calm failure. That is poor advice; they ought rather to encourage Samson to use his wisdom in the hope of moderating the effects of his failure. But Samson has put a straight question—"do [men] not say, how well / Are come upon him his deserts?"— and the Chorus goes on to give him a true answer: "men wonder / Why thou shouldst wed *Philistian* women." Samson's reply marks the second time the concept of "inner light" appears in the play. He married outside his own tribe because he knew "from intimate impulse" that what he proposed "was of God" in that it provided the occasion to begin the liberation of Israel. He chose Dalila as his second wife in the same manner he chose his first, from among the overlord, unclean, and forbidden tribe, because of the earlier divine guidance and its recognized intention.

The Chorus reminds Samson, however, that *"Israel* still serves," implying that an "intimate impulse" must be judged by its result. In Samson's intelligent but emotional answer there is strong evidence of a potential reintegration of his conflicting impulses. Israel's continued servitude cannot be held to disprove the validity of inner light; as Samson was free to attend to the impulse to offer deliverance, so Israel was free to cooperate or not in the difficult task of realizing it. Samson was not coerced by God, Israel was not coerced by Samson; coercion cannot deliver men into freedom, but their own corruption and sloth can deliver them into servitude. The Chorus responds to the truth in Samson's contention and groups him, as Paul had, with Gideon and Jephtha as elect saints who were potential, but disregarded, believers. Samson's answer is ambiguous; it is vengeful, yet thoughtful, and it has within it the hinted beginning of integration. When he says, "Mee easily indeed mine may neglect, / But Gods propos'd deliverance not so," he implies both that *it is easy (safe) enough to disregard me, but not so safe to disregard what God proposes* and that *it makes no difference to me if my efforts are disregarded, but it makes a great difference to me if God's are.* The second statement does not invoke God as a self-justifying device but as higher and holier than His self-critical chosen instrument. Samson's scorn of his slavish people is not a form of special pleading for himself; it is directed against them in support of God. Samson is not championing himself but God. Moreover, the lines posit a future as well as a past. If it turns out that the Chorus is right in assuming that a cause must be measured by its effects, perhaps the full effects are not yet known. It may be, however, that God's justice implies that the quality of an act will be judged by the quality of its intention.

The first stasimon attempts a preliminary resolution of the themes on which Samson and the Chorus have touched. God's justice is simply asserted in language recalling both Job and the Psalmist. God is just, but His ways are difficult to understand; He must be trusted even when He seems not only to condone the breach of His own laws but to inspire that breach. The Chorus speaks both to Samson and to themselves, continuing the comforting and cautioning. But the Chorus is not troubled with the most difficult form of attack on God's justice: how is it just to prompt a man to expose himself to continual temptation and neither make him strong enough to resist nor forgive and rescue him if he fail? When they noted earlier that fallen men *are* examples to others of the instability of the human state, they did not say that men fall *in order to be* such mirrors. The question of God's justice remains for them a question of means and causes, not of ends and effects. They ask, did God act fairly? Their stasimon contains a minimal justification of God, a minimal bleak comfort for Samson. The problem that preoccupies them is simply this: if God commands a man to do something He has earlier said is unholy, does God Himself not connive at sin? The Chorus no longer doubts that Samson was prompted by God; they simply define God as above the law He makes and free from all constraint. God can place a "National obstriction" on Jews not to marry Gentiles and can remove that "legal debt" for a particular Nazarite because "with his own Laws he can best dispence," or, as Milton said in *De Doctrina Christiana*, "he is omnipotent and utterly free in his actions." The pains the Chorus takes to absolve God from responsibility to His own laws are, however, sandwiched between warning men and vindicating God. They begin by asserting the folly of atheism and end by asserting the folly of speculation.

As the first episode ends, the reader has been shown an interior dialogue of a divided mind in the prologue, a balancing attempt to weigh the distance between past and present in the parode, and a series of questions and answers in the first episode, with a preliminary resolution in the first stasimon. Samson fell because he was insufficiently armed by wisdom against the woman he was prompted to marry. The human failure is absolute, yet the divine prompting was just because God is omnipotent and can legitimately do whatever He wills to do. The total structure of Act I is dialectical and traces the following steps: Samson is in a terrifying state, unable to think; he is in a pitiable state, unable to act. How did it happen and what can come of it? He was at fault and nothing can be done. But men must not doubt God in any event; God acts as He wills; it is impious to think He does not. Since God has finished with Samson, human beings can do nothing more than soothe him. His future can only be resigned waiting for death.

LOUIS L. MARTZ

"Samson Agonistes": The Breath of Heaven

Sam. A little onward lend thy guiding hand
To these dark steps, a little further on;
For yonder bank hath choice of Sun or shade,
There I am wont to sit, when any chance
Relieves me from my task of servile toyl,
Daily in the common Prison else enjoyn'd me,
Where I a Prisoner chain'd, scarce freely draw
The air imprison'd also, close and damp,
Unwholsom draught: but here I feel amends,
The breath of Heav'n fresh-blowing, pure and sweet,
With day-spring born; here leave me to respire.

This is an opening rich with implica
tions, for the situation suggests the opening of Sophocles' redemptive
tragedy, *Oedipus at Colonus*, where the blind Oedipus is led on stage by his
daughter Antigone. We know that Samson will also be accepted by the
divine power, as Oedipus was at last accepted and transfigured by the
divine powers at the close of that Greek play. At the same time Milton's
phrasing in these opening lines contains a redemptive overtone drawn
from the first chapter of the Gospel of Luke, where Zacharias prophesies
the redemption of God's people: "Through the tender mercy of our God;
whereby the *dayspring* from on high hath visited us, to give light *to them*

From *Poet of Exile: A Study of Milton's Poetry.* Copyright © 1980 by Yale University Press.

that sit in darkness and in the shadow of death, *to guide our feet* into the way of peace." So the guiding hand that Samson speaks of here is a human hand, literally, and the breath of Heaven that he enjoys is a physical breeze, literally; but this opening, with Milton's characteristic mingling of classical and Christian evocations, will suggest the presence of a higher power, still to be revealed.

Samson's long prologue here displays a remarkable combination of self-control and turbulent emotional power. Although he bitterly laments his captivity and his loss of sight, he refuses the temptation to blame God for his fate:

> Promise was that I
> Should *Israel* from *Philistian* yoke deliver;
> Ask for this great Deliverer now, and find him
> Eyeless in *Gaza* at the Mill with slaves,
> Himself in bonds under *Philistian* yoke;
> Yet stay, let me not rashly call in doubt
> Divine Prediction; what if all foretold
> Had been fulfilld but through mine own default,
> Whom have I to complain of but my self?
> (38–46)

But as his agony swells out, the temptation returns, and is again refused:

> God, when he gave me strength, to shew withal
> How slight the gift was, hung it in my Hair.
> But peace, I must not quarrel with the will
> Of highest dispensation, which herein
> Happ'ly had ends above my reach to know:
> Suffices that to me strength is my bane,
> And proves the sourse of all my miseries;
> So many, and so huge, that each apart
> Would ask a life to wail, but chief of all,
> O loss of sight, of thee I most complain!
> Blind among enemies, O worse then chains,
> Dungeon, or beggery, or decrepit age!
> (58–69)

And so on into that famous lamentation where the steady flow of the blank verse breaks under the strain and is transformed into a lyric utterance of short and long lines, ebbing and flowing with the speaker's almost unbearable pain:

O dark, dark, dark, amid the blaze of noon,
Irrecoverably dark, total Eclipse
Without all hope of day!
O first created Beam, and thou great Word,
Let there be light, and light was over all;
Why am I thus bereav'd thy prime decree?
The Sun to me is dark
And silent as the Moon,
When she deserts the night
Hid in her vacant interlunar cave.

(80–89)

How poorly the chorus understands this man, as they enter now,
judging him only by outward appearances. "Can this be hee?" they ask,
recalling the physical grandeur of his exploits:

Can this be hee,
That Heroic, that Renown'd,
Irresistible *Samson?* whom unarm'd
No strength of man, or fiercest wild beast could withstand;
Who tore the Lion, as the Lion tears the Kid,
Ran on embattelld Armies clad in Iron
And weaponless himself,
Made Arms ridiculous, useless the forgery
Of brazen shield and spear, the hammer'd Cuirass,
Chalybean temper'd steel, and frock of mail
Adamantean Proof.

(124–34)

But more deeply, Samson's prologue has shown him to be a man whose
mind and character still retain a great potential. The function of the
various episodes that we now watch is to release and develop that deep
potential.

In the first episode the "Consolation" of the chorus does not lead
Samson to blame God or lose his faith in God's justice, although the
"Counsel" offered by Samson's friends is full of painful queries:

Chor. Tax not divine disposal, wisest Men
Have err'd, and by bad Women been deceiv'd;
And shall again, pretend they ne're so wise.
Deject not then so overmuch thy self,
Who hast of sorrow thy full load besides;
Yet truth to say, I oft have heard men wonder
Why thou shouldst wed *Philistian* women rather
Then of thine own Tribe fairer, or as fair,
At least of thy own Nation, and as noble.

(210–18)

But Samson defends his first Philistine marriage on the grounds that he "knew / From intimate impulse" that it was ordained by God for Israel's deliverance: "The work to which I was divinely call'd." And he adds that he "thought" the same was true for Dalila—though there is a tacit admission of possible error here, perhaps an error of self-deception caused by the "specious" charms of Dalila.

The chorus wryly concedes Samson's ability "to provoke" the Philistines—but to what end? "Yet *Israel* still serves with all his Sons." Here, surprisingly, Samson leaps to defend both himself and God. In spite of his weaknesses, he declares, Israel had many opportunities to throw off the Philistine yoke, if they had supported him on many different occasions:

> *Sam.* That fault I take not on me, but transfer
> On *Israel's* Governours, and Heads of Tribes,
> Who seeing those great acts which God had done
> Singly by me against their Conquerours
> Acknowledg'd not, or not at all consider'd
> Deliverance offerd.
>
> (241–46)

With the memory of his deeds and the grandeur of his language Samson convinces the chorus that the fault is indeed in the Israelites, who have before this deserted their heroes. Milton skillfully conveys the distance between such heroes and the ordinary man by a curiously deflating use of rhyme at the close of this choric response:

> *Chor.* Thy words to my remembrance bring
> How *Succoth* and the Fort of *Penuel*
> Thir great Deliverer contemn'd,
> The matchless *Gideon* in pursuit
> Of *Madian* and her vanquisht Kings:
> And how ingrateful *Ephraim*
> Had dealt with *Jephtha*, who by argument,
> Not worse then by his shield and spear
> Defended *Israel* from the *Ammonite*,
> Had not his prowess quell'd thir pride
> In that sore battel when so many dy'd
> Without Reprieve adjudg'd to death,
> For want of well pronouncing *Shibboleth*.
>
> (277–89)

One of the astonishing things about Milton's art in this whole drama is the way in which he has, it seems, deliberately played down the choruses in the middle of the drama, refusing to give the chorus very good lines, except toward the beginning (where they are uplifted by the memory of Samson's physical prowess), and toward the end (where they are strengthened by Samson's recovery and ultimate victory). After each of the first three episodes, Milton has given the chorus words that are, for the most part, dry and commonplace, often surprisingly flat, as here at the end of the first episode:

> Yet more there be who doubt his ways not just,
> As to his own *edicts*, found *contradicting*,
> Then give the rains to wandring thought,
> Regardless of his glories *diminution*:
> Till by thir own perplexities *involv'd*
> They ravel more, still less *resolv'd*,
> But never find self-satisfying *solution*.
>   As if they would confine th' Interminable,
> And tie him to his own *prescript*,
> Who made our Laws to bind us, not himself,
> And hath full right to *exempt*
> Whom so it pleases him by *choice*
> From National obstriction, without *taint*
> Of sin, or legal *debt*;
> For with his own Laws he can best *dispence*.
>
> (300–14)

The rhymes and partial rhymes here (which I have italicized) create by their "jingling" an effect of something like triviality in the chorus; and since Milton elsewhere in the play writes so very well, we are bound to ask whether there is not some deliberate effect in thus making the chorus speak so flatly. Indeed, the heavy-handed use of rhyme and partial rhyme here seems almost to mirror the contempt for rhymed verse that Milton had expressed several years earlier in the prefatory note to *Paradise Lost*:

> The Measure is *English* Heroic Verse without Rime, as that of *Homer* in *Greek*, and of *Virgil* in *Latin*; Rime being no necessary Adjunct or true Ornament of Poem or good Verse, in longer Works especially, but the Invention of a barbarous Age, to set off wretched matter and lame Meeter; grac't indeed since by the use of some famous modern Poets, carried away by Custom, but much to thir own vexation, hindrance, and constraint to express many things otherwise, and for the most part worse then else they would have exprest them.

Rhyme, he declares, is "a thing of it self, to all judicious eares, trivial and of no true musical delight," which cannot be found "in the jingling sound of like endings." The choric stanzas that I have just quoted seem to prove the point. Is this an instance of Milton's sardonic humor—to give the chorus stanzas of deliberate flatness? At the very least it would appear that Milton's use of rhyme here has the effect of lowering the tone of high seriousness and making impossible any great dignity in this choric speech. The effect is thus to stress, by contrast, the grandeur of Samson, the glory of his poetry, the greatness of his mind: his difference from ordinary men.

This difference also appears by contrast with his father Manoa, who now enters to begin the second episode. Manoa complains bitterly to his son and seems so deeply involved in his own grief that he cannot think about the effect that his words may have upon Samson:

> Nay what thing good
> Pray'd for, but often proves our woe, our bane?
> I pray'd for Children, and thought barrenness
> In wedlock a reproach; I gain'd a Son,
> And such a Son as all Men hail'd me happy;
> Who would be now a Father in my stead?
>
> Alas methinks whom God hath chosen once
> To worthiest deeds, if he through frailty err,
> He should not so o'rewhelm, and as a thrall
> Subject him to so foul indignities,
> Be it but for honours sake of former deeds.
> (350–55, 368–72)

But Samson is far from being shaken by these moans; he has faced all this long ago; and he answers with self-control and dignity:

> Appoint not heavenly disposition, Father,
> Nothing of all these evils hath befall'n me
> But justly; I my self have brought them on,
> Sole Author I, sole cause . . .
> (373–76)

And he ends, as in his great prologue, with a surge of immense vitality, though turned against himself:

> O indignity, O blot
> To Honour and Religion! servil mind
> Rewarded well with servil punishment!
> The base degree to which I now am fall'n,
> These rags, this grinding, is not yet so base
> As was my former servitude, ignoble,
> Unmanly, ignominious, infamous,
> True slavery, and that blindness worse then this,
> That saw not how degeneratly I serv'd.
> (411–19)

The distance between Samson and ordinary men is at once emphasized by Manoa, as he proceeds to ignore the power of Samson's self-
castigation and answers at first with a querulous (and, to the reader,
half-comic) understatement: "I cannot praise thy Marriage choises, Son, /
Rather approv'd them not;" and this is followed by obvious doubt of his
son's divine inspiration in these matters:

> but thou didst plead
> Divine impulsion prompting how thou might'st
> Find some occasion to infest our Foes.
> I state not that; this I am sure; our Foes
> Found soon occasion thereby to make thee
> Thir Captive, and thir triumph; thou the sooner
> Temptation found'st, or over-potent charms
> To violate the sacred trust of silence
> Deposited within thee.
>
> (420–29)

Then Manoa, returning to his self-centered complaint, adds, "A worse
thing yet remains": the Philistines are today celebrating Dagon's victory in
delivering Samson into their hands (one may hear the voice of aged
self-pity):

> So *Dagon* shall be magnifi'd, and God,
> Besides whom is no God, compar'd with Idols,
> Disglorifi'd, blasphem'd, and had in scorn
> By th' Idolatrous rout amidst thir wine;
> Which to have come to pass by means of thee,
> *Samson*, of all thy sufferings think the heaviest,
> Of all reproach the most with shame that ever
> Could have befall'n thee and thy Fathers house.
>
> (440–47)

Here again, Samson acknowledges his fault with dignity and rational
power, but he goes beyond his earlier self-denunciation to assert his
unbroken faith that God will triumph, even though Samson himself is
now cast out from grace:

> This only hope relieves me, that the strife
> With me hath end; all the contest is now
> 'Twixt God and *Dagon; Dagon* hath presum'd,
> Me overthrown, to enter lists with God,
> His Deity comparing and preferring
> Before the God of *Abraham*. He, be sure,
> Will not connive, or linger, thus provok'd,
> But will arise and his great name assert:

> *Dagon* must stoop, and shall e're long receive
> Such a discomfit, as shall quite despoil him
> Of all these boasted Trophies won on me,
> And with confusion blank his Worshippers.
>
> (460–71)

Manoa agrees, in a perfunctory tone, and then goes on to show that his mind is not at all on such matters, but is fixed upon his hope to ransom his son and take him home: "But for thee what shall be done?" Manoa here represents the terms of household common sense, the encouragement to believe that God somehow will perhaps relent, that things simply cannot go on being as unhappy as they are. Samson rejects all these easy consolations in one of the simplest and noblest speeches of the entire play, when Manoa suggests that he might even possibly regain his sight, if only he has patience:

> All otherwise to me my thoughts portend,
> That these dark orbs no more shall treat with light,
> Nor th' other light of life continue long,
> But yield to double darkness nigh at hand:
> So much I feel my genial spirits droop,
> My hopes all flat, nature within me seems
> In all her functions weary of herself;
> My race of glory run, and race of shame,
> And I shall shortly be with them that rest.
>
> (590–98)

The effect of his father's "consolations" has been to make Samson realize to the full his "sense of Heav'ns desertion," as he cries out in the great lyrical utterance that follows, a passage expressed, again, not in blank verse, but in undulating long and short lines which begin with a few scarcely noticed rhymes, and then utterly give up all rhymes, as the ode reaches its climax:

> I was his nursling once and choice delight,
> His destin'd from the womb,
> Promisd by Heavenly message twice descending.
> Under his special eie
> Abstemious I grew up and thriv'd amain;
> He led me on to mightiest deeds
> Above the nerve of mortal arm
> Against the uncircumcis'd, our enemies.
> But now hath cast me off as never known,
> And to those cruel enemies,
> Whom I by his appointment had provok't,
> Left me all helpless with th' irreparable loss

Of sight, reserv'd alive to be repeated
The subject of this cruelty, or scorn.
Not am I in the list of them that hope;
Hopeless are all my evils, all remediless;
This one prayer yet remains, might I be heard,
No long petition, speedy death,
The close of all my miseries, and the balm.

(633–51)

That prayer will soon be answered; through the dark night of this despair, his thoughts are moving in the right way.

Immediately, the contrast between Samson's grandeur of despair and the commonplace musing of the chorus is enforced by some of the flattest lines and weakest rhymes that Milton ever wrote:

God of our Fathers, what is man!
That thou towards him with hand so *various*,
Or might I say *contrarious*,
Temperst thy providence through his short course,
Not evenly, as thou rul'st
The Angelic orders and inferiour creatures *mute*,
Irrational and *brute*.
Nor do I name of men the common *rout*,
That wandring loose *about*
Grow up and perish, as the summer flie.

(667–76)

The chorus is confused and bewildered; but the chosen man is greater than the chorus can here realize, as we are soon to see.

Now, as Samson faces utterly his agonized sense of loss, the external cause of that loss sails into sight with all her streamers waving, perfumed, beautiful, seductive, weeping, penitent (she says), declaring her "conjugal affection," begging forgiveness, asking if she may take him home to her bed and board. Samson's fierceness toward Dalila is a measure of the seductive power that she still holds for him:

My Wife, my Traytress, let her not come near me.

(725)

Out, out *Hyæna*; these are thy wonted arts.

(748)

And artful she certainly is. Our opinion of Samson's character is improved here, since we see from the subtlety of her arguments and the appeal of her excuses why and how Samson fell before her earlier persuasions, as he has eloquently described her blandishments in the scene with Manoa. She uses, at first, three arguments, which may be summed up thus: (1) You say I'm weak; well, you're weak too; so let's be weak together. Forgive my weaknesses so that man may forgive your weaknesses. (2) It was love that caused it. I did it to keep you with me:

> I knew that liberty
> Would draw thee forth to perilous enterprises,
> While I at home sate full of cares and fears
> Wailing thy absence in my widow'd bed;
> Here I should still enjoy thee day and night
> Mine and Loves prisoner, not the *Philistines*,
> Whole to my self, unhazarded abroad,
> Fearless at home of partners in my love.
> These reasons in Loves law have past for good,
> Though fond and reasonless to some perhaps:
> And Love hath oft, well meaning, wrought much wo,
> Yet always pity or pardon hath obtain'd.
>
> (803–14)

(3) I did it for my country:

> thou know'st the Magistrates
> And Princes of my countrey came in person,
> Sollicited, commanded, threatn'd, urg'd,
> Adjur'd by all the bonds of civil Duty
> And of Religion, press'd how just it was,
> How honourable, how glorious to entrap
> A common enemy, who had destroy'd
> Such numbers of our Nation.
>
> (850–57)

Samson answers her throughout with careful, steady reasoning; he is fully in command of his mental powers, as Dalila at last realizes, when she tries to win him with a hurt and humble manner:

> In argument with men a woman ever
> Goes by the worse, whatever be her cause.
>
> (903–04)

But he answers with strong and bitter wit:

> For want of words no doubt, or lack of breath,
> Witness when I was worried with thy peals.
>
> (905–06)

Seeing him so resolved, she tries the last appeal: whatever is past is past; let me take care of you; let me make it up to you. We notice the insidious nature of the temptation she here offers to the blind man:

> though sight be lost,
> Life yet hath many solace, unjoy'd
> Where other senses want not their delights
> At home in leisure and domestic ease,
> Exempt from many a care and chance to which
> Eye-sight exposes daily men abroad.
> I to the Lords will intercede, not doubting
> Thir favourable ear, that I may fetch thee
> From forth this loathsom prison-house, to abide
> With me, where my redoubl'd love and care
> With nursing diligence, to me glad office,
> May ever tend about thee to old age
> With all things grateful chear'd, and so suppli'd,
> That what by me thou hast lost thou least shalt miss.
> (914–27)

Samson himself seems almost to believe her here, for at first he responds more gently:

> No, no, of my condition take no care;
> It fits not; thou and I long since are twain.
> (928–29)

But he soon moves on into the tone of more rigorous rejection:

> Nor think me so unwary or accurst
> To bring my feet again into the snare
> Where once I have been caught; I know thy trains
> Though dearly to my cost, thy ginns, and toyls;
> Thy fair enchanted cup, and warbling charms
> No more on me have power, their force is null'd,
> So much of Adders wisdom I have learn't
> To fence my ear against thy sorceries.
> (930–37)

Nevertheless, the relative mildness of Samson's manner here seems to make her bolder and to urge her into one final plea: "Let me approach at least, and touch thy hand." Samson's fierce revulsion is a sign of the powerful attraction which she still holds:

> Not for thy life, lest fierce remembrance wake
> My sudden rage to tear thee joint by joint.
> (952–53)

And he concludes with a tense and guarded manner, maintaining his firm self-control through bitter and fierce irony:

At distance I forgive thee, go with that;
Bewail thy falshood, and the pious works
It hath brought forth to make thee memorable
Among illustrious women, faithful wives;
Cherish thy hast'n'd widowhood with the gold
Of Matrimonial treason: so farewel.

                                        (954–59)

What shall we make of Dalila here? To what extent does she mean what she says? Is it true, as Samson says, "That malice not repentance brought thee hither"? Is she, as the chorus says, "a manifest Serpent by her sting / Discover'd in the end"? Dalila remains an enigma that neither Samson, nor the chorus, nor the audience, can resolve. Her speeches suggest a complex tissue of motives and impulses: curiosity, a challenge to see if she can draw him back, regret that it turned out worse than she thought it would, physical desire to have Samson back with her again, a desire to defend herself, to prove to herself perhaps that she is not as bad as it may seem. And then at the end we have the natural anger of a woman scorned, which does not necessarily prove her to be a hypocrite throughout, though Samson is surely right in thinking that she would betray him again if he went back. Whatever her nature, whatever her motives, the power of her appeal has certainly accomplished a remarkable change in Samson; she has stirred him out of his sense of loss, stung him into more positive responses.

Samson looks even stronger here if we compare this scene with the scene in Euripides' *The Trojan Women* which it evokes: that scene where Menelaus at last confronts his wife Helen. Menelaus enters cursing Helen, saying that he will kill her now, or take her home and have her killed there. His manner, however, is that of indecisive bluster and torment; and every Greek who watched the play knew perfectly well that Menelaus would never kill her, because in Homer's *Odyssey*, they knew, Telemachus had visited Menelaus and Helen, and had seen them living together again, not at all happily, after the Trojan War. So Menelaus looks weak here in the Greek play, and Helen's cool arguments and unrepentant ways, we know, will overcome his threats. Dalila is far more impressive than the Helen of Euripides, whose brazen reliance on her beauty shows in all her lines; and for this reason too Samson here seems to have much greater strength of mind than Menelaus.

Samson, we see, has now arisen beyond all temptations—and also far beyond the denunciation of the evils of women which we now hear presented in the chorus's inadequate commentary on this complex and moving scene. The chorus presents its conventional anti-feminist satire in what might fairly be called the weakest rhyming of the entire play:

> It is not vertue, wisdom, valour, *wit*,
> Strength, comliness of shape, or amplest *merit*
> That womans love can win or long *inherit*,
> But what it is, hard is to *say*,
> Harder to *hit*,
> (Which way soever men refer *it*)
> Much like thy riddle, *Samson*, in one *day*
> Or seven, though one should musing *sit.*
>
> (1010–17)

The loss of dignity in the poetry is clear: Milton, it seems, is here drastically lowering the tone and manner of the poetry for some particular effect.

> Is it for that such outward *ornament*
> Was lavish't on thir *Sex*, that inward *gifts*
> Were left for hast unfinish't, judgment *scant*,
> Capacity not rais'd to appre*hend*
> Or value what is *best*
> In choice, but oftest to affect the *wrong?*
> Or was too much of self-love *mixt*,
> Of constancy no root *infixt*,
> That either they love nothing, or not *long?*

> Therefore Gods universal *Law*
> Gave to the man despotic *power*
> Over his female in due *awe*,
> Nor from that right to part an *hour*,
> Smile she or *lowre:*
> So shall he least confusion *draw*
> On his whole life, not *sway'd*
> By female usurpation, nor *dismay'd.*
>
> (1025–60)

The jarring impact of the endings here should help to indicate that this is hardly John Milton's final word of wisdom about women. We are warned against this by the weakness of the verse, by the one-sided quality of the view, and by the exaggeration of man's proper power over women. Authority man has—or should have—according to Milton, but never quite a power of this grim variety. Why, then, has Milton brought in such a choric utterance here, weak in itself, and out of tone with the central tendency of Samson's own self-denunciation? True, Samson blames Dalila furiously, for showing the "arts of every woman false like thee," but that is far from saying that nearly every woman is false. The chorus has picked up one aspect of the previous scene and has driven it to the point of caricature. The effect is to relieve the violent tension of the previous scene by a touch of satirical humor, and thus to prepare the way for the next scene, which develops a robustly comic tone, as Samson deflates the bragging and fastidious giant Harapha. Here is the one portion of the play in which we have a glimpse of the old folk-hero: taunting, audacious, primitive in his total confidence in his physical strength:

> I only with an Oak'n staff will meet thee,
> And raise such out-cries on thy clatter'd Iron,
> Which long shall not with-hold mee from thy head,
> That in a little time while breath remains thee,
> Thou oft shalt wish thy self at *Gath* to boast
> Again in safety what thou wouldst have done
> To *Samson*, but shalt never see *Gath* more.
> (1123–29)

But the glimpse of the primitive hero is brief; Milton very soon transmutes Samson into the dignified champion of God, as Samson declares (with a significant use of the word "Nativity"):

> My trust is in the living God who gave me
> At my Nativity this strength, diffus'd
> No less through all my sinews, joints and bones,
> Then thine, while I preserv'd these locks unshorn,
> The pledge of my unviolated vow.
> (1140–44)

And soon Samson declares his willingness to resume the role of God's champion against Dagon, as he proceeds to accept the hope that he had earlier refused to allow:

> All these indignities, for such they are
> From thine, these evils I deserve and more,
> Acknowledge them from God inflicted on me
> Justly, yet despair not of his final pardon
> Whose ear is ever open; and his eye
> Gracious to re-admit the suppliant;
> In confidence whereof I once again
> Defie thee to the trial of mortal fight,
> By combat to decide whose god is God,
> Thine or whom I with *Israel's* Sons adore.
> (1168–77)

The hero is fully restored; his great potential has now been revealed; and the play can continue rapidly towards the fulfillment of its triumphant catastrophe. But even in this ending, where the chorus is given many lines of much greater power than in the middle scenes, Milton creates the impression that these men, along with Manoa, have difficulty in grasping the true greatness of Samson's achievement. Their spirits are lifted by the scene with Harapha—to the point where their fine ode, "Oh how comely it is and how reviving," proceeds for thirty fervent lines without a single rhyme—but during the scene with Samson and the Officer, and in the scene with Manoa following Samson's departure, the chorus shows itself bewildered: "How thou wilt here come off surmounts my reach," they say in one deflating line (1380), and they agree completely with Manoa in his hopes for ransoming his son:

> Thy hopes are not ill founded nor seem vain
> Of his delivery, and thy joy thereon
> Conceiv'd, agreeable to a Fathers love,
> In both which we, as next participate.
> (1504–07)

The Messenger then describes the center of Samson's great achievement in these words:

> with head a while enclin'd,
> And eyes fast fixt he stood, as one who pray'd,
> Or some great matter in his mind revolv'd.
> At last with head erect thus cryed aloud,
> Hitherto, Lords, what your commands impos'd
> I have perform'd, as reason was, obeying,
> Not without wonder or delight beheld.
> Now of my own accord such other tryal
> I mean to shew you of my strength, yet greater;
> As with amaze shall strike all who behold.
> (1636–45)

We note the emphasis on mental action, on reason, and on choice: "Now of my own accord." Samson's greatness lies in his rational choice of a God-given opportunity. But here is what the chorus, in its immediate response, makes of this rational act:

> O dearly-bought revenge, yet glorious!
> Living or dying thou hast fulfill'd
> The work for which thou wast foretold
> To *Israel*, and now ly'st victorious
> Among thy slain self-kill'd
> Not willingly, but tangl'd in the fold
> Of dire necessity, whose law in death conjoin'd

> Thee with thy slaughter'd foes in number more
> Then all thy life had slain before.
>
> (1660–68)

Does the heavy rhyme, once again, help to suggest that this view is not to be taken as the whole truth? The "law" of "dire necessity" plays no part in Milton's universe: by saying that Samson has died "self-kill'd / Not willingly," the chorus shows its initial failure to grasp the deeper meaning of Samson's triumph. Yet, as the chorus proceeds here, the realization of some inward act of "vertue," "illuminated" by God, breaks through:

> But he though blind of sight,
> Despis'd and thought extinguish't quite,
> With inward eyes illuminated
> His fierie vertue rouz'd
> From under ashes into sudden flame . . .
>
> (1687–91)

The latent contradiction between "necessity" and "inward eyes" is not to be reconciled—nor need it be; it is enough to know that the chorus at the close has glimpsed something of the essential truth. As for Manoa, one wonders: his final thoughts are all external—on washing the "enemies blood" off Samson's body, on having a proper funeral, on building a proper monument, where

> The Virgins also shall on feastful days
> Visit his Tomb with flowers, only bewailing
> His lot unfortunate in nuptial choice,
> From whence captivity and loss of eyes.
>
> (1741–44)

Still harping on those foreign wives, Manoa can see no relation between Samson's "nuptial choice" and the opportunity to achieve, by another choice, his final victory. As Samson knows, it was not his nuptial choice that led to his "captivity and loss of eyes"; it was his weakness in dealing with the blandishments of his chosen mate.

Can we, amid these circumstances, wholly believe Manoa when he says the words that for some readers have seemed to explain why the play is not a true tragedy?

> Nothing is here for tears, nothing to wail
> Or knock the breast, no weakness, no contempt,
> Dispraise, or blame, nothing but well and fair,
> And what may quiet us in a death so noble.
>
> (1721–24)

Like everything else that Manoa has said in the play, this is at best a
half-truth, a partial understanding. There is much that is here for tears,
much that is not well and fair. Samson, like all tragic heroes, has gained
his victory within the self, but at terrible cost. It is the cost of his final
understanding that we must ponder, as the chorus brings the tragedy to a
quiet and conventional close. In these final lines the chorus speaks with
an effective firmness, while the conventionality is marked by its expression in fourteen lines, rhymed in sonnet-style:

> All is best, though we oft doubt,
> What th' unsearchable dispose
> Of highest wisdom brings about,
> And ever best found in the close.
> Oft he seems to hide his face,
> But unexpectedly returns
> And to his faithful Champion hath in place
> Bore witness gloriously; whence *Gaza* mourns
> And all that band them to resist
> His uncontroulable intent,
> His servants he with new acquist
> Of true experience from this great event
> With peace and consolation hath dismist,
> And calm of mind all passion spent.

Certainly the chorus and Manoa have been uplifted by Samson's
achievement; they have received "new acquist / Of true experience" that
reaffirms their faith and opens the way toward their salvation. And yet
even at the close they seem not quite to grasp the complex meaning of
Samson's victory. They stress the "uncontroulable intent" of God, while
neglecting the free intent of Samson. They stress the way in which God
has borne "witness" to his "faithful Champion," rather than the way in
which this faithful man has borne witness to God. The distance between
the "Elect" and the "rest" has been maintained. The chorus and Manoa
have missed the deep self-discovery of the hero: that he is, by his own
willing choice, a chosen son of God.

Nothing could show more clearly the range and reach of Milton's
poetical career than a comparison between his volumes of 1645 and 1671.
The earlier book derives from a pastoral joy in the physical creation, a
sense of relationship between man and nature, though shadowed in places
by a growing awareness of mortality and of moral and political evil at work
in the world of man. In the later book that joy in the physical creation
has been rigorously restrained, and that restraint is conveyed by the
rigorous control over sensuous imagery, pagan allusion, and the burgeon-

ing language of Milton's grand style. *Paradise Regain'd*, with its desert setting, is an anti-pastoral, played in the gray country of the mind, without recourse to the fruits of earth. Or perhaps it is better called a pastoral of a kind peculiar to the Bible, a retreat from the city to the wilderness and the sparse pasturing hills of Judaea, such as the Israelites and their prophets made in answer to "the voice of him that crieth in the wilderness, Prepare ye the way of the Lord, make straight in the desert a highway for our God" (Isaiah 40:3). The contest of styles that is won by the Son of God in *Paradise Regain'd* finds its fulfillment in the relatively plain style of *Samson Agonistes*, where the play of sensuous imagery is severely pruned and the mode of reasoned speech prevails. The result is a volume of austere greatness, a grandeur of self-abnegation that demon-strates, in both poems, the discovery of the true inner self of the chosen son.

Thus Milton's three great volumes of 1645, 1667, and 1671 might be seen as a triptych. On one side lies the green, youthful, chiefly joyous work of pastoral creation, and on the other the austere, ascetic, reasoned, rigorous work of age. In between lies the master piece, where a pastoral joy in God's Creation lives at the center of the vision, while the sombre tones of a wise and suffering maturity enfold that vision within scenes that reveal the possibilities of tragic failure and redemptive hope. Each of the three panels has an individual integrity, and can be viewed apart. Yet the measure of Milton's greatness lies in a realization of the full ensemble.

JOHN HOLLANDER

Echo Schematic

We might dwell for a moment on one of the most famous fragments of broken refrain in our literature, the nonce burden in Keats' "Ode to a Nightingale" following the mention of the "perilous seas in faery lands forlorn" (70). The next strophe begins "Forlorn! the very word is like a bell / To toll me back from thee to my sole self!" (71–72). The echoing repetition returns, as has often been observed, another sense of the word *forlorn*, as if some of the perils of the seas lay in the fragility of the vision which they helped compose. The word is, even here, Miltonic, with its resounding of a literal and a figurative meaning. It recalls Adam's sense of life without Eve in Paradise: "To live again in these wild Woods forlorn" (*Paradise Lost* IX, 910), where the last word trails away in a cloud of sad prophetic irony: "these wild Woods forlorn" are not the wilderness of fallen nature. Adam thinks he means Eden figuratively, but he is, alas, literally invoking both the fallen world and the lost unfallen one: his trope of the place of loss is an unwittingly literal designation of the loss of place. Keats' "forlorn" is like a very echo from within his text, but it reaches back to another voice behind it.

The scheme of refrain is likewise linked to the echo of affirmation and acknowledgment that we have already remarked in Hesiod, pastoral tradition, and so forth, in the mythopoeic account of its origination in *Paradise Lost*. The First Hymn (V, 153–208) invokes heavenly powers for aid in amplification of its praising voice, even as the Lady invokes Echo's amplification in *Comus*. But the unfallen hymn of praise transcends the

From *The Figure of Echo*. Copyright © 1981 by The Regents of the University of California. University of California Press.

anaphora and catalogue of its precursor Psalm 148 by seeming to generate its refrain—indeed, the very idea of refrain—during the course of its unfolding. Before moving on from echoing schemes to ad hoc tropes of echo, we might examine the Original Refrain in detail.

Adam and Eve (V, 147–52) are in Paradise

> to praise
> Thir Maker, in fit strains pronounct or sung
> Unmediated, such prompt eloquence
> Flow'd from thir lips, in Prose or numerous Verse,
> More tuneable than needed Lute or Harp
> To add more sweetness

—or, as we might continue, to add more of the significance which Schopenhauer felt, and Nietzsche quoted him as feeling, accompanying instrumental music gave to utterance and action. Adam and Eve's language, we are implicitly told, needed no supplementary *ethos* or *pathos*, and certainly none of the *logos* which, for romantic thought, purely instrumental music came to embody as well.

In this total *a capella* song, classical and unfallen, the original pair first observe—echoing, *sotto voce*, Psalm 19—that even God's "lowest works" "declare / Thy goodness beyond thought, and Power Divine" (V, 158–59). Then they move into the imperative, hortatory mode of the hymn which follows. They call for the "Sons of Light" to "speak," thus reversing the great pattern of fallen praise (in Pindar's first Pythian Ode, and in the myth of the statue of Memnon) in which light strikes a figurative echo in literal sound from a body, instead of merely casting a shadow: "Thou Sun, of this great World both Eye and Soul, / Acknowledge him thy Greater, sound his praise / In thy eternal course" (V, 171–73).

This is the hymn's own primary voice. Its first *Nachklang* is picked up tentatively, across an enjambment which cuts the amplifying echo, the distant *epistrophe*, in half:

> Moon, that now meet'st the orient Sun, now fli'st
> With the first Stars, fixt in thir Orb that flies,
> And yee five other wand'ring Fires that move
> In mystic Dance not without Song, resound
> His praise, who out of Darkness call'd up Light.
> (V, 175–79)

Adam, who will soon himself call up Sound out of Silence, then establishes the formula / (verb) + "his praise" / in the second half of the significantly varied end-stopped lines that grow into the refrain of the remainder of the hymn:

Air, and ye Elements of eldest birth
Of Nature's Womb, that in quaternion run
Perpetual Circle, multiform, and mix
And nourish all things, let your ceaseless change
Vary to our great Maker still new praise.

Ye Mists and Exhalations that now rise
From Hill or steaming Lake, dusky or grey,
Till the Sun paint your fleecy skirts with Gold,
In honor to the World's great Author rise,
Whether to deck with Clouds th'uncolor'd sky,
Or wet the thirsty Earth with falling showers,
Rising or falling still advance his praise.

His praise ye Winds, that from four Quarters blow,
Breathe soft or loud; and wave your tops, ye Pines,
With every Plant, in sign of Worship wave.
Fountains and yee, that warble as ye flow,
Melodious murmurs, warbling tune his praise.

Join voices all ye living Souls; ye Birds,
That singing up to Heaven Gate ascend,
Bear on your wings and in your notes his praise;

Yee that in Waters glide, and yee that walk
The Earth, and stately tread, or lowly creep;
Witness if I be silent, Morn or Even,
To Hill, or Valley, Fountain or fresh shade
Made vocal by my Song, and taught his praise.
(V, 180–204)

This is not glossed by the narration as "the First Refrain," but such, indeed, it is. Like the famous "cras amet qui numquam amavit, quiquam amavit cras amet" line of the *Pervigilium Veneris* ("tomorrow those who have never loved will love, and those who have will love tomorrow"), the broken echo concludes, and builds up, "stanzas" of various lengths, summing up the essential qualities of the different choral voices. The elements "vary" the praise, as the rest of the hymn will "vary" the refrain. Thus, the "Mists and Exhalations," "Rising or falling still advance his praise" (with an echo of "still" from line 184); then the lovely anadiplosis of line 192, where the winds pick up the motion of the clouds, transmit it to the visible waving of the trees, and complete a traditional symphony of the *locus amoenus* with the warbling of the water's eloquence, followed by the bird song.

The final stanza (200–204) returns to the singers themselves. A *tornata* that, like the conclusion of *Lycidas*, frames as well as completes, it is self-referential. Its self-reference is like that of the prayer, which con-cludes in a kind of caudal or meta-prayer for its own efficacy (and which, in Herbert's poems in *The Temple*, is frequently disposed throughout the main text in a constant figurative undersong). In addition, it invokes the primary world of pastoral. The sounding landscape is "made vocal" by poetry by means of that primary animation which, for Vico, is the "most luminous" of tropes, in that it makes fables of the inanimate by giving "sense and passion" to things, here both embodied in voice. The authen-ticity of the hymn itself is here avowedly confined to a realm of figure: all that can bear witness to unfallen man's praising voice are the stock fictions of pastoral fable, "taught" his praise. This echoes Virgil's first eclogue, "formosam resonare doces Amaryllida in silvas," even as they are both reechoed, in fallen modulations, in Adam's forlorn cry in Book X (860–62):

> O Woods, O Fountains, Hillocks, Dales and Bow'rs,
> With other echo late I taught your Shades
> To answer, and resound far other Song.

Adam here is already like Virgil's Tityrus and the "starv'd lover" of Book IV, line 769. Even the Original Song is full of echoes, although in *Paradise Lost*, an internal *Nachklang* frequently generates a proleptic *Vorklang*, or preecho. In the poem's pattern of unfallen organization, we must take this hymn to be the true *locus amoenus* (Milton's *locus classicus*) of pastoral echo, and its rhetoric to be that of pastoral praise, not loss.

But perhaps the most remarkable aspect of the scheme of echoing refrain here is that it is employed tropically. The first "echo" of the series which increases, rather than diminishes, in significatory volume is itself a metaphor of the reflection of light. The sun (as Conti says, "author of light to the other stars") "sounds / His praise"; the other heavenly bodies "resound / His praise"in echo, and in conceptual parallel to their return of solar light.

The Original Hymn, then, manifests not only the First Refrain, but the First Echo. Even the angelic choir's "sacred Song" in Book III (372–415) has no refrain, nor indeed any other echoing schemes. It is like sung doctrine, and requires the accompaniment of "Harps ever tun'd, that glittering by thir side / Like Quivers hung"—that is, aside from the shade of pun on "quaver" as musical ornament, harps with strings like the glittering arrows of erotic putti. It concludes with the neoclassical lyric formula "never shall my Harp thy praise / Forget." The only natural acoustical echoes occurring previously in *Paradise Lost* are in the demonic regions of Book II, where they are used in carefully turned figures to

describe the nature of damned assent. The fallen angels agreeing with
Mammon after his speech produce a sound likened to that of winds stored
in hollow rocks, played back later "with hoarse cadence" to "lull" an-
chored ships (284–90). But we must remember that this concord will only
lead to the full disclosure of its own acoustic nature in the transformed
hisses later on (Book X). And so, too, with the assent given to Satan's
words further on:

> If chance the radiant Sun with farewell sweet
> Extend his ev'ning beam, the fields revive,
> The birds thir notes renew, and bleating herds
> Attest thir joy, that hill and valley rings.
>   (II, 492–95)

(Here, too, light strikes forth sound, and "herds" half-echo "birds.") But
this very simile, his epic need to use it, and its lamentable success in the
poem cause Milton to interject, in one of those rare moments of intrusion,
his revulsion. In Book IV, he cries out "Honor dishonorable" in disgust at
the notion that postlapsarian *pudeur* about nudity was present in Paradise.
Here in Book II, he cries out: "O shame to men! Devil with Devil damn'd
/ Firm concord holds, men only disagree." Both this damnable echoing
and the unechoing, unfigured music of the heavenly choir in Book III,
then, are recalled and transcended in their echoes in the First Hymn.
They are cancelled and transformed in a process analogous in Milton to
what Hegel calls *Aufhebung*.

The Original Hymn not only originates refrain, but interprets the
scheme as a trope of echo—as assent, consent, concert, consonance,
approval, and witness. Moreover, its relation to older utterances of the
trope is itself resonant. This affirmative aspect of echo's figure completely
obliterates a negative, mocking one, which appears in a starkly literal way
earlier, again in the demonic milieu of Book II. Sin's account to Satan of
her parturition of Death concludes as her son, "he my inbred enemy,"
"forth issu'd, brandishing his fatal Dart / Made to destroy." The following
lines are strongly Ovidian: "I fled, and cri'd out *Death*; / Hell trembl'd at
the hideous Name, and sigh'd / From all her Caves, and back resounded
Death" (II, 787–89).

This is an instance of a negation more profound than even the
reductive mockery which Milton draws upon, and Sin anticipates for
fallen human poetry. She cries out her son's name in a blend of erotic fear
and mother love; she names him directly and screams out the general
human alarm (as in "Murder!"). Hell's return of the word is the sound of
revulsion from caves whose hollowed emptiness has now for the first time

been (1) employed as a physical locus of echo, and (2) figuratively identified with negation, nonbeing, and death. And yet the whole event uses the materials of pastoral affirmative echo, perverted in the Satanic mode of eternally twisted tropings. "The forest wide is fitter to resound / The hollow Echo of my careful cryes" says Spenser's Cuddie in his sestina (*Shepheardes Calender*, "August," 159–60), thus importing the hollowness of the nymph's abode into the sound of all the body she has left. But most poetic echoes are far from hollow; rather are they crowded with sound and rebound or, like Milton's echo of "Death," with dialectic. Never again would negative echo resound so immediately and so clearly. In American poetry from Emerson through Whitman, Frost, and Stevens, the seascape or landscape will only be able to utter the word *death* in a barely decipherable whisper.

The comic or satiric echo song depends for its force, then, on the dramatic irony sustained by the primary voice's not "hearing," as it were, the nasty synecdochic echo (else it would surely, we feel, shut up after a couplet or two). An even stronger dramatic irony is generated when the speaker is made inadvertently to echo a prior voice: dramatic form is an implicit echo chamber in this respect. (One has only to think of the role of words like *natural* and *nature* in *King Lear* or *honest* in *Othello*, whose reboundings define the tragic contingencies of those who give them voice. The operation of the trope of dramatic irony in such cases seems dialectical. Is it because of the anterior enunciations of such words that a tragic hero is known to all but himself as an echoer, rather than as a propounder? Or does the classical analysis of the dramatic irony as an inadvertent foreshadowing, an un-self-comprehended prophecy, reveal the more central twisting of the ironic machine?) In the narrative realm, such instances abound in *Paradise Lost*. "Or when we lay," argues Belial, invoking recent pains (II, 168–69), "Chain'd on the burning Lake? that sure was worse," unaware that he is echoing the narrator's previous description of the nature of Satan's vastness: "So stretcht out huge in length the Arch-fiend lay / Chain'd on the burning Lake" (I, 209–10). The echo, which includes the enjambed "lay," is of a voice Belial has never heard, an epic narrator possessed of some "Foreknowledge absolute." The reader is reminded again how Belial is limited by his ignorance of the script written for him (once he has surrendered his freedom by choosing Satan and the fiction of self-createdness). Even as the modern reader hears a secondary echo, in this and other instances of repeated phrase throughout *Paradise Lost*, of the classical formulaic epithet, he implicitly surveys the distance between fallen angels such as Belial and the Homeric personages who are both his poetic forbears and, in the remodeled mythological history of *Paradise Lost*, his historical descendants.

In general, when Milton's poem echoes itself, whether from nearby or at a great distance, there is no ironic shift of voice, as in the previous case. In its wordplay, for example, *Paradise Lost* favors the echoing sort, rather than the compact form of the single word: *antanaclasis* rather than strict pun. In the rhetoric of wit, this is usually the weaker form (imagine, for example, "Now is the winter of our discontent / Made glorious summer by this sun of York's / Own son"), where the repetition has the plonking quality of self-glossing in the worst way. In many cases in Shakespeare's sonnets, or in lines like Donne's "When thou hast done, thou hast not done," the antanaclastic repetition embodies a compact pun (so that in order to gloss itself, the line would have to end "thou hast not done [Donne]," and it is only the second "done" which is being played upon). It is likely that the excessively unfunny antanaclasis with which Satan sneaks into Paradise, when "in contempt, / At one slight bound high overleap'd all bound / Of Hill or highest Wall" (IV, 181–82), is mimetically bad—even if Satan's leap is as graceful as that of the winner over the tennis net, the epic voice, in describing it, must change its notes to corny. At such close range, echoing repetition controls the ironies that inhere in the relation of the punning meanings, rather than those dramatic ironies that change of time and place will make literal.

More typical in *Paradise Lost* is the slightly deformed antanaclasis which Abraham Fraunce in *The Arcadian Rhetorike* (1588) reserved for the usual term *paranomasia* (which he also calls "allusion," interestingly enough, from the *ludus* of wordplay): thus Satan in Book I sneers at the benign rule of the King of Heaven (whom he has just accused of being *tyrannos* rather than *basileus* anyway), who "still his strength conceal'd, / Which tempted our attempt, and wrought our fall" (I, 641–42). Milton has given Satan the advertent wordplay here, as Adam is given the gentler and more loving wit, the beautiful and beautifully complex invocation to Eve in Book IV (411): "Sole partner and sole part of all these joys." (Here, as Alistair Fowler points out, the two meanings of *sole*—"only" and "unrivalled"—are also at work.) But love commands more intricate wit than hate does, and the way in which we are reminded that *part* is part of *partner*—an echo of stem rather than of suffix—is one worthy of George Herbert.

Closely related to Belial's echo of the voice of the narration—indeed, a kind of antitype of it—is Satan's echo of an earlier formula in his speech on Mt. Niphates (IV, 42–45). At a strange moment of inadvertent admission of a truth about his relation to God that he had previously (and publicly) denied, he avers that

> he deserv'd no such return
> From me, whom he created when I was
> In that bright eminence, and with his good
> Upbraided none . . .

This is the Satan who, enthroned at the beginning of Book II in a fierce but inauthentic splendor—its description may itself echo Spenser's representation of the throne of Lucifera (*Faerie Queene* I. iv. 8)—"exalted sat, by merit rais'd / To that bad eminence" (II, 5–6). The memory of the "bright eminence" echoes the reader's earlier apprehension of the bad one, but the dramatic irony is softer here than it was in the case of Belial. An even more poignant echo of the inexorable narrative voice occurs in Book IX, where Satan is at one of his most moving moments in the poem.

He has just made his second mistake about Paradise. (The first is in Book IV, 505–8, where he attributes to the unfallen Adam and Eve, as they make love in a sight to him "hateful" and "tormenting," the necessity for the consolations and errors of fallen eroticism. He says of them that they were "Imparadis't in one another's arms / The happier Eden." Satan is wrong because they are "imparadis't" indeed in Paradise; the notion that an erotic embrace is a bower of bliss is a desperate, lovely fiction of fallen humanity.) A complementary mistake also results from Satan's being smitten with beauty in Paradise: addressing Earth (IX, 99ff), Satan praises the scene before him, feels the need of rhetorical elevation, then rationalizes the hyperbole: "O Earth, how like to Heav'n, if not preferr'd / More justly, Seat worthier of Gods, as built / With second thoughts, reforming what was old!" Then comes a second order of rationalization: Earth is better because it is the newer model, "For what God after better worse would build?" Again, *le pauvre*, Satan can only respond in fallen human terms of work, enterprise, and progress. It reciprocates for the mistake about love in Book IV. From the beauty of Earth and the nobility of its inhabitants ("Growth, Sense, Reason all summ'd up in Man"—a purely humanist notion), Satan moves to the deep pleasure yielded by landscape, pleasure unfallen yet, for humanity or for the seventeenth century, into the declensions of Beautiful, Picturesque, and Sublime, but summing them all up:

> If I could joy in aught, sweet interchange
> Of Hill and Valley, Rivers, Woods and Plains,
> Now Land, now Sea, and Shores with Forest crown'd,
> Rocks, Dens, and Caves; but I in none of these
> Find place or refuge . . .
>
> (IX, 115–19)

"Rocks, Dens and Caves . . ." Satan finds no refuge in these, and particularly in the dialectic of array and design in pictures and spectacles of them. The reader will remember that the adventurous Drakes and Magellans of Pandemonium in Book II passed "O'er many a Frozen, many a Fiery Alp, / Rocks, Caves, Lakes, Fens, Bogs, Dens, and shades of Death" (II, 620–21). That famous line of monosyllables over which the steps of prosodic theorists have for so long tripped is immediately echoed in the next line, "A Universe of death. . . ." Not only is Satan's longing catalogue of the joys of contemplated landscape bound to conclude in the places of retreat and darkness, prefiguring the meaning of shadiness that will eventually become attached to dark places after Adam and Eve first guiltily hide themselves there. He is, moreover, echoing the narration's understanding of the proleptically fallen relation, in Book II's prophetic vision of human culture, of rocks and dens and caves with death.

Adam's reflex of this kind of Satanic echoing—echoing of what has already, and in just those words, been propounded—can be heard in his patently rhetorical antanaclasis at IX, 1067. The first words he says to Eve after they awaken, "as from unrest," from their first fallen fucking in a "shady bank, / Thick overhead with verdant roof imbowr'd" (IX, 1037–38) are: "O Eve, in evil hour thou didst give ear / To that false Worm . . ." (IX, 1067–68). This is the same rhetorical Adam of the "sole partner and sole part," affirming the new fallen phenomenology of Eve's name: it no longer echoes "even," "eve," "evening," but now, as henceforth, "evil." In addition, he, like Satan, is echoing the narration. Less than three hundred lines before, Eve had stretched out her hand "in evil hour / Forth reaching to the Fruit" (IX, 780–81). Adam speaks almost with a tone of "indeed, Milton was right in saying that it was 'in evil hour' that this occurred," a tinct of wisdom never given to Satan. It is only the poetry of fallen man that will need to employ tropes and fables, similes, echoes, and allusions, in order to represent Truth. We somehow know that Adam is far less mocked by the dramatic irony of the narrative echo than Satan is, tortured ironist though he may be.

The chorus of echoes which accompanies the scenes of loss and regret surrounding the Fall is completed by the narration's own playback of an already resounding phrase. It occurs in the digression on the nature of the fig leaves with which human nakedness—the fallen form of nudity, ever to require *clothing*, as nudity itself, if concealed, is always to be veiled by visionary *drapery*—first hides itself ("Honor dishonorable!"). The fig tree is associated with a benign primitive role in a Rousseauian nature: the "Indian Herdsman shunning heat / Shelters in cool" (IX, 1108–9). It is

this exotic tree, benevolent and protective in the more exotic and childlike of human cultures, that

> spreads her arms
> Branching so broad and long, that in the ground
> The bended Twigs take root, and Daughters grow
> About the Mother tree, a Pillar'd shade
> High overarch't, and echoing walks between.
>
> (IX, 1103–7)

Shade in Paradise is a lovely variation from sunlight; this "Pillar'd shade,"
and that of the "shady bank / Thick overhead with verdant roof imbowr'd"
have already been imprinted with the shadowy type of death. In Book I,
301–3, the famous and heavily allusive image of the fallen legions of the
rebel "Angel Forms" shows them as lying "Thick as autumnal Leaves that
strow the Brooks / In Vallombrosa, where th' Etrurian shades / *High
overarch't* imbower" (my italics). The specific verbal echo accompanies
the shadows cast by the earlier text on the futurity of all shady places.
And, as elsewhere in Milton, the rhetorical echo calls up the literal
acoustical event: "echoing walks between."

There is something like a dramatic irony in a character's inadvertent echo of the narrative voice by which even his own utterance is
recounted. There is also, as we have been seeing, a kind of allusive
typology in the more possibly self-aware echo of an earlier moment
in Miltonic narration by a later one. We might compare these two conditions with the different kinds of irony revealed by the sense of unwitting
literalness. In a phrase like Miranda's "O brave new world . . . ," the
audience recognizes an allusion to a literal hemisphere, of which the
speaker is ignorant. Much more like Miltonic allusive irony is Abraham's
remark to Isaac, in response to the boy's question about what lamb will be
used for the sacrifice. "God will provide his own lamb," replies the
Kierkegaardian religious hero; the dramatic irony is again generated by the
unwitting literalness of what had been propounded as a trope, here a trope
of evasion. But the Christian reading of this episode (not the *akeda* of the
Hebrew Bible, but the first figurative sacrifice foreshadowing the trope of
Christ as lamb), gives the literalness another dimension. What Abraham
offers figuratively, the narrative literalizes when the ram is discovered
entangled in the thicket. But the literalization is only a movement into
the fullness of antitype: the foreshadowing will be literally fulfilled in the
typological completion of the episode in the New Testament when the
Lamb of God is finally provided by, and of, him.

It is this kind of dramatic and typological irony that is at work in

so many of those highly charged rhetorical moments in *Paradise Lost*. It
looks in the contortions of Satan's manipulations of the literal and the
figurative, the local and the general ("Evil be thou my Good" completed
by the whining of "All good to me becomes / Bane" in Book IX, for
example). Indeed, we might learn from the shadows of the unwitting in
Satan's rhetoric, and in that of Adam when he echoes Satan in syntax
and tone (as in IX, 755–75), how central to dramatic irony this question
of inadvertent literalness can be. (Kafka's great parable *On Parables* also
sheds fierce light on this.) Dramatic irony is often a matter of an utterance
striking an unwitting *Vorklang*, as it were, of an eventual echo, of a
situation to which it will turn out to have alluded. It might be redefined
in terms of manifest rhetorical figuration turning out, horribly, to have
been literal. Certainly, Satanic rhetoric provides an origination of this.

One kind of self-echo in Milton occurs in the almost leitmotivic
reappearance of phrases and cadences in *Paradise Lost* to which sophisticated critical attention of the past few decades has been so attentive.
These form a subclass of their own. As echoes, their voices do not come
from afar, or from absent places, so much as from a memory of the poem's
own utterance. Their region of origin is usually schematically related to
that of the echoic answer: thus, in Book V, the Son sits "Amidst as from a
flaming Mount, whose top / Brightness had made invisible" (V, 598–99);
the reversal of "No light, but rather darkness visible" (I, 63) points up the
radically different character of the flaming. But such patterns are quite
basic to the fabric of *Paradise Lost*, and might be considered as elements in
what seems to be the poem's memory of itself.

WILLIAM KERRIGAN

Oedipus and Sacred Oedipus

In "The Theme of the Three Caskets" Freud shows the recurrence in myth, folklore, and art of a grouping of three women. Their true faces are worn by the Fates. But often, in wishful disguises, they are posed before a man who must choose one of them in the context of love or affection. Havoc may ensue, as it does in *King Lear*, when the man fails to choose the third woman. Unlike Bassanio in *The Merchant of Venice*, Lear is blinded by the obvious, and his refusal to see through appearances represents, in Freud's view, a disavowal of fate. To all appearances, that is, the old King acknowledges his death in the act of dividing his kingdom, but his unreadiness for the promised end is betrayed in his denial of the cold and reserved Cordelia. Despite her many transformations—Aphrodite for Paris, Cinderella for the Prince, Cordelia for Lear—the third woman preserves in some fashion her true character. She is the figure of Death, the inexorable one, the woman who, as Milton wrote in one of his most haunting phrases, "slits the thin-spun life." This theme also calls forth the best in Freud. At the end of the essay he returns to *King Lear* for his finest moment as a literary critic, which is, not surprisingly, the finest moment in psychoanalytic criticism:

> Lear is an old man. . . . But Lear is not only an old man: he is a dying man. In this way the extraordinary premise of the division of his inheritance loses all its strangeness. But the doomed man is not willing to renounce the love of women; he insists on hearing how much he is loved. Let us now recall the moving final scene, one of the culminating points of tragedy in modern drama. Lear carries Cordelia's dead body on

From *The Sacred Complex: On the Psychogenesis of Paradise Lost.* Copyright © 1983 by The President and Fellows of Harvard College. Harvard University Press.

to the stage. Cordelia is Death. If we reverse the situation it becomes intelligible and familiar to us. She is the Death-goddess who, like the Valkyrie in German mythology, carries away the dead hero from the battlefield. Eternal wisdom, clothed in the primaeval myth, bids the old man renounce love, choose death and make friends with the necessity of dying.

The dramatist brings us nearer to the ancient theme by representing the man who makes the choice between the three sisters as aged and dying. The regressive revision which he has thus applied to the myth, distorted as it was by wishful transformation, allows us enough glimpses of its original meaning to enable us perhaps to reach as well a superficial allegorical interpretation of the three female figures in the theme. We might argue that what is represented here are the three inevitable relations that a man has with a woman—the woman who bears him, the woman who is his mate and the woman who destroys him; or that they are the three forms taken by the figure of the mother in the course of a man's life—the mother herself, the beloved one who is chosen after her pattern, and lastly the Mother Earth who receives him once more. But it is in vain that an old man yearns for the love of woman as he had it first from his mother; the third of the Fates alone, the silent Goddess of Death, will take him into her arms.

These two paragraphs are worthy to be set next to any statements that have been elicited by the plays of Shakespeare. There was a side to Freud, this man whose thought, like his therapy, starves illusion, that resembled the implacability of natural law, and it led him directly to the heart of *Lear.*

If *Hamlet* is the great tragedy of the absent father, whose hero finds God, *Lear* is the great tragedy of the absent mother, whose hero finds Nature. It is unbearable. Once he has denied Cordelia, Lear drops into a disillusionment without bottom. When he might finally be able to say "This is the worst," he is dead and unable to speak. Everything maternal in the world save for Death, the mother as natural law, divested of every illusion, fails him. For all the rant about the hell of the vagina and the curse of procreation, the old King conspicuously lacks a Queen. He searches the faces of his daughters for the face of his missing wife. Inside him, meanwhile, another mother presses toward his heart. As he says, during one of those onslaughts of psychosomatic distress scattered throughout the play,

> O, how this mother swells up toward my heart!
> Hysterica passio, down, thou climbing sorrow,
> Thy element's below!—Where is this daughter?
> (II.iv.54–56)

Before he will weep, "this heart / Shall break into a hundred thousand fluws" (II.iv.282). By the final scene the "sorrow" of "this mother" climbs to his heart. In one of the reversals Freud points to, Mother Earth bearing dead children, the weight of all sorrow and all flaw, becomes Lear bearing Cordelia. "Break heart!"—Kent wishes him death. "Vex not his ghost. Oh, let him pass!" The "break" and the "pass" are imaginatively accomplished by the "hysterica passio" residual from the first and deepest mother. She gave him life once, and she does not repeat herself. It does not matter how many times we say "never," for the third mother is already inside of us, the gift of the first. Like Satan, Lear also lives the riddle of the Sphinx backward: the last mother is the rediscovery in total disillusionment of what the first has wrought.

Eve became the figure of Death when she "knew not eating Death" (9.792). Thereafter she is doomed to have the children of Satan, who can only sire Death, by oral impregnation. The vacillations in fallen Adam's attitude toward her follow the cleavage in the two common etymologies given for her name, *hevia* (serpent) and *eva* (life):

> Out of my sight, thou Serpent, that name best
> Befits thee with him leagu'd, thyself as false
> And hateful; nothing wants, but that thy shape,
> Like his, and color Serpentine may show
> Thy inward fraud, to warn all Creatures from thee
> Henceforth; lest that too heav'nly form, pretended
> To hellish falsehood, snare them. But for thee
> I had persisted happy.
>
> (10.867–874)

> peace return'd
> Home to my Breast, and to my memory
> His promise, that thy Seed shall bruise our Foe;
> Which then not minded in dismay, yet now
> Assures me that the bitterness of death
> Is past, and we shall live. Whence Hail to thee,
> *Eve* rightly call'd, Mother of all Mankind,
> Mother of all things living, since by thee
> Man is to live, and all things live for Man.
>
> (11.153–161)

In the first passage, Adam foreshadows his children in feeling that he has inherited death and woe from Eve, that fate is the consequence of his love for Eve. But in the second he senses that "Man is to live" through Eve, and Christ will perfect this refiguring or "rightly calling" of Eve. *Paradise Regained* is a happy repetition of Book 9 of *Paradise Lost*: now Eve stays at home, Adam goes forth to be tempted, and comes home having redeemed the meaning of Eve. The Christian mother is life, Cordelia with the promise of a new futurity. Through Christ, peace returns "Home" to the breast of man, not the wandering womb that overtakes the heart of Lear. How does this renovation establish itself in the symbolism of the brief epic?

Let us return to the pinnacle, bearing with us Freud's evocation of the three mothers in the life of a man—the mother who gives life and nourishment; the mother regained in mature erotic love; and the Earth who receives us when, in the words of Michael to Adam, "like ripe Fruit thou drop / Into my Mother's lap" (11.535–536). For Antaeus the first mother will become the third, as in a pagan Pietà. For Oedipus, returned to his father's house, the first mother will become the second. It is the work of Christ on earth to redeem tragic man by transforming the third mother into the first:

> he unobserv'd
> Home to his Mother's house private returned.

Like Antaeus after the bout with Hercules, like Oedipus after answering the riddle, Christ in the end returns to his first mother. As we will see, the Miltonic psychology of redemption demands that there be nothing compulsive or fatal about this attachment; and, unlike the Laius who made his deserted son Oedipus ("swell-foot"), Christ's Father will not permit his Son "to dash" his "foot against a stone." Still, two factors orient the closure of the poem toward this tragic fate: the typological identities of Christ and Mary, and its symmetry with the closure of the parent poem. Is this not the home of second Adam and second Eve, toward which our first parents began wandering, providence their guide, at the end of *Paradise Lost*? But while Adam was the mother of Eve (called his "Daughter" at 9.291), new Eve is the mother of new Adam, and the old husband has now become a son. The conventional typology Milton exploits has retained, latent in its symbolism, the idea of their oedipal marriage. As dramatized in *Paradise Regained*, the work of redemption is the sacred complex by means of which this marriage, and much of what it means in psychic life, is transcended through its latent repetition.

The double simile unmistakably urges separation from the first mother. Antaeus is defeated because his strength, depending wholly on this attachment, is also his weakness; Oedipus became, in the words of Neville's Seneca, "the most unhappiest wretch that ever sun did see," because he too delivered his manliness to the first mother; and we might recall here that Death and "th' incestuous Mother" (10.602) are inseparable companions in *Paradise Lost*. Severing this primal attachment is, in the life of every man, the task of forming a self—provisionally completed by the institution of the superego. The savior of *Paradise Regained* makes this severance absolute. He follows the call of his Father into the wilderness, leaving mother and home behind. As a prelude to temptation he fasts, asserting his freedom from the primordial gift of the mother. The meaning of these actions becomes explicit in the first temptation: as the Word is more nourishing than bread, so the Father replaces the mother as provider of strength.

By "separation" from the mother I do not mean simple distance. Milton reveals a psychological aspect to the theological contention that Mary supplies the humanity of Christ. The hero has assimilated his mother, grieved and identified. She is an internal presence, contributing from within to his work of salvation, and when Christ descends into himself to set his life before him (as Mary does in the matching soliloquy at 2.63–104, calming her pure breast in the absence of her son), the words of his mother appear inside these "deep thoughts" (1.190). Given the context we are evolving now, the speech of Mary still resounding in the mind of her son may be appreciated as one of Milton's shrewdest triumphs. Christ remembers the day she took him "apart" to teach the lesson of apartness:

> High are thy thoughts
> O Son, but nourish them and let them soar
> To what height sacred virtue and true worth
> Can raise them, though above example high;
> By matchless Deeds express thy matchless Sire.
> For know, thou art no Son of mortal man;
> Though men esteem thee low of Parentage,
> Thy Father is th'Eternal King, who rules
> All Heaven and Earth, Angels and Sons of men.
> A messenger from God foretold thy birth
> Conceiv'd in me a Virgin; he foretold
> Thou shouldst be great and sit on *David's* Throne,
> And of thy Kingdom there should be no end.
>   (1.229–241)

He for God only, she for God in him: before the voice of the Father proclaims his lineage to the world at the baptism, second Eve makes her private annunciation. This mother removes from the life of her heroic son any possibility of duplicating the tragedy of Oedipus, which was predicated on his ignorance of his progenitors; when Christ returns home, he knows who he is. She gives him the answer, in a sense, to the riddle of the

Sphinx, which Freud interpreted as symbolic of the earliest riddle whose unfolding cannot be extricated from the process of psychic organization: where do babies come from? Christ has the facts of his life. On the pinnacle he will do no more than what Mary has urged. She initiates his separation from her, a mother who does not tempt or retard, but rather propels her son to the paternal identification that resolves the oedipus complex and organizes his autonomy. At the beginning of her beautifully direct and complete disclosure, she tells him to "nourish" his thoughts (she herself being part of that nourishment, since Christ is thinking this speech), and at the end she points him toward the symbolism of the Bible ("*David's* Throne," "thy Kingdom") he will prefer to material nourishment in the first temptation.

Heir to the oedipus complex, the superego is the universal solution to the tragedy of Oedipus. Yet in preventing this catastrophe, the superego brings its own agony in the either/or of ambition and veneration, rivalry and submission, being oneself and obeying another. When Satan parodies the speech of Mary on the pinnacle, he assumes that Christ's attempt to be "highest" *must entail a conflict with his Father.* But in a speech that gives Christ the wherewithal to rise above Antaeus who could not live separated from his mother, Hercules who did the bidding of women, the Sphinx who must be conquered with the knowledge of humanity, and Oedipus who actualized the marriage latent in the symbolism of second Adam and second Eve, Mary also prepares Christ to outriddle the fallacious Satan. The wisest line in her speech, "By matchless Deeds express thy matchless Sire," the one Christ fulfills on the pinnacle, promises that this son can strive to be *matchless* without competing with his father. The Christian superego, it is suggested, will allow a certain relief from the disjunctions that burden the first superego. Pursuing the highest ambition, "above example high," the Son of God remains, indeed becomes, the image of his "matchless Sire."

"Milton keeps reminding us of Christ's hunger," Watkins writes, "which is his unifying symbol, modulated from food to truth to glory." Satan can be termed "Insatiable of glory" (3.148), and Christ can term himself "hung'ring more to do my Father's will" (2.259): both hunger. By his extension of this vocabulary Milton evolves in metaphor a concept not dissimilar from Freud's libido, which also has its beginnings in hunger. Through the ordeal of his temptation, the Son of God destroys and regenerates the hunger that is Death, Son of Satan.

In the wilderness Christ relives symbolically the entire history of the libido, regaining for the prospect of choice what all the children of Eve undergo as a process. There are two temptations of food. In the first

Satan asks Christ to provide nourishment for himself and others in want; in the second Satan would provide food for Christ. The first answers to the narcissism of the undifferentiated infant, for whom the mother is a part of himself and food can be summoned, as if "By Miracle" (1.337), through the agency of his magical cry. The luxurious banquet, by contrast, acknowledges that nourishment depends on an external source. It is suggestive that Christ first *feels* hunger after the initial temptation (2.244), for the two temptations correspond to a fateful metamorphosis in the history of the libido. At the beginning of life libido is need—biological, appeasable, finite. Soon, however, need yields to the transgressions of desire, psychological and restless; instead of satisfying a mere emptiness, nourishment comes to *mean* something, and as the sign of a desire, becomes caught up in the early dialectic of self and other. Thereafter libido is an energy of infinite "wanting," our involuntary response to the absent and the lost, proceeding from object to object with the excess characteristic of wish—the force in us that will not welcome reality. Far down this line we find the exotic Ovidian banquet conjured by Satan, every dish a sign of wealth, privilege, and cultural refinement, so different from the bread of the first temptation.

For Milton the great symbol of this break in the life of the libido is the fall. Blameless midday hunger took flight into desire, and narcissism was no longer innocent. Doubtless the fasting of *Paradise Regained*, the long debates about the proper objects of desire, are meant to purify that first transgression:

> But now I feel I hunger, which declares
> Nature hath need of what she asks; yet God
> Can satisfy that need some other way,
> Though hunger still remain.
>
> (2.252–255)

Fasting reestablishes the difference between need and desire. Anything beyond the constant pressure of hunger is a superfluity—and this entire dimension of excess, the sphere of desire, is referred to God. All the temptations represent a continuation of Christ's separation from Mary. As the source of his humanity, she is the source of his hunger. Taking "some other way," Christ repudiates the long chain of worldly desires that issues from the first mother and ends only in death. God may not give what nature asks, but with hunger in abeyance, the way is clear for God to satisfy in "some other way," creating desire anew. "Me hung'ring more to do my Father's will." The will of the Father *is* the desire of the Son.

But the summary movement from need to desire, the oedipal

mother who succeeds the nourishing mother, has been removed from the chain by the tempter himself. Unlike the Lady of *Comus*, Christ will not be made to declare the sage and serious doctrine of virginity, even though his own life will become its primary sanction for Christian culture. When Belial proposes to tempt Christ with women, Satan seems to be tempted himself, and he reacts with an indignation oddly resembling that of his opponent in the wilderness. This greater man will not, like "*Adam* first of men," fall by "Wife's allurement" (2.133–134):

> for Beauty stands
> In th'admiration only of weak minds
> Led captive; cease to admire, and all her Plumes
> Fall flat and shrink into a trivial toy,
> At every sudden slighting quite abasht:
> Therefore with manlier objects we must try
> His constancy, with such as have more show
> Of worth, of honor, glory, and popular praise;
> Rocks whereon greatest men have oftest wreck'd.
> (2.220–228)

If there is a coherent figure in the opening lines of this passage (a peacock with tail first spread, then closed, as Dunster suggested?), it soon suffers a puzzling seachange in which the word "shrink" signals both a diminishment of what "stands" within the weak beholder of beauty and a metamorphosis of the plumed object beheld, now "a trivial toy." This likeness of a failed erection leads Satan instantly to "manlier objects," the "Rocks" of his new strategy—a metaphor that seems to have leapt out of the "hard stones" of the first temptation (1.343). Ironically, what Satan says of women is true of everything he offers Christ, who is not destined to dash himself on a stone. Christ is rather the "solid rock" (4.18) on which Satan wrecks, "a rock / Of Adamant" (4.533–534), "firm" (4.534), a proven metal. The triumph is Christ standing on the pinnacle, "highest."

The important thing to remember about "phallic symbols" is that the phallus, as its name proclaims, is itself a symbol—the "signifier of desire," in Lacan's elegant phrase. The tempter displays impressive objects. Is *that* the signified of your desire? Yet Satan has laid down in his own account of diminished female beauty the motif that runs through all of Christ's refusals until, on the pinnacle, the tempter himself falls down in amazement: the Son of God only desires to be the Son of God. The mockery and belittlement of Satan's impressive objects by the unmoved Christ betrays an almost physical conception of desire. When something appears desirable to us, we have lost to this something in the external world a power in us. "Weak minds" find female beauty strong; it is actually their own expelled strength that binds them. This sense of desire as an investment of mental power answers in Christian terms to the doctrine of *cupiditas*, and in psychoanalytic terms to the cathectic energy of the libido. One can feel the might of Christ grow as his desire is withheld again and again from the objects of the world Satan parades before him:

> Extol not Riches then, the toil of Fools,
> The wise man's cumbrance if not snare, more apt
> To slacken Virtue and abate her edge.
>
> (2.453–455)

> Conquerors, who leave behind
> Nothing but ruin wheresoe'er they rove . . .
> Till Conqueror Death discover them scarce men,
> Rolling in brutish vices, and deform'd,
> Violent or shameful death their due reward.
>
> (3.78–88)

In the end it is as if all the strength of the world has flowed into him as a consequence of his very rejection of the world. The libido of the sons of men, dispersed like the body of Osiris among the objects desire deifies, is gathered and consecrated in the virgin wholeness of Christ. In the sacred oedipus complex, castration is in part this chosen withdrawal from the profane world, which no longer signifies desire, no longer calls forth power and energy from their interior fortress. This attempt to reclaim desire for volition presents us with a mature derivative of the idealized virginity, the narcissistic form of castration, found in *Comus*. By disassembling the phallus as symbolic bridge between desire and its external objects, Christ gains an interior and spiritual potency—a oneness with the paternal will.

The repressed temptation returns in the vision of Athens, "Mother of Arts" nestled "in her sweet recess" (4.240–242). Satan speaks of women as "such toys" (2.177) and, in rebuking Belial, as "a trivial toy." When he rejects Athenian wisdom, Christ speaks of shallow men reading books as "collecting toys," "Children gathering pebbles on the shore" (4.328–330), and soon thereafter of "swelling epithets thick laid / As varnish on a Harlot's cheek" (343–344). Why are toys a symbol of the despicable, of what desire has vacated? These allusions to toys in the vicinity of women and books may remind us that learning begins in playing. Successors to the body of the mother, toys are the second objects of knowledge, and books themselves emerge from pebbles and whatnots, the array of playthings. The fact that Christ petulantly claims, "When I was yet a child, no childish play / To me was pleasing, all my mind was set /

Serious to learn and know" (1.201–203) alerts us to the possibility that our author associated danger with the learning that is playing. Milton probably began to learn under the aegis of women: son of a charitable mother, he also had an older sister. Perhaps all boys in the full career of their learning move from the maternal matrix of early playing to the more paternal realm of formal education, where the superego oversees their exercises, but that transition was abrupt and the two genders distinctly marked in the Renaissance.

He thanked his father for providing him with this male wisdom in both poetry and prose. Milton scholars know, better than anyone, that he learned. But what was his experience with those books? Why does Satan annul the erotic temptation and conclude the expansion of desire with old teachers and old texts wherein Christ discerns whorish epithets, things "past shame"? When we quote the famous passages on trial and temptation in *Areopagitica*—"He that can apprehend and consider vice with all her baits and seeming pleasures, and yet abstain, and yet distinguish, and yet prefer that which is truly better, he is the true warfaring Christian"—we sometimes forget that their local context is a defense of the reading of tainted books as the safest way for a good man to learn about vice. I suspect that classical literature, which does not blush at "seeming pleasures," was like vernacular romance a play world for Milton, where conflicts of the home took root in culture. That he acquired culturally erotic ways we know from the Ovidian Elegy 5, which equates erection with poetic power, and particularly from Elegy 7, which he printed in 1645 with a retraction dated 1630: the "wantonness" of his youth has been reformed by "the shady Academy" and "its Socratic streams," for "thenceforward my breast has been rigid under a thick case of ice, of which the boy himself fears the frost for his arrows, and Venus herself is afraid of my Diomedean strength" (p. 16). It is the posture of the Lady of Christ's, the Lady, and Christ, all of them strong through the exercise of repudiation. But as we gather from "Il Penseroso," reading is the social life of a solitary man, and it was precisely "the solitariness of man" (CP II, 246) that the divine institution of marriage was intended to assuage. Milton could be the master of luxurious books, bringing to them, in Christ's words, "A spirit and judgment equal or superior" (4.324), but nothing in the play world of culture had prepared him for Mary Powell.

After his impetuous marriage, Milton expounded the sage and serious doctrine of divorce (not for "gross and vulgar apprehensions") with an evident bitterness over the consequences of his chaste and literary youth. Those who sport with Amaryllis in the shade "prove most successful in their matches, because their wild affections . . . have been as so many divorces to teach their experience" (CP II, 249–250). The women that Milton knew from books were fantasy women: harlots to be repulsed, virgins to be guarded, "Fairy Damsels" (2.359) like those decorating Satan's banquet. In his maturity Milton had reason enough to denounce a moral life lived by the turning of pages.

The autobiographical sources of the Athenian temptation reach beyond the treacherous instruction Milton had received concerning the second mother in a man's life to the meaning he ascribed to *scientia* itself. The genetic sequence that leads from the body of the mother to toys to books curled back on itself for Milton; books unveiled and exhibited the maternal body of the world. *Ad Patrem* contains the most interesting of Milton's several accounts of his education. Written in the tongue to which his father had given him access, it is our sole record of a disagreement between them. The father, we infer, has expressed some dissatisfaction over the son's dalliance with poetry at the expense of more practical pursuits. As Milton thanks him for his education, he offers high praise unconsciously as well, for the father has given him a mother:

> I do not mention a father's usual generosities, for greater things have a claim on me. It was at your expense, dear father, after I had got the mastery of the language of Romulus and the graces of Latin, and acquired the lofty speech of the magniloquent Greeks, which is fit for the lips of Jove himself, that you persuaded me to add the flowers which France boasts and the eloquence which the modern Italian pours from his degenerate mouth . . . and the mysteries uttered by the Palestinian prophet. And finally, all that heaven contains and earth, our mother, beneath the sky, and the air that flows between earth and heaven, and whatever the waters and the trembling surface of the sea cover, your kindness gives me the means to know, if I care for the knowledge that your kindness offers. From the opening cloud science appears and, naked, she bends her face to my kisses, unless I should wish to run away or unless I should find her enjoyment irksome. . . . What greater gift could come from a father, or from Jove himself if he had given everything, with the single exception of heaven.

The gift of male culture might have proven "irksome," inciting a "wish to run away," were it not for the process of erotic sublimation that managed to seduce an oedipal mother (the *publica mater* of "Naturam Non Pati Senium," unwrinkled and ever fertile) in the lessons of the schoolroom. Knowledge, Milton writes in the last Prolusion, is our conquest of Mother Nature:

> almost nothing can happen without warning or by accident to a man who is in possession of the stronghold of wisdom. Truly he will seem to

have the stars under his control and domination, land and sea at his command, and the winds and storms submissive to his will. Mother Nature herself has surrendered to him. It is as if some god had abdicated the government of the world and committed its justice, laws, and administration to him as ruler.

Not unlike the abdicating Father of Book 3 of *Paradise Lost*, Milton's father had relinquished the privileged hold over knowledge that all fathers enjoy for a time, transferring the dominion of Mother Nature to a son who would one day design the entire universe, including the incomparable account of Creation in Book 7 of *Paradise Lost*. But the elder Milton had also opened the mysteries of the prophet, and that was the downfall of his paternity. As Milton reveals early in *Ad Patrem*, divine poetry "preserves some spark of Promethean fire and is the unrivalled glory of the heaven-born human mind and an evidence of our ethereal origin and celestial descent." In the religious form of the family romance, the prophetic poet is a son of God.

How can a son assert himself against a revered father? Divide him. "Insofar as I am a poet, I am not your son; my origins are divine, my authority is God, and it is with my God that the struggle we are here engaged in must be adjudicated. Are you not holding now, in your hands, my *Promethean fire?*" Symbolized in *Paradise Regained* in the difference between "son of Joseph" and "Son of God," this splitting of the imago of the father constitutes the major psychological strategy of Milton's life and work.

His father first, then all the derivatives of his father in earthly authority—teachers, bishops, kings, parliaments, theologians—could be deposed and abused by a rebellious son, while Milton at the same time remained the obedient son of his divine father. This is the generative core of the strong poet Harold Bloom has discerned for us, the unintimidated poet who read his precursors with a "judgment equal or superior," bowing to none of them, not even to Moses and the Evangelists. The two attitudes characteristic of his authorship, celebration and belligerence, derive from the psychological formula of the divided father. Milton's great lesson is that obedience is freedom—and so it is, if one is obedient to what lies outside the world and if through obedience one can do what is otherwise forbidden. His ability to pursue rebellious courses as the injunction of obedience chartered his apartness from social confinements. Guilt could always be overcome. He was not wrong to mature slowly, to desire divorce, to entertain the fantasies that interested him in polygamy, to oppose the church and comply with the killing of the King. When the spurious *Eikon Basilike* was causing some of its readers to regret that execution, Parliament could have found no man in all of Europe whose temperament was better suited to defend their nation against self-recrimination. Tillyard condensed a good deal of insight in remarking that if Milton had been Adam, he would have eaten the apple and commenced to write a pamphlet justifying himself. This man came to the Spirit of Protestantism with a tremendous oedipal defiance.

In *Comus* the split is obscured by the fact that earthly and heavenly authorities promote the same law. Only when the epilogue moves us toward a representation of transcendent destiny do we feel the aggressive desires locked prematurely in the obedience of the Lady. In *Paradise Regained*, written after the sacred complex had been articulated, profane and sacred law oppose each other in lethal combat.

The evolution of paternal defiance into spiritual power is close to being the manifest plot of the brief epic. In exchange for his gifts and his advice, the tempter wants to be worshipped as the Son's god. He hopes to exact from Christ a single acknowledgment: that *Satan is Christ's father*. Has he not always wished to be God? He first appears as an old man. He offers to feed Christ, then to plan his career and tender sound advice, to secure him wealth and power and statecraft, to hurry him and educate him, finally to define his name—and the one thing he expressly withholds from the Son is women. Who played this role in the life of Milton? Somewhere at the ground of the imaginative act that created this Satan (not the Satan of *Paradise Lost*) was the imago of John Milton, Sr., fixed in the unconscious of a troubled oedipal son. In place of the mother he had offered a cultural world to some degree symbolic of, but therefore alienated from, the genuine desire of the son. In this world, it is true, the son had found sublime means for restoring an archaic self-esteem. But he had also become entangled and belated there, weakening his eyes to learn every lesson but the one that matters most to a man—how to be happy with a woman. In *Paradise Regained* the best teacher takes revenge on the impositions of the Renaissance Name-of-the-Father.

Satan was not Milton's only idea of his father. We are speaking of a split, and if one current was murderous enough to produce a vision of the devil, the other must have lent its veneration to the Miltonic God. As we read in *Ad Patrem*,

> Now, since it is my lot to have been born a poet, why does it seem strange to you that we, who are so closely united by blood, should pursue sister arts and kindred interests? Phoebus himself, wishing to part himself between us two, gave some gifts to me and others to my father; and, father and son, we share the possession of the divided god.

The father had some renown as an organist and composer. It was music, the paternal half of the divided god, "Married to immortal verse" that ravished the "meeting soul" of L'Allegro, and the "pealing Organ" in concert with the anthems of the choir that dissolved the embodied soul of Il Penseroso. Blind but not deaf, Milton again unified this divided god in the operatic heaven of *Paradise Lost.*

Yet Milton cherished at the center of his strength a blasphemous profanation of the father internalized at the resolution of the first oedipal complex. Freud repeatedly noted the "immortality" or conservatism of the superego: the father passes his values to the son, whereupon the son, having embodied them, passes these values to his son. The dimension of futurity opened to the ego by the oedipal resolution, as we said earlier, is readily enthralled to the vanities and timidities of social life. From the perspective of the sacred complex unfolded in *Paradise Regained,* the substitutional propulsion of worldly desires under the guidance of the superego is a bondage—a closed arc of hungers that stretches from mother to fatal mother, and those who live solely within this arc, blind mouths from cradle to grave. John Smith maintained that "the only way to *unite* man firmly to himself is by uniting him to God, and establishing in him a firm amity and agreement with the First and Primitive Being": religion *"restores a Good man to a just power and dominion over himself and his own Will, enables him to overcome himself, his own Self-will and Passions, and to command himself & all his Powers for God."* This "First and Primitive Being," for Smith and the other members of the Cambridge school an innate idea of God associated with innate principles of virtue, becomes in our psychoanalysis of faith a return to the primitive oedipal father, unspoiled by the ways of tradition, in whose place the ego searches for God. Denouncing Satan, Christ denounces the earthly father as guide to earthly desire. When God dethrones this father at the resolution of the sacred complex, the new Adam can overcome the old antimony of veneration and ambition. Hostile rivalry toward the father, forbidden by the ego-ideal of the first complex, is recovered in the superiority of the interior Spirit to all other "forcers of conscience" (the Westminister Assembly, Milton wrote in "On the New Forcers of Conscience," would "force our Consciences that Christ set free").

The doubling on the pinnacle now appears in a new light. In the name of righteousness, a new ownership of the will, the sacred superego licenses an attack on its rival, the profane superego; but insofar as the complex is being repeated, this sacred obedience duplicates the rivalrous disobedience of the first complex. The ego of new Adam has repossessed the evil energy of old Adam. The structure—temptation, renunciation,

obedience—remains the same, yet the sacred complex subverts the profane one.

I have not given much content to the religious superego. Were we
to find there some culture-bound list of Christian duties, I would feel that
my efforts to discern psychological advent in religious symbolism had been
in vain: the new superego would be the old one glorified, a mental space
upon which laws can be inscribed. But *Paradise Regained* is notable for the
absence of such prescriptions. Christ delivers maxims, yet they are mostly
negative ones; we do not even hear the golden rule. He shows how not to
become ensnared by the limited vision of the world. The major function
of reason in the poem is to refute commonplace conceptions of a successful lifetime, placing our trust in the "inward Oracle" and its "Spirit of
Truth" (1.462–463). The poem is a struggle between guides, one of whom
is palpable and manifest as the way of the world, whereas the other is
secret, interior, waited upon. Guided in this second way, Christ on the
pinnacle gains unique selfhood at the moment he claims his Father's
name.

Milton attended a college named for him. But this Christ has no
need for the "Socratic streams" of the "shady Academy" that had protected the young Milton from wantonness:

> To sage Philosophy next lend thine eare,
> From Heaven descended to the low-rooft house
> Of Socrates, see there his Tenement,
> Whom well inspired the Oracle pronounc'd
> Wisest of men; from whose mouth issu'd forth
> Mellifluous streams that water'd all the schools
> Of Academics old and new.
>
> (4.272–278)

Satan speaks beautifully here. Socrates, like Christ an oral man, no
writer, "from whose mouth issu'd forth" the virtuous discourse that became Plato's Idea of the Good, Aristotle's magnanimity, the Stoa's *sui
potestas*—a great fiat of mind whose reissue in scriptural form has been
guarded and systematized by the Western Academy . . . as then in Greece,
so later in England. The alternative wisdom that illuminates Christ comes not
only from the horizontal stream of history "in our native tongue" (333),
but instantaneously from above:

> he who receives
> Light from above, from the fountain of light,
> No other doctrine needs, though granted true.
>
> (288–290)

But in what sense is this light a doctrine? It is not handed down. It is not taught in an Academy. To quote Smith again: "Divine Truth is better understood, as it unfolds itself in the purity of mens hearts and lives, then in all those subtil Niceties into which curious Wits may lay it forth. And therefore our Savior, who is the great Master of it, would not, while he was here on earth, draw it up into any *System* or *Body*, nor would his Disciples after him; He would not lay it out to us in any Canons or *Articles* of *Belief*, not being indeed so careful to stock and enrich the World with Opinions and Notions, as with true Piety, and a Godlike pattern of purity, as the best way to thrive in all spiritual understanding. His main scope was to promote an *Holy life*, as the best and most compendious way to a *right Belief*. He hangs all true acquaintance with Divinity upon the doing of God's will, *If any man will doe his will, he shall know of the doctrine, whether it be of God* (John 7.17)." Like More and Cudworth, Smith sought to restrain the potential anarchy of the inward light by arguing that innate principles of virtue would become universally self-evident once the innate idea of God had exfoliated. I doubt whether Milton would have assented to this restraint. From *Areopagitica* to the preface of the *Christian Doctrine* it is clear that the inward light does not tell all men the same thing. But this description of what Christ brought into the world, with its subordination of specific belief to holy life and reason to will, is compatible with the religious vision of *Paradise Regained*. The only paraphrase for the doctrine of "Light from above" is the matchless life of a unique man. The question at issue in the poem is not the ethical "what did Christ tell us to do?" but the existential "who is Christ?" Except in the medium of symbolism, the answer eludes our saying. Christ refuses to be contained by the rational and psychological categories of the world. More akin to oracle than to argument, his unclassifiable doctrine founds a culture whose ideal is forever outside of cultural systems. The interior light makes possible an iconoclastic purgation of the profane superego in which the laws and traditions, the "ways" of a society, reside. This revolutionary culture of free individuals anticipates the future, and its native art is prompted, unpremeditated.

As early as *Comus* Milton knew that reason is choice, but the full implications of this idea are not apparent in his work until the last books of *Paradise Lost*. The poet has celebrated the right reason of prelapsarian man and mourned its failure. In the choosing of the final lines, where the world lies ready to be entered by the guided deliberation of Adam and Eve, Milton foreshadows the starker Protestantism of *Samson Agonistes* and *Paradise Regained*, where choices are not made by a rational faculty invested with universal principles. The old role of right reason is collapsed into the choosing itself, an intuitive act performed in response to the urgings of God. As intellectual intuition transforms the rational pursuit of knowledge into immediate possession, so volitional intuition transforms the rational pursuit of virtue, invariably involving the application of law to circumstance, into the immediate presence of a prompting will. In both cases the ego simply consents to what is there. Reason now becomes the guardian of readiness, keeping the hero from imprudent action during his agon of waiting. One aspect of this guardianship is the management of theodicial doubts, the "patience to prevent / That murmur" (Sonnet XIX) which might inspire action in the absence of divine will. When rousing motions come to Christ on the pinnacle and to Samson after he has refused to be humiliated before Dagon, there is no negotiation with them, no trace of *that* sort of agonizing: "Master's commands come with a power resistless / To such as owe them absolute subjection" (*SA* 1404–1405). In the two poems generally assumed to have been written after *Paradise Lost*, Saurat concluded, Milton "frees himself from dogma; all he keeps of it is God-Destiny." Obedient to an inward oracle, the ego no longer seeks virtue in struggling to free itself, through a rationally motivated ethics, from the superego. The religious life has accomplished a transvaluation, or recapture at a higher level, of the voluntarism of the primitive superego.

There are obvious risks in this surrender. How many of us, told that writing a book would mean going blind, would proceed to write the book? The otherness within us, the eye that watches and the voice that calls, can become concrete to the point of hallucination in pathological states. It can indeed command irresistible forces. Born of conflict, the superego generates conflict by its presence: the rational ego that would be a law unto itself must always encounter a dispensation of guilt whose habits of accusing and esteeming the ego remain to a large degree incorrigibly irrational. But in the sacred complex Milton came to grips with these conflicts, working through them as well as repeating them. Theodicy itself provides the most lucid example. We have noted that the rough draft of a theodicy undertaken by the oedipal child will confront him with the dark irony that the father, bearer of the law forbidding intercourse with the mother, is precisely the one who disobeys his own law: the desire to be the father is both the model for evil and the model for good. Here we encounter the religious transposition of this embryonic theodicy. God is dark and God is light, for what is it to be evil in *Paradise Lost*? To be evil is to be God, a law unto oneself. In philosophy and symbol the theodicial argument of *Paradise Lost* expansively reworks an outrage intrinsic to the history of conscience.

The superego celebrated in *Paradise Regained* and *Samson Agonistes* has made the prerational otherness at its origins sacred and suprarational. In its passage to the sacred, the superego acquires what I would call a feminine aspect—not in the vulgar sense that women are intuitive, which is a lesser way to think, but in the sense that intuition in all people, men and women, is a form of knowing or being rooted in the early matrix of sudden attunements and shared promptings.

Waller has suggested that the voluntarism of Luther and Calvin encouraged an anxious and fragmented experience of time, since if every moment expresses the will of an unknowable God toward the individual, every next moment can be discontinuous with the present one. Such anxiety proceeds from the assumption that one is set *against* time, experiencing the dramaturgy of a God external to the self. In the voluntarist world of his last poems, presided over by a riddling God, Milton shows how this anxiety may be conquered by recovering, in an oedipal structure, basic trust. Christ knows that Satan has been given "permission from above" (1.496) to impose his temptations. But the Son's interior attunement to the otherness of the Father allows him to become the master of circumstance, undefined by circumstance. The foreseeing God of *Paradise Lost* prepared well for the ordeals of fallen man:

> And I will place within them as a guide
> My Umpire *Conscience*, whom if they will hear,
> Light after light well us'd they shall attain,
> And to the end persisting, safe arrive.
> (3.195–197)

The soul is not solitary. Trusting the God who speaks and illuminates in the felt alterity of conscience, we are led through riddling discontinuities to moments of clarity, light after light, until we come to the end. The father as superego, the father as culture, the father as God—it is through the third father in the life of Renaissance man, less a lawgiver than a guide, that the last mother can regain the power of the first. The oedipus complex is made mortal in order that the ego can be made immortal.

SANFORD BUDICK

Milton's Image
of Divine Analysis:
Provenance and Meaning

The logical structures of seventeenth-century poetic images in general and of Milton's imagery in particular have been the object of considerable though inconsistent attention in modern scholarship. James Whaler and Rosemond Tuve early made us aware that few poets and few ages have more systematically exploited the potentialities of poetic images to embody logical contents. During the past forty years a host of perceptive commentators have discussed, from diverse points of view, the logical components of many of Milton's images. But in most of these discussions it has seemed to be a foregone conclusion that the analytic role played by Milton's imagery cannot be coextensive with the larger meanings of his finished poetic products. His imagistic use of logical analysis, in other words, is in this view necessarily a handmaiden of art, which, at the crucial moment, discreetly defers to the grander business of synthesis and resolution that we necessarily expect of truly poetic completions.

These assumptions, it seems to me, do not finally clarify (and perhaps they even obscure) the unique meanings of Milton's poems. Geoffrey Hartman has begun persuasively to counter the formulas of synthesis and resolution that have pervaded Milton scholarship. By analyzing a series of images of "the observer ab extra" in *Paradise Lost*, he has argued that the "poet constantly suggests, destroys and recreates the idea

From *The Dividing Muse: Images of Sacred Disjunction in Milton's Poetry*. Copyright © 1985 by Yale University Press.

of an imperturbably transcendent discrimination." Analytic reason of a higher order is thus assigned by Hartman a special figural centrality in Milton's verse. The abiding significance of such figuration is greater even and more deeply founded, I believe, than Hartman's insightful remarks indicate. As I have suggested, Milton's poetic meanings depend upon theological structures that are themselves organized by continuous division and distinction. At this point, however, a mild caveat is in order. Even if the well-accustomed view that Milton's images everywhere create harmony out of discord, synthesis from analysis, is rejected, it does not necessarily follow that, where Milton is concerned, the concept of poetic unity must altogether be abandoned. Varieties of reader-oriented poetics have undoubtedly proved to be very fruitful in interpreting Milton's poems. But even those works that are accessible to such interpretations may establish criteria of independent wholeness that are of a different order from those shown to be absent by affective readings. We must, that is, consider the general possibility that Milton's images of divine analysis have a denotative meaning that has so far been grasped incompletely. And we should consider the further, specific possibility that Milton's compositions regularly accord analytic structures a theological value that is primary rather than secondary, ultimate rather than penultimate.

My aim here is to describe in more or less systematic fashion the intellectual origins and poetic meanings of one particular image of deific division that recurs frequently in Milton's writing. The image, which stands as divine rationality itself, is markedly analytic in its own form and is associated with a significant theme or activity of dialectical discrimination. This dialectic, like the analytic shape of its characteristic image, is highly individual. So too is the context of intellectual and religious history in which Milton found it and deployed it for his own purposes. I shall survey briefly some additional representations of this divine analysis in Milton's poetry, and then attempt to identify its roots and efflorescence in his theological milieu. For an awareness of the depth of these affiliations can, I believe, enlarge our ultimate understanding of the kinds of meaning and poetic unity achieved in Milton's works.

THE MUSE THAT DIVIDES

It is quite possible that Milton himself announced the link between poetic analysis and divine division in the Nativity Ode. In the opening lines of *The Passion*, composed within a year of the Ode, he had this to say about the genre or method of the earlier poem:

> Erewhile of Music and Ethereal mirth,
> Wherewith the stage of Air and Earth did ring,
> And joyous news of heav'nly Infant's birth,
> My muse with Angels did divide to sing.

Of course, divide can mean only to "execute 'division', or rapid melodic passages," as Carey puts it, though as he adds, "elsewhere in Milton's poetry 'divide' means either 'share' or 'separate'." But given what we have seen of the thematic significance of division or "parting" in the Ode, it seems likely that Milton's direct reference to the dividing muse of the Nativity Ode is to the specialized muse that (among other things) proceeds by acts of systematic separation. The musical meaning is not thereby cancelled. Quite the contrary. In the Ode, divine division and the angelic new music occur in integral relation.

Two other examples, which will come in for fuller discussion later, will help illustrate the number and variety of Milton's poems that recur to mercy-seat division. The predicament of his sonnet When I Consider . . . (ca. 1652) can be formulated in many ways, but in all of them a central element must be the contradictory claims of passive acceptance of God's will and the obligation to act in order to fulfill other expressions of that same will. The apparent resolution of these counterclaims comes as a realization of an underlying theological verity. In the much-glossed closing lines, patience speaks from a transcendent realm. She states the one unchanging truth that stands behind our life of shadow objects:

> Thousands at his bidding speed
> And post o'er Land and Ocean without rest:
> They also serve who only stand and wait.

The scholarly quest for the exact order and neighborhood of the angelic thousands and the standing attendants is well worth pursuing, for it is plausible to assume that the precise quality of Milton's acceptance of his fate is minutely reflected in these heavenly specifications. But the goals of the present restricted inquiry can be served even by focusing on a point made by Grierson seventy years ago and reiterated recently by Harry Robins: in the last line of the poem Milton re-creates an image of the divine throne that was given special emphasis in a long tradition exemplified by Pseudo-Dionysius and Aquinas. For Milton's more immediate exegetical milieu, the same point may be made more simply by noting Calvin's frequently quoted gloss on the extended wings of the propitiatory cherubim in Exodus 25:18: "to mark the readiness of their obedience, for the extension of their wings is equivalent to their being prepared for the performance of whatever God might command. Thus they are said to turn their faces towards the mercy-seat, because they are attentive to the will of God."

In Milton's description as in Calvin's, divine being intervenes between its emanated potencies. The contradiction of fulfilling active being in perfect stasis is resolved in a discrimination of incoincident potentialities. Placed at the very end of the sonnet, the described structure itself suggests a terminal stasis. It is an immovable band of division that subsists beyond and within the emanations of motion that constitute the created world. Milton elevates and redeems the shattering disruption of life and creativity by suggestively incorporating it within God's own pattern of immobility within deputed motion. That framed image—part visual and part nonvisual—of intervening, unmoved, moving godhead is revealed as the source image of divine power, divine presence, and divine grace. Thus the unstated, invisible, dividing component of the last line— God's medial throne—has the effect of raising the image and the sonnet towards the condition of a sublime idea.

My second example is from the very end of Milton's career, from *Paradise Regained*. The thematic significance of the mercy-seat division in this instance is extensive and complex. . . . The appearance and function of the image are sufficiently schematized, however, for even a brief sketch to produce a working acquaintance.

In the Nativity Ode the fulfillment of God's meaning is somehow prophesied in the extension of the symmetry of the propitiatory to the opening wide of heaven's gates. In *Paradise Regained* the same image life is compassed in an elongated series of very similar image movements. Here Milton begins slowly, almost in a retarded movement, with a triple iteration of the opening of heaven's doors (I.29–32, 79–85, 280–88). In spite of the repetitions, the significance of the opening doors is left unexplained and mysterious, just as the image counterparts of the opened doors are for the time being left unmentioned.

In the third of these passages, for example, Christ recounts,

> as I rose out of the laving stream,
> Heaven open'd her eternal doors, from whence
> The Spirit descended on me like a Dove;
> And last the sum of all, my Father's voice,
> Audibly heard from Heav'n, pronounc'd me his,
> Mee his beloved Son, in whom alone
> He was well pleas'd; by which I knew the time
> Now full, that I no more should live obscure,
> But openly begin.

Somewhat reductively stated, the drama of *Paradise Regained* concerns the fact that in spite of the declared centrality of the baptism revelation and in spite of Christ's unequivocally spoken understanding of its meaning, he does not at all openly begin. Instead he is immediately moved to retire into the wilderness. He does just so, once more, in the final moment of the poem. Directly after the angels have sung, "on thy glorious work / Now enter, and begin to save mankind" (IV.634–35), Christ emphatically returns, unobserved and private, home "to his Mother's house" (IV.638–39). The time may well be full (I.287) for Christ's fulfillment of his mission, but fullness clearly has a special meaning in this poem.

The initial image pattern of the heavenly temple, with its symmetrical portals from which issue the divine spirit and voice, is itself fulfilled by the image of the godlike man as "Holiest of Holies" (IV.348–49). It is summed or gathered up, that is, in Christ the "true Image of the Father . . . enshrin'd / In fleshly Tabernacle . . . Wand'ring the Wilderness" (IV 596–600). Milton thus borrows Paul's theme of "edification" or of transposition of the pre-Christian, material temple to the immaterial, inward, and heavenly temple, a favorite topos in Puritan writing. The cherubim of glory that the author of Hebrews (revising Exodus 25) similarly envisions around the transposed propitiatory are also not forgotten by Milton. At the moment of symbolic triumph over Satan, before Christ again retires rather than enter on his glorious work, the fixed Old Testament mercy seat is reconstituted as a propitiatory "couch" without specified location:

> straight a fiery Globe
> Of Angels on full sail of wing flew nigh,
> Who on their plumy Vans receiv'd him soft
> From his uneasy station, and upbore
> As on a floating couch through the blithe Air.
> (IV. 581–85)

The most striking aspect of Milton's use of the mercy-seat pattern must for the time being be stated even more skeletally than the above points, for it is the most intricate and requires the most ample commentary. In the final temptation Satan imagines that by bringing Christ to the highest pinnacle of his father's house (IV.549–52) he will either heighten his humiliation or ensnare him in hubris. Instead, he only aids Christ in fulfilling triumphantly his subordinate elevation as Word or voice of God. How this fulfillment relates to the holiest of holies, the mercy seat, and the cherubic wings that surround him is not yet clear. But here too a particular image of divinely centered symmetry is intimately associated with Christ's office.

IMAGES OF DIVINE DICHOTOMY

In the cases briefly reviewed above I have suggested that Milton pays special attention to the images of divine division that for him constitute a particularly vital species of analytic image, and that these images are generally found in a derivative or familial relationship with the biblical pattern of the propitiatory throne of God. Let us next consider the parent images of that family and, following that, some of the characteristic ways in which Milton's age regarded them. Few other periods have been as systematic in their attempts to discover and delineate the shapes and functions of rational images, especially those of sacred origin. Perhaps it was a perfectly natural gesture for the last pre-Enlightenment age.

The two largest biblical images of propitiatory pattern have become so commonplace in Christian thought that they are in a sense always beyond, or rather nearer than, the reach of ordinary allusion. They recur in a multitude of ways throughout the prophetic literature and they are so frequently dissolved, in high concentration, in Christian writing, that they may be precipitated or redissolved at any moment. God's instructions to Moses in Exodus 25:20–22 are the starting text:

> And the cherubims shall stretch forth their wings on high, covering the mercy seat with their wings, and their faces shall look one to another. . . .
>
> And thou shalt put the mercy seat above upon the ark; and in the ark thou shalt put the testimony that I shall give thee.
>
> And there I will meet with thee, and I will commune with thee from above the mercy seat, from between the two cherubims.

No other Old Testament text specifies so precisely the habitation of divine presence; and no other text is more central, architecturally as well as thematically, to the delineation of the holy temple. It was, of course, just this geographical location of centralized meaning that was transposed in the New Testament into a divine process without place. In Hebrews the process of incarnation and atonement is represented as an internalized and universally available structure of intercessory holiness. Here again is the movement from Old to New Covenant that is expressed by the Pauline idea of edification. In Milton's terms it is the preference of God for the redeemed heart, upright and pure, before all material temples.

The most direct New Testament commentary on these matters and on the above verses in Exodus is the following passage of Hebrews 9:

> 1   Then verily the first covenant had also ordinances of divine service, and a worldly sanctuary.
>
> 2   For there was a tabernacle made; the first, wherein was the

candlestick, and the table, and the shewbread; which is called the sanctuary.

3 And after the second veil, the tabernacle which is called the Holiest of all;

4 Which had the golden censer, and the ark of the covenant overlaid round about with gold, wherein was the golden pot that had manna, and Aaron's rod that budded, and the tables of the covenant;

5 And over it the cherubims of glory shadowing the mercyseat; of which we cannot now speak particularly.

6 Now when these things were thus ordained, the priests went always into the first tabernacle, accomplishing the service of God.

7 But into the second went the high priest alone once every year, not without blood, which he offered for himself, and for the errors of the people:

8 The Holy Ghost this signifying, that the way into the holiest of all was not yet made manifest, while as the first tabernacle was yet standing;

9 Which was a figure for the time then present, in which were offered both gifts and sacrifices, that could not make him that did the service perfect, as pertaining to the conscience. . . .

11 But Christ being come an high priest of things to come, by a greater and more perfect tabernacle, not made with hands, that is to say, not of this building;

12 Neither by the blood of goats and calves, but by his own blood he entered in once into the holy place, having obtained eternal redemption for us. . . .

15 And for this cause he is the mediator of the new testament, that by means of death, for the redemption of the transgressions that were under the first testament, they which are called might receive the promise of eternal inheritance.

The *occupatio* or *occultatio* of the fifth verse, concerning the mercy seat itself, was traditionally understood to be the key to the entire description. The mystery shadowed forth by the mercy seat is too great to be spoken of directly; but the meanings elaborated in all the verses relating to the tabernacle as a figure of Christ's redemption are extensions of the central structure of propitiation and interposition. And in the fifteenth verse, the Old Testament placement of the propitiatory above the tables of the law and below the point of God's communion is reflected in the structure of mediation.

Milton's learned acquaintance John Diodati nicely sums up this complex of relationships in his *Annotations* (a work that at least one contemporary believed Milton himself had translated into English, or had at least seen through the press). On the word *kapporeth* in Exodus 25:17 Diodati writes:

the Hebr. word signifieth also a mercy-seat; and so the Apostle calls it, *Heb.* 9.5. *viz.* a means of purging and expiating sin; because that this cover signified Christ, who with his righteousness covereth all our sins, and containeth within himself all the Churches righteousness, as the tables of the Law were inclosed under the cover; and interposeth himself as Mediator, between the Law which accuseth us, and God our Judge, as the cover was between the said Tables, and the majestie of God, which shewed it self present over the Cherubims of this Cover, as sitting upon his throne.

Diodati emphasizes that for the author of Hebrews the mystery shaded between the two ends of the mercy seat, and between man's transgressions against the law and the wrath of God, is the grace of separation, division, and mediation. Christ interposes himself as separator and divider.

Another of Milton's contemporaries, Gervase Babington, extends the application of the same theme to Hebrews 12:29, "For our God is a consuming fire." His comment on Exodus 25:17 begins as does Diodati's:

How notable a Figure again this was of Christ, I pray you see: for first, it was the cover of the *Arke* where the law of *Moses* lay; and who hideth and covereth us from the wrath of God, and from the accusation of the Law but Jesus Christ?

Next comes his compounding of Hebrews 9:15 and Hebrews 12:29:

He is like a coole shadow to flie unto in the scorching heat of Gods deserved displeasure, which is a *consuming fire.*

The Satan of *Paradise Regained* knows, or at least senses, the value of such interposition. Willingly or not, he foretells the fulfillment of Christ's propitiatory role; and he does so almost precisely in Babington's terms:

> to that gentle brow
> Willingly I could fly, and hope thy reign,
> From that placid aspect and meek regard,
> Rather than aggravate my evil state,
> Would stand between me and thy Father's ire
> (Whose ire I dread more than the fire of Hell)
> A shelter and a kind of shading cool
> Interposition, as a summer's cloud.
> (III. 215–22)

Carey is right to object to Northrop Frye's assertion that this passage describes "the direct opposite of Christ's true nature." As a possible source that is also a familar text for the explication of Christ's soteriology, Carey cites Isaiah 25:4–5, "For thou hast been . . . a shadow from the heat . . . even the heat with the shadow of a cloud." This is surely

germane. But I must go further. The interposition described by Milton in
those images very likely prefigures Christ's fulfillment of his mercy-seat
office as separator and mediator. This was the office described in Hebrews
in connection with Exodus 25 and frequently elaborated in the manner of
Diodati or Babington.

What else could the same exegetical milieu, especially the parts
that Milton showed himself particularly drawn to, provide with regard to
these biblical places? Milton and his contemporaries were surely well
aware that the theme of divine separation or division is characteristic of
more than one passage in Hebrews. David Berkeley has pointed out, for
example, that the opening phrases of *Lycidas* almost certainly allude to the
following formula for separation of things transitory from things eternal in
Hebrews 12:26 27:

> . . . now he hath promised, saying, *Yet once more* I shake not the earth
> only, but also heaven.
> And this word, *Yet once more*, signifieth the removing of those
> things that are shaken, as of things that are made, that those things which
> cannot be shaken may remain [emphases added].

Seventeenth-century awareness of extensive themes of separation in Hebrews was often not only broad and deep but even minutely focused. But I
am concerned here only with the most striking of the relevant texts and
with two of the richest forms of that awareness.

For the description of a divine agency or process of division, the
most significant and best known figure in Hebrews is undoubtedly verse 12
of chapter 4, which I will cite whole:

> For the word of God is quick, and powerful, and sharper than any
> twoedged sword, piercing even to the dividing asunder of soul and spirit,
> and of the joints and marrow, and is a discerner of the thoughts and
> intents of the heart.

In this declaration (which has repeatedly been put forth as a possible
component of the background for the mysterious two-handed engine of
Lycidas) some readers of Milton's time believed they could find a warrant
for understanding God's Word as being analytic or even dichotomizing in
function. The Cambridge of Milton's time, which served as the principal
host of Ramist thought in England, and which nurtured Milton's own
substantial interest in Ramist logic, was fertile ground for such interpretation.

In discussing Ramist method, Rosemond Tuve emphasized the
ways in which the logic and rhetoric of Ramus and his followers could
extend the realm of poetic imagery to include novel kinds of verse
argumentation. One of her principal assumptions was that Ramism could

explain how the tendency to abstraction in much sixteenth and seventeenth century verse could be brought home to roost in one obviously
valid criterion of poetic value: the concrete and the visual. But Frances
Yates has shown that the drift of Ramist method is usually quite different
from, even opposite to, the implications proposed by Tuve. Tuve consciously and completely ignored the schematization of dichotomies that
was conventionally identified as the programmatic core of Ramist method.
She did so, one may suppose, because she considered it totally lacking in
philosophical meaning or because she could not see how it might form a
part of the influence of Ramism on poetic practice.

Before bringing Yates's more comprehensive account to bear, I
should acknowledge that, indeed, Ramist dichotomization was in itself
without significant or distinctive philosophical content. The totally general, almost banal, nature of that content is usefully characterized by
Father Ong:

> The Ramist dichotomies have little, if any real theoretical foundation.
> There is a bipolarity in being, which echoes everywhere through philo-
> sophical history; form and matter, act and potency, Yang and Yin, thesis
> and antithesis, the one and the many, and so on through an indefinite
> number of epiphanies. This includes perhaps the Neo-Platonic teaching,
> well known to Aquinas, that from any given unity only one other unity
> can be generated, further generation requiring the combination of these
> two originals. The Ramist dichotomy can be regarded as a reflection or
> correlative of this bipolarity. But it does not arise from any penetrating
> insight on Ramus' part into the principles of the bipolarity. . . . There is
> simply no one ground on which we can account for Ramus' dichotomies.

Yet, as Ong is the first to acknowledge, all this does not detract from the
fact that, as he says, "the cult of dichotomies which reaches its peak
development" with Ramus and his highly dedicated followers had an
immense influence on the day to day thinking and writing of countless
educated Europeans from the middle of the sixteenth century to at least
the end of the seventeenth. By themselves the Ramist dichotomies may
mean virtually nothing. But there can be no doubt that they expressed a
contemporary general tendency to heavily schematized thought of a binary
kind; and when they were joined to a structure of thought or belief that
did have a distinctive poetic, philosophical, or theological content the
result could be powerfully and deeply meaningful.

Yates has shown that the place of Ramist method within the
historical development of the art of memory (which is its parent) be-
stowed upon it an identifiable antagonist and polemical meaning, even a
sectarian religious character. Yates explains:

Though many surviving influences of the old art of memory may be
detected in the Ramist "method" of memorizing through dialectical
order, yet he deliberately gets rid of its most characteristic feature, the
use of the imagination. And, above all, gone in the Ramist system are
the images, the emotionally striking and stimulating images the uses of
which had come down through the centuries from the art of classical
rhetoric. The "natural" stimulus for memory is now not the emotionally
exciting memory image; it is the abstract order of dialectical analysis
which is yet, for Ramus, "natural," since dialectical order is natural to
the mind. . . .

The extraordinary success of Ramism, in itself rather a superficial
pedagogic method, in Protestant countries like England may perhaps be
partly accounted for by the fact that it provided a kind of inner iconoclasm, corresponding to the outer iconoclasm. . . .

Ramism cannot be entirely identified with Protestantism for it seems
to have been popular with some French Catholics. . . . Nevertheless,
Ramus became a Protestant martyr after his death in the Massacre of St.
Bartholomew, a fact which certainly had much to do with the popularity
of Ramism in England. And there can be no doubt that an art of memory
based on imageless dialectical order as the true natural order of the mind
goes well with Calvinist theology.

As vivid evidence, Yates cites the dicta of the Ramist Puritan William
Perkins: "So soone as the minde frames unto it selfe any forme of God (as
when he is popishly conceiued to be like an old man sitting in heauen in a
throne with a sceptre in his hand) an idol is set up in the minde. . . . A
thing faigned in the mind by imagination is an idol." Clearly the imageless
dialectical order of Ramism was to be achieved by an iconoclastic purgation of the iconographic arts of memory.

But from Perkins's pronouncements and Yates's commentary it is
not clear how, short of simply ignoring the idols spawned by degenerate
imagination, the Ramist method was to attack the images themselves—
how it was to convert the image of God as an old man sitting on a throne
(with a scepter in his hand) into a manifestation of an imageless dialectic.
Ong remarks in this connection that by the use of the "dichotomized
branching outline" instead of the iconographic arts, the inner iconoclasm
described by Yates was in effect already accomplished: "The images were
annihilated and the visualism of the age was redirected to a text, to
visualizable words." But I would like to suggest that the attempt to subdue
the rampagings of imagination was by some Ramists conceived to be far
more direct than this.

Returning now to Hebrews 4:12 and the exegetical undercurrents
of Milton's age, there are clear indications that, indeed, for at least some
Ramists the Word of God offered itself as the great instrument of aggres-

sive dichotomization. The Word was the dividing sword that was to be used in the mind's rational battle against mystification, confusion, and self-deluding emotionalism. William Gouge (1578–1653), fellow of King's College, Cambridge, and one of the best known English defenders of Ramus in the early part of the century, expressed what was after all the inevitable Ramist view of Hebrews 4:12. In two of his principal works Gouge expatiated upon the sword-like dividing Word, wielded by God and man, waging an incessant warfare of divinely willed dichotomization. In his posthumous *Commentary on the Whole Epistle to the Hebrews*, published in 1655, Gouge explains the key phrases in Hebrews—the "word of God . . . quick, and powerful and sharper than any twoedged sword, piercing even to the dividing asunder of soul and spirit"—as circumstantial description of the means "whereby Christ exerciseth his Propheticall Office." Soul for Gouge is "will and affections"; spirit is "understanding or mind . . . the highest faculty." The two must not be confused: "the severall Metaphors whereby the power of the word is set out, may most fitly be applied," he says, "to Gods Word preached," by Christ the arch-preacher and by the generations of his apostle preachers. The work of all such preachers is to cut the knot that ties the rational faculty to the will and affections.

As part of his Calvinist understanding of our fallen condition Gouge envisions a universal mental enslavement to the sensory and sensual manifestations of the will and affections. He does not explicitly call this enslavement imagination, but the equivalent of that power is clearly his concern when he describes the need to separate will and mind as well as to weed out the growth of will and affections in pure mind:

> The soul and spirit are as nearly and firmly knit together as any parts of the body can be: yet the Word can divide them asunder, and that not only by distinguishing the one from the other, but also by discovering the severall desires and delights, or dislikings and loathings of the soul; and likewise of the castings, plottings, and contrivements of the spirit; and all these both in good and evil things.

The preaching or use of God's Word in this way, says Gouge, must be pursued aggressively: "As with a two-edged sword a man may defend and offend, so with the Word. Verity and virtue may be maintained and defended, and errour and every enormity may be refelled and repelled. See *The whole armour of God*. . . ." By offend Gouge means take the offensive by attacking directly the confusion of sensory and rational faculties. How the divisions of the Word are to manage this work Gouge does not say here. He comes closest to an explicit description of the procedures for achieving this in the work to which he refers us, his own *The Whole Armour of God* (1619). Here the dividing functions of the Word detailed in Hebrews 4:12 are said to be directly expressed by Ramist method incorporated into public preaching, as well as private prayer or meditation. One of mankind's principal ways of wielding God's dividing Word, Gouge explains, is to apply it reflexively in "dividing the Word aright." In saying this, it is clear that Gouge intends exegetical as well as polemical uses of the method:

> In laying downe this doctrine of Prayer, the Apostle doth so skilfully couch together many severall and distinct points, as every word almost affordeth a severall Doctrine: he contenteth not himselfe in generall to exhort unto the duty of prayer, but also declareth divers circumstances appertaining thereunto: Whence observe, that
>
>> *It is a warrantable course of teaching, to set forth Principles of Religion in their severall and particular branches. This is one kinde of dividing the Word aright.*
>
> Thus will the understanding of hearers be much informed with a distinct knowledge of the mysteries of godliness, and thus shall they much better discerne the great depth of those mysteries, and the rich treasure that is contained in them. Yea, thus also shall their memory be much helped in retaining them: for severall branches distinctly and in order set downe are a great means to strengthen memory.
>
> This iustifieth that manner of teaching, which is (as we speake) *Common-place-wise*: by particular defining, dividing, subdividing, and distinct handling of particular branches of the Principles of Religion.

Gouge shows himself well aware of the monomania to which Ramist dichotomization could lead and therefore warns preachers not to be "over-curious in multiplying their divisions, or over-tedious in amplifying them." But his commitment is clear. The divisions of the Word described in Hebrews signal for him a "distinct" process of attaining divine truth, as well as a structure for embodying it.

The Oxford anti-Ramist, Thomas Jackson, president of Corpus Christi, shows us that the view of Hebrews 4:12 expressed by Gouge was familiar fare in mid-seventeenth-century England. And of course Jackson's demurrer extended its currency. In the final sermons of his *Commentaries upon these Articles of the Creed*, completed before his death in 1640 and published in 1657, Jackson had this to say about the Ramist capitalization on Hebrews 4:12:

> Some Late Writers . . . there be, which doubt, whether by *The Word of God* in the Text, the Son of God be punctually meant: who yet grant, That those *Attributes* ver. 13 (*Neither is there any Creature which is not manifested in his sight, but all things are naked and open unto the eyes of him*

with whom we have to do) can be meant of none, but the Son of God, and the ever-living Judge of quick and dead.

But this Interpretation doth contradict it self, doth divide and separate those things which the Spirit of God hath conjoyned; and if it were true, would rend asunder the *very Subject of all the Propositions* in my Text, which is Indivisibly One; it cannot abide the touch or test of any Logick, unlesse it be of his Logick who opposeth *Invention* unto *Judgment*, unto whose followers nothing more usual than to turn the greatest *Mysteries* in Divinitie into bare *Metaphors* or *Rhetorical Tropes*: Nothing more familiar, than to interpret those Prophetical Passages by which the Holy Ghost doth delineat [sic] the Incarnation of the *Word*, to be meant of God only . . . in a common vulgar, not in any mystical sense.

If Jackson is not thinking of Gouge's *Whole Armour* and of his *Commentary* (first preached in almost a thousand sermons at Blackfriars), he surely has in mind Gouge's intellectual twins. What Gouge thinks of as informing the understanding "with a distinct knowledge of the mysteries of godliness" is precisely for Jackson the perverse analytic process of turning "the greatest *Mysteries* in Divinitie into bare *Metaphors* or *Rhetorical Tropes*." On Hebrews 4:12–13 Gouge's *Commentary* offers fourteen pages of metaphorical and rhetorical analysis, folio!

Jackson has clearly not distorted or focused on a side issue by accusing the analytic Ramists of denying that the dividing Word is one and the same with the mysterious Son of God. In discussing the word *discerner* of 4:12, Gouge carefully disagrees with "they who interpret the Word of God to be the *Sonne of God*" and exploits for purposes of disagreement the conventional gloss that "we in English according to the notation of the Greek call such a one a *Critick*." It was important for Gouge to think of the Word of God as an analytic instrument distinct from Christ. Jackson was vexed by the analytic impulse that required such a separation. As Jackson may have sensed, the deeper motive of this impulse was related to a newly emerging zeitgeist that was to be extremely dangerous for organized religion of all kinds. The nature of that zeitgeist was very difficult to talk about. The terms for describing it were only just then being crystallized in rudimentary form by the harbinger philosophers of the Enlightenment. But the reasoning immediately behind Gouge's manifestation of the analytic impulse was easily located. As Jackson aptly noted, it represented something virtually identical to the Ramist program of opposing *inventio* to *dispositio* or *iudicium* as the binary parts or antitheses of Ramist logic. In the Ramist universe any kind of creativity can be reduced to its separable components.

Something of real significance was indeed at stake in the tense difference of opinion registered by Gouge and Jackson in their disparate ways of understanding God's dividing Word. In his important essay "Logic and the Epic Muse: Reflections on Noetic Structures in Milton's Milieu," Ong has illuminated the background issues that philosophical and historical retrospection has since identified in the Ramist controversies. Viewed contextually within the history of man's successive attempts to organize his understanding of reality, logic of all kinds, Ong explains, is deeply "antithetical" to its "antecedent rhetorical stage." In its every gesture it proclaims antagonism to the rotund, unrigorous emotionalism that is easily (not always justly) associated with rhetoric. In addition, Ong points out, logic is antithetical "in its very being":

> Logic is polarized in one way toward negativity and violent destruction. It moves toward greater and greater explicitation, typified especially by stress on definition. But, since definition (de-finire, to mark off the limits) manifests what a thing is by making clear what it is not, logic proceeds by setting up greater and greater antitheses, typified by stress on division and distinctions—in the case of Ramist logic dichotomies, the most divisive of divisions, modeled on the difference between yes and no, and featured today in the binary structures of computer operations.

Like the Enlightenment world view it helped usher in, Ramist method "symbolized and fostered the aggressive, no-quarter given, intently analytic habits of mind which are at the base of modern science and technology."

It is clear that whether or not Gouge fully understood the implications of his commentary, his elaboration of the meaning of God's dividing Word expressed a large philosophical and religious shift. Jackson felt it in his pulse and cried out. He knew that men like Gouge were giving voice to a powerful need to find a center of rationality—conceived in contemporary logical, dialectical terms—within religion and within the scriptural texts themselves. Jackson saw the growing need and feared the delimiting, reductive consequences of an analytic process that would transform the greatest mysteries in divinity into what Gouge called a distinct knowledge. He foresaw or intuited that the mystical, transcendent principle symbolized by the Incarnation of the Word could easily be squeezed out and discarded in such a process. Jackson particularly stressed the Ramists' unwillingness to identify the Son with the Word of God because he understood that with this point he had snared them in their own den. Gouge was visibly nervous about identifying the Son with the Word as analytic procedure, as Ramist method, because the equation limited and defined the Redeemer too strictly. There must be an escape clause. The Son must be let be in the next verse. Let him remain outside and above the two-edged system.

Without referring to Hebrews or Gouge or Jackson, Ong explains beautifully the larger Ramist issue that lies behind such exclusions and relates it to important questions in Milton's poetry. The exclusiveness of the Ramist dialectical procedures and structures Ong calls a radical form of closure:

> Closure marks Ramist thought conspicuously. Ramist "arts" are totalities, purportedly embracing all there is of their subjects, and doing so in a way which admits readily of being diagrammed. This sense of closure—which can be identified more or less with the rationalism maturing in the Enlightenment—certainly plagued Milton in his effort to pack the reality of Christian revelation into *Paradise Lost*. . . .
>
> Milton's place in the long-range development of the epic and of logic can . . . be described rather neatly, if not with full inclusiveness, in terms of open and closed existence. The epic, which came into being as (among other things) a massive knowledge-storage creation of the prephilosophic world, projected an open cosmology, one in which explanation is at best partial and incompleteness is a permanent quality of mortal life. Epic was based on *agonia*, struggle, typically between persons, which is never-ending, but continues generation after generation. . . .
>
> Logic, on the other hand, the paradigmatic knowledge-storage device of the post-philosophical or rationalist world, symbolizes closed existence: the logical universe, certainly as conceived by Ramus and Milton's age generally, purports to carry within itself a full explanation of itself. . . . In actuality Milton's commitment to a closed system of existence was less than total. No man can live or write by method alone. But the rational didactic aim in *Paradise Lost*—"to justifie the wayes of God to men"—and his attraction to Ramist logic (which led him in his own *Logic* to suggest that the divine Trinity was illogical), with much else in his writings and career, suggest how strongly Milton was attracted to ultimate closure.

All this is extremely pertinent and illuminating. Yet we must consider the possibility that, having faced the implications of this ultimate closure, Milton and others in his age may have sought a way to open it significantly. They may have turned to an instrumentality, in other words, that was deeply systematic and authoritative, yet not at all a reversion to a nonrational position, Trinitarian (in Ong's terms), mystical (in Jackson's), or otherwise.

A means of this sort would optimally represent a further intensification of the analytic interpretation of God's dividing Word, even while it placed at the center of reality the Christian deity and revelation that had to be packed into a Christian epic. Ideally it would also open the epic to a never-ending struggle ruled by the transcendent principle itself. And, lastly, it would offer a finely balanced environment for a Christian poet whose commitment to a closed system of existence was great indeed, but, in principle, dramatically less than total.

A list of such conditions constitutes a very tall order. It is unlikely that any one investigation will provide the one true key that answers to all these needs. But we can, I think, hope to find a single, integral grouping of seventeenth-century conceptions that will satisfy—or at least point the way in which an imaginative writer might on good authority satisfy—most of the requirements mentioned. The Ramists who explicated Hebrews with logic in mind were not the most advanced purveyors of a sacred analytic image. Even while they labored, an image of this kind was made available that was from many points of view far more intensely and extensively analytic than the Ramist variety. And this image too had profound Reformation affiliations with the dividing topoi of Hebrews.

PHILO, GROTIUS, AND THE DIVIDING WORD OF HEBREWS 4:12

Through a different but related access I now return, therefore, to Hebrews. It is time to attempt to explain to ourselves—especially since Milton's age was the first to explain to itself—the immediate philosophical origins of the general patterns of division in Hebrews and, in particular, of the images controlled by the dividing Word of God. I should first leap ahead from Milton's epoch and note that since the publication of Johann Benedict Carpzov's voluminous *Sacrae Exercitationes in S. Paulli Epistolam ad Hebraeos ex Philone Alexandrino* at Helmstadt in 1750, biblical scholars of all schools and creeds have recognized that the Epistle to the Hebrews derives significantly from the Alexandrianism of Philo. Carpzov insisted upon an immensely detailed philological and conceptual relationship between Hebrews and Philo's texts. At the end of the nineteenth century, F. W. Farrar summed up the view of the matter that has remained standard to the present day: "the most marked feature of the Epistle to the Hebrews is its Alexandrian character, and the resemblances which it contains to the writings of Philo." On the other hand, notes Farrar, despite the many obvious borrowings from Philo, such as the images of Hebrews 4:12 and of Hebrews 9, in its general theology and in its way of relating to the Old Testament, Hebrews is worlds apart from Philo's Judaism. It is Philo's imagery, then, especially the structure of that imagery, that exercised a pervasive influence on Hebrews. Much of this was circumstantially understood in Milton's own time.

Moffatt has remarked that the Philonic and Alexandrian traditions behind Hebrews were in effect suppressed until the Reformation, when the revival of Greek learning made it possible to bring the necessary Hellenistic knowledge to bear. Perhaps the most notable of all the Philo-oriented investigations of the later Renaissance was the Hebrews commentary of Milton's friend, Hugo Grotius, whose *Adamus Exul* served Milton as a model for important elements of *Paradise Lost*. Grotius's and other Protestants' interest in the Alexandrian aspects of early Christianity, like the interest in Ante-Nicene Christianity, expressed part of a Reformation hope (Milton devoutly shared it) of diminishing or even bypassing reliance on Roman Catholic learning. Considering the early date of Grotius's *Bibelwissenschaft* (a full generation before the highly controversial work of Richard Simon), it is clear that there is more than a little of the avant-garde in his lengthy citations of parallel passages from Philo.

Grotius's long extracts from Philo proclaim a self-evident and unique relationship to verses of unquestioned sacred authority. The exegetical case was a rare one indeed. For a Christian of the mid-seventeenth century there could be no difference in scriptural status between verses in Exodus 25 and Hebrews 9, or Genesis 15 and Hebrews 4. They were all the Scriptures. Since, in this case, they were inevitably seen as treating of the same subject they even came together as the same text. If anything, the later exemplars of the text contained aspects of divine value that had not yet emerged in the earlier ones. Here, therefore, was an instance in which an exegesis (Philo's cited by Grotius) was absolutely authoritative, for it had preceded the text in one of its sacred forms and had actually helped to create it. So it must have struck an intelligent contemporary. Indeed, this may have been one of the reasons for placing Grotius in the final position of the *Critici Sacri*, the highly popular multiple commentary published in London in 1660. Grotius's Philonic glosses may not have been viewed by Milton's contemporaries as the final word, but they were surely seen as being among the very latest and most exciting.

On the dividing Word of God in Hebrews 4:12 Grotius quoted extensively from Philo's commentary on Genesis 15. It was this exegetical occasion that Philo had used to elaborate one of his most vivid and most central symbols, that of the logos severer or dividing Word who disposes the parts or opposites of reality. Grotius quotes as follows from the *Quis Rerum Divinarum Heres*:

> He wishes you to think of God who cannot be shewn, as severing through the Severer of all things, that is his Word, the whole succession of things material and immaterial whose natures appear to us to be knitted together and united. That severing Word whetted to an edge of utmost sharpness never ceases to divide.
>
> (XXVI.130)

As the rest of his Hebrews commentary shows, Grotius is well aware both of the conceptual significance of Philo's logos severer and of the detailed correspondence between Philo's symbols and the themes and images of Hebrews.

For a seventeenth-century Ramist who had a special interest in Hebrews and its thematics of division, and who yet sought to escape the most extreme consequences of Ramist closure, few representations of divine power could have been more congenial. The image of the logos severer not only obviated the need for excluding the transcendent principle from the analytic acts of the dividing Word; it actually placed that very principle at the center of universal division. Here the logos creator is seen as the logos analyzer who keeps himself at the center of division. Around that center, Philo repeatedly explains, the dichotomies or opposites of reality contend in a struggle that is not only never-ending but that is the key to grasping the fact that the divine nature is beyond boundaries or definition. The logos center of division divides and defines but is itself infinite. The opposites were divided and set into motion by the logos. The logos stands between, unmoved: he is the great interposer who mediates the peace of the cosmos. Emplaced within creation he expresses the form of the divine office. Indeed, in Philo's view we mortals can expect no higher knowledge of divinity. Philo explains that this is the image projected from the tabernacle, the holiest of holies, the propitiatory, the wings of the cherubim, and the imageless voice or logos that speaks from above and between the cherubim. This was the explanation that had contributed significantly to forming the images and themes of divine division in the Epistle to the Hebrews. Indeed, as Grotius's quotations from Philo suggest, the explanation of the meaning of those images had become part of the sacred images themselves.

THE WORD, THE TOWER, AND THE MERCY SEAT

Seventeenth-century commentators on the biblical archetypes of Milton's images of divine division help make us aware of the structural individuality of these images. But in addition to highlighting the structures, the same commentators suggest how the place or activity of separation in these particular dialectical images could be associated with a densely interrelated set of theological values. These values may explain a good deal about the meanings of Milton's poems. For one thing, they suggest that when we find ourselves in the neighborhood of recurring images of this kind we are very likely face to face with a special form of rational

Christian theology. This species of images and conceptions dramatically shifts the writer's theological emphasis from the deferred eschatological materialization of Christ's redemption to the immediate realization of Christian meanings in the renewal of a particular divine dialectic. In the events of his life, Christ the logos fulfills the propitiatory image of mediating division or separation. The word is the iconoclast that divides the images of reality to produce an "imageless" dialectical ordering. Taken together, the agent, the activity, and the objects of that activity are the divine image redeemed. For writers with such convictions, creating and recognizing that unique image can serve as a theological end in itself.

A complex of dividing imagination redeems the divine image in Milton's epics. In the creation of his vast poetic forms, Milton does not work emblematically. Nevertheless his largest structures significantly project the image of divine division described in this chapter; and at climactic moments in the epics, Milton even focuses his work of image redemption in what may justifiably be called poetic emblems.

One such emblem is offered in the tower scene of *Paradise Regained*. I noted before that the tower scene provides a final instance of the mercy-seat pattern in explicit relation to Christ the voice or Word of God. The poem's concluding action is thus played out on the geographical site of the historical mercy seat. If it did nothing more than establish this connection between mercy seat and triumphant logos, the moment would be a dramatic one for the story of Milton's sacred images. But the tower scene is vital in still another way. For Milton does not simply re-create an image that, for him, had immense historical and theological significance. He re-forms that image and redefines it, making it consonant with his most deeply Christian feelings about the difference between the Old Covenant and the New.

As I observed earlier, in this scene Satan believes that he has forced Christ into a posture of presumption against the Father. Inadvertently, of course, he has only succeeded in expediting Christ's fulfillment as God's Word. That fulfillment includes the emplacement of Christ as ordained, dividing Word on an enlarged mercy seat. In other words, Christ is able to perfect the propitiatory design so crucial to the divine structure of the world only by standing on the highest pinnacle and speaking—or being—the Word: "Also it is written, / Tempt not the Lord thy God."

But this is not all. Milton gives the Pauline idea of edification its largest possible dimensions by opening it infinitely, yet preserving for it an integral form. In the Old Covenant, the place of the logos was above the midpoint of the mercy seat within the temple edifice. Milton's representation of the New Covenant preserves and enlarges the supervenient relation—

but with a substantial Christian difference. Now the floating mercy seat (IV 585) is sent throughout the world as a pattern of universal logos division. The redeemed image of a dividing dialectic is no longer localized and restricted in a particular place, but is made infinitely accessible in the mercy of Christ's intervention. In Milton's specific terms, the grace of the Word's mediatorial division against Satan, on the enlarged mercy seat, is the temple made available to the minds and hearts of all humankind. In the Nativity Ode, immediately after prophesying the fulfillment of the propitiatory pattern, with "Mercy set between," the poet had stepped back and said, "But wisest Fate says no, / This must not yet be so" (149–50). At the close of his career, Milton continued to view Christ the logos as the central part of a permanently established serviceable design. But if in 1629 his conception of the required instauration was of a historical and eschatological nature and required a delayed fulfillment ("This must not yet be so"), in his later years he came to conceive of individual spiritual life as a panorama sufficient for the enactment of the largest Christian revolutions, in every present moment.

The implications of setting afloat the mercy seat and its dividing dialectic are enormous, not only for *Paradise Regained*, but for *Paradise Lost* as well. In both *Paradise Lost* and *Paradise Regained*, Milton projects the time and space not only of history but of the individual Christian mind. In the climaxes of both epics, he celebrates privately, for every man, the feast of dividing mercy postponed from the Nativity Ode—that which *must now be so*.

PETER M. SACKS

"Lycidas"

In reading "Lycidas," one might well
begin by recognizing how many different yet mutually reinforcing "works"
the poem performs. Admittedly, a great many circumstances converged on
the genesis of the poem; but it was Milton's extraordinarily ambitious
imagination that so thoroughly amplified the complexity of his occasion.
At least two characteristics of Milton's temperament, apart from his
ambition, fitted him for seizing the occasion in this way: his combative
spirit, in which the desire to write was never more strongly aroused than
by some obstacle or challenge; and his closely related fascination with
loss, where, again, his desire and imagination seemed to stir most powerfully against deprivation or constraint. Indeed, Milton's motto might have
been "So much the rather. . . ." I shall speak of this more concretely
during what follows, but for the moment we may agree that another way
of inquiring into the occasion of "Lycidas" is to ask what adversaries in
addition to death—what circumstances, powers, even traditions—Milton
chose to range himself against, and to surpass.

We have already remarked on the decline of the pastoral elegy
during the three decades preceding "Lycidas," a decline confirmed by the
fact that Milton was conspicuously alone among more than a score of
elegists in his choice of what by 1637 was regarded as an unconvincing,
even trivial, form for a poem of mourning. Milton was no doubt excited
by the opportunity to reconquer the ground lost by the genre and to
carry the tradition onward to unprecedented greatness. Here occurs one of
the convergences that so distinguish the creation of this poem. For Milton

From *The English Elegy: Studies in the Genre From Spenser to Yeats.* Copyright © 1985 by
Johns Hopkins University Press.

himself was at this time straining to herald his future career as an epic poet by mastering and surpassing the pastoral mode. The historical needs of the declining genre thus interlocked with the personal needs of a rising poet.

This interlocking is, however, far more profound, for Milton's ambition was not merely to write a consummate pastoral poem but to secure immortality. In the often-cited letter to Diodati, written in September, two months before "Lycidas," Milton wrote, "You ask what I am thinking of? So may the good Deity help me, of immortality!" Now what could agitate that desire for immortality more urgently than death itself, which in the year of King's death had already carried off not only Ben Jonson, the reigning poet, in whose wake men spoke of poetry's demise, and not only numerous victims of the plague (some even in Milton's village of Horton), but also, in April, Sara Milton, mother of the poet? And what could appease that same desire for immortality more fully than a work that was itself not merely a promise of approaching fame but a poem designed precisely to create a figure for what surpasses death?

None of Milton's earlier elegies are strictly pastoral, and it was not until King's death that Milton had a subject truly suited to that form. An obvious suitability is the fact that Milton and King both had been "nursed upon the self same hill" of Cambridge. This allowed the pastoral fiction of a shared locale and common pursuits. The convention of mourning a fellow shepherd was now legitimate, and what is more important, Milton's relative closeness to King (compared to his remote relation to previously elegized figures) provoked the poet's defense against his *own* mortality more strongly than had hitherto been the case.

Furthermore, King died at an age (25 years) that lent itself to an association with the martyred vegetation deities, an association augmented by King's having been both a poet and a clergyman, two roles well suited to the allegorical conventions of the genre. Here was a set of circumstances that permitted Milton to attempt an elegy, which, unlike his earlier exercises, could be measured against a definable and hence surpassable series of works. Joining company with Theocritus, Virgil, Sannazaro, and Spenser, Milton was now where he felt most at home and most inspired: in the arena with and against the tradition he had so carefully absorbed.

By reflecting on the abrupt death of a young clergyman (who had in fact died en route to his first parish, in Ireland), Milton also saw his chance to exploit fully the pastoral elegy's potential for theological criticism or political satire. This tradition was not new, having had strong practitioners in Mantuan and Spenser, to name only two of whom Milton was aware. But no elegy had ever mounted an attack so magisterially swingeing and so menacingly prophetic as the speech of Saint Peter in "Lycidas." Here again, we face a convergence of personal and historical forces in Milton's poem.

What, then, was the historical context in which Milton mourned the death of a young member of an oppressed minority of good clergymen? While most critics have noted Milton's antagonism toward Roman Catholicism, and more especially toward the tyranny and corruption of the high Anglican clergy, few have examined the situation as closely as they might.

During the years preceding 1637 the courts of James I and Charles I had severely increased their repression of Puritanism. Archbishop Laud, Primate of England since 1633, had extended the power of the High Commission Court and had added that vigorous instrument of nationwide surveillance and suppression, the Metropolitan Visitation. At the same time, the church exercised absolute rights of censorship, preventing or punishing the publication of any seditious works. To clinch his reactionary campaign, Laud prescribed certain elements of ceremony in all services and proscribed the Puritan practice of sermons or lectures, hence denying Milton a potential source of income, leaving him "church-outed by the prelates" ("and shove away the worthy bidden guest").

It was partly in reaction to this dramatic extension of church tyranny that the nation began to reassert liberty of conscience and expression; and a reader of "Lycidas" should be aware that 1637 was indeed the first year of the so-called revolutionary epoch. In this year, Scotland rebelled against the *Book of Common Prayer*, Hampden's ship-money case drove in a wedge against authority, and in June, in the presence of vast numbers of outraged sympathizers in the palace yard at Westminster, the Puritans Prynne, Bastwick, and Burton were cut and branded for sedition.

These men had written and circulated an outspoken attack entitled *A Breviate of the Prelates intollerable usurpations, both upon the Kings Prerogative Royall, and the Subjects Liberties*. In this work they decried the abrogation of the rule of law and the perversion of the entire fabric of justice by churchmen who had "crept up above all." They denounced the wolfish clergy for preying upon instead of nourishing their congregations, and they prophesied the vengeance of God upon the nation. The language and the stance prefigure part of Milton's poem, and the fate of the three men must have harshly sealed their influence on the poet.

Milton may actually have been in London in late June on one of the periodic visits he is known to have made from Horton. Even were he not among the crowds at Westminster, he would certainly have heard of the events and of the eloquent orations made from the pillory, since a sympathetic *Relation* of the entire execution, together with a report of the speeches, was rapidly circulated. What is significant for us is the *manner* in which the victims and their supporters perceived the event. For the *Relation* is marked by a combination of denunciatory, vengeful anger, together with a sense of martyrdom, ceremony, and grace.

The account speaks of the three "Servants of Jesus Christ . . . having their way strawed with sweet hearbes from the house out of which they came to the Pillory, with all the honour that could be done unto them." They might have been the subjects of an elegy or of a funeral procession. And their own language on the pillory has a ring that we hear again in Milton's poem written only five months later. Here is Dr. Bastwick, moments before his ears were hacked off: "If the Presses were as open to us, as formerly they have beene, we would shatter his Kingdome about his eares." And here is Prynne after he had been cut and branded: "The more I am beate down, the more am I lift up." These phrases happen to coincide with words and figures in "Lycidas," but beyond them, the entire drama, with its currents of wrath and resilience and its fervid revolutionary appeal to a retribution and consolation that derive from beyond this world, is part of what we must recognize as Milton's chosen occasion.

King's death was an accident—there was no one to blame. And yet Milton, no doubt realizing that he needed some actual target for his anger, chose to rage against the conspiracy of those "perfidious" forces that strike down the good while leaving the wicked in triumph. It is this channeling of wrath outward to revenge that contributes so fully to his resolution of the question of justice, and to his completion of the work of mourning. Our appreciation of this should be especially keen after the study of revenge tragedies [earlier], and we shall recognize how Milton stages a displaced, verbal revenge, while also managing to conjure a transcendent context in which such vengeance is sanctified.

We have not yet quite exhausted the complex nature of the occasion. Another set of problems was provoked by King's having died so young and so abruptly, just as he was literally making his passage from years of diligent preparation to what may have been years of fruition. Milton's preparation for his own work and for his future claim to immortality was even now just coming to an end after several years of ascetic self-discipline. In a letter to Diodati, Milton spoke of his undistracted labors: "Whereas my genius is such that no delay, no rest, no care or thought almost of anything, holds me aside until I reach the end I am making for, and round off, as it were, some great period of my studies."

The very rhythm and balance of his phrasing suggest the dogged purpo-
siveness of his drive, while the goal is expressed in a conventional figure
of sublimation. As he writes in his next letter, "And what am I doing?
Growing my wings and meditating flight; but as yet our Pegasus raises
himself on very tender pinions. Let us be lowly wise."

It is clear, therefore, that before writing "Lycidas," Milton had
already made a rather decisive deflection of desire, channeling it not into
such enjoyments as the blithe Diodati suggested but rather into projects of
a more spiritual elevation. Not a little energy must have been bound to
this pursuit, and the effect of King's sudden death was, therefore, to cut
the entire knot of Milton's intended transaction. He would now have to
question and renegotiate the supposed exchange by which renunciation
buys its own reward and self-sacrifice defends against mortality. At the
same time, he would have to retain control of the energy itself, which
must have threatened to come unbound as the justification for its constraint was so abruptly threatened. As we have seen, these are tasks
crucial to the work of mourning. By confronting them at their most
pressing, Milton forced his poem to its particular intensity.

> Yet once more, O ye Laurels, and once more
> Ye Myrtles brown, with Ivy never sere,
> I come to pluck your Berries harsh and crude,
> And with forc'd fingers rude,
> Shatter your leaves before the mellowing year.
> Bitter constraint, and sad occasion dear,
> Compels me to disturb your season due:
>
> (1–7)

I have [previously] said much about the elegiac "Yet once more," so
I will not repeat the earlier account of the various functions of repetition.
In Milton's case, the statement has an obvious literal as well as rhetorical
meaning in that he is writing yet another elegy within his own career, as
well as within the career, so to speak, of pastoral elegy itself. (It is typical
of Milton to associate the careers in this way.) One may be sure, therefore, that the repetition itself deliberately repeats such usages in Theocritus,
Virgil, Sannazaro, and others, this being but the first of many indications
that Milton is not only adding to but recapitulating the tradition. As one
reads on, one realizes how fully the assembly of allusions and echoes in
this poem allows the poet to gather up the genre as though to carry it
forward in his own poem.

The mention of laurels, myrtle, and ivy is another obvious use of
the conventional symbols, and Milton's phrasing, too, recalls a specific

line from Virgil's "Eclogue II": "Et vos, o lauri, carpam, et te, proxima myrte." But in these lines Milton already extends what he inherits. At least two elements should be dwelt on briefly: (1) he contrives both to quicken the original meaning of the old symbols and at the same time to widen their reference; and (2) he begins immediately to exploit the rhetorical power of the vocative mood, which so distinguishes this poem.

Laurels, myrtle, and ivy are of course ancient tokens of poethood, but by using them as figures for poetic offerings, Milton adds his personal urgency regarding the question of his own ripeness as a poet. Related figures had marked his anxiety previously in sonnet 7: "But my late spring no bud or blossoms show'th . . . inward ripeness doth much less appear." It is a common device, but Milton's real achievement is to associate the prematurity of the unmellowed King's death with the possibly premature verse of the elegist, thereby confronting the possibility that he himself and his career may be as mortally vulnerable as King.

Furthermore, by subjecting the figures to a curious literalization, Milton allows a reemergence of latent symbolic meanings. We are shown not the immutable, conventional tokens but leaves and berries, which may be shattered or plucked—the action is jarringly physical, as though the figurative status of these plants were itself breaking in the poet's hands. We recall Spenser's similar literalization of the Astrophel flower, his rejection of its traditionally consoling symbolism, allowing the flower to be "untimely cropt." And it is interesting to note that Milton's original version of these lines in the Trinity Manuscript reads "and crop your young" in place of the later "shatter your leaves." Milton's effect is similar to Spenser's, for it, too, literally breaks the traditional figures of compensation in order to prepare a substitution of more spiritualized "plants." He shatters the brittle signs of a merely earthly fame in order to make way for the higher variant that "lives and spreads aloft" in heaven.

The harsh, emphatically physical violation of the plants evokes a further meaning, one whose implications are underscored by the language of reluctance and compulsion ("Forc'd fingers," "constraint," "compels me"). As previously suggested, the work of mourning involves a castrative moment of submission to death and to a necessary deflection of desire. The way in which the poet here is being forced to a bitter shattering and plucking of leaves and of berries "harsh and crude" is not unlike the compulsion to an act of symbolic castration, which the subsequent images of the decapitated Orpheus and the abhorred shears confirm. And it is against the cluster of this and other related imagery that the consolation of a resurgent yet displaced and spiritualized sexual energy will have to triumph.

In addition to his revision of the familiar plant symbols, I mentioned Milton's intense use of the vocative mood, which extends throughout the poem; and it is important to see how the energy of the poem is braced from the outset by being directed to some kind of addressee. The poem is thus tautened by a sinew of address, a compelling tone of engagement. The near-magical manner in which Milton keeps changing fictive addressees is also crucial to the development of the poem, for the long passage from the personified laurels to the Genius of the shore may be read as an intensifying exercise in making up or evoking a presence where there is none—a fundamentally elegiac enterprise. So, too, the repeated vocative mood not only palliates the solitude of the bereaved but grips the reader as though he, too, were being continually addressed.

> For Lycidas is dead, dead ere his prime,
> Young Lycidas, and hath not left his peer:
> Who would not sing for Lycidas? he knew
> Himself to sing, and build the lofty rhyme.
> He must not float upon his wat'ry bier
> Unwept, and welter to the parching wind,
> Without the meed of some melodious tear.
> (8–14)

I referred earlier to the repetitive calling of the dead by name. Certainly the ceremonial practice of invocation and the psychological *anáklisis*, or propping, are at work here, but in a flexible and unobtrusive way. The mourner calls, but his call is worked into his discourse, and once again Milton reveals his nuance and control, his way of allowing the conventions to function even as he subordinates them to his personal manner.

The opposed images in lines 11–14 initiate the contrast between entire clusters of images throughout the poem. While individual elements of this contrast have been noted by several critics, the "cluster" aspect, the close relation between apparently different kinds of images, has not been stressed. This is largely due to the neglect of the more original meanings of such figures and of their relation to the energy and consciousness of the griever. For example, the purposeful, ultimately consoling elevation of the "lofty rhyme" opposes the random and desolate horizontality of a "wat'ry bier," a contrast repeated in several versions and culminating in that between the guarded mount and the risen soul on the one hand and the whelming tide and far-flung corpse on the other. But what is the relation of this contrast to that between a consoling, invigorating liquid and a barren, parching wind, or between reward and an almost punitive neglect?

What does a cluster such as that of elevation, poetry, liquid, and reward imply? We have spoken of consolation as the achievement of a deflected sexual assertion, of a trope for a procreative force that outlasts individual mortality. The erection of tombs or stelae or indeed of a survivor's verse may be seen, therefore, as understandably associated with images of an invigorating liquid. The dew that Colin Clout sought to inherit from the dead Tityrus was such a liquid—an originally sexual power allegorized as poetic creativity. In "Lycidas" the imagery of a saving and surviving liquid, the figure for ongoing desire and creativity, hence of successful mourning, is even included in mythological form in the Arethusa-Alpheus legend (also present in Virgil's "Eclogue X"), as well as in the form of the swift Hebrus who bears the gory visage of continuing song to the Lesbian shore. These are the liquids that, unlike the barren diffusion of the sea, retain a direction and a continuing force, associated as they must be with the melodious tear and the lofty rhyme. It is in no way surprising, therefore, that Milton immediately associates his inspiration with the sacred well.

> Begin then, Sisters of the sacred well,
> That from beneath the seat of *Jove* doth spring,
> Begin, and somewhat loudly sweep the string.
> Hence with denial vain, and coy excuse,
> So may some gentle Muse
> With lucky words favor my destin'd Urn,
> And as he passes turn,
> And bid fair peace be to my sable shroud.
>   (15–22)

Significantly, the sacred well "springs" (reinforcing the suggestion of lofty rhyme and of an originally seminal power) from Jove's seat, as though this were somehow *his* liquid power. The line alludes not only to the opening of Hesiod's *Theogony*:

> With the Heliconian Muses let us start
> Our song: they hold the great and godly mount
> Of Helicon, and on their delicate feet
> They dance around the darkly bubbling spring
> And round the altar of the mighty Zeus.

It also alludes to the barely Christianized version in Revelation 22: "And he showed me a pure river of water of life, clear as crystal, proceeding out of the throne of God and of the Lamb." Almost like Alpheus, this liquid will surface again at the end of the poem in images of those "other streams" and that "Nectar pure."

Furthermore, the presence of the Sister Muses deepens our recognition that the poet is asserting a residually sexual poetic power, particularly as he urges, "Hence with denial vain, and coy excuse," as though
this were indeed an erotic relationship. We notice how the vocative has
shifted to an imperative mood, a clue to Milton's desire to control the
personages of his poem. Nor is this imperiousness a matter of chance as he
addresses the Muses. The very echo in "somewhat loudly" of Virgil's *paulo
maiora* alerts us to the fact that Milton has his eye on Virgil's "Eclogue
IV," with its move from pastoral to prophetic utterance.

After this summons, the poet suddenly confesses much of his
motivation, his desire for a defense against his own obliteration, in short,
for immortality, a power that, after death, may yet compel a later poet to
turn to him in homage and benediction. Milton seems to wrestle with the
timing of this statement. The urgency of his need is, I think, at odds with
his tact. What results is an uneasy compromise: on the one hand the
undeniably abrupt admission, as though the expressed intention could not
be restrained a moment longer; on the other the clever ambiguity of the
"so may," which tempers the boldness of purpose (*so* meaning "in order
that") by the more neutral possibility of a mere analogy (*so* meaning "just
as").

The expression of personal motive and anxiety increases the urgent
intimacy of the poem, carrying us forward into the prolonged identification of the mourner with his lost friend and predisposing us to recognize
the degree of self-mourning that gathers in the following lines. The past
and its landscape, together with the figure of the dead shepherd, are, after
all, versions of a lost self.

> For we were nurst upon the self-same hill,
> Fed the same flock, by fountain, shade, and rill.
> Together both, ere the high Lawns appear'd
> Under the opening eyelids of the morn,
> We drove afield, and both together heard
> What time the Gray-fly winds her sultry horn,
> Batt'ning our flocks with the fresh dews of night,
> Oft till the Star that rose, at Ev'ning, bright
> Toward Heav'n's descent had slop'd his westering wheel.
> Meanwhile the Rural ditties were not mute,
> Temper'd to th'Oaten Flute;
> Rough *Satyrs* danc'd, and *Fauns* with clov'n heel
> From the glad sound would not be absent long,
> And old *Damaetas* lov'd to hear our song.
>
> (23–36)

Only a few features of these lines need be remarked here. The figure of nursing suggests the benevolent, nourishing mother, the loss of whom I have claimed to be an inescapably recapitulated element of any mourning. By attachment to the mother I mean attachment to a unity that seems to precede a sense of individuation and of separate mortality. Figures for this matrix could be the flowery lap of Nature or the Muse. In this poem, written a mere seven months after Milton had lost his own mother, that grief is overwhelmingly important, as we shall see. In keeping with the evocation of life in the presence of the mother, time and place are described as strangely seamless, both encompassed by an unbroken circle of natural routine, a kind of rhythmic browsing. The poem's larger temporality (a day's song) will enlarge and repeat this particular figure of the diurnal round, healing, in fact, the "heavy change" which suddenly comes to rob the inset, recollected pastoral of its perfection.

The high lawns repeat the motif of elevation, which is brought into significant association now with eyes and morning, both figuring the virile, watchful sun, a symbol of paternal power and of totemic immortality. Here the young sons set off *before* that power has fully risen. They are still close to a nursing nature, as yet evading, one might say, the father's fully opened eyes, the pure eyes of all-judging Jove which the poet will come to know more intimately through loss.

While the songs of this idyllic day are equally unmarked by loss or even by a more than momentary absence, Milton does contrive to insinuate the idea of loss, as the double negatives allow the possibility of deprivation to surface in consciousness: "were not mute . . . would not be absent long." The effect is reminiscent of Spenser's almost subliminal warnings in "Astrophel": "Both wise and hardie (too hardie alas!) . . . He vanquisht all, and vanquisht was of none," signals preparing and cushioning the mind against a sudden loss. Milton's narrative timing, like Spenser's and like that of many elegists in the tradition, is carefully designed to situate the recollected idyll after the mere statement of loss but before the fuller narration and elaboration of that loss. The reader is, therefore, somehow both prepared for loss and yet forced to reexperience its reality. The mourned subject is made to die again.

Even were the idyll not explicitly framed by loss, it has an unmistakable air of unreality, a vulnerable, fictive quality, as though the recollection were a wish-fulfilling dream. Hence the curiously self-englobed temporality, a perfect wheel of time made to revolve within the larger narrative. Hence, too, the way in which the idyll concludes with an unobtrusive clue to its own fictionality. For while the conventional pastoral fiction (shepherds for poets, the hill for Cambridge) can be reduced to its literal referents, the mention of satyrs and fauns introduces a further, less reducible level of fictionality, and from here the entire idyll seems to be retrospectively illuminated by the brightened light of unreality. It is a subtle version of the poet's later, more explicit admissions of fond dream or false surmise, and it is difficult to imagine a more superb and gentle manner of both indulging and yet distancing one's recollections of the past and of the dead.

The idyll concludes with a mention of Damaetas's approval, and it is fitting that this period of innocent nursing, of small rural ditties, and of proximity to nature, should be unthreatened by any truly powerful figure of authority. Unlike that of all-judging Jove, Damaetas's approval is not contingent upon sacrifice or loss. Yet old Damaetas does, however mildly, prefigure the later judge. And our understanding of the genre and of the work of mourning makes us appreciate why a mention of this figure terminates the recollected idyll. So, too, we are less unprepared to follow this first mention of an older figure of authority by what might otherwise, despite the fictionality of the idyll, appear to be a surprisingly abrupt turn to the confrontation of disastrous loss.

> But O the heavy change, now thou art gone,
> Now thou art gone, and never must return!
> Thee Shepherd, thee the Woods, and desert Caves,
> With wild Thyme and the gadding Vine o'ergrown,
> And all their echoes mourn.
> The Willows and the Hazel Copses green
> Shall now no more be seen,
> Fanning their joyous Leaves to thy soft lays.
> As killing as the Canker to the Rose,
> Or Taint-worm to the weanling Herds that graze,
> Or Frost to Flowers, that their gay wardrobe wear,
> When first the White-thorn blows;
> Such, *Lycidas*, thy loss to Shepherd's ear.
>
> (37–49)

Here is the harshly elaborated loss of that ideal, recollected world, whose images of freshness and nurture have given way to those of insidious disease and of a specifically premature ruin. While Milton's use of the pathetic fallacy is conventional, he nevertheless modulates the passage away from fallacy into extended simile, thereby adding a measure of sophistication (he *declares* the figurative nature of such comparisons) and control (he uses the similes to *define* the precise nature of the loss). In fact, as though it were moving toward a single destination, the entire passage accumulates and converges upon a center of loss, the shepherd's

ear. This emphatic focus deserves more interpretation than it has received, and some elements of our theoretical approach may be of help.

It is not enough to say merely that the ear has been deprived of
what it used to hear. That is *not* the exact nature of its loss. Rather, as the
tenor of the similes urgently suggests, the ear is itself an object of ruin: as
Canker (cankerworm, a caterpillar that destroys leaves) kills the rose, as
Taint-worm invades the weanling herds, and as frost destroys the flowers,
so this loss assaults the ear. The worm imagery is especially well chosen,
the worm's motion being so perfectly menacing to the labyrinth of the ear.

We may, therefore, regard the loss as not only *to* but *of* the
shepherd's ear. At a simple level we can point, as anthropologists and
psychologists might, to the practice whereby a mourner isolates a part of
his body as the locus of pain—the synecdoche allowing him to localize an
otherwise diffuse hurt. But beyond this is the crucial practice of symbolic
self-injury or castration in relation to the work of mourning. Just as the
child performs a voluntary symbolic castration to avoid death or what he
fears as actual castration, and just as the vegetation deity suffers a particularly castrative martyrdom so that the phallic principle of fertility may be
renewed, so, too, the griever wounds his own sexuality, deflecting his
desire, in order to erect a consoling figure for an ongoing, if displaced,
generative power. We have already seen how an act of shattering and
plucking will eventually, by the power of Jove, yield the immortal plant of
heavenly praise. Similarly, the wounded and trembling ear will yet be
touched and more than repaired by the ministry of Apollo. The ear that
loses its capacity to hear the songs to which it was attached is granted the
power to hear strains of a "higher mood." We recall the refrain of Saint
John: "He that hath an ear let him hear what the spirit saith." The
movement is from a physical to a spiritual organ. It is what happens
visually in *Paradise Lost*, where the poet's blindness to the external world
yields a higher, inner vision: "So much the rather thou Celestial Light /
Shine inward." In each case, a castrative loss or curbing yields a higher,
almost always immortalizing strength.

> Where were ye Nymphs when the remorseless deep
> Clos'd o'er the head of your lov'd *Lycidas*?
> For neither were ye playing on the steep,
> Where your old *Bards*, the famous *Druids*, lie,
> Nor on the shaggy top of *Mona* high,
> Nor yet where *Deva* spreads her wizard stream:
> Ay me, I fondly dream!
> Had ye been there—for what could that have done?
> What could the Muse herself that *Orpheus* bore,

The Muse herself, for her enchanting son
Whom Universal nature did lament,
When by the rout that made the hideous roar,
His gory visage down the stream was sent,
Down the swift *Hebrus* to the *Lesbian* shore?
(50 63)

We may recall how such conventional questioning is in large part designed not only to avert potential self-accusation but also to *create* the fictive addressees, substituting the pretence of temporary absence for the suspicion of nonexistence or permanent neglect. At least three features of Milton's personal use of the conventions deserve notice. First, Milton revises Virgil's own revision of Theocritus. In his "First Idyl," Theocritus had Thyrsis ask where in Sicily (i.e., his own recollected locale) the nymphs had been. Virgil's "Eclogue X," however, shifts the scenario to Arcadia, a realm quite remote from himself or Gallus. Milton follows Theocritus in using his own national locale—Bardsey, Anglesey, and the river Dee. The effect is an added immediacy, as well as the vigor of an achieved rather than received transfiguration of geography.

Second, the imagined locations of the nymphs share aspects of the positive, consoling images in lines 11–14 noted above. They are associated either with elevations ("the steep . . . the top of Mona high") or with a special, purposeful liquid force ("Where Deva spreads her wizard stream"). Yet now these haunts are empty and remote. Their associated images of protection and strength are brought into question.

The third and more significant feature of this address is Milton's characteristic, self-critical rejection of an indulged fiction. As usual, Milton curbs in order to surpass himself—an essentially elegiac maneuver. The wish fulfillment is renounced "in deference to reality," and the loss is more fully confronted. Here the realization is that of the Muses' inefficacy, and it precipitates the most complicated crisis in the poem.

The poet has to mourn the loss of Lycidas *and* his own loss of belief in the Muses' protection, in particular that of Calliope, the mother of Orpheus. This loss is made especially catastrophic by being cast in terms that recapitulate Orpheus's violent death. We are thus brought to that crux in mourning: a recapitulated loss of the mother, together with a scenario of castration. "Lycidas" confronts this with such unparalleled force in part because Milton always seems to renovate conventional images and myths. But it is difficult in this case to exclude additional, biographical factors—Milton's obsessive sense of his own career (his relation to the Muse) and the death, seven months previously, of his mother. A full discussion of the issues involved here carries us at last into the immediately following section of the poem.

> Alas! What boots it with uncessant care
> To tend the homely slighted shepherd's trade,
> And strictly meditate the thankless Muse?
> Were it not better done as others use,
> To sport with *Amaryllis* in the shade,
> Or with the tangles of *Neaera's* hair?
> *Fame* is the spur that the clear spirit doth raise
> (That last infirmity of Noble mind)
> To scorn delights, and live laborious days;
> But the fair Guerdon when we hope to find,
> And think to burst out into sudden blaze,
> Comes the blind *Fury* with th'abhorred shears,
> And slits the thin-spun life. "But not the praise,"
> *Phoebus* repli'd, and touch'd my trembling ears;
> "*Fame* is no plant that grows on mortal soil,
> Nor in the glistering foil
> Set off to th'world, nor in broad rumor lies,
> But lives and spreads aloft by those pure eyes
> And perfect witness of all-judging *Jove*;
> As he pronounces lastly on each deed,
> Of so much fame in Heav'n expect thy meed."
>
> (64–84)

The cruel cutting short of a career arouses the poet to question his own defense against mortality and to redefine the possible regard, if any, for his own ascetic pursuits. In discussing the occasion of this poem, I noted that one of the tasks facing Milton was that of controlling the energy that is suddenly released once the object or rationale of its binding attachment is threatened. Not surprisingly, therefore, Milton questions the value of his asceticism, wondering whether an unsublimated eroticism is not worth indulging after all. Presumably the justification for strictly meditating the Muse was a promise of fame, and a special relation to that motherly figure, the Muse. By curbing desire, diverting it into poetic ambition, he could retain the close relationship. Or so he might have thought had he not abruptly discovered that the Muse may not be interested, may be quite thankless, and may, after all, show an alarming ability to give way to a kind of anti-Muse, one who mocks at and even causes martyrdom—an Atropos malevolently wielding the shears. By dwelling with horror on the decapitation of Orpheus, Milton not only reenacts the harsh event but does so with a bitter momentary ignorance of what it may achieve. It seems to be a lose-lose situation, one that may remind us

of Titus sacrificing his hand for the severed heads of his sons. The
economy of sacrifice and reward has collapsed. Or is it that the notion of
reward must be revised, a revision somehow earned more fully, after all,
by this very submission?

Immediately following this cry of outrage, therefore, the poem
turns to what the harsh fate *does* in fact secure: not an earthly fame,
which is made to seem an insufficiently displaced or sublimated object of
desire, but rather a more spiritualized version—the divine approval granted
by an otherworldly judge. We have seen the attendant imagery of reward
prepared earlier, in the figures of shattered foliage and of the shepherd's
blighted ear. The damage to these is now repaired as they, too, make way
for more spiritual versions and functions.

There is, however, a residual cautioning in Apollo's gesture, as any
reader of Virgil's "Eclogue VI" will recall: in Virgil's poem the gesture
signified Apollo's rebuke to the poet's premature ambition. In "Lycidas"
the criticism takes the form of a more extended chastisement, preparing
us, surely, for a Christian reading of this entire episode. From that
perspective, achieved more clearly later in the poem, the fate of Orpheus
represents the chastening of man's soul in submission to a divine father.
Paul's epistle to the Hebrews spells out the Christian version of the
oedipal transaction:

> . . . My son, despise not thou the chastening of the Lord, nor faint
> when thou art rebuked of him:
> For whom the Lord loveth he chasteneth, and scourgeth every son whom
> he receiveth.
>
> If ye endure chastening, God dealeth with you as with sons; for
> what son is he whom the father chasteneth not?
>
> Furthermore we have had fathers of our flesh which corrected *us*, and we
> gave *them* reverence: shall we not much rather be in subjection unto the
> Father of spirits, and live?
>
> (Heb. 12.5–9)

Milton's focus on the authority of the father is marked in the
dramatic movement from female to male figures, a movement that is itself
part of the work of mourning: the separation from the primary object of
desire associated with the mother and an identification with the father
and his symbols of power. Hence the movement away from the sisters, the
nymphs, and Calliope toward Apollo and Jove, with particular attention
to the powerful, even seminal, influence of Jove's eyes. Eyes are the
emblems of virility and of a father's gaze. Here, the spiritual version of

that virility still has the power to raise aloft, and its totemic prestige is firmly linked to a judging power.

With these ideas in mind, we are now in a position to return to Milton's biography, where we discover not only that Sara Milton died in April 1637 but that this death left the poet with a father who happened at this very time to be as powerful a figure of judgment as Milton could possibly have faced. Since 1634, Milton had in fact struggled with his father's distrust of a poetic career. He had devoted himself primarily to the study of Church history and was at least partly trying to accommodate his father's directive, namely, to engage the clerical issues of the time in sermon and debate. Certainly, he was biding his time, preparing for epic pursuits, but the fact remains that "Lycidas" was probably the first poem Milton wrote following his final revision of *Comus*. The poem therefore had to bear a heavy burden of proof if Milton were to convince his father that poetry could in fact engage serious concerns. Milton writes a poem not only affected by the loss of his mother but also designed for the eyes of his father.

There is still the unanswered question of why, on a clear summer's day, a ship mysteriously foundered and sank in the Irish sea, carrying to his death a twenty-five-year-old clergyman and poet.

> O Fountain *Arethuse*, and thou honor'd flood,
> Smooth-sliding *Mincius*; crown'd with vocal reeds,
> That strain I heard was of a higher mood:
> But now my Oat proceeds,
> And listens to the Herald of the Sea
> That came in *Neptune's* plea.
> He ask'd the Waves, and ask'd the Felon winds,
> What hard mishap hath doom'd this gentle swain?
> And question'd every gust of rugged wings
> That blows from off each beaked Promontory.
> They knew not of his story,
> And sage *Hippotades* their answer brings,
> That not a blast was from his dungeon stray'd,
> The air was calm, and on the level brine,
> Sleek *Panope* with all her sisters play'd.
>
> (85–99)

The poet modulates back to the more strictly pastoral mode symbolized by Arethuse and Mincius, doing so in a way that deliberately calls attention to the manner in which he has surpassed this mode. The stage-managing device is thus inseparable from a continuing act of self-commentary.

Triton learns from Hippotades (Aeolus) that neither had there been any disturbance nor had the waves and winds so much as heard of Lycidas's fate. While maintaining the opposition between male constraint (his dungeon) and feminine pleasure (the sport of Panope), the lines present further, disquieting separations, not only between man and nature but between man and the mythological presences he may once have cherished. The poem is indeed moving, in a typically Miltonic manner, to a Christian distancing or revaluation of Classical myth. There is no sympathy here between the nymphs and a drowning man. Worse yet, they play while he sinks. It is precisely this blend of remoteness and suspected triviality that characterizes the "merely" pastoral world that Milton is even now so thoroughly undertaking to surpass. The play of Panope thus becomes associated with the dance of fauns and satyrs to the rural ditties, glad sounds that we now seem to have heard so long ago.

As if to increase this remoteness, the following three lines move to a blend of harsh diction with religious rhetoric:

> It was that fatal and perfidious Bark
> Built in th'eclipse, and rigg'd with curses dark,
> That sunk so low that sacred head of thine.
>
> (100–102)

The Orphic figure is already undergoing the kind of Christianizing that we studied [elsewhere]. Perhaps it was with a view to this that Milton carefully revised the Orpheus episode in such a way as to delay until now the Christian revision: for example, he began with "goarie scalpe," then altered it to "divine head," then "divine visage," but then, significantly, went back to "gory visage," deleting mention of the divinity. So, too, the rout of savage maenads is now replaced by a suggested agent of Sin, associated with perfidiousness and with the eclipse. The eclipse evokes both the crucifixion (hence moving the subject yet further from a pagan to a Christian martyrdom) and the original Fall. We recall how in *Paradise Lost* the first sign of Eve's sin is precisely an eclipse.

The catastrophe thus begins to find its place more securely within a Christian context of sin, Fall, and redemption, as the later sections of the poem will elaborate.

> Next *Camus*, reverend Sire, went footing slow,
> His Mantle hairy, and his Bonnet sedge,
> Inwrought with figures dim, and on the edge
> Like to that sanguine flower inscrib'd with woe.
> "Ah! Who hath reft" (quoth he) "my dearest pledge?"
>
> (103–7)

Camus, personification of the river Cam and of Cambridge University, recalls the mild figure of old Damaetas. But Camus has an added dignity: he is a "reverend Sire," his "footing slow" is different from the light steps that accompanied Damaetas's well-loved songs, and his attire enhances his majestic sadness. We have [previously] studied how the imagery of weaving and embroidery is so frequently associated with the work of mourning; I shall therefore merely note its careful contrivance in these lines. Apart from their customary connotations, and their allusion to prior elegiac weavings, the lines seem to achieve a close yet unobtrusive metaphorical blending of the natural and the human worlds: the garments and embroidery are also the actual margins of the stream, where, amid dim reeds and sedge, one may discern apparent figures, brighter growths inscribed into the fabric like Apollo's words of grief, *ai, ai,* inscribed upon the hyacinth. It is as though the differing worlds can overlap only by metaphor and artifice occasioned by loss. Camus himself seems to pace at the borders of the pastoral world, a world now ineradicably embroidered with mortality. His single utterance is that questioning cry of deprivation, which can be answered only from another realm, in a "dread voice."

> Last came, and last did go,
> The Pilot of the *Galilean* lake.
> Two massy Keys he bore of metals twain
> (The Golden opes, the Iron shuts amain).
> He shook his Mitred locks, and stern bespake:
> "How well could I have spar'd for thee, young swain,
> Enough of such as for their bellies' sake,
> Creep and intrude and climb into the fold?
> Of other care they little reck'ning make,
> Than how to scramble at the shearers' feast,
> And shove away the worthy bidden guest;
> Blind mouths! that scarce themselves know how to hold
> A Sheep-hook, or have learn'd aught else the least
> That to the faithful Herdman's art belongs!
> What recks it them? What need they? They are sped;
> And when they list, their lean and flashy songs
> Grate on their scrannel Pipes of wretched straw.
> The hungry Sheep look up, and are not fed,
> But swoln with wind, and the rank mist they draw,
> Rot inwardly, and foul contagion spread:
> Besides what the grim Wolf with privy paw
> Daily devours apace, and nothing said;
> But that two-handed engine at the door
> Stands ready to smite once, and smite no more."
> (108–31)

For the physical appearance of Saint Peter we are given only two items, but they are rich in significance. The keys have been amply glossed, but our understanding of the sexual economies of loss and consolation, together with our sense of more primitive totemic representations of authority and resurrection, should alert us to a wider range of connotation than is customarily evoked.

So, too, the "Mitred locks" deserve a fuller interpretation. The figure of the abhorred shears had certainly emphasized the castrative nature of loss, and the emphasis will be repeated by Saint Peter's mention of the shearers' feast. Hair is a traditional symbol of sexual power, and Saint Peter's locks represent an immortal version of that power. We notice that the locks are not merely worn but shaken like an instrument, and their power is sanctified by the totemic headdress that they support. The association between locks of hair and a resurrected vitality will be reinforced by the figure of the rising sun tricking his beams and flaming in the forehead of the morning sky and ultimately by that of Lycidas, whose oozy locks are laved in heaven with nectar pure. It is with a sense, then, of Saint Peter's particular totemic attributes that we hear his speech.

What is the real significance and function of Saint Peter's opening words? I do not think that the purpose of his "How well could I have spar'd thee . . . Enough of such" has been adequately noted. He is making an equation, and it is important in the light of what follows to recognize this as the essential equation of the revenger. One Lycidas is worth enough of such, and it is against that number—that tally—that the entire speech unrolls like a single act of vengeance. Here is the controlled release of rage that we have seen to be so crucial to the work of mourning. Once again, it involves the locating of a target for a wrath that must be turned outward; the shifting of the burden of pain; the reversal from the passive suffering of hurt to the active causing of it; and above all, the assumption of the power to hurt, a power that we have studied in its relation to the totemic force associated with a metaphoric sexual immortality. This may well account for the penumbra of mystery and awe surrounding the two-handed engine. Its strangeness and apartness is surely an aspect of its power as a totemic instrument, and as such, it must be associated with the two keys and with the miter, which we know to be tall, conical, and two-peaked.

So much of the poet's energy pours into Saint Peter's tirade that it is difficult and artificial to separate its elements. We can at least point to the following: the accumulated frustration of the questions, Where were ye? What hard mishap? Who hath reft?; the energy bound to years of laborious preparation and self-denial (here, whatever energy could not quite be rededicated to the pursuit of divine praise could be marshaled into a legitimized rage); the anger against those who had prevented Milton from the possibility of church lecturing; the bitter fury against those who had punished Burton, Bastwick, and Prynne; the anger against a mother or Muse who deserted the son she should have protected; the anger at having to mourn, at having one's rude fingers forced to their shattering work; the anger, finally, of any ambitious poet against his own thus far (to him, and to his father) inadequate work. The last-named element finds it way, I think, into the contempt for those who "grate on their scrannel pipes of wretched straw."

Before leaving this speech, we may admire Milton's resolution of the revenger's problematic sense of separation from the agents or source of justice. We have seen Titus and Hieronimo petitioning the gods in vain and receiving only neglect or scorn from the human courts. For them, language loses its efficacy; their grief itself is mocked. Milton heals the breach by the radical device of summoning Saint Peter in person—a summons enabled only by Milton's extremely Protestant internalization of divinity. That is to say, whereas Titus and Hieronimo regard divine power as impossibly remote and external, withdrawn somewhere beyond a diamantine wall, Milton regards it as potentially within the self. So much so that he can give it voice. Milton's words become Saint Peter's. They give him presence. In a sense, they create him. If we balk at supposing that Saint Peter is somehow within Milton, we have no choice but to conclude that Milton is somehow within the saint.

> Return *Alpheus*, the dread voice is past
> That shrunk thy streams; Return *Sicilian* Muse,
> And call the Vales, and bid them hither cast
> Their Bells and Flowrets of a thousand hues.
> Ye valleys low where the mild whispers use
> Of shades and wanton winds and gushing brooks,
> On whose fresh lap the swart Star sparely looks,
> Throw hither all your quaint enamell'd eyes,
> That on the green turf suck the honied showers,
> And purple all the ground with vernal flowers.
> Bring the rathe Primrose that forsaken dies,
> The tufted Crow-toe, and pale Jessamine,
> The white Pink, and the Pansy freakt with jet,
> The glowing Violet,
> The Musk-rose, and the well-attir'd Woodbine,
> With Cowslips wan that hang the pensive head,
> And every flower that sad embroidery wears:
> Bid *Amaranthus* all his beauty shed,

And Daffadillies fill their cups with tears
To strew the Laureate Hearse where Lycid lies.
For so to interpose a little ease,
Let our frail thoughts dally with false surmise.
                    (132–53)

When well expressed, wrath itself is sweet, like honey; and Milton, as he turned from the diatribe of Peter to the sweet yield of the valleys, must have felt something of what Homer and Plato meant. Milton coaches Alpheus to renew the current of his desire. As we know, Alpheus, the stream, is a figure for an already once-deflected passion: the youth underwent a transformation in order to continue his pursuit. The stream is a figure, in other words, for the mourner's sexuality, and for its necessary willingness to accept not only a detour but a sacrificial change. And despite the great beauty and apparent relaxation in this so-called interlude, the work of sacrifice is minutely continued.

It is important to view the present offering in contrast to the bitter plucking of the poem's start. Now, the anger has been purged, and the rewards (the undying flowers of praise) have been established. The process can be repeated in a sweeter, more decorative manner, even while the clues of sacrifice are unmistakable: the offering of "quaint enamell'd eyes" (the "white Pink," incidentally, also connotes a little eye, pink meaning "eyelet"); the hanging, pensive heads (not only of cowslips but of pansies too); the flowers chosen as emblems of frustrated or forlorn young love ("the rathe Primrose that forsaken dies"); or flowers like the "tufted Crow-toe" (orcus mascula) or the amaranth, here explicitly urged to shed his beauty (the amaranth is, literally, the unfading flower, the never-quenched life flame. Its tiny red spires revive in water long after plucking—perfect emblems for a sacrificed but resurrected power).

While essential to the poem's development and to its high level of self-awareness, the recognition of "false surmise" reflects not only on the fictive presence of the dead in "Lycidas" but on the figurative action that underlies any such ceremonial offering, any such imagining that the dead person—someone addressed as he or thou rather than it—is actually in the mourner's presence. In this sense, the interposing tribute is any elegy, any invention of farewell addressed to one who has already gone. And in the turbulent lines that follow, however much one feels a certain harsh confrontation with the unadorned ugliness of death, the fiction of address is being maintained, even as the exact locating of that address is forcibly bewildered.

Ay me! Whilst thee the shores and sounding Seas
Wash far away, where'er thy bones are hurl'd,
Whether beyond the stormy Hebrides,

Where thou perhaps under the whelming tide
Visit'st the bottom of the monstrous world;
Or whether thou to our moist vows denied,
Sleep'st by the fable of *Bellerus* old,
Where the great vision of the guarded Mount
Looks toward *Namancos* and *Bayona's* hold;
Look homeward Angel now, and melt with ruth.
And, O ye *Dolphins*, waft the hapless youth.
(154–64)

The movement away from the fictive hearse to the great diffusion of the rolling sea definitely accelerates the withdrawal of attachment from the dead. And the distance opened up by those *whethers* and *ors* prepares, as it should, for the necessary reattachment of love to a substitute. That substitute is, as we know, a transfigured version of the lost Lycidas, and it is fascinating to note how Milton actually combines the movement of detachment with a subtle premonition of the apotheosis to come. For the diffusion of place hints, in however painful a voice, at the kind of omnipresence of a deity. The hint is strengthened by the orotund language ("the bottom of the monstrous world") and by the possible suggestion of Christ's visit to harrow hell. It is furthered by reference to Bellerus, Saint Michael, and the legendary figure of Palaemon.

Palaemon was the drowned youth whom dolphins carried to the shore. A temple was erected in homage to him as the guardian of sailors, a role to be accorded Lycidas. Bellerus is the fabled giant who will arise from his slumbers as though from death. And Saint Michael is not only the patron of mariners (hence again prefiguring the "Genius of the shore") but also the agent of Justice, wielding a sword that should remind us of the two-handed engine of divine vengeance. Tradition has it that men of faith could see the apparition of Michael on the mountain at Land's End. There Milton places him, on his fortified elevation guarding against the Spanish strongholds across the sea. The image of consolidated defense surely reflects on the poet's own increasingly assured defense, his conviction that a concentrated power (be it his lofty rhyme, his praise aloft, or even the power of his reinforced repression, his rededication to an ascetic quest) will stand erect against less high desires and against death itself. It is because these lines so brilliantly affect that distancing of the lost object, the relic of the actual Lycidas, *and* so fully prefigure the new object of attachment, the resurrected Lycidas, that the poem can now finally move to the lines that follow.

Weep no more, woeful Shepherds weep no more,
For *Lycidas* your sorrow is not dead,

Sunk though he be beneath the wat'ry floor,
So sinks the day star in the Ocean bed,
And yet anon repairs his drooping head,
And tricks his beams, and with new-spangled Ore,
Flames in the forehead of the morning sky:
So *Lycidas*, sunk low, but mounted high,
Through the dear might of him that walk'd the waves,
Where other groves, and other streams along,
With *Nectar* pure his oozy Locks he laves,
And hears the unexpressive nuptial Song,
In the blest Kingdoms meek of joy and love.
There entertain him all the Saints above,
In solemn troops, and sweet Societies
That sing, and singing in their glory move,
And wipe the tears for ever from his eyes.
Now *Lycidas*, the Shepherds weep no more;
Henceforth thou art the Genius of the shore,
In thy large recompense, and shalt be good
To all that wander in that perilous flood.

(165–85)

Here, then, is the act of substitution, without which no work of mourning is complete, the reattachment to a new object of love, in this case a troped, indeed apotheosized, version of the physical Lycidas who had sunk "beneath the wat'ry floor." The turn to the mounted Lycidas thus necessarily reflects a spiritualization of the poet's own attachment, a refined reassertion of desire evident in the accompanying imagery (the emphasis on mounting, on repairing a drooping head, on laving the oozy locks, and finally on the nuptial song in the kingdom of joy and love). We discern not merely the mourner's reinvestment of desire but the conclusion of the archaic funeral rites for the vegetation god—the retrieval or establishment of an emblem of renewed fertility and the celebration of a reunion that regenerates the natural world. Here, of course, in a Christianized version we have the elevation of the soul (still imaged, however, by the sun) and its entry into a spiritually raised, rather than physically renewed, natural world, a world now of other streams and groves, where the nuptial song celebrates the marriage of the Lamb, or of the human spirit, to God. The pastoral world is reinscribed in heaven.

As for the figure of the sun, apart from its totemic power and its history as a crucial elegiac trope, it has been carefully contextualized in "Lycidas," situated in relation to so many other images and prefigurations that it now gathers up a vast range of meaning in its final, triumphant rise. It recalls the opening eyelids of the morn; it fulfills the aborted sudden blaze of fame; it sheds the eclipse; it raises all those fallen, pensive, sunk, or severed heads.

Yet it is intriguing to notice how the poet, even while he exploits this figure of the sun as a simile for the rising soul, manages to supersede it by the Christian force that according to Milton makes that simile possible. Lycidas rises like the sun but does so through the dear might of Christ. We are invited to see how this power, as a force that can *cause* a sunlike rise, exceeds that of the sun. We may even be reminded that in a Christian cosmos God is the creator or cause of the sun itself. This set of ideas is important to the coda of the poem, and it is stressed further by the motif of an enabling or *positing* power manifested in the poet's *fiat*: "Henceforth thou art the Genius of the shore." The accent is very nearly that of command. Is the poet himself now playing a Christ-like role?

> Thus sang the uncouth Swain to th'Oaks and rills,
> While the still morn went out with Sandals gray;
> He touch't the tender stops of various Quills,
> With eager thought warbling his *Doric* lay:
> And now the Sun had stretch't out all the hills,
> And now was dropt into the Western bay;
> At last he rose, and twitch't his Mantle blue:
> Tomorrow to fresh Woods, and Pastures new.
>   (186–93)

The mourner's act of self-distancing and self-surpassing, so essential to mourning, is here taken one step further. Even the successful mourner is suddenly superseded, in a way that reminds us of the place of this poem in the context of Milton's developing career. He has written his consummate pastoral, and has achieved within it instances and proofs of epic power. Not only is this coda written in *ottava rima*, the form for Italian epic, but it reads precisely like those moments in epic poetry when the narrator follows the speech of a protagonist with "Thus sang. . . ." It is as though Milton, in ending and describing his elegy, has already entered an epic.

The line "He touch't the tender stops of various Quills" is surely meant to counterpoint, in a gentle fashion, the forced fingers rudely shattering the leaves. And "touch't the tender stops" ought, too, to recall "touch't my trembling ears," thereby suggesting a development that the poet has now made, an assimilation of the Apollonian, epic touch within the Doric "warble." Once again we admire the mourner's absorption of the gestures of authority, which culminates in the assimilation of the elegist to the guiding figure and power of the poem, the sun. Assimilation and yet, as always, surpassal.

First, there is the power deriving from an accelerated description of the sun's motion, as though the poet's act of description were hurrying the sun, somehow even causing tenses to collapse into the timeless now of eternity, or indeed of poetry: "And now the Sun . . . And now was dropt." Following this is the master stroke of replacing the sun by the elegist, sliding from one to the other via a deliberately ambiguous pronoun, *he*. That ambiguity is even prepared for by the attribution to the elegist of a "Mantle blue," somehow part of the same attire as the "Sandals gray;" and by the brilliant succession "And now was dropt . . . At last he rose." The physical Lycidas had sunk; his spirit has mounted high. The sun sinks; the poet rises.

The "Mantle blue" calls for a few comments. It is perhaps only the coventry blue cloak of a shepherd. But how to distinguish it now from the blue sky surrounding the sun? What is more interesting, it is a consoling revision of the "mantle black" that surrounded a disconsolate Colin Clout at the end of "January." It is the last and perhaps most pointed of Milton's allusions to the tradition he has overgone.

The way in which the elegist preempts the rising of the sun reflects back on Christ's power to effect a spiritual sunlike rise for man. But Milton has calmly assumed that power himself: *he* makes the uncouth swain rise, and he himself has risen, as though he were another sun. We find it hard to avoid the recognition that it is, after all, the poet who has Christ raise Lycidas. The frame of fictionality encompasses even that supreme action; which brings us to the disquieting region of conjecture, so important to Milton, of whether Christianity may be no more than a superior product (superior to Classical mythology, for example) of man's imagination. What we have already seen to be the poem's repeated questioning of its own fictions cannot entirely be escaped. (The accelerated temporality of the sun's motion is no more real than the rhythmic circle of the idyll. And the sun, in order to behave as a symbol for resurrection, has to *appear* to have a nocturnal demise, another of man's fictions. And how is he who walked the waves so different from Palaemon? Is he more real? or is he simply more powerful?)

Near the end of Revelation, a text we see alluded to and even quoted in "Lycidas," there is a verse that reads:

> And the city had no need of the sun, neither of the moon, to shine in it;
> for the glory of God did lighten it, and the Lamb is the light thereof.
>
> (21:23)

John's highly rhetorical imaging of God as the light of the new Jerusalem depends on substituting God for the original solar figure. But "Lycidas," moving as it does from submissive gestures of compulsion and loss to an internalizing counterusurpation of totemic power, has substituted the figure of the elegist for both the sun and God. As we see the rising poet imaginatively projecting, as no sun can, the landscape of the future, we may think ahead to Ruskin's statement regarding "invention spiritual":

> Man is the sun of the world; more than the real sun. The fire of his . . . heart is the only light and heat worth gauge or measure. Where he is, are the tropics; where he is not, the ice-world.

WILLIAM FLESCH

The Majesty of Darkness

Thou art immortal and this tongue is known
But to the uncommunicating dead.
—P. B. SHELLEY

Abyss is its own apology.
—DICKINSON

This essay undertakes to urge what I only half-jokingly call the novel view that Milton is of God's party in *Paradise Lost*. Novel, because axioms of philosophy are not axioms until they are proved upon the pulse, and most readers, on both sides of this vexed issue, have had to go elsewhere even for the terms of an argument about God's justifiability (for example, to theology). On my reading, *Paradise Lost* dramatizes a series of more or less mistaken interpretations of God in order to claim a terrific prerogative for poetry as the only human endeavor pitched high enough to be adequate to the God the poem imagines. The poem may load the deck in poetry's favor, then, but it still must convince you to play with that deck: that, I argue, is what Milton conceived of as his task. Justifying the ways of God to men becomes equivalent to proving poetry upon the pulse: making the reader go the same steps as the author, till she or he reaches the point where God is his own apology. It will become clear, I hope, that this is not a claim for the vatic fullness of poetry, a fullness which would attest to the presence of God. Rather, Milton's God is justified through poetry, and one way of

First published in this volume. Copyright © 1985 by William Flesch.

putting this is to say that he derives his own authority from poetry. For poetry, I shall argue, is the only thing that Milton conceived of as being inherently antipathetic to idolatry.

People are agreed on Milton's hatred of idolatry. Christopher Hill is most succinct on political implications: "Idolatry is a short summary of all he detested: regarding places as holier than people; interfering with the strongly-held convictions of Christians about how they should and should not worship God; use of financial and corporal punishments in spiritual matters; all the sordidness of church courts progging and pandering for fees." The concept of idolatry does much—even all—of the work of coordinating the poetical, political, and religious dimensions of Milton's thought: readers of all stripes agree to find Eve's worshipping of the tree the clearest sign of her degradation, a degradation to find its latest avatar in what he calls, in "Of Reformation," "the new-vomited Paganisme of sensuall Idolatry" which was the target of the Puritan revolution. Idolatry makes the soul forget "her heavenly flight" (1.520,522). For Milton it was the exact antithesis of freedom, the alienation of one's own free will. Even Calvinism becomes a mode of idolatry; the Arminian rejection of Calvinist predestination in the "Christian Doctrine" is couched in the terms of iconoclasm:

> It seems, then, that predestination and election are not particular but only general: that is, they belong to all who believe in their hearts and persist in their belief. Peter is not predestined or elected as Peter, or John as John, but each only insofar as he believes and persists in his belief.
> (6.176)

Determining which party Milton was of, then, depends on deciding which is the party of the iconoclasts. Percy Shelley—who can represent the radical tradition from Blake to Empson—sees Satan as a forerunner of his own explicitly revolutionary hero Prometheus, and it's hard to quarrel with him that even for Milton Satan was on the side which saw itself as resisting oppression. I agree that there are problems with Satan— I'll insist on it—but certainly he spends a lot of time defending his attempted regicide in terms like those of Milton's defenses of the English people. If we are to admire Milton's refusal to idolize the name of king—"a name then which there needs no more among the blockish vulgar, to make it wise, and excellent, and admir'd, nay to set it next the Bible, though otherwise containing little els but the common grounds of tyranny and popery, drest up, the better to deceiv" (3.339)—it is difficult not to admire much of what Satan says to the same purpose. Throughout the first two Books Satan denounces what he sees as "the Tyranny of

Heav'n" (1.124), or what Mammon calls a "state / Of splendid vassalage" (2.251 52). His incitement of the rebel angels can couch itself as a plea for liberty from servile pomp, whose ceremonies seem to be important in heaven. Satan's objection to God's command about the Son that "to him shall bow / All knees in Heav'n, and shall confess him Lord" (5.607–8), seems perfectly justified since the Son has not yet demonstrated his worth. While Milton wants us to admire the Son because he volunteers to redeem humanity through his sacrifice, this reason for exaltation comes after Satan's rebellion (although earlier in the poem). Satan's objection to the Son stems, at least in part, from the same impulse that caused Milton to inveigh against arbitrariness in law-giving. It wouldn't be out of character for Satan to urge, with Milton, that "In the publishing of humane lawes, which for the most part aime not beyond the good of civill society, to set them barely forth to the people without reason or Preface, like a physicall prescript, or only with threatnings, as it were a lordly command, in the judgment of *Plato* was thought to be done neither generously nor wisely." The judgment Milton is approving is about human and civil laws, it is true, but Milton's heaven (and at this point, Milton's God) doesn't seem fundamentally different in quality from civil society. If God's purpose is to evoke love in the angels, one would think he'd do better to use persuasion which is "a more winning and more manlike way to keepe men in obedience than feare," since it "would so incite, and in a manner, charme the multitude into the love of that which is really good, as to imbrace it ever after, not of custome and awe, which most men do, but of choice and purpose, with true and constant delight" (1:746). But God doesn't give Satan any persuasive reason for the law proclaiming the Son's glorification; to Satan it does seem an arbitrary and lordly command:

> . . . by Decree
> Another now hath to himself ingross't
> All Power, and us eclipst under the name
> Of King annointed.
>
> (5.774–77)

And there is no reason to doubt that Satan's expectations were encouraged by a genuine belief that God ruled only through what Milton scornfully calls "custome and awe" and Satan calls "old repute / Consent or custom" (1.639–40). Satan's grandeur, even if it is the grandeur of archangel ruined, comes from his iconoclasm, from his desire for liberty.

Obviously, though, there are problems with Satan. His superiority to his conception of God may consist in his perseverance "in some purpose which he has conceived to be excellent, in spite of adversity and torture" as Shelley put it in his "Defence of Poetry" (498), but it is not at all clear how excellent his purpose is. Empson and Bloom see *Paradise Lost* as chronicling Milton's struggle with the nobility of his own conception of Satan, a struggle which forced him into debasing or "rotting" his own noble conception as Satan's grandeur threatened to get out of hand. But Shelley's analysis of Satan in the preface to *Prometheus Unbound*, that he is not "exempt from the taints of ambition, envy, revenge, and a desire for personal aggrandisement" (133), seems as true of Satan early (both in the poem and in the time frame) as later. Satan desires to conquer God so that he can reign in God's place: the liberty he would achieve would be for himself alone. His rejection of Christ's authority comes ultimately from his sense that his own power is being diminished. He refuses to worship the name of king in God: yet for himself and his crew he claims that their "Imperial Titles assert / Our being ordain'd to govern, not to serve" (6.801–2). He will not acknowledge as true of himself what he argues against God, that titles of nobility are "merely titular" (6.774). Satan's revolt is not against tyranny. It is against a tyrant whose place he wishes to usurp.

We should admire, then, the iconoclastic traits that urge Satan to revolt against a figure who does look and act very much like a tyrant, but we should not overlook his own similar tendencies. Satan never sustains the iconoclasm which makes him admirable, since side by side with it exists a desire to be the worshipped icon. I think this accounts for our ambivalent feelings about Satan: heroic in his rebellion against idolatry, he never gets finally beyond it himself.

Even his analysis of his fall reifies the dubious battle. The rebels (with the partial and hypocritical exception of Mammon) all follow Satan in ascribing God's victory only to the superior *degree* of his power, a degree they might hope to match. Beelzebub articulates their idolatrous conception of the true God (and yet it is this idolatrous conception that allows them to imagine themselves iconoclasts) when he anticipates Satan's claim that God has overcome them by force. His name for God is "our Conqueror":

> . . . whom I now
> Of force believe Almighty, since no less
> Than such could have o'erpow'rd such force as ours.
> (1.143–45)

As in Satan's speech about testing God's traditional kingship, the idolatrous strain subverts the speaker's iconoclasm. Beelzebub's pun echoes Milton's objections to imposing laws by force instead of reason, but at the same time it takes the term "Almighty" to refer only to superior force. For the rebel angels, the war in heaven was a war to determine who was first in strength. Their rejection of traditional power offers nothing but a new power in its place. So that their conception of God is that he is great because of his power; he is the victor "whom Thunder hath made greater" (1.258).

To be fair to Satan, he is different from the other rebels by being the only one of them who seems really (if inconsistently) to be outraged by the equation of greatness with power. He is most noble when most stoical, when least impressed by the force that has vanquished him. His claim that thunder made God greater misconceives God, but it also rejects such a conception of greatness. Although he ends up by repeating it, Satan deplores what he takes to be God's idolatry of force:

> Hail, horrors, hail
> Infernal world, and thou profoundest Hell
> Receive thy new Possessor: One who brings
> A mind not to be chang'd by Place or Time.
> The mind is its own place, and in itself
> Can make a Heav'n of Hell, a Hell of Heav'n.
> What matter where, if I be still the same,
> And what I should be, all but less than hee,
> Whom Thunder hath made greater? Here at least
> We shall be free. . . .
>
> (1.250–59)

Satan is the only one of the rebels whose character is complex, and that complexity manifests itself in almost all his speeches. His irreconcilable impulses towards self-sufficient iconoclasm and towards his own iconic glory besiege him with contraries. We feel the authentic power of his affirmation of self-reliant freedom, independent of place: he anticipates Michael's doctrine that "God attributes to place / No sanctity . . ." (11.836–37). But that freedom too often resolves into meaning nothing more than freedom to attempt to regain only the lost place, "once more / With rallied Arms to try what may be yet / Regain'd in Heav'n . . ." (1.249–71).

We do get a sense of the nobility of Satan's rebellion when we hear that one of its results was to have his name blotted out of the book of life. There is unintended pathos in Raphael's sneer, "Nameless in dark oblivion let them dwell" (7.380). Satan's willingness to give up his name stems from that part of him which scorns terms of honor, what Milton, writing as Charles' iconoclast, calls "the gaudy name of majesty." All the angelic names double as titles, deriving their glory from God, who appears in all of them (via the -el suffix) except Zephon's. In the "Christian Doctrine" Milton says that angels take on God's name to image him:

> The name of God seems to have been attributed to the angels because they were sent from heaven bearing the likeness of the divine glory and person and, indeed the very words of God. . . . Angels or messengers, even though they may seem to take upon themselves, when they speak, the name and character of God, do not speak their own words but those specified by God, who sent them. . . . Exod. xxxiii. 20: *no one can see me and live.* Also John 1.18: *no one has ever seen God,* and v. 37: *you have never heard his voice nor seen his shape;* I Tim. vi. 16: *dwelling in unapproachable light, whom no man has seen or can see.* It follows, then, that whoever was heard or seen was not God. . . .
>
> (236–37)

Although this is primarily about the identity of the messengers who speak to humans, I think that for Milton the names of all the angels implied their conditions as images of God, just as Adam is created in God's image. (I will insist, however, on the importance for Milton of the interpretation that Adam's *name* alludes to the ground he comes from.) Satan's rebellion entails the loss of his Godlike name, and this loss would mean two things to him. It would first of all signify his own kenosis, his refusal to bear the name and be the image of God, in favor of a radically unidolatrous freedom. Following Althusser and Deleuze, I see the act of naming—of calling by name—as forming and fixing the subject, and, as Foucault says, the moment of subjectivity is also the moment of subjection, of the insertion of a link in the great chain of power relations; if this claim has any intuitive force to it there's no reason to deny that intuition to Milton. But for Satan this freedom would also come to mean supplanting God.

By giving up a title which invests him with God's image, Satan comes to attempt to rival God's invisibility and inaccessibility. This attempt is double-edged. It proceeds out of a less iconic and more admirable understanding of God than the other angels (both fallen and unfallen) possess (as I'll claim later, even the unfallen angels think that they can see God); but it erroneously and idolatrously considers a visible, accessible, irremediably subjective being like Satan capable of rivaling God. Pride engenders Satan's fall, but I think that that pride is not accurately described as pride of place alone. Satan's nobility *does*, for many acute and powerful readers, rival and even exceed God's. As a projection of Milton's repressed pride in his own insightfulness, an insightfulness which tempts him (if Sandler is right) to reject the authority of the Bible, Satan can be understood to be imagining himself to know more about Godlike inaccessibility than any of the other angels, and perhaps even than God himself. But Satan is idolatrously proud of his own unidolatrousness. I think this is the feeling behind Satan's scorn at God's being made greater by thunder. Satan (or Milton in Satan) thinks, and not without some very good evidence, that his conception of Godliness is poetically superior to God's. He certainly speaks better poetry than God is allowed to. I am going to argue that not only is Satan's conception of God inadequate, but also his conception of Godliness; nevertheless Satan comes closer than any of the other angels to the understanding of Godliness which was Milton's.

The loss of his name indicates Satan's nobility, and his reaction to it distinguishes him, for a time at least, from the rest of the fallen angels. Milton's scorn for the other rebels is boundless. Not complex like Satan, their only desires are gluttonous: to be feasted and adored as idols. Satan sustains for a time (and only partially) his noble and impossible condition of namelessness, a truer image of God's invisible glory than are the idols. But the other rebels seem avid to get themselves new names, avid to be idolized in their own names:

> . . . of their Names in heav'nly Records now
> Be no memorial, blotted out and ras'd
> By thir Rebellion, from the Books of Life.
> Nor had they yet among the Sons of *Eve*
> Got them new Names, till wand'ring o'er the Earth,
> Through God's high sufferance for the trial of man,
> By falsities and lies the greatest part
> Of Mankind they corrupted to forsake
> God thir creator; and th'invisible
> Glory of him that made them, to transform
> Oft to the Image of a Brute, adorn'd
> With gay Religions full of Pomp and Gold,
> And Devils to adore for Deities:
> Then were they known to men by various Names,
> And various Idols through the Heathen World.
> (1.361–75)

This passage catches one of the profoundest contrasts in the poem— that between the puerile, cartoonish infestation of these ridiculous deities and "God's high sufferance" which inflects "all our woe" with the sense that it is God's as well (otherwise why *high* sufferance?). To the extent that the rebels find their greatest delight in "gay Religions full of Pomp and Gold" they're ridiculous. And yet, Satan does differ from them. Milton arouses our disgust at these lesser rebels. But in large part we are disgusted because they contrast with Satan. They are parasites, ready to swarm in when he's done his job, for the rewards only. But no reader can see this passage as referring to Satan, and Milton explicitly aligns himself with Satan's distrust of names when, at the beginning of Book 7, his invocation of the Muse is to the "meaning, not the Name" (7.5).

But Satan is not able to maintain his impossible namelessness. To be like God he would really have to be unchanged by place or time, but his response to his fall is too often close to the obsessive concern with outward show that characterizes the pervasive idolatry of the fallen angels. For the most part, Satan's actions are ultimately reactions, and so are based, however indirectly, on the exterior constraints that Satan as iconoclast wants to think himself entirely independent of. Even in Book 1 he spends a lot of time playing the adolescent inverter that Harold Bloom finds he has become by Book 9. His first speech to Beelzebub asserts his desire for revenge, a reactive passion (1.107), and fifty lines later he takes up his adversarial role decisively: "To do aught good will never be our task, / But ever to do ill our sole delight, / As being contrary to his high will / Whom we resist" (1.159–62). This resolution finally leads to his ultimate degradation, in which he wholly accepts the adversarial *name* that heaven has given him, and revels in its meaning: "Satan (for I glory in the name, / Antagonist of Heav'n's Almighty King)" (10.386–87). The Son ultimately manifests himself as Satan's better when he refuses this reactive, adversarial role in Book 10; his willingness "to clothe his Enemies" (10.219) enriches the possibilities of human life instead of turning the world into the silly theatre of antagonism that Satan wants it to be.

At the end of Book 2 Milton provides an objective correlative to the fallen angels' idolatrous overestimation of names. Many readers echo Johnson's discomfort with the allegorization of Sin and Death, as being unworthy of the grandeur that has come before. But this unworthiness itself allegorizes the idolatry of the rebels. They never learn, what it will be Adam and Eve's burden to discover, that sin and death are something more than the names of horrid personages. For Satan, the words "sin" and "death" become the names of exterior beings, instead of being felt as interior states. The externalization of sin and death allegorizes Satan's refusal to understand the pertinency of a figurative understanding of allegory. He takes the image for the essence, and he worships the image. According to Sin's account—the force of which neither of them understands—Satan "full oft / Thyself in me thy perfect image viewing, / Becam'st enamored" (2.763–65). He falls in love with sin as a narcissistic self-image, and so evinces his sinful idolatry of himself. That he could find a sufficient, a perfect, idol for himself within so decayed an allegory shows how debased his self-idolatry has become.

Idolatrous narcissism is on one level the cause of all the falls in the poem. Abdiel interprets it as the opposite of real liberty, when he upbraids Satan, echoing Sin, as being "Thyself not free, but to thyself enthralled" (6.181). Satan tempts Eve, who has already manifested her narcissistic tendencies in her attraction to her reflection at the pool (4.460–66), with the promise of what she might become; Adam's reproach to her, that she insisted on going off alone because she was "longing to be seen" (10.877) doesn't seem unfair. But Adam consents to eat when he finds that Eve has fallen because he feels "The Link of Nature draw me: Flesh of Flesh, / Bone of my Bone thou art" (9.914–15), and that "to lose thee were to lose myself" (9.959).

Commentators often try to distinguish Satan's narcissistic attraction to Sin from what looks like a similar trait in God by calling it a parodic version of the Father's glorification of his Son. The Son is supposed to be worthy of God's surpassing love because he is "The radiant image of his Glory" (3.63); God praises him as "thou, in whom my glory I behold / In full resplendence" (5.719–20), and when he addresses him "O Son, in whom my soul hath chief delight, / Son of my bosom, Son who art alone / My Word, my wisdom, and effectual might" (3.168–70), the Son seems to have sprung out of God's bosom as Sin will spring out of Satan's head and Eve from Adam's side. Obviously Milton did feel a difference between God's love for his Son and Satan's desire for Sin, but the difference doesn't ilable for the heavenly audience, except by decree.

In fact, it's impossible, from a heavenly perspective, to distinguish between Satan and God except as different in degree. I have been arguing that one of the signs of the rebel angels' idolatry is their belief that might makes right, that only force ratifies the pretension to sovereignty, and so that the only difference between Satan and God is one of degree (except that Satan sometimes imagines himself as deploring this state of things). A less vicious version of the rebels' doctrine manifests itself in the idea of the great chain of being, in which every link has its place in a hierarchy. A defense of hierarchy can of course be mounted: "Orders and Degrees / Jar not with liberty, but well consist" (5.792–93)—but this is Satan speaking. His initial objection is not to the chain but to having his position as its second link (after God) usurped by the Son. Abdiel is exceptional among the angels in perceiving a radical discontinuity between the highest of the angels and the Son (5.841–45), who is himself, according to the Arian "Christian Doctrine," only the first of all created beings (Part I, Chapter V and passim). But Abdiel's interpretation isn't the one encouraged in Heaven, since the Father's prediction that "God shall be All in All"

(3.341) seems an easy induction from the continuous version of the chain that Raphael explains to Adam. Thus his repetition of "all" enforces a continuity in being—a continuity which does seem to attribute sanctity to place:

> O *Adam*, one Almighty is, from whom
> All things proceed, and up to him return,
> If not deprav'd from good, created all
> Such to perfection, one first matter all,
> Indu'd with various forms, various degrees
> Of substance, and in things that live, of life;
> But more refin'd, more spiritous, and pure,
> As nearer to him plac't or nearer tending
> Each in thir several active Spheres assign'd,
> Till body up to spirit work, in bounds
> Proportion'd to each kind. . . .
>   time may come when men
> With angels may participate . . .
> And from these corporal nutriments perhaps
> Your body may at last turn all to spirit,
> Improv'd by tract of time, and wing'd ascend
> Ethereal, as wee. . . .
>
> (5.469–99)

Empson notices some of Raphael's unwitting echoes of Satan's dream temptation in this passage (147ff). I want to build on his insight by arguing that Raphael sounds so much like Satan because they have very similar ideas about God and heaven. Raphael and Beelzebub both seem to have the same conception of what it means to be almighty. For Beelzebub, in his claim that God demonstrated himself to be almighty by defeating a force next in power to his (1.144–45), almightiness implies a position at the top of the scale of power, commensurable with lesser might. Raphael takes a similar view when he describes Michael and Satan battling with "next to Almighty Arm" (6.316). For both of them, God is a Platonic form: if he is the origin of ontology, he is likewise approachable through ontology, with being becoming purer (or mightier) as one is placed or tends nearer to him.

Again, Raphael doesn't seem far from the lesser rebels in his conception of God's *invisibility*. Milton subscribes to the Arian tenet that the Father is absolutely unknowable. He is radically different from all created beings, even the Son, who is the voice we hear and the sight we see when we imagine that we are seeing God: "*The Word* must be audible, but God is inaudible just as he is invisible, John v. 37; therefore the Word is not of the same essence as God" (6.239). The rebels, with (as I have argued) the intermittent exception of Satan, possess a debased notion of this doctrine. God's inaudibility and invisibility get parodied when the rebels corrupt human beings "th'invisible / Glory of him that made them, to transform / Oft to the Image of a Brute" (1.369–71), which is to have the unknown degenerate into the monstrous. Mammon's attempt to persuade the fallen angels that they can make a material heaven of hell also presents God's invisibility in material terms:

> This deep world
> Of darkness do we dread? How oft amidst
> Thick clouds and dark doth Heav'n's all-ruling Sire
> Choose to reside, his Glory unobscur'd,
> And with the majesty of darkness round
> Covers his throne, from whence deep thunders roar
> Must'ring thir rage, and Heav'n resembles hell?
> (2.262–68)

But this somewhat literal-minded conception of God's hidden state is not restricted to hell. Raphael always presents God as either within a covering cloud (e.g. 6.28 and 56–57), or hidden by a dazzling brightness. It is worth comparing Milton's conception of God's dazzling invisibility with Raphael's. One's impression is that Raphael believes his inability to tolerate the direct sight of God comes merely from his being too far down on the chain of being. God is dazzling, yes, but his inaccessibility is finally relative. Raphael and the other angels can't see God, but they take this invisibility as proceeding from the weakness of their own sight (a weakness Satan refuses to acknowledge), not as one of God's fundamental attributes. Adam echoes Raphael when he laments the weakness that the fall has produced in him:

> How shall I behold the face
> Henceforth of God or Angel, erst with joy
> And rapture so oft beheld? those heav'nly shapes
> Will dazzle now this earthly, with thir blaze
> Insufferably bright.
> (9.1080–84)

For Raphael, God speaks "as from a Flaming Mount, whose top / Brightness had made invisible" (5.598–99), which—at first—looks like Milton's hymn in Book 3 to:

> . . . thee Author of all being,
> Fountain of Light, thyself invisible
> Amidst the glorious brightness where thou sit'st
> Thron'd inaccessible, but when thou shad'st

> The full blaze of thy beams, and through a cloud
> Drawn round about thee like a radiant Shrine,
> Dark with excessive bright thy skirts appear,
> Yet dazzle Heav'n, that brightest Seraphim
> Approach not, but with both wings veil thir eyes.
> Thee next they sang of all Creation first,
> Begotten Son, Divine Similitude,
> In whose conspicuous count'nance, without cloud
> Made visible, th'Almighty Father shines,
> Whom else no Creature can behold. . . .
>
> (3.374–87)

I think that after reading the whole of *Paradise Lost* a reader coming back to these lines should understand God's invisibility in the second line as fundamental, as preceding the glorious brightness he expresses, not proceeding from it as an effect. We can infer from the last three lines that, far from hiding God, clouds make him visible, like the clothes the invisible man wears in Wells, since it is only in the Son that God is visible without clouds. The reference to the brightness of the Seraphim invites the reader to see in this hymn another allusion to the great chain of being, since there is an implicit comparison of their brightness with God's. But in addition to the difference between God's invisibility and his dazzling light, Milton introduces another discontinuity when clouds shade the full blaze. It is this doubly distanced expression of God that the angels find insufferably bright, and it appears that Raphael mistakes this tertiary inaccessibility for God's invisibility. Milton, on the other hand, would see this attenuated brightness as the end of the great chain of being (or even already beyond it, since *brightest* Seraphim shade their eyes). Beyond that is God's fundamental inaccessibility.

My claim is that the Platonic doctrine which Raphael speaks for is mistaken and that it is this same mistaken doctrine that ultimately tempts the rebels' attempt. Following Deleuze, I want to argue for a Gnostic (but not, I hope, Bloomian) alternative to Platonic doctrine—an alternative which focuses the drama of *Paradise Lost* not on the staged opposition God/Satan but on the complex relationship of a different kind of God with human beings. Deleuze underlines a kind of idolatry in Plato when he contrasts the Timaean god Chronos (who represents the "moving image of eternity") with the temporality of human beings as "actors." The task of the actor, says Deleuze, is intensity: he or she must concentrate in the most fleeting of presents the weight of the entire past and future of the character represented. The ephemerality of the means of representation— its inadequacy to what it represents—becomes itself an intensity which figures the charge of time more adequately than any more leisurely present (that is a present whose inherent evanescence is not at issue). "Instead of going from the most ample present towards a future and past which can only be expressed by a present more transitory than they are, you go from a future and past become limitless to the most transitory present—a pure instant which ceaselessly subdivides" (my translation). The actor, then, is anti-Platonic, since the soul of acting is that it should be only fictional (which is not the same as third-rate being). It should have the poignancy of what is only fictional, the poignancy that belongs to Calliope when she turns out to be an empty dream. Deleuze is good at relating that poignancy to temporality, in a way that could gloss Proust, but which I want to make gloss *Paradise Lost*:

> The actor is not like a god, but like a counter-god. God and the actor are opposed to each other in their reading of time. What humans grasp as past or future, the god lives in his eternal presence. The god is Chronos: the divine present is the circle in its entirety, while the past and the future are dimensions relative to some highlighted segment of the circle. But for the actor, the present is the narrowest, tightest, most ephemeral, most punctual point on a straight line, never ceasing to divide that line, and dividing itself into past/future. The actor has the essence of the Aeon: instead of the fullest, profoundest present—a present spreading out like an oil stain, embracing past and future—here arises a limitless past/future reflected in an empty present with no more thickness than a mirror.
>
> (my translation)

I'll want to argue that Milton's true God was the Gnostic Aeon, not Raphael's debased and serenely self-present manifestation of complacency. Raphael's understanding of God's secrecy and invisibility is pretty tame. He resolves his uncertainty about how to "relate / To human sense th'invisible exploits / Of warring Spirits; how . . . unfold / The secrets of another World" by concluding that they really aren't so different from the common knowledge of this world. The hint to Adam indicates his Platonism fairly strongly, with its allusion to the allegory of the cave: "what if Earth / Be but the shadow of Heav'n, and things therein / Each to other like, more than on Earth is thought?" (5.564–76). In Books 7 and 8 he thinks of God as guarding only state secrets from the angels, by a sort of divine executive privilege, suppressing what apparently *could* be revealed. He tells Adam not to inquire too closely about the nature of the universe, "nor let thine own inventions hope / Things not reveal'd, which th'invisible King, / Only Omniscient, hath supprest in Night. . . ." (7.121–23). This makes it sound as though invisibility were an accidental, not an essential, feature of the things that are closest to God. Near the beginning of Book 8 Raphael praises God for doing "wisely to conceal" the mechanism of his astronomy, "and not divulge / His secrets to be scanned by them who ought / Rather admire. . . ." (8.73–75). This God comes out of Machiavelli, deriving his power not so much from what he keeps to himself as from the fact that he keeps things to himself, which allows him to be the only omniscient one. As a representative of the angels' conception of God, Raphael unwittingly explains how the rebels could have thought themselves capable of replacing him. The angels don't really understand God to be entirely different from themselves. For none of them are secrecy and invisibility *inherent* attributes of the things they do not know. One gets the feeling that, like Bentley, they would emend "secret" to "sacred" in "the secret top of Horeb" (except that at least Bentley feels there's a possible difference there, which they do not).

Adam and Eve start off with an understanding similar to the angels'. They believe that their inability to see God is a function of their place, and their morning hymn in Book 5 conceives of him as being "to *us* invisible." They think that higher up on the chain they would be able to see him; thus they praise the angels, "for yee behold him" (5.157 and 161), and Raphael confirms what Milton surely considered an error. Raphael claims that it is the angels' "happy state" to "stand / In sight of God enthron'd" (5.535–36). What does this do but ratify Satan's dream temptation of Eve? There she was encouraged to equate "high exaltation" with the ability to "*see* / What life the Gods live there, and such live thou" (5.90 and 80–81): thus visibility would mean commensurability—and so susceptibility to being equalled (and, as Satan continues, overthrown). Again, in Book 9, Satan's temptation encourages Eve to attempt the clearer sight that Raphael has already told her belongs to the angels:

> Why then was this forbid? Why but to awe,
> Why but to keep ye low and ignorant,
> His worshippers; he knows that in the day
> Ye Eat thereof, your Eyes that seem so clear,
> Yet are but dim, shall perfetly be then
> Op'n'd and clear'd, and ye shall be as Gods,
> Knowing both Good and Evil as they know.
> That ye should be as Gods, since I as Man,
> Internal Man, is but proportion meet. . . .
>   (9.702–11)

Eve is receptive to Satan's argument here because it is based on the Platonic conception of "proportion meet." Raphael has described the possibility of moving up on the great chain of being; he promised the humans that they could eventually attain to the angelic vision that does have sight of God. Satan exploits both Raphael and Eve's naive notion that God is within the possible reach of sight in order to encourage her to attempt that reach. One of the immediate consequences of Eve's disobedience is a further degradation of her understanding of secrecy and invisibility. She thanks Experience because "it op'n'st Wisdom's way, / And giv'st access, though secret she retire. / And I perhaps am secret; Heav'n is high, / High and remote to see from thence distinct / Each thing on Earth. . . ." (9.810–14). Already she senses that eating the fruit does not provide an easy way up to heaven, which is high and remote; what momentarily sounds like a claim to God-head—"I perhaps am secret" —immediately reduces to the hope that what she has done will be overlooked. (But the expression of that hope is wonderful. already she's speaking great poetry.)

There is, then, something seriously deficient about the angelic and unfallen conception of God. Empson remarks that Book 6 reads like bad science fiction, which seems a good way of summing up our discomfort with heaven according to Raphael. Therefore, I want to suggest that the fall of humanity turns out to be fortunate (to argue that it's not, as Danielson does, is inevitably to prefer God's poetry in Book 3 to Milton's) because it enables a much deeper understanding of God. Satan verges on such an understanding when he is closest to Milton, when he is thinking most poetically, most like an Arian. If the angels are Arians at all, it is in a trivial way; for them God is only unknowable and inaccessible because he's just the other side of knowledge and accessibility. But for Adam and Eve the fall produces a sense of drastic discontinuity between finite intelligences and the unknowable God. This sense of discontinuity is at first primarily negative (as when Adam asks how he will be able henceforth to tolerate the insupportably dazzling sight of God or Angel, or when Eve feels that heaven is high and remote), but even in its negative aspect Milton equates it with poetic power. His dismissal, in his invocation to Book 9, of Raphael's account of the war in heaven seems every bit as imperious as Empson's. It is for the "sad task" of describing the *fall* that Milton requests "answerable style" (9.13 and 20); this seems a bit odd at first, since he'd shown very little anxiety about whether he'd be able to ventriloquize a seraphic description of the war in heaven. But he goes on in the invocation to reject poetry about "tilting Furniture" (9.34), and thereby himself voices our half-suppressed embarrassment about the silliness of what's gone on in heaven. He's not interested in the standard topics that give "Heroic name / To Person or to Poem" (9.40–41):

> Mee of these
> Nor skill'd nor studious, higher Argument
> Remains, sufficient of itself to raise
> That name, unless an age too late, or cold
> Climate, or Years damp my intended wing
> Deprest; and much they may, if all be mine,
> Nor Hers who brings it nightly to my Ear.
>
> (9.41–47)

More interesting than the implication that Raphael's narrative is not up to the poetry Milton finally aspires to is the contrast with twilit Eden presented by the opening of Book 9. There is more poetic affect in Milton's intense apprehension of his mortality in these lines than in any of the descriptions of the events in heaven. Even the cautious optimism of the last two lines is suffused with a sense of loss. Perhaps he'll live to finish the poem, but he'll still be susceptible to all the dampening influences of his mortal condition. These lines feel rather like *The Tempest*: the island is magical, but when you leave it every third thought will be of death. I think this passage is so moving because of the contrast between Urania's radiance and Milton's mortal blindness. We get a sense of her radiance, but also a sense that its power is not a saving but a consoling one. "Nightly" seems to be the key word. For Urania, night is like the nights in Paradise before the fall, illumined by the stars, planets and moon, or like night in heaven: "grateful Twilight (for Night comes not there / In darker veil)" (5.645–46). But for Milton it ultimately means the night of Sonnet XXIII, forgotten for a moment but returning after his nightly muse has fled. The radiance which illuminates him also intensifies his sense of loss, as when Caliban wakes and cries to sleep again.

In the invocation to Book 9, Milton both asserts and demonstrates that loss of Eden, the fall into mortality, produces poetic affect. Of course, this is a position that he cannot be comfortable with. One feels that the choiring angels hymning praise to the works of God provide the model of poetry that Milton is least anxious about. But the affect actually derives from the impossibility of sustaining the apparent radiance of that poetry in a fallen condition. For a long time, I think, Milton felt ambivalent about his sense that poetic power is enabled by loss, and at least twice before he tried to dissipate that ambivalence by splitting its antinomies into paired poems: "L'Allegro" / "Il Penseroso" and "On the Morning of Christ's Nativity" / "The Passion." But in *Paradise Lost* he combines celebration and lamentation. This combination reflects Milton's ambivalence about the poetry he finds himself writing most powerfully; but this ambivalence also produces the most powerful moments in that poetry. As an evil

rhetorician whose language is sublimely intensified in hell, Satan represents the negative side of that ambivalence. But the Romantics seem right
in thinking that Milton couldn't avoid, through much of the poem,
feeling a strong identity with Satan, an identity which he understood as a
real problem: as I have argued, the identification seems to stem from their
both having a deeper conception of Godliness than the rest of heaven.
And this conception seems indissolubly linked to ambivalence. Satan
and Milton are both suspicious of the origins of their poetic power, but
Satan's final response is to get rid of ambivalence by reifying that origin,
by making it either an icon to be rejected (if the icon is God) or
worshipped (if it is himself). Milton, on the other hand, had a lot
invested in not identifying poetic and iconic thinking. If he calls books
the image of God in "Areopagitica" (2.492), by the 1660s he was very
careful to explode the notion that one could call "idols the layman's
books" (6.693). Satan cannot sustain the drastically iconoclastic sense
that his poetic power springs from something radically unknowable, from
unknowability itself. He does not have the negative capability that would
enable him to accept ambivalence itself as a condition of power. This is
not just another way of saying what the angels say, that his overweening
pride made him reject an invisible God who nevertheless should obviously
be obeyed. Satan's deep sense that the origin of power is inaccessible far
outdoes, in its deep and powerful sublimity, the angels' conceptions of
God. But it finally founders, while Milton's does not.

Empson and Bloom see Milton's response to his ambivalence as
being finally to cut the Gordian knot by scapegoating Satan, by making
him despicable (or, more subtly, by recounting how unjust rebellion
necessarily makes the highest nobility vile). But *Paradise Lost* seems
ultimately to respond to this problem positively too, which is I think its
greatest strength. In giving up Satan it doesn't give up God or its
ambivalent conception of God. Early on, Milton was ambivalent about a
poetry based on loss; in *Paradise Lost* he bases his poetry on the very loss
that that ambivalence entails, the loss of angelic certainty about the
origin of power.

II

It is a version of the abyss as somehow God's element, in the same way
that night is Milton's, that Adam will eventually learn. The way he learns
it is via his learning that his own element is really dust, that his name
images, not Platonic forms, but the formless, the scattered. His lamenta-

tion in Book 10 recognizes dust as "our final rest and native home" (10.1085) when he speaks the lines Mary Shelley used as her powerful epigraph: "Did I request thee, Maker, from my clay / To mould me Man, did I solicit thee / From darkness to promote me . . . ?" (10.743–45). The knowledge that "we are dust, / And thither must return and be no more" (11.199) is the knowledge of death that the fruit of the tree instilled. Milton insists on the *quality* of this knowledge, altering Genesis to have Adam and Eve "know" but not appreciate their origin before the fall. So when God climaxes his judgment with the phrase "know thy birth" before the line from Genesis, "For dust thou art, and shalt to dust return" (10.207–8), there is a strong implication that this knowledge is incommunicable to the immortals. Adam and Eve did not know what this meant, even though they were acquainted with its content, when they were immortal. Knowledge has come to mean something different to them now. The power of the judgment is not available to the unfallen. The judgment is powerful because it reveals the dark nativity of life as being the abyss. The knowledge available to human beings of their natural element produces the poetic affect that Milton associates with Godliness. Humans go beyond the fallen angels in this knowledge, since the rebels keep asserting that "in our proper motion we ascend / Up to our native seat" (2.75–76). The rebels reject the apprehension of the abyss that establishes poetic power, and in this refusal of the unknowable they prove themselves as ultimately not like God. But Adam's final statement that the fall was fortunate doesn't refuse the unknowable. He goes beyond the foreknowledge vouchsafed to Michael when he sees beyond the end of time. Here he as last speaks Milton's words, achieves Milton's insight into the unknowable:

> How soon hath thy prediction, Seer blest,
> Measur'd this transient World, the Race of time,
> Till time stand fixt: beyond is all abyss,
> Eternity, whose end no eye can reach.
> (12.553–56)

One of the consequences of my argument is the claim that God does not ever appear in *Paradise Lost*: "whoever was heard or seen was not God." That claim seems to be worth making since it saves God from sounding ridiculous. As I read the poem, the figure of God is an emanation constructed for the dwarfish understandings of the angels. In the "Christian Doctrine" Milton tells us:

> It is safest for us to form an image of God in our minds which corresponds to his representation and description of himself in the sacred writ-

ings. Admittedly, God is always described or outlined not as he really is but in such a way as will make him comprehensible to us. Nevertheless, we ought to form just such a mental image of him as he, in bringing himself within the limits of our understanding, wishes us to form. Indeed he has brought himself down to our level expressly to prevent our being carried beyond the reach of human comprehension, and outside the written authority of scripture, into vague subtleties of speculation.

(6.133–34)

The "safest" way is the way taken by the loyal angels, who are content to form an image of God in their minds. H. R. McCallum uses the injunction in this passage to argue that Milton wants us also to take the safe way out. I agree that part of Milton very much wanted to repress his Satanic sense that his idea of God was deeper than that of the Scriptures. But *Paradise Lost* is most powerful when Milton allows that sense full rein. Bloom remarks on the outrageousness of Milton's pursuit of "Things unattempted yet in Prose or Rhyme" (1.16), since one of the prose attempts of the story narrated in *Paradise Lost* is the Bible (*Vessels*, 83). Milton at his most powerful refuses the safest way. He calls his song "advent'rous" (1.13), and I think we feel some surprise when Adam gives Eve the same epithet after the fall (9.921). We could read this either way: the angelic reading would be that Milton is casting suspicion on his own enterprise by comparing it with Eve's sin; but more interesting (or adventurous), I think, is the idea that Eve's adventurous deed ultimately results as Satan has predicted; results in enlarging human apprehensions of God.

Milton certainly would not countenance an image of God which went beyond the received images. But the important point is that he doesn't countenance them either. The extreme Puritanism of his definition of idolatry in the "Christian Doctrine" cuts against an unadventurous literalism: "Idolatry means making or owning an idol for religious purposes, or worshiping it, *whether it be a representation of the true God* or of some false god" (6.690–91, my emphasis). Milton at his darkest and most powerful—at his most mortal—goes beyond received images, not to another image, but to meditations on loss and exile which share the inessential essence of what Valentinus—writing against Raphael's hero Plato—called the forefathering abyss.

Chronology

1608	Born in London, December 9.
1617	Enters St. Paul's School, London.
1625	Enters Christ's College, Cambridge.
1629	B.A., Cambridge.
1632	M.A., Cambridge.
1632–38	Studies at home in London and at Horton, Buckinghamshire.
1634	Presentation of masque, Comus, at Ludlow Castle.
1638–39	Visit to Italy.
1641	Of Reformation in England.
1642	The Reason of Church-Government. Marries Mary Powell, who subsequently returns to her parents.
1643	The Doctrine and Discipline of Divorce.
1644	Areopagitica.
1645	Mary Powell Milton returns to her husband in London. Poems of Mr. John Milton, Both English and Latin.
1649	The Tenure of Kings and Magistrates. Becomes Secretary of Foreign Tongues to Cromwell's Council of State.
1651	Latin Defense of the English People.
1652	Blindness. Death of Mary Powell Milton and of their son.
1656	Marries Katherine Woodcock.
1658	Death of Katherine Woodcock Milton.
1660	The Ready and Easy Way to Establish a Free Commonwealth.
1663	Marries Elizabeth Minshull.
1667	Paradise Lost (in ten books).
1671	Paradise Regained and Samson Agonistes.
1674	Paradise Lost (in twelve books). Dies November 8.

Contributors

HAROLD BLOOM, Sterling Professor of the Humanities at Yale University, is the author of *The Anxiety of Influence, Poetry and Repression* and many other volumes of literary criticism. His forthcoming study, *Freud: Transference and Authority*, attempts a full-scale reading of all of Freud's major writings. He is the general editor of *The Chelsea House Library of Literary Criticism.*

F. T. PRINCE was Professor of English at Southampton University. A noted poet, his best known collection is *Soldiers Bathing*. Besides *The Italian Element in Milton's Verse*, his scholarly work includes the New Arden edition of Shakespeare's *Poems*.

ISABEL G. MacCAFFREY was Professor of History and Literature at Harvard University. She published notable books on Milton and on Spenser, and several crucial critical essays on Wallace Stevens.

SIR WILLIAM EMPSON was one of the most eminent of modern poet-critics. He taught for many years in China, and later at Sheffield University. His principal writings include his *Collected Poems, Seven Types of Ambiguity, Some Versions of Pastoral* and *The Structure of Complex Words.*

THOMAS GREENE is Professor of Renaissance Studies and Comparative Literature at Yale. His books include a study of Rabelais and *The Light in Troy.*

NORTHROP FRYE, University Professor at Victoria College, Toronto, is the most eminent of living critics. He is best known for *Anatomy of Criticism, The Great Code of Art* and his study of William Blake, *Fearful Symmetry.*

GEOFFREY H. HARTMAN is Karl Young Professor of English and Comparative Literature at Yale. His books include *Wordsworth's Poetry* and *Saving the Text*, a study of Jacques Derrida.

ANGUS FLETCHER is Professor of English at the Graduate School of the City University of New York. His best known works are *Allegory* and *The Prophetic Moment*, a study of Spenser.

STANLEY E. FISH, Professor of English at the Johns Hopkins University, is the author of *Surprised by Sin: The Reader in Paradise Lost* and *Is There a Text in this Class?*

LESLIE BRISMAN is Professor of English at Yale University. His books include *Milton's Poetry of Choice and Its Romantic Heirs* and *Romantic Origins*.

MARY ANN RADZINOWICZ is Professor of English at Cornell University, and the author of a study of *Samson Agonistes*.

LOUIS L. MARTZ, Sterling Professor Emeritus of English at Yale, is the author of *The Poetry of Meditation* and *The Poem of the Mind*.

JOHN HOLLANDER, poet and critic, teaches at Yale. His books include *Spectral Emanations: New and Selected Poems* and *Vision and Resonance*.

WILLIAM KERRIGAN, Professor of English at the University of Virginia, has published two critical studies of Milton and a number of essays on Freud and Kierkegaard.

SANFORD BUDICK is Director of the Institute of Literary Studies at the Hebrew University, Jerusalem.

PETER M. SACKS, poet and critic, teaches at the Johns Hopkins University.

WILLIAM FLESCH teaches at Brandeis University, and is finishing a book on Milton and Renaissance poetry.

Bibliography

Adams, Richard P. "The Archetypal Pattern of Death and Rebirth in Milton's *Lycidas*." *PMLA* 64 (1949): 183–88.

Adams, Robert M. *Ikon: John Milton and the Modern Critics*. Ithaca: Cornell University Press, 1955.

Allen, D.C. *The Harmonious Vision: Studies in Milton's Poetry*. Baltimore: Johns Hopkins University Press, 1953.

————. "Milton's Eve and the Evening Angels." *Modern Language Notes* 75 (1960): 108–09.

Arthos, John. *Dante, Michelangelo and Milton*. New York: Humanities Press, 1963.

Banks, Theodore H., Jr. *Milton's Imagery*. New York: Columbia University Press, 1956.

Barber, C. L. " 'A Masque Presented at Ludlow Castle': The Masque as a Masque." In *The Lyric and Dramatic Milton*. Edited by J. H. Summers. New York: Columbia University Press, 1965.

Barker, Arthur E. *Milton and the Puritan Dilemma, 1641–1660*. Toronto: University of Toronto Press, 1942.

————. "Structural Pattern in *Paradise Lost*." *Philological Quarterly* 28 (1949): 17–30.

————, ed. *Milton: Modern Essays in Criticism*. New York: Oxford University Press, 1965.

Baruch, Franklin R. "Time, Body, and Spirit at the Close of *Samson Agonistes*." *English Literary History* 36 (1969): 319–39.

Berger, Harry, Jr. "Archaism, Vision, and Revision: Studies in Virgil, Plato, and Milton." *Centennial Review* 11 (1967): 24–52.

————. "*Paradise Lost* Evolving: Books I–VI." *Centennial Review* 11 (1967).

Berry, Boyd M. *Process of Speech: Puritan Religious Writing and Paradise Lost*. Baltimore: Johns Hopkins University Press, 1976.

Bloom, Harold. *A Map of Misreading*. New York: Oxford University Press, 1975.

Bridges, Robert. *Milton's Prosody*. Oxford: Clarendon Press, 1921.

Brisman, Leslie. *Milton's Poetry of Choice and its Romantic Heirs*. Ithaca: Cornell University Press, 1973.

Broadbent, J. B. *Some Graver Subjects: An Essay on Paradise Lost*. London: Chatto and Windus, 1960.

Brockbank, Philip. " 'Within the Visible Diurnal Spheare': The Moving World of *Paradise Lost*." In *Approaches to Paradise Lost*. Edited by C. A. Patrides. London: Edward Arnold, 1968.

Brooks, Cleanth. "The Light Symbolism in 'L'Allegro-Il Penseroso'." In *The Well-Wrought Urn*. New York: Harcourt Brace Jovanovich, 1975.

———. "Eve's Awakening." In *A Shaping Joy*. London: Methuen, 1971.

Brooks, Cleanth and Hardy, John Edward, eds. *Poems of Mr. John Milton: The 1642 Edition, with Essays in Analysis*. New York: Harcourt, Brace, 1952.

Burden, Dennis H. *The Logical Epic*. Cambridge: At the University Press, 1967.

Bush, Douglas. *Mythology and the Renaissance Tradition in English Poetry*. Minneapolis: University of Minnesota Press, 1932.

———. *"Paradise Lost" in Our Time: Some Comments*. Ithaca: Cornell University Press, 1945.

Carrithers, Gale. "Milton's Ludlow *Masque*: From Chaos to Community." *English Literary History* 33 (1966): 23–42.

Cirillo, Albert R. "Noon-Midnight and the Temporal Structure of *Paradise Lost*." *English Literary History* 29 (1962): 372–95.

Colie, Rosalie. "Time and Eternity: Paradox and Structure in *Paradise Lost*." *Journal of the Warburg and Courtauld Institutes* 23 (1960): 127—38.

Cope, Jackson I. *The Metaphoric Structure of "Paradise Lost."* Baltimore: Johns Hopkins University Press, 1962.

Cox, Lee Sheridan. "The 'Ev'ning Dragon' in *Samson Agonistes*: A Reappraisal." *Modern Language Notes* 76 (1961): 577–84.

———. "Natural Science and Figurative Design in *Samson Agonistes*." *English Literary History* 35 (1968): 51–74.

Curry, Walter Clyde. *Milton's Ontology, Cosmology and Physics*. Lexington: University of Kentucky Press, 1957.

Daiches, David. *Milton*. London: Hutchinson University Library, 1957.

———. "The Opening of *Paradise Lost*." In *The Living Milton*. Edited by Frank Kermode. London: Routledge and Kegan Paul, 1960.

Daniells, Roy. *Milton, Mannerism and Baroque*. Toronto: University of Toronto Press, 1963.

Darbishire, Helen. *Milton's Paradise Lost*. Oxford: Clarendon Press, 1951.

———. "Milton's Poetic Language." *English Studies at the English Association* 10 (1957): 31–52.

Davie, Donald. "Syntax and Music in *Paradise Lost*." In *The Living Milton*. Edited by Frank Kermode. London: Routledge and Kegan Paul, 1960.

Davies, Stevie. *Images of Kingship in Paradise Lost*. Columbia: University of Missouri Press, 1983.

Demaray, John G. *Milton and the Masque Tradition*. Cambridge: Harvard University Press, 1968.

———. *Milton's Theatrical Epic: The Invention and Design of Paradise Lost*. Cambridge: Harvard University Press, 1980.

Diekhoff, John S. *Milton's Paradise Lost: A Commentary on the Argument*. New York: Columbia University Press, 1946.

———. "The Trinity Manuscript and the Dictation of *Paradise Lost*." *Philological Quarterly* 28 (1949): 44–52.

————, ed. *A Maske at Ludlow: Essays on Milton's Comus*. Cleveland: Case Western Reserve University Press, 1968.

Duncan, Joseph E. *Milton's Earthly Paradise*. Minneapolis: University of Minnesota Press, 1972.

Durling, Robert M. *The Figure of the Poet in the Renaissance Epic*. Cambridge: Harvard University Press, 1965.

Eliot, T. S. "Milton" and "A Note on the Verse of John Milton." In *On Poetry and Poets*. London: Faber and Faber, 1957.

Empson, William. *Some Versions of Pastoral*. New York: New Directions, 1950.

————. *Milton's God*. London: Chatto and Windus, 1965.

Evans, John Martin. *"Paradise Lost" and the Genesis Tradition*. Oxford: Clarendon Press, 1968.

Fell, Kenneth. "From Myth to Martyrdom: Toward a View of Milton's *Samson Agonistes*." *English Studies* 34 (1953): 145–55

Ferry, Anne Davidson. *Milton's Epic Voice: The Narrator in Paradise Lost*. Cambridge: Harvard University Press, 1963.

Fish, Stanley. *Surprised by Sin: The Reader in Paradise Lost*. New York: St. Martin's Press, 1967.

————. "Interpreting the Variorum." *Critical Inquiry*, vol. 2 (1976): 465–85.

Fixler, Michael. *Milton and the Kingdoms of God*. Evanston: Northwestern University Press, 1964.

Fletcher, Angus. *The Transcendental Masque: An Essay on Milton's Comus*. Ithaca: Cornell University Press, 1971.

Freeman, James A. *Milton and The Martial Muse*. Princeton: Princeton University Press, 1980.

Frye, Northrop. "Literature as Context: Milton's *Lycidas*." In *Fables of Identity: Studies in Poetic Mythology*. New York: Harcourt, Brace and World, 1963.

————. *The Return of Eden: Five Essays on Milton's Epics*. Toronto: University of Toronto Press, 1965.

Frye, Roland Mushat. *God, Man and Satan: Patterns of Christian Thought and Life in "Paradise Lost," "Pilgrim's Progress" and the Great Theologians*. Princeton: Princeton University Press, 1960.

Fuller, Elizabeth Ely. *Milton's Kinesthetic Vision in Paradise Lost*. Lewisburg: Bucknell University Press, 1983.

Gallagher, Philip. " 'Real or Allegoric': The Ontology of Sin and Death in *Paradise Lost*." *English Literary Renaissance* 6 (1976): 317–33.

Gardner, H. L. *A Reading of Paradise Lost*. Oxford: Clarendon Press, 1965.

Giamatti, A. Bartlett. *The Earthly Paradise and the Renaissance Epic*. Princeton: Princeton University Press, 1966.

Gilbert, Sandra M. "Patriarchal Poetry and Women Readers: Reflections on Milton's Bogey." *PMLA* 93 (1978): 368–82.

Goodman, Paul. "Milton's 'On His Blindness': Stanzas, Motion of Thought." In *The Structure of Literature*. Chicago: University of Chicago Press, 1954.

Gossman, Ann. "Milton's Samson as the Tragic Hero Purified by Trial." *Journal of English and Germanic Philology* 61 (1962): 528–41.

Grace, William J. "Orthodoxy and the Aesthetic Method in *Paradise Lost* and *The Divine Comedy*." *Comparative Literature* 1 (1949): 173–87.

Greene, Thomas. *The Descent from Heaven: A Study in Epic Continuity*. New Haven: Yale University Press, 1963.

Grierson, H. J. C. *Milton and Wordsworth: Poets and Prophets*. Cambridge: At the University Press, 1936.

Guillory, John. *Poetic Authority*. New York: Columbia University Press, 1983.

Halkett, John. *Milton and the Idea of Matrimony*. New Haven: Yale University Press, 1970.

Haller, William. "Order and Progress in *Paradise Lost*." *PMLA* 35 (1920): 218–25.

Hanford, James Holley. *John Milton, Poet and Humanist*. Cleveland: Press of Case Western Reserve University, 1966.

Harding, David P. *Milton and the Renaissance Ovid*. Urbana: University of Illinois Press, 1946.

———. *The Club of Hercules: Studies in the Classical Background of "Paradise Lost."* Urbana: University of Illinois Press, 1962.

Harris, William O. "Despair and 'Patience as the Truest Fortitude' in *Samson Agonistes*." *English Literary History* 30 (1963): 107–20.

Hartman, Geoffrey. "Milton's Counterplot" and "Adam on the Grass with Balsamum." In *Beyond Formalism: Literary Essays 1958–1970*. New Haven: Yale University Press, 1970.

Hertz, Neil. "Wordsworth and the Tears of Adam." *Studies in Romanticism* 7 (1967): 15–33.

Hill, Christopher. *Milton and the English Revolution*. London: Faber and Faber, 1977.

Hollander, John. *The Untuning of the Sky: Ideas of Music in English Poetry 1500–1700*. Princeton: Princeton University Press, 1961.

———. *The Figure of Echo: A Mode of Allusion in Milton and After*. Berkeley: University of California Press, 1981.

Hughes, Merritt Y. *Ten Perspectives on Milton*. New Haven: Yale University Press, 1965.

Hunter, William B. "Milton and Thrice-Great Hermes." *Journal of English and Germanic Philology* 45 (1946): 327–36.

———. "Milton's Materialistic Life Principle." *Journal of English and Germanic Philology* 45 (1946): 68–76.

Hunter, William B.; Patrides, C. A.; and Adamson, J. H., eds. *Bright Essence: Studies in Milton's Theology*. Salt Lake City: University of Utah Press, 1971.

Kelley, Maurice. *This Great Argument: A Study of Milton's "De Doctrina Christiana" as a Gloss Upon "Paradise Lost."* Princeton: Princeton University Press, 1941.

Kermode, Frank. "Milton's Hero." *Review of English Studies* 4 (1953): 317–30.

———, ed. *The Living Milton*. London: Routledge and Kegan Paul, 1960.

Kerrigan, William. *The Prophetic Milton*. Charlottesville: The University of Virginia Press, 1974

———. *The Sacred Complex: On the Psychogenesis of Paradise Lost*. Cambridge: Harvard University Press, 1983.

Knight, Douglas. "The Dramatic Center of *Paradise Lost*." *Stuttgarter Arbeiten zur Germanistik* 63 (1964): 44–59.

Knight, G. Wilson. *The Burning Oracle: Studies in the Poetry of Action*. London: Oxford University Press, 1939.

———. *Chariot of Wrath: The Message of John Milton to Democracy at War*. London: Faber and Faber, 1942.

Knott, John Ray. *Milton's Pastoral Vision*. Chicago: University of Chicago Press, 1971.

Kranidas, Thomas. *The Fierce Equation: A Study of Milton's Decorum*. The Hague: Mouton, 1965.

Krouse, Michael. *Milton's Samson and the Christian Tradition*. Princeton: Princeton University Press, 1949.

Langdon, Ida. *Milton's Theory of Poetry and Fine Art*. New Haven: Yale University Press, 1924.

Lawry, Jon S. *The Shadow of Heaven: Matter and Stance in Milton's Poetry*. Ithaca: Cornell University Press, 1968.

Leavis, F. R. "Milton's Verse." In *Revaluation*. London: Chatto and Windus, 1956.

Leishman, J. B. *Milton's Minor Poems*. London: Hutchinson, 1969.

Lewalski, Barbara Kieffer. "Structure and the Symbolism of Vision in Michael's Prophecy, *Paradise Lost*, XI–XII." *Philological Quarterly* 42 (1963): 23–35.

———. *Milton's Brief Epic*. Providence: Brown University Press, 1966.

———. "*Samson Agonistes* and the 'Tragedy' of the Apocalypse." *PMLA* 85 (1970): 1050–62.

Lewis, C. S. "A Note on *Comus*." *Review of English Studies* 8 (1932):170–76.

———. *A Preface to Paradise Lost*. London: Oxford University Press, 1942.

Lieb, Michael. *The Dialectics of Creation: Patterns of Birth and Regeneration in "Paradise Lost."* Amherst: University of Massachusetts Press, 1970.

Lieb, Michael and Shawcross, John T., eds. *Achievements of the Left Hand: Essays on the Prose of John Milton*. Amherst: University of Massachusetts Press, 1974.

Loewenstein, Joseph. " 'Translated to the Skies': Echoic Silence in *Comus*." In *Responsive Readings: Versions of Echo in Pastoral, Epic and Jonsonian Masque*. New Haven: Yale University Press, 1984.

Lord, George deForest. "*Paradise Regain'd*: Self-Discovery in the Waste Land." In *Trials of the Self: Heroic Ordeals in the Epic Tradition*. Hamden, Conn.: Archon Books, 1983.

Lovejoy, Arthur O. "Milton and the Paradox of the Fortunate Fall." *English Literary History* 4 (1937):16–179.

MacCaffrey, Isabel G. *Paradise Lost as "Myth."* Cambridge: Harvard University Press: 1959.

MacCallum, H. R. "Milton and Figurative Interpretation of the Bible." *University of Toronto Quarterly* 31 (1962): 397–415.

———. "Milton and Sacred History: Books XI and XII of *Paradise Lost*." In *Essays in English Literature from the Renaissance to the Victorian Age Present to A. S. P. Woodhouse*. Edited by Millar MacLure and F. W. Watt. Toronto: University of Toronto Press, 1964.

MacLean, Hugh N. "Milton's Fair Infant." *English Literary History* 24 (1957): 269–305.

Madsen, William G. "The Fortunate Fall in *Paradise Lost*." *Modern Language Notes* 74 (1959): 103–05.

———. *From Shadowy Types to Truth*. New Haven: Yale University Press, 1968.

Marshall, W. H. "*Paradise Lost: Felix Culpa* and the Problem of Structure." *Modern Language Notes* 76 (1961): 15–20.

Martz, Louis. *The Paradise Within: Studies in Vaughn, Traherne and Milton*. New Haven: Yale University Press, 1964.

———. *The Poet of Exile: A Study of Milton's Poetry*. New Haven: Yale University Press, 1980.

———, ed. *Milton: A Collection of Critical Essays*. Englewood Cliffs, N.J.: Prentice-Hall, 1966.

Mayerson, Caroline W. "The Orpheus Image in *Lycidas*." *PMLA* 64 (1949): 189–207.

Miller, Milton. "*Paradise Lost*: The Double Standard." *University of Toronto Quarterly* 20 (1950–51): 183–99.

Milner, Andrew. *John Milton and the English Revolution*. London: The Macmillan Press, 1981.

Mueller, Martin. "*Pathos* and *Katharsis* in *Samson Agonistes*." *English Literary History* 31 (1964): 156–74.

Neuse, Richard. "Metamorphosis and Symbolic Action in *Comus*." *English Literary History* 34 (1967): 49–64.

———. "Milton and Spenser: The Virgilian Triad Revisited." *English Literary History* 45 (1978): 606–39.

Nicolson, Marjorie Hope. "The Spirit World of Milton and More." *Studies in Philology* 22 (1925): 433–52.

———. "Milton and Hobbes." *Studies in Philology* 23 (1926): 405–33.

———. "The Telescope and Imagination." *Modern Philology* 32 (1935): 233–60.

Nohrnberg, James. "*Paradise Regained* by One Greater Man: Milton's Wisdom Epic as a 'Fable of Identity'." In *Centre and Labyrinth: Essays in Honor of Northrop Frye*. Edited by Eleanor Cook et al. Toronto: University of Toronto Press, 1983.

Parker, Patricia. *Inescapable Romance: Studies in the Poetics of a Mode*. Princeton: Princeton University Press, 1979.

———, "Eve, Evening and the Labor of Reading in *Paradise Lost*." *English Literary Renaissance* 9 (1979): 319–42.

Patrides, C. A. *Milton and the Christian Tradition*. Oxford: Oxford University Press, 1966.

————, ed. *Milton's Epic Poetry*. Baltimore: Penguin Books, 1967.

————, ed. *Milton's Lycidas: The Tradition and the Poem*. Columbia: University of Missouri Press, 1983.

Peter, John D. *A Critique of "Paradise Lost."* New York: Columbia University Press, 1960.

Pointon, Marcia R. *Milton and English Art*. Toronto: University of Toronto Press, 1970.

Pope, Elizabeth M. *Paradise Regained: The Tradition and the Poem*. Baltimore: Johns Hopkins University Press, 1947.

Prince, Frank Templeton. *The Italian Element in Milton's Verse*. Oxford: Oxford University Press, 1954.

Rajan, Balachandra. *"Paradise Lost" and the Seventeenth Century Reader*. London: Chatto and Windus, 1947.

Ransom, John Crowe. "A Poem Nearly Anonymous." In *The World's Body*. New York: Charles Scribners' Sons, 1938.

Reesing, John. *Milton's Poetic Art*. Cambridge: Harvard University Press, 1968.

Richmond, Hugh M. *The Christian Revolutionary: John Milton*. Berkeley: University of California Press, 1974.

Ricks, Christopher. *Milton's Grand Style*. Oxford: Clarendon Press, 1963.

Riggs, William G. *The Christian Poet in Paradise Lost*. Berkeley: University of California Press, 1972.

————. "The Poet and Satan in *Paradise Lost*." In *Milton Studies II*. Edited by James D. Simmonds. Pittsburgh: University of Pittsburgh Press, 1970.

Ross, Malcom M. *Milton's Royalism*. Ithaca: Cornell University Press, 1943.

————. "Milton and the Protestant Aesthetic." In *Poetry and Dogma*. New Brunswick: Rutgers University Press, 1954.

Ryken, Leland. *The Apocalyptic Vision in "Paradise Lost."* Ithaca: Cornell University Press, 1970.

Samuel, Irene. *Plato and Milton*. Ithaca: Cornell University Press, 1947.

————. *Dante and Milton: The "Commedia" and "Paradise Lost."* Ithaca: Cornell University Press, 1966.

Sewell, Arthur. *A Study in Milton's Christian Doctrine*. London: Oxford University Press, 1939.

Shawcross, John T. "The Chronology of Milton's Major Poems." *PMLA* 76 (1961): 45–58.

————. "The Balanced Structure of *Paradise Lost*." *Studies in Philology* 62 (1965): 696–718.

————. "The Metaphor of Inspiration in *Paradise Lost*." In *Th' Upright Heart and Pure*. Edited by Amdeus P. Fiore. Pittsburgh: Duquesne University Press, 1967.

Shumaker, Wayne. "'Flowerets and Sounding Seas' A Study in the Affective Structure of *Lycidas*." *PMLA* 66 (1951): 485–494.

Sirluck, Ernest. "Milton Revises the *Faerie Queene*." *Modern Philology* 48 (1950): 90–96.

Spaeth, Sigmund G. *Milton's Knowledge of Music*. Ann Arbor: University of Michigan Press, 1963.

Sprott, Ernest S. *Milton's Art of Prosody.* Oxford: Clarendon Press, 1958.

Stapleton, Laurence. "Milton's Conception of Time in the *Christian Doctrine.*" *Harvard Theological Review* 57 (1964): 9–22.

Steadman, John M. "Image and Idol: Satan and the Elements of Illusion in *Paradise Lost.*" *Journal of English and Germanic Philology* 59 (1960): 640–54.

———. *Milton and the Renaissance Hero.* Oxford: Clarendon Press, 1967.

———. *Milton's Epic Characters.* Chapel Hill: University of North Carolina Press, 1968.

Stein, Arnold. *Answerable Style: Essays on "Paradise Lost."* Minneapolis: University of Minnesota Press, 1953.

———. *The Art of Presence: The Poet and Paradise Lost.* Berkeley: University of California Press, 1977.

Stone, C. F. "Milton's Self-Concerns and Manuscript Revision in *Lycidas.*" *Modern Language Notes* 83 (1968): 867–81.

Summers, Joseph H. *The Muse's Method: An Introduction to "Paradise Lost."* Cambridge: Harvard University Press, 1962.

Svendsen, Kester. *Milton and Science.* Cambridge: Harvard University Press, 1956.

Taylor, Edward W. "Milton's Firedrake." *Milton Quarterly* 6 (1972): 7–10.

Tillyard, E. M. W. *Studies in Milton.* London: Chatto and Windus, 1951.

———. *The English Epic and its Background.* London: Chatto and Windus, 1954.

———. *The Miltonic Setting, Past and Present.* London: Chatto and Windus, 1957.

Tolliver, Harold E. "Complicity of Voice in *Paradise Lost.*" *Modern Language Quarterly* 25 (1964): 153–70.

Tuve, Rosemond. *Images and Themes in Five Poems by Milton.* Cambridge: Harvard University Press, 1957.

———. "Baroque and Mannerist Milton." *Journal of English and Germanic Philology* 60 (1961): 817–33.

Waldock, A. J. *"Paradise Lost" and its Critics.* Cambridge: At the University Press, 1947.

Wallace, John M. "Milton's Arcades." *Journal of English and Germanic Philology* 58 (1959): 627–36.

Wallerstein, Ruth. *Studies in Seventeenth Century Poetic.* Madison: University of1 Wisconsin Press, 1950.

Weiskel, Thomas. *The Romantic Sublime: Studies in the Structure and Psychology of Transcendence.* Baltimore: Johns Hopkins University Press, 1976.

Whaler, James. "The Miltonic Simile." *PMLA* 46 (1931): 1034–74.

Wheeler, Thomas. "Milton's Twenty-Third Sonnet." *Studies in Philology* 58 (1961): 510–15.

Whiting, G. W. and Gossman, Ann. "Siloa's Brook, the Pool of Siloa and Milton's Muse." *Studies in Philology* 58 (1961): 193–205.

Widmer, Kingsley. "The Iconography of Renunciation: The Miltonic Simile." In

Milton's Epic Poetry: Essays on Paradise Lost and Paradise Regained. Edited by C. A. Patrides. Middlesex: Penguin Books, 1967.

Wilkenfield, Roger B. "Act and Emblem: The Conclusion of *Samson Agonistes.*" *English Literary History* 32 (1965): 160–68.

———. "The Seat at the Center: An Interpretation of *Comus.*" *English Literary History* 33 (1966): 170–97.

Wilkinson, David. "The Escape from Pollution: A Comment on 'Comus'." *Essays in Criticism* 10 (1960): 32–43.

Williamson, George. "The Education of Adam." *Modern Philology* 61 (1963): 96–109.

Wittreich, Joseph Anthony, Jr. *Visionary Poetics: Milton's Tradition and His Legacy.* San Marino, Cal.: Huntington Library Press, 1979.

———, ed. *Calm of Mind.* Cleveland: Case Western Reserve University Press, 1971.

———, ed. *Milton and the Line of Vision.* Madison: University of Wisconsin Press, 1975.

———, ed. *The Romantics on Milton.* Cleveland: Case Western Reserve University Press, 1975.

Woodhouse, A. S. P. "The Argument of Milton's *Comus.*" *University of Toronto Quarterly* 11 (1941–2): 46–71.

———. "Notes on Milton's View of Creation: The Initial Phases." *Philological Quarterly* 28 (1949): 211–36.

———. "*Comus* Once More." *University of Toronto Quarterly* 19 (1950): 218–23.

———. "Pattern in *Paradise Lost.*" *University of Toronto Quarterly* 22 (1952–3): 109–27.

———. "Tragic Effect in *Samson Agonistes.*" *University of Toronto Quarterly* 28 (1958–9): 205–22.

Wright, B. A. *Milton's "Paradise Lost."* London: Methuen, 1962.

Acknowledgments

"Milton's Minor Poems" by F. T. Prince from *The Italian Element in Milton's Verse* by F. T. Prince, copyright © 1954 by Oxford University Press. Reprinted by permission.

"Satan's Voyage" by Isabel G. MacCaffrey from *Paradise Lost as "Myth"* by Isabel G. MacCaffrey, copyright © 1959 by The President and Fellows of Harvard College. Reprinted by permission.

"Heaven" by William Empson from *Milton's God* by William Empson, copyright © 1961 by William Empson. Reprinted by permission.

"The Descent from Heaven" by Thomas Greene from *The Descent from Heaven: A Study in Epic Continuity* by Thomas Greene, copyright © 1963 by Yale University Press. Reprinted by permission.

"Revolt in the Desert" by Northrop Frye from *The Return of Eden* by Northrop Frye, copyright © 1965 by University of Toronto Press. Reprinted by permission.

"Milton's Counterplot" by Geoffrey H. Hartman from *English Literary History* (1958), copyright © 1958 by Johns Hopkins University Press. Reprinted by permission.

"The Transcendental Masque" by Angus Fletcher from *The Transcendental Masque: An Essay on Milton's Cosmos*, copyright © 1971 by Cornell University Press. Reprinted by permission.

"Reason in *The Reason of Church Government*" by Stanley E. Fish from *Self-Consuming Artifacts* by Stanley E. Fish, copyright © 1972 by The Regents of the University of California. Reprinted by permission.

"Edenic Time" by Leslie Brisman from *Milton's Poetry of Choice and Its Romantic Heros* by Leslie Brisman, copyright © 1973 by Cornell University Press. Reprinted by permission.

"Milton and His Precursors" by Harold Bloom from *A Map of Misreading* by Harold Bloom, copyright © 1975 by Oxford University Press. Reprinted by permission.

"*Samson Agonistes:* The Divided Mind" by Mary Ann Radzinowicz from *Toward Samson Agonistes: The Growth of Milton's Mind* by Mary Ann Radzinowicz, copyright © 1978 by Princeton University Press. Reprinted by permission.

"*Samson Agonistes:* The Breath of Heaven" by Louis L. Martz from *Poet of Exile: A Study of Milton's Poetry* by Louis L. Martz, copyright © 1980 by Yale University Press. Reprinted by permission.

"Echo Schematic" by John Hollander from *The Figure of Echo* by John Hollander, copyright © 1981 by The Regents of the University of California. Reprinted by permission.

"Oedipus and Sacred Oedipus" by William Kerrigan from *The Sacred Complex: On the Psychogenesis of Paradise Lost*" by William Kerrigan, copyright © 1983 by The President and Fellows of Harvard College. Reprinted by permission.

"Milton's Image of Divine Analysis: Provenance and Meaning" from *The Dividing Muse: Images of a Sacred Disjunction in Milton's Poetry*, copyright © 1985 by Yale University Press. Reprinted by permission.

"*Lycidas*" by Peter M. Sacks from *The English Elegy: Studies in the Genre from Spenser to Yeats* by Peter M. Sacks, copyright © 1985 by Johns Hopkins University Press. Reprinted by permission.

"The Majesty of Darkness" by William Flesch, copyright © 1985 by William Flesch. Published for the first time in this volume. Printed by permission.

Index